Praise for *Travelling to Infinity*

"Stephen Hawking may think in 11 dimensions, but his
first wife has learnt to love in several."
The Times

"Jane Hawking has written a book about what it was like
to be pivotal to her husband's celebrated existence...
but it is much more a shout from the outer darkness."
The Daily Telegraph

"What becomes of time when a marriage unravels? And
what becomes of the woman who has located her whole self
within its sphere? For Jane Hawking, the physics of love and
loss are set in a private universe."
The Guardian

"Jane describes the final, painful years of her
marriage in candid detail."
The Independent

"Jane Hawking's harrowing and compelling
account... rings very true."
Irish Times

"This is not a vindictive book, although the agony she went
through is palpable; if Stephen's struggle to keep his mind clear
is heroic, so is her determination to balance his escalating needs
and those of their three children."
Independent on Sunday

"Jane writes about her former husband with tenderness,
respect and protectiveness."
Sunday Express

P9-DMY-110

TRAVELLING TO INFINITY

MY LIFE WITH STEPHEN

TRAVELLING TO INFINITY

MY LIFE WITH STEPHEN

JANE HAWKING

ALMA BOOKS

ALMA BOOKS LTD
London House
243–253 Lower Mortlake Road
Richmond
Surrey TW9 2LL
United Kingdom
www.almabooks.com

Travelling to Infinity: My Life with Stephen is an extensively revised
version (with new material) of *Music to Move the Stars*, first published by
Macmillan in 1999
Travelling to Infinity: My Life with Stephen first published by Alma
Books Limited in 2007
First paperback edition first published in 2008, reprinted 2010
This new edition first published by Alma Books in 2014
Copyright © Jane Hawking, 1999–2014
All rights reserved

Jane Hawking asserts her moral right to be identified as the author of this
work in accordance with the Copyright, Designs and Patents Act 1988

ISBN: 978-1-84688-347-7
EBOOK: 978-1-84688-356-9 (mobi)

Printed in the USA by Edwards Brothers Malloy, Inc.

Contents

For my family

*La parole humaine est comme un chaudron
fêlé où nous battons des mélodies à faire
danser les ours quand on voudrait attendrir
les étoiles.*

– Gustave Flaubert

Human expression is like a cracked kettle
on which we beat out music for bears to
dance to, when really we long to move the
stars to pity.

Part One

1

Wings to Fly

The story of my life with Stephen Hawking began in the summer of 1962, though possibly it began ten or so years earlier than that without my being aware of it. When I entered St Albans High School for Girls as a seven-year-old first-former in the early Fifties, there was for a short spell a boy with floppy, golden-brown hair who used to sit by the wall in the next-door classroom. The school took boys, including my brother Christopher in the junior department, but I only saw the boy with the floppy hair on the occasions when, in the absence of our own teacher, we first-formers were squeezed into the same classroom as the older children. We never spoke to each other, but I am sure this early memory is to be trusted, because Stephen was a pupil at the school for a term at that time before going to a preparatory school a few miles away.

Stephen's sisters were more recognizable, because they were at the school for longer. Only eighteen months younger than Stephen, Mary, the elder of the two girls, was a distinctively eccentric figure – plump, always dishevelled, absent-minded, given to solitary pursuits. Her great asset, a translucent complexion, was masked by thick, unflattering spectacles. Philippa, five years younger than Stephen, was bright-eyed, nervous and excitable, with short fair plaits and a round, pink face. The school demanded rigid conformity both academically and in discipline, and the pupils, like schoolchildren everywhere, could be cruelly intolerant of individuality. It was fine to have a Rolls Royce and a house in the country, but if, like me, your means of transport was a pre-war Standard 10 – or even worse, like the Hawkings, an ancient London taxi – you were a figure of fun or the object of pitying contempt. The Hawking children used to lie on the floor of their taxi to avoid being seen by their peers. Unfortunately there was not room on the floor of the Standard 10 for such evasive action. Both the Hawking girls left before reaching the upper school.

Their mother had long been a familiar figure. A small, wiry person dressed in a fur coat, she used to stand on the corner by the zebra crossing near my school, waiting for her youngest son, Edward, to arrive by bus from his preparatory school in the country. My brother also went to that school after his kindergarten year at St Albans High School: it was called Aylesford House and there the boys wore pink – pink blazers and pink caps. In all other respects it was a paradise for small boys, especially for those who were not of an academic inclination. Games, cubs, camping and gang shows, for which my father often played the piano, appeared to be the major activities. Charming and very good-looking, Edward, at the age of eight, was having some difficulty relating to his adoptive family when I first knew the Hawkings – possibly because of their habit of bringing their reading matter to the dinner table and ignoring any non-bookworms present.

A school friend of mine, Diana King, had experienced this particular Hawking habit – which may have been why, on hearing some time later of my engagement to Stephen, she exclaimed, "Oh, Jane! You are marrying into a mad, mad family!" It was Diana who first pointed Stephen out to me in that summer of 1962 when, after the exams, she, my best friend Gillian and I were enjoying the blissful period of semi-idleness before the end of term. Thanks to my father's position as a senior civil servant, I had already made a couple of sorties into the adult world beyond school, homework and exams – to a dinner in the House of Commons and on a hot sunny day to a garden party at Buckingham Palace. Diana and Gillian were leaving school that summer, while I was to stay on as Head Girl for the autumn term, when I would be applying for university entrance. That Friday afternoon we collected our bags and, adjusting our straw boaters, we decided to drift into town for tea. We had scarcely gone a hundred yards when a strange sight met our eyes on the other side of the road: there, lolloping along in the opposite direction, was a young man with an awkward gait, his head down, his face shielded from the world under an unruly mass of straight brown hair. Immersed in his own thoughts, he looked neither to right nor left, unaware of the group of schoolgirls across the road. He was an eccentric phenomenon for strait-laced, sleepy St Albans. Gillian and I stared rather rudely in amazement but Diana remained impassive.

"That's Stephen Hawking. I've been out with him actually," she announced to her speechless companions.

"No! You haven't!" we laughed incredulously.

"Yes I have. He's strange but very clever, he's a friend of Basil's [her brother]. He took me to the theatre once, and I've been to his house. He goes on 'Ban the Bomb' marches."

Raising our eyebrows, we continued into town, but I did not enjoy the outing because, without being able to explain why, I felt uneasy about the young man we had just seen. Perhaps there was something about his very eccentricity that fascinated me in my rather conventional existence. Perhaps I had some strange premonition that I would be seeing him again. Whatever it was, that scene etched itself deeply on my mind.

The holidays of that summer were a dream for a teenager on the verge of independence, though they may well have been a nightmare for her parents, since my destination, a summer school in Spain, was in 1962 quite as remote, mysterious and fraught with hazards as, say, Nepal is for teenagers today. With all the confidence of my eighteen years, I was quite sure that I could look after myself, and I was right. The course was well organized, and we students were lodged in groups in private homes. At weekends we were taken on conducted tours of all the sights – to Pamplona where the bulls run the streets, to the only bullfight I have seen, brutal and savage, but spectacular and enthralling as well, and to Loyola, the home of St Ignatius, the author of a prayer I and every other pupil at St Albans High School had had instilled into us from constant repetition:

Teach us, O Lord,
to serve Thee as Thou deservest,
to give and not to count the cost...

Otherwise we spent our afternoons on the beach and the evenings out down by the port in restaurants and bars, participating in the fiestas and the dancing, listening to the raucous bands and gasping at the fireworks. I quickly made new friends outside the limited St Albans scene, primarily among the other teenagers on the course, and with them, in the glorious, exotic atmosphere of Spain, experimented with a taste of adult independence away from home, family and the stultifying discipline of school.

On my return to England, I was whisked away almost immediately by my parents who, relieved at my safe return, had arranged a family holiday in the Low Countries and Luxembourg. This was yet another broadening experience, one of those holidays in which my father specialized and which he had been arranging for us for many years – ever since my first trip to Brittany at the age of ten. Thanks to his enthusiasms we found ourselves in the vanguard of the tourist movement, travelling hundreds of miles along meandering country roads across a Europe in the process of emerging from its wartime trauma, visiting cities, cathedrals and art museums, which my parents were also discovering for the first time. It was a typically inspired combination of education, through art and history, and enjoyment of the good things of life – wine, food and summer sun – all intermingled with the war memorials and cemeteries of Flanders' fields.

Back in school that autumn, the summer's experiences lent me an unprecedented feeling of self-assurance. As I emerged from my chrysalis, school provided only the palest reflection of the awareness and self-reliance I had acquired through travelling. Taking my cue from the new forms of satire appearing on television, I, the Head Girl, devised a fashion show for the sixth-form entertainment, with the difference that all the fashions were constructed from bizarrely adapted items of school uniform. Discipline collapsed as the whole school clamoured for entry on the staircase outside the hall, and Miss Meiklejohn (otherwise know as Mick), the stocky, weather-beaten games mistress on whose terrifyingly masculine bark the smooth running of the school depended, was for once reduced to apoplexy, unable to make herself heard in the din. In desperation, she resorted to the megaphone – which usually only came out for a blasting on Sports Day, at the pet show, and for the purpose of controlling those interminable crocodiles we had to form when marching down through every possible back street of St Albans for the once-termly services in the Abbey.

That term long ago in the autumn of 1962 was not supposed to be about putting on shows. It was supposed to be about university entrance. Sadly it was not a success for me in academic terms. However great our adulation for President Kennedy, the Cuban missile crisis that October had well and truly shaken the sense of security of my generation and dashed our hopes for the future. With the superpowers playing such dangerous games with our lives, it was not at all certain that we had any future to look forward to. As we prayed for peace in school assembly under the direction of the Dean, I remembered a prediction made by

Field Marshall Montgomery in the late Fifties that there would be a nuclear war within a decade. Everyone, young and old alike, knew that we would have just four minutes' warning of a nuclear attack, which would spell the abrupt end of all civilization. My mother's comment, calmly philosophical and sensible as ever, at the prospect of a third world war in her lifetime, was that she would much rather be obliterated with everything and everyone else than endure the agony of seeing her husband and son conscripted for warfare from which they would never return.

Quite apart from the almighty threat of the international scene, I felt that I had burnt myself out with the A-level exams and lacked enthusiasm for school work after my taste of freedom in the summer. The serious business of university entrance held only humiliation when neither Oxford nor Cambridge expressed any interest in me. It was all the more painful because my father had been cherishing the hope that I would gain a place at Cambridge since I was about six years old. Aware of my sense of failure, Miss Gent, the Headmistress, sympathetically went to some lengths to point out that there was no disgrace in not getting a place at Cambridge, because many of the men at that university were far inferior intellectually to the women who had been turned away for want of places. In those days the ratio was roughly ten men to one woman at Oxford and Cambridge. She recommended taking up the offer of an interview at Westfield College, London, a women's college on the Girtonian model, situated in Hampstead at some distance from the rest of the University. Thus one cold, wet December day, I set off from St Albans by bus for the fifteen-mile journey to Hampstead.

The day was such a disaster that it was a relief at the end of it to be on the bus home again, travelling through the same bleak, grey sleet and snow of the outward journey. After the uncomfortable exercise in the Spanish Department of bluffing my way through an interview which seemed to hinge entirely on T.S. Eliot, about whom I knew next to nothing, I was sent to join the queue outside the Principal's study. When my turn came, she brought the style of a former civil servant to the interview, scarcely looking up from her papers over her horn-rimmed spectacles. Feeling exceedingly ruffled from the fiasco of the earlier interview, I decided it was better to make her notice me even if in the process I ruined my chances. So when in a bored, dry voice, she asked, "And why have you put down Spanish rather than French as your main language?", I answered in an equally bored, dry voice, "Because Spain is hotter than France." Her papers fell from her hands and she did indeed look up.

To my astonishment, I was offered a place at Westfield, but by that Christmas much of the optimism and enthusiasm that I had discovered in Spain had worn thin. When Diana invited me to a New Year's party which she was giving with her brother on 1st January 1963, I went along, neatly dressed in a dark-green silky outfit – synthetic, of course – with my hair back-brushed in an extravagant bouffant roll, inwardly shy and very unsure of myself. There, slight of frame, leaning against the wall in a corner with his back to the light, gesticulating with long thin fingers as he spoke – his hair falling across his face over his glasses – and wearing a dusty black-velvet jacket and red-velvet bow tie, stood Stephen Hawking, the young man I had seen lolloping along the street in the summer.

Standing apart from the other groups, he was talking to an Oxford friend, explaining that he had begun research in cosmology in Cambridge – not, as he had hoped, under the auspices of Fred Hoyle, the popular television scientist, but with the unusually named Dennis Sciama. At first, Stephen had thought his unknown supervisor's name was *Skeearma*, but on his arrival in Cambridge he had discovered that the correct pronunciation was *Sharma*. He admitted that he had learnt with some relief, the previous summer – when I was doing A levels – that he had gained a First Class degree at Oxford. This was the happy result of a viva, an oral exam, conducted by the perplexed examiners to decide whether the singularly inept candidate whose papers also revealed flashes of brilliance should be given a First, an Upper Second or a Pass degree, the latter being tantamount to failure. He nonchalantly informed the examiners that if they gave him a First he would go to Cambridge to do a PhD, thus giving them the opportunity of introducing a Trojan horse into the rival camp, whereas if they gave him an Upper Second (which would also allow him to do research), he would stay in Oxford. The examiners played for safety and gave him a First.

Stephen went on to explain to his audience of two, his Oxford friend and me, how he had also taken steps to play for safety, realizing that it was extremely unlikely that he would get a First at Oxford on the little work he had done. He had never been to a lecture – it was not the done thing to be seen working when friends called – and the legendary tale of his tearing up a piece of work and flinging it into his tutor's wastepaper basket on leaving a tutorial is quite true. Fearing for his chances in academia, Stephen had applied to join the Civil Service and had passed the preliminary stages of selection at a country-house weekend, so he was all set to take the Civil Service exams just after Finals. One morning he woke late as usual, with the niggling feeling that there was something he ought to be doing that day, apart from his normal pursuit of listening to his taped recording of the entire *Ring Cycle*. As he did not keep a diary but trusted everything to memory, he had no way of finding out what it was until some hours later, when it dawned on him that that day was the day of the Civil Service exams.

I listened in amused fascination, drawn to this unusual character by his sense of humour and his independent personality. His tales made very appealing listening, particularly because of his way of hiccoughing with laughter, almost suffocating himself, at the jokes he told, many of them against himself. Clearly here was someone, like me, who tended to stumble through life and managed to see the funny side of situations. Someone who, like me, was fairly shy, yet not averse to expressing his opinions; someone who unlike me had a developed sense of his own worth and had the effrontery to convey it. As the party drew to a close, we exchanged names and addresses, but I did not expect to see him again, except perhaps casually in passing. The floppy hair and the bow tie were a façade, a statement of independence of mind, and in future I could afford to overlook them, as Diana had, rather than gape in astonishment, if I came across him again in the street.

2

On Stage

Only a couple of days later, a card came from Stephen, inviting me to a party on 8th January. It was written in a beautiful copperplate hand which I envied but, despite laborious efforts, had never mastered. I consulted Diana, who had also received an invitation. She said that the party was for Stephen's twenty-first birthday – information not conveyed on the invitation – and she promised to come and pick me up. It was difficult to choose a present for someone I had only just met, so I took a record token.

The house in Hillside Road, St Albans, was a monument to thrift and economy. Not that that was unusual in those days, because in the postwar era we were all brought up to treat money with respect, to search out bargains and to avoid waste. Built in the early years of the twentieth century, 14 Hillside Road, a vast red-brick three-storey house, had a certain charm about it, since it was preserved entirely in its original state, with no interference from modernizing trends, such as central heating or wall-to-wall carpeting. Nature, the elements and a family of four children had all left their marks on the shabby façade which hid behind an unruly hedge. Wisteria overhung the decrepit glass porch, and much of the coloured glass in the leaded diamond panes of the upper panels of the front door was missing. Although no immediate response came from pressing the bell, the door was eventually opened by the same person who used to wait wrapped in a fur coat by the zebra crossing. She was introduced to me as Isobel Hawking, Stephen's mother. She was accompanied by an enchanting small boy with dark curly hair and bright blue eyes. Behind them a single light bulb illuminated a long yellow-tiled hallway, heavy furniture – including a grandfather clock – and the original, now darkened, William-Morris wallpaper.

As different members of the family began to appear round the living-room door to greet the new arrivals, I discovered that I knew them all: Stephen's mother was well known from her vigils by the crossing; his young brother, Edward, was evidently the small boy in the pink cap; the sisters, Mary and Philippa, were recognizable from school, and the tall, white-haired, distinguished father of the family, Frank Hawking, had once come to collect a swarm of bees from our own back garden. My brother Chris and I had wanted to watch, but to our disappointment he had shooed us away with a gruff taciturnity. In addition to being the city's only beekeeper, Frank Hawking must also have been one of the few people in St Albans to own a pair of skis. In winter he would ski down the hill past our house on his way to the golf course, where we used to picnic and gather bluebells in spring and summer and toboggan on tin trays in winter. It was like fitting a jigsaw together: all these people were individually quite familiar to me, but I had never realized that they were related. Indeed there was yet another member of that household whom I recognized: she lodged in her own self-contained room in the attic, but came down to join in family occasions such as this. Agnes Walker, Stephen's Scottish grandmother, was a well-known figure in St Albans in her own right on account of her prowess at the piano, publicly displayed once a month when she joined forces in the Town Hall with Molly Du Cane, our splendidly jolly-hockey-sticks folk-dance leader.

Dancing and tennis had been just about my only social activities throughout my teenage years. Through them, I had acquired a group of friends of both sexes from various schools and differing backgrounds. Out of school we went everywhere in a crowd – coffee on Saturday mornings, tennis in the evenings and socials at the tennis club in summer, ballroom-dancing classes and folk dancing in the winter. The fact that our mothers also attended the folk-dance evenings along with many of St Albans' elderly and infirm population did not embarrass us at all. We sat apart and danced in our own sets, well out of the way of the older generation. Romances blossomed occasionally in our corner, giving rise to plenty of gossip and a few squabbles, then usually faded as quickly as they had bloomed. We were an easygoing, friendly bunch of teenagers, leading simpler lives than our modern counterparts, and the atmosphere at the dances was carefree and wholesome, inspired by Molly Du Cane's infectious enthusiasm for her energetic art. Fiddle on her shoulder, she called the dances with authority, while Stephen's grandmother, her corpulent frame upright at the grand piano, applied her fingers with nimble artistry to the ivories, not once allowing the sausage bang of tight curls on her forehead to become ruffled. An august figure, she would turn to survey the dancers with a curiously impassive stare. She, of course, came downstairs to greet the guests at Stephen's twenty-first birthday party.

The party consisted of a mixture of friends and relations. A few hailed from Stephen's Oxford days, but most had been his contemporaries or near contemporaries at St Albans School and had contributed to that school's success in the Oxbridge entrance exams of 1959. At seventeen, Stephen had been younger than his peer group at school, and consequently was rather young for university entrance that autumn, especially as many of his fellow undergraduates were not just one year older than him, but older by several years because they had all come up to Oxford after doing National Service, which had since been abolished. Later Stephen admitted that he failed to get the best out of Oxford because of the difference in age between him and his fellow undergraduates.

Certainly he maintained closer ties with his school friends than with any acquaintances from Oxford. Apart from Basil King, Diana's brother, I knew them only by repute as the new elite of St Albans' society. They were said to be the intellectual adventurers of our generation, passionately dedicated to a critical rejection of every truism, to the ridicule of every trite or clichéd remark, to the assertion of their own independence of thought and to the exploration of the outer reaches of the mind. Our local paper, *The Herts Advertiser*, had trumpeted the success of the school four years earlier, splashing their names and faces across its pages. Whereas I was just about to embark on my undergraduate career, their student years were now already behind them. They were, of course, very different from my friends, and I, a bright but ordinary eighteen-year-old, felt intimidated. None of this crowd would ever spend their evenings folk-dancing. Painfully aware of my own lack of sophistication, I settled in a corner as close to the fire as possible with Edward on my knee and listened to the conversation, not attempting to participate. Some people were seated, others leant against the wall of the large chilly dining room, where the only source of heat was from a glass-fronted stove. The conversation was halting and consisted mostly of jokes, none of which were even remotely as highbrow as I was expecting. The only part of it I can remember was not a joke, but a riddle, about a man in New York who wanted to get to the fiftieth floor of a building but only took the lift to the forty-sixth. Why? Because he was not tall enough to reach the button for the fiftieth floor...

It was some time before I saw or heard of Stephen again. I was busily engaged in London following a secretarial course in a revolutionary type of shorthand, which used the alphabet instead of hieroglyphs and omitted all vowels. Initially I accompanied my father to the station at a sprint to catch the 8 a.m. train every morning, until I discovered that I was not required to be at the school in Oxford Street quite so early. I could travel at a more leisurely pace than my dedicated, hard-working father, so I ambled to the station for the nine o'clock train and met a completely different commuting public from the jam-packed, harassed-looking, middle-aged breadwinners in dark suits. Rarely did a day go by when I did not meet someone I knew – unhurried and casually dressed, either going back to college after a weekend at home or going up to London for an interview. This was a welcome start to the day, because for the rest of it, apart from a short break for lunch, I was confined to the classroom, surrounded by the clatter of massed old-fashioned typewriters and the chatter of ex-debs whose main claim to distinction seemed to be the number of times they had been invited to Buckingham Palace, Kensington Palace or Clarence House.

The revolutionary form of shorthand was easy enough to pick up, but the touch-typing was a nightmare. I could see the sense of the shorthand, for that was going to be useful for note-taking at university, but the typing was tiresome in the extreme and I was hopeless at it, still struggling to reach forty words a minute when the rest of the class had finished the course and mastered all the additional skills of the secretarial art. Actually the shorthand would be of short-term value while the typing skills would prove themselves over and over again.

At weekends I could forget the horrors of typing and keep up with old friends. One Saturday morning in February, I met Diana, who was now a student nurse at St Thomas's Hospital, and Elizabeth Chant, another school friend, who was training to become a primary-school teacher, in our favourite haunt, the coffee bar in Greens', St Albans' only department store. We compared notes on our courses and then started talking about our friends and acquaintances. Suddenly Diana asked, "Have you heard about Stephen?" "Oh, yes," said Elizabeth, "it's awful, isn't it?" I realized that they were talking about Stephen Hawking. "What do you mean?" I asked. "I haven't heard anything." "Well, apparently he's been in hospital for two weeks – Bart's I think, because that's where his father trained and that's where Mary is training." Diana explained, "He kept stumbling and couldn't tie his shoelaces." She paused. "They did lots of horrible tests and have found that he's suffering from some terrible, paralysing incurable disease. It's a bit like multiple sclerosis, but it's not multiple sclerosis and they reckon he's probably only got a couple of years to live."

I was stunned. I had only just met Stephen and for all his eccentricity I liked him. We both seemed shy in the presence of others, but were confident within ourselves. It was unthinkable that someone only a couple of years older than me should be facing the prospect of his own death. Mortality was not a concept that played any part in our existence. We were still young enough to be immortal. "How is he?" I enquired, shaken by the news. "Basil's been to see him," she continued, "and says he's pretty depressed: the tests are really unpleasant, and a boy from St Albans in the bed opposite died the other day." She sighed, "Stephen insisted on being on the ward, because of his socialist principles, and would not have a private room as his parents wanted." "Do they know the cause of this illness?" I asked blankly. "Not really," Diana replied. "They think he may have been given a non-sterile smallpox vaccination when he went to Persia a couple of years ago, and that introduced a virus to his spine – but they don't really know, that's only speculation."

I went home in silence, thinking about Stephen. My mother noticed my preoccupation. She had not met him, but knew of him and also knew that I liked him. I had taken the precaution of warning her that he was very eccentric, in case she should come across him unannounced. With the sensible assurance of the deep-seated faith which had sustained her through the war, through the terminal illness of her beloved father and through my own father's bouts of depression, she quietly said, "Why don't you pray for him? It might help."

I was astonished therefore when, a week or so later, as I was waiting for a 9 a.m. train, Stephen came sauntering down the platform carrying a brown canvas suitcase. He looked perfect-ly cheerful and pleased to see me. His appearance was more conventional and actually rather more attractive than on past occasions: the features of the old image which he had doubtless cultivated at Oxford – the bow tie, the black-velvet jacket, even the long hair – had given way to a red necktie, a beige raincoat and a tidier, shorter hairstyle. Our two previous meetings had been in the evening in subdued lighting: daylight revealed his broad, winning smile and his limpid grey eyes to advantage. Behind the owlish spectacles there was something about the set of his features which attracted me, reminding me, perhaps even subconsciously, of my Norfolk hero, Lord Nelson. We sat together on the train to London talking quite happily, though we scarcely touched on the question of his illness. I mentioned how sorry I had been to hear of his stay in hospital, whereupon he wrinkled his nose and said nothing. He behaved so convincingly as if everything were fine, and I felt it would have been cruel to have pursued the subject further. He was on his way back to Cambridge, he said, and as we neared St Pancras, he announced that he came home quite often at weekends. Would I like to go to the theatre with him sometime? Of course I said I would.

We met one Friday evening at an Italian restaurant in Soho, which in itself would have been a sufficiently lavish evening out. However Stephen had tickets for the theatre as well, and the meal had to be brought to a hasty and rather embarrassingly expensive conclusion to enable us to make our way south of the river to the Old Vic, in time for a performance of *Volpone*. Arriving at the theatre in a rush, we just managed to throw our belongings under our seats at the back of the stalls when the play began. My parents were fairly keen theatre-goers, so I had already seen Jonson's other great play *The Alchemist* and had enjoyed it thoroughly; *Volpone* was just as entertaining, and soon enough I was totally absorbed in the intrigues of the old fox who wanted to test the sincerity of his heirs but whose plans went badly wrong.

Elated by the performance, we stood discussing it afterwards at the bus stop. A tramp came by and politely asked Stephen if he had any loose change. Stephen felt in his pocket and exclaimed in embarrassment, "I'm sorry, I don't think I have anything left!" The tramp grinned and looked at me. "That's all right, guv'," he said, winking in my direction, "I understand." At that moment the bus drew up and we clambered on. As we sat down, Stephen turned to me apologetically, "I'm terribly sorry," he said, "but

I don't even have the money for the fare. Have you got any?" Guiltily aware of how much he must have spent on our evening, I was only too happy to oblige. The conductor approached and hovered over us as I searched for my purse in the depths of my handbag. My embarrassment equalled Stephen's as I discovered that it was missing. We jumped off the bus at the next set of traffic lights and fairly ran all the way back to the Old Vic. The main entrance to the theatre was closed, but Stephen pressed on – to the stage door at the side. It was open and the passage inside was lit. Cautiously we ventured in, but there was no one to be seen. Directly at the end of the passage we found ourselves on the deserted but still brightly lit stage. Awestruck, we tiptoed across it and down the steps into the darkened auditorium. In no time at all, to our joint relief, we found the green leather purse under the seat where I had been sitting. Just as we were heading back towards the stage, the lights went out, and there we were in total darkness. "Take my hand," said Stephen authoritatively. I held his hand and my breath in silent admiration as he led me back to the steps, up across the stage and out into the passage. Fortunately the stage door was still open, and as we tumbled out into the street we burst into laughter. We had been on the stage at the Old Vic!

3

A Glass Coach

Some weeks after the Old Vic episode, as the speed-writing course was officially coming to an end, my mother met me on my return home one evening excitedly waving a message from Stephen, who had telephoned to invite me to a May Ball in Cambridge. The prospect was tantalizing. In the Lower Sixth at school, a girl had been invited to a May Ball, and the rest of us were green with envy lapping up every detail of a gala occasion which seemed to be the stuff of fairy tales. Now, unbelievably, my turn had come. When Stephen rang to confirm the invitation, I accepted with pleasure. The problem of what to wear was soon solved when I found a dress in white-and-navy silk in a shop near the speed-writing school in Oxford Street, which was just within my means.

The May Balls, which with typical Cambridge contrariness take place in June, were still some months away. In the meantime I had to start replenishing my funds, depleted by the purchase of the ball gown, for my travels around Spain later in the summer, so I signed on with a temporary-employment agency in St Albans. My first assignment was a one-and-a-half-day stint – Thursday afternoon and the whole of Friday – in the Westminster Bank in Hatfield, where the manager of the branch, Mr Abercrombie, a patient, kindly man, was a friend of my father's. I was first directed to the telephone switchboard, but with no inkling of what to do, I panicked at the flashing lights and frantically pulled out some leads on the board while desperately trying to push others into the vacant holes. I succeeded only in cutting off all outside callers and in connecting up the telephones of people who were sitting opposite each other. After that, I gradually settled into a variety of temporary jobs as the spring advanced into early summer and the night of the May Ball approached.

When Stephen arrived one hot afternoon in early June to take me to Cambridge, I was shocked by the deterioration in his condition since that evening of the Old Vic escapade, and

I doubted that he was really strong enough to drive his father's car, a huge old Ford Zephyr. Built like a tank, it had apparently forded rivers in Kashmir when the family – minus Stephen who had stayed at school in England – had lived in India some years earlier. I feared that the snorting vehicle might well go much too fast for the present driver, a slight, frail, limping figure who appeared to use the steering wheel to hoist himself up to see over the dashboard. I introduced Stephen to my mother. She showed no signs of surprise or of alarm, but waved us away as if she were the fairy godmother, sending me off to the ball – with Prince Charming – in a runaway glass coach.

The journey was terrifying. It transpired that Stephen's role model for driving was his father, who drove fast and furiously, overtaking on hills and at corners – he had even been known to drive down a dual carriageway in the wrong direction. Drowning out all attempts at conversation, the wind roared through the open windows as we sped at take-off speed past the fields and trees of Hertfordshire into the exposed landscape of Cambridgeshire. I scarcely dared look at the road in front while Stephen, on the other hand, seemed to be looking at everything except the road. He probably felt that he could afford to live dangerously since fate had already dealt him such a cruel blow. This however was of scant reassurance to me, so I secretly vowed that I would travel home by train. I was definitely beginning to have my doubts about this supposedly fairy-tale experience of a May Ball.

Defying all road-accident statistics, we actually arrived in one piece at Stephen's lodgings, in a fine Thirties-style graduate house set in a shady garden, where the other revellers were busy with last-minute preparations. When I had changed in the upstairs room allotted to me by the housekeeper, I was introduced to Stephen's fellow lodgers and research students, whose seemingly contradictory attitudes towards him baffled me. They talked to him in his own intellectual terms, sometimes caustically sarcastic, sometimes crushingly critical, always humorous. In personal terms, however, they treated him with a gentle consideration which was almost loving. I found it hard to reconcile these two extremes of behaviour. I was used to consistency of attitude and approach, and was perplexed by these people who confidently played devil's advocate, arguing ferociously with someone – that is Stephen – one minute, and the next not only treating him as if nothing were amiss, but attending caringly to his personal needs, as if his word were their command. I had not learnt to distinguish reason from emotion, the intellect from the heart. In my innocence I had some hard lessons to learn. Such innocence, by Cambridge standards, was boring and predictable.

We all went off to a late dinner in a first-floor restaurant on the corner of King's Parade. From where I sat, I gazed out at the pinnacles and spires of King's College, the Chapel and the gatehouse, darkly silhouetted against the vast, luminous panorama of an East Anglian sunset. That in itself was magical enough. We returned to the house for last-minute adjustments before setting out on the ten-minute walk across the watery green spaces of the Backs to the old courts of Trinity Hall, Stephen's College. He insisted on taking his tape recorder and collection of tapes across to the College to install in a friend's room, put at our disposal when we needed a break from the jollifications, but he could not carry them himself. "Oh, come on," one of his friends grumbled benevolently, "I suppose I shall have to carry them for you." And he did.

Relatively small, unpretentious and tucked away from public view, Trinity Hall consists of a motley collection of buildings – very old, old, Victorian and, most recently, modern – enclosing lawns, flower beds and a terrace which overlooks the river. We approached the College from the other side of the Cam, standing briefly on the high arch of a new bridge which, Stephen seriously impressed upon me, had recently been built in memory of a student, Timothy Morgan, who had died tragically in 1960 having just completed his design for it. From that bridge we were regaled with a fairy-tale spectacle: it reminded me of the mysterious country house in one of my favourite French novels, *Le Grand Meaulnes* by Alain-Fournier, where the hero, Augustin Meaulnes, chances across a brightly lit château in the dark depths of the countryside and, from being a bemused observer, finds himself drawn into the revelries, the music and the dancing, never quite knowing what to expect. Here in Trinity Hall, bands were sending their strains out on the night air, the lawn leading down to the river was decorated with twinkling lights, as was the magnificent copper beech in the centre, and couples were already dancing on a raised platform under the tree. In the marquee at the top of the lawn I was introduced to more friends of Stephen's, and together we made a beeline for our ration of champagne, which was being served from a bath, then on to the buffet and to the various entertainments: to the tightly packed Hall where on a distant stage an inaudible cabaret was taking place, to an elegantly panelled room where a string quartet was attempting to compete with the Jamaican-steel band out on the lawn outside, and to a corner by the Old Library where chestnuts were being served from a glowing brazier. Our companions had drifted away, leaving us sitting up on the terrace by the river, watching the dancers writhe to the hypnotic rhythms of the steel band. "I'm sorry I don't dance." Stephen apologized. "That's quite all right – it doesn't matter," I lied.

Dancing was not totally out of the question however, because later, after yet another buffet and more champagne, we discovered a jazz band secreted away in a cellar. The room was dark, apart from some weird blueish lights. The men were invisible except for their cuffs and shirt-fronts, which shone with a bright-purple luminosity, while the girls could hardly be seen at all. I was fascinated. Stephen explained that the lights were picking up the fluorescent element contained in washing powder, which was why the men's shirts were so visible, but that, as the girls' new dresses would not have been contaminated with *Tide* or *Daz* or any other detergent, they did not show up with the same ghostly light. In the darkness of the underground room, I persuaded Stephen to take to the floor. We swayed gently to and fro, laughing at the dancing patterns of purple light until, to our disappointment, the band packed up and went.

In the early hours of the morning, the other colleges which had been hosting May Balls traditionally opened their doors to all-comers. As day dawned, we staggered down Trinity Street to Trinity College where, in a spacious set of rooms, somebody's extremely well-organized and mature girlfriend was preparing breakfast, but I just sank into an armchair and fell asleep. Some kind person must have led me back sleepwalking to the lodging house in Adams Road, where I slept comfortably until mid-morning.

The day's programme for the May Ball partners had been planned with the efficiency of a modern tour operator, except that it was much more stimulating. As well as researching their PhDs in Chemistry, Stephen's friends, Nick Hughes and Tom Wesley, were much involved, as editors, in the production of a guide to the post-war buildings of Cambridge, *Cambridge New Architecture*, which was to be published in 1964. Stephen shared their interest and acted as a part-time consultant in the project. They were all anxious therefore to show the objects of their deliberations to any interested parties. However sceptically these buildings are viewed today, in the Sixties they were the cause of great excitement, the assertive excitement of post-war development and expansion, unconcerned for old properties, meadows or trees which might inhibit the new wave of roads, buildings and university development. Conservation was not yet a popular concern.

With a zealous, pioneering fervour, our guides pointed out to us – their impressionably ignorant female guests – the features of a selection of new sites, either recently finished or still under construction. These included the Hugh Casson development of the Sidgwick Site, and Churchill College – the memorial to Sir Winston, whose concern at the lack of provision for scientists and technologists in this country led to the foundation of the College in 1958. We were also taken to Harvey Court, the Gonville and Caius development, which left even the contributors to *Cambridge New Architecture* lost for words. They described it hopefully as "an experiment which may eventually bully its occupants into enjoying the pattern of life it imposes", and added in its defence: "and it is Cambridge's most courageous attempt at finding some new ideal solution to the problems of college residence". Little did I know that some twelve years later I would be living next door to this particular experiment in modern living. Finally, as a sop to tradition, we visitors from less richly endowed universities were allowed to take a quick peep inside King's College Chapel.

After lunch we all went out for a ride in a punt, and then the question of the return journey loomed. "I think it would be better if I went by train," I hesitantly suggested to Stephen, but he would not hear of it. Anxious not to offend him, I took my place once again in the passenger seat of the dreaded Zephyr. The journey home was every bit as terrifying as the outward journey, and by the time we reached St Albans, I decided that, much as I appreciated the May Ball, I did not want to subject myself to that sort of dodgem ride ever again. My mother was in the front garden when we drew up at the gate. I tersely said "thank you and goodbye" to Stephen, and, with never a backwards glance, marched into the house. My mother followed me in and reprimanded me severely: "You're not going to send that poor young man away without even a cup of tea are you?" she said, shocked at my indifference. Her words pricked my conscience. I ran out of the house to try and catch Stephen. He was still there, parked at the gate, trying to start the car. Slowly the car began to roll back down the steep hill, because he had let the brake off before getting the engine started. He jammed the brake on and, with alacrity, came in for tea, sitting with me in the sun by the garden door. As we excitedly recounted the events of the ball to my mother, he was attentive and charming. I decided that I really rather liked him and could forgive his road madness providing I did not have to experience it too often.

4

Hidden Truths

A couple of weeks later we temporarily acquired an addition to our family as my parents had responded to a call for accommodation for visiting French teenagers and were taking care of a sixteen year-old girl whose best friend, by an uncanny coincidence, was lodging with the Hawkings. One Saturday in June, not long after the May Ball, Isobel Hawking invited the two French girls and me to join her on a visit to Cambridge. To my relief, she drove sensibly, talked in a jovially concentrated intellectual fashion and brought a splendid picnic – "a cold collation" she called it – which we ate on the veranda of Stephen's ground-floor room in Adams Road. Thus my family and I were brought into closer and more regular contact with the Hawkings, and when Stephen came back to St Albans for a weekend, my parents invited him to dinner. They treated him with faultless hospitality, outwardly unperturbed by his appearance. He had reverted to his old Oxford ways. His lank, straight hair was longer than ever, and the black-velvet smoking jacket and the red bow tie had become a uniform, adopted to defy the very conformity which my parents represented. They, for their part, may have taken comfort from the fact that this was to be our last meeting for some time, as I was on the point of setting off yet again for Spain.

Early one morning in July 1963, my father drove me to Gatwick for a student flight which was due to leave at 9 a.m. and arrive in Madrid at one o'clock, but take-off was delayed while repairs were carried out to an engine. I was not at all concerned by the delay, nor by the need for repairs, nor by the fact that, after take-off, water – which eventually turned to icicles – dripped through the roof of the aircraft. Nor was I worried by the discovery that the captain and his co-pilot were happily enjoying a glass of beer when we students were invited to look into the cockpit. Bill Lewis, an acquaintance of our local GP, who was meeting me in Madrid, was much more anxious. "I thought you must be coming via the North Pole!" he joked when, at last, I emerged from customs at five in the afternoon. He took me home to meet his wife, who assured me of a warm welcome at their apartment every evening from six onwards, and then he delivered me to the lodgings he had found for me. Pilar, the landlady, was a small, vivacious, sharp-nosed, black-haired single lady who lived in a extraordinarily large, well-appointed flat just round the corner from the Lewises. Pilar's other lodger, Sylvia, was also English and worked at the British Embassy. Sylvia was not happy about some of Pilar's friends, who would turn up at all hours of the day and the night, and when she told me her concerns I hastened to lay my plans for leaving Madrid at the earliest opportunity, but not before taking advantage of every precious moment in the capital city and its environs to visit the Prado Museum and join many a tourist bus to the royal palaces at Aranjuez and the Escorial. Of course I also went to Toledo, the medieval city perched on a rock above the river Tajo, where in the thirteenth century Jews, Arabs and Christians had worked in perfect harmony in the pursuit of learning, and where in the seventeeth century El Greco executed some of his finest paintings. With a group of students I went on the pilgrimage to the Valley of the Fallen, el Valle de los Caídos, supposedly the monument to the dead of both sides in the Civil War but in fact a burial place only for the Fascists – and eventually Franco himself – constructed by Republican prisoners of war. I began to realize that the many mutilated beggars on the streets of Madrid were the tragic, living remnants of the Civil War, revealing an ugly, schizoid streak to Spain. In the mid-twentieth century, the country still bore out the disturbing contrasts depicted by Goya in the eighteenth- and early-nineteenth-century paintings and drawings I had seen in the Prado.

Back in Pilar's establishment, Sylvia and I had the uncomfortable sensation that things were coming to crisis point. We had persistently refused to go out with her in the evenings and, just as regularly, saucepans were now clattering through the air in the kitchen, while meals and mealtimes became a matter of chance. Feeling slightly guilty at leaving Sylvia in the lurch, I took evasive action and set off by air-conditioned train for the safety of Granada, where I settled in for a protracted stay at an international student hostel which housed a stimulating and unpredictable crowd, particularly the Spaniards among them, whose discussions could range from politics to poetry in the space of a single breath. To preserve my own sanity, I would sometimes have to escape from the intensity of their arguments to wander the streets of Granada in the heat of the day, watching the gypsy children at play in front of their caves, or to stroll through the Moorish palace, the Alhambra and the gardens of the Generalife, astounded at the sheer extravagant beauty of the place.

Lulled into a dreamy slumber by the perfume of the roses and the playing of the fountains, I would sit alone for hours under the arches in the courtyard of streams, in the Generalife, and from there would gaze across to the forbidding walls which concealed the intricate, creamy lacework of the inner courtyards of the Alhambra. Dazzling in the sun, the city lay at my feet, its glare broken only by the tall bottle-green spikes of the cypresses and the violent purple and pink patches of bougainvillea tumbling over reflecting white walls. A beautiful city but also a very cruel city. What other city could claim to have murdered its own most famous son? It was in Granada at the outbreak of the Spanish Civil War that the rebellious right-wing Francoist forces slaughtered the greatest Spanish poet of the twentieth century, Federico García Lorca, the poet who, through the colour, rhythm and vision of his verse, had introduced me to Andalucía long before I had set foot on its soil.

During these long periods of solitary contemplation in a setting of such dramatically haunting beauty, I found myself overcome by waves of loneliness. In the past I had known moments of extreme dejection without being able to identify a precise cause. The reason for them was now becoming apparent and it was natural enough: I longed to have someone with whom to share my experiences. Moreover, I realized that the person I most wanted to share them with was Stephen. The early rapport between us had held much promise of harmony and compatibility. Because of his illness, any relationship with him was bound to be precarious, short-lived and probably heartbreaking. Could I help him fulfil himself and find even a brief happiness? I doubted whether I was up to the task, but when I confided in my new-found friends of all nationalities they urged me to go ahead. "If he needs you, you must do it," they said.

Competing against this inner turmoil, the strong pull of adventure finally tore me away from the brooding magic of Granada and deposited me on a hot, smelly bus, crowded with

37

market vendors and their wares – mostly still alive and flapping and squawking – on the slow crawl over the hills to Málaga. I was waiting in the bus station for the connection to La Línea, the last Spanish outpost before Gibraltar, when a man came up to me and asked if I would like to train as a Spanish dancer. To my surprise he explained that I had the right looks and figure. Although I was by now an old hand at fending off the predatory Spanish male, I was flattered. Despite my misgivings, the man appeared genuine. He was neither oily nor ingratiating, but quite straightforward in his approach. He handed me a card bearing the address of his dance studio. I was weighing up his offer when the bus for La Línea lumbered into view and hauled me out of temptation's way. Sometimes I have a faint twinge of regret at how that bus broke all known records for timekeeping in Spain by arriving on schedule. Who knows what my story might have been, had it arrived just a few minutes later?

From La Línea I passed through the very physical border between Spain and Gibraltar, a barricade of green iron railings about twenty feet high with a gate at the customs post. Gibraltar, with all its incongruous trappings of British colonialism, was a convenient stepping stone for my one and only trip to Africa, to Tangiers for my first encounter with the descendants of the people who had invaded Spain in 711 and stayed there for more than seven hundred years – the Arabs. I liked them. They treated me, a young English girl travelling alone, with great courtesy and, unlike the Spaniards, who automatically harassed any passing foreign female, they showed no such disrespect. They were a dignified people, proud of their artistic skills, which were everywhere on display in the booths of the Kazbah. They were also gentle and hospitable, curious to learn about life in Europe, as I discovered over many glasses of the hot, sweet mint tea with which they plied me whenever I bought the smallest item in their shops.

Quite a few saucepans had been flung around in Madrid during my absence, according to Sylvia. Pilar was more and more dissatisfied with the return that she was getting from her paying guests, having doubtless anticipated sizeable bonuses of one sort or another, and had turned Sylvia out of her room, so she was now sharing with me. This we decided was a good thing, because there was safety in numbers, but it was no good for Sylvia as a long-term prospect, since I would shortly be leaving and she could not possibly stay in the house on her own. I had deliberately refrained from telling the Lewises the truth about the lodgings they had kindly found for me, as I did not want to appear ungrateful for their help or their hospitality, but the time had now come to apprise them of the goings-on at *la casa de Pilar*. Sylvia came with me to the Lewises' six o'clock cocktail hour, and together we told them about the succession of decidedly repulsive male visitors to the apartment – for, albeit on a small scale, Pilar was running a disorderly house and was intent on procuring nice English girls for some of the flabby, ageing men of her acquaintance. We recounted how they attempted to grab us when we returned home at night, usually sheltering behind the *sereno*, the nightwatchman, who kept the keys to the front doors of all the apartment houses in the street and who would appear at a clap of the hands to open the main door. We lightly glossed over the shenanigans which went on all night in the other rooms in the flat, and the ominous rattlings of the locked bedroom door handle.

As Sylvia and I recounted these tales to the captive audience of British expatriates on my final evening in Madrid, Mrs Lewis spluttered over her gin and tonic, while her other guests grinned in amusement. Immediately the tendrils of the local grapevine started reaching out to find new lodgings for Sylvia as a matter of urgency. Most of the Lewis regulars, like Sylvia, worked at the British Embassy, though she had not met any of them before. They were amusing but modest, a good advertisement for the Diplomatic Service, which began to beckon as an exciting career prospect. I returned to England the next day, by student flight, sad to have left behind so many experiences, sights, sounds, acquaintances and intrigues, but dazzled at the array of contrasting, maybe even conflicting, possibilities that were opening up before me.

5

Uncertain Principles

My attempts to get in touch with Stephen on my return home from Spain were unavailing. According to his mother, he had already gone back to Cambridge and was not at all well. I was busy preparing to leave home to embark on a new stage of my life in London and, for the next few weeks that autumn, my attention was totally absorbed as I was drawn into the academic and social whirl of the Westfield scene in particular, and London in general. Concerts, the theatre and the ballet were all within easy reach. This was how I came to be travelling on the London Underground with a group of friends when we glimpsed the headlines announcing President Kennedy's assassination. It was at about that time, November 1963, that I heard from Stephen again. He was coming to London for dental treatment and asked if I would like to go to the opera with him. This was a much more enticing prospect than any of the Freshers' hops, which despite Beatlemania were dire occasions where the boys stayed stuck to the walls until the last dance. Though I had loved music since early childhood, I had had little formal training and had been to the opera only once – with the school to a performance of *The Marriage of Figaro* at Sadler's Wells. My single attempt to learn an instrument, the flute, had been quickly aborted at the age of thirteen, when I broke both arms trying to ice-skate on the frozen lake in the park at Verulamium, the site of the Roman city on which St Albans was founded.

One Friday afternoon that November, I met Stephen in Harley Street, where Russell Cole, his Australian uncle by marriage, had his dental practice. He walked haltingly, lurching from side to side, making taxis an expensive necessity for journeys of any great distance. Curiously, as his gait became more unsteady, so his opinions became more forceful and defiant. On our way to visit the Wallace Collection, only a short distance from Harley Street, he announced quite adamantly that he did not share the general hero-worship of the assassinated President. In his opinion, the manner of Kennedy's handling of the Cuban Missile Crisis could only be described as foolhardy: he had brought the world to the brink of nuclear war and it was he, not the Russians, who had threatened a military confrontation. What's more, Stephen declared, it was preposterous for the United States to claim a victory, because Kennedy had agreed to remove US missiles from Turkey to appease Kruschev. Despite the force with which he expressed his ideas and his difficulty in walking, Stephen was indefatigable, so, from the Wallace Collection, we made our way down Regent Street in search of a restaurant. We were just crossing Lower Regent Street when, in the middle of the road, as the lights were turning green, he stumbled and fell. With the help of a passer-by, I dragged him to his feet and thereafter gave him my arm to lean on. Shaken, we hailed a taxi for Sadler's Wells.

The opera for which Stephen had tickets was *The Flying Dutchman*. It was magnificent, sweeping us away in the power of its music and the drama of its legendary tale. The Dutchman, cursed to roam the seas through storm and wind until he could find someone who would sacrifice herself for love of him, was a wild, hounded figure, loudly lamenting his fate from the rigging of his tossing ship. Senta, the girl who fell in love with him, was pure and innocent. Like most Wagnerian sopranos, however, her weight kept her pretty firmly moored to her spinning wheel. Sensing that Stephen identified closely with the hero, I began to understand his demonic driving tactics. His father's car was the vehicle for his fury at the trick that Fate had dealt him. He too was flying hither and thither in search of rescue – in a manner that could only be described as foolhardy.

After that evening, I felt that I needed to find out more for myself about Stephen's condition. I made several sorties into London, searching out old acquaintances who had become medical students, and investigating the poky offices of various charities dealing in neurological illnesses. Everywhere I drew a blank. Perhaps it was better not to know. Was Stephen's fate any worse, I wondered, than the fate which loomed over us all? We lived under the shadow of the nuclear cloud, and none of us could count on our full threescore years and ten.

In the lull of the bleak winter days between Christmas and the New Year, I called on Stephen at home in St Albans. He was on the point of leaving for London to go to the opera with his father and sisters. However he was so obviously delighted to see me that

I readily accepted his spontaneous invitation – to accompany him and his father in a week's time to yet another opera, Strauss's *Der Rosenkavalier*. The opera seemed to be an established family pastime in the Hawking household, whereas I, a newcomer, was still assessing this hybrid art form. Though undoubtedly it could exert tremendous emotional power through the combination of music and drama, it could also appear ludicrous if for the merest second one's concentration lapsed. During the next term Stephen seemed to have access to an inexhaustible supply of opera tickets and was forever coming to London to take me to Covent Garden or Sadler's Wells. I once ventured to suggest that I would rather like to go to the ballet, as the ballet had been my passion since the age of four, but that suggestion was quashed with withering scorn. Ballet was a waste of time, and the music was trivial, not worth the effort of listening, I was told. Chastened, I refrained from telling Stephen when I managed to get myself a ticket for Tchaikovsky's *Romeo and Juliet*, with Fonteyn and Nureyev, through the student union. We went in a party of girls and sat in the cheap seats, far back and high up in the amphitheatre at Covent Garden, way above the Grand Circle where the Hawkings usually sat. That performance was sublime, and it left me deeply moved.

Stephen was still coming to London frequently for seminars or for dental appointments and, increasingly, I found myself travelling to Cambridge to visit him on Saturdays or Sundays. Those visits, though urgently awaited, often proved disappointing to both of us. The fare – at ten shillings return – made quite a hole in my allowance of ten pounds a month, and the course of love did not run at all smoothly. It did not need much imagination to realize that Stephen could not contemplate embarking on a long-term, stable relationship because of the dismal prognosis of his illness. A quick fling was probably all he could envisage, and that was not what I – in my innocence and in the puritanical climate of the early Sixties, when the fear of an unwanted pregnancy was a potent constraint – dared imagine. These opposing perspectives led to such tension between us that I often returned to London in tears, and Stephen probably felt that my presence was rubbing salt into the wound of his trauma. He revealed little where emotional matters were concerned and he refused to talk about his illness. For fear of hurting him, I tried to intuit his feelings without forcing him to voice them, thus unwittingly establishing a tradition of non-communication, which eventually would become intolerable. I met him yet again in Harley Street later that winter, after an appointment with his consultant. "How did you get on?" I asked. He grimaced. "He told me not to bother to come back, because there's nothing he can do," he said.

At Westfield, Margaret Smithson, my room-mate, came with me to the meetings of the Christian Union, where I hoped to gain some supportive insights for a situation which was becoming very confusing as I became more and more involved in it. Like his parents, Stephen had no hesitation in declaring himself an atheist, despite the strong Methodist background of his Yorkshire grandparents. It was understandable that, as a cosmologist examining the laws that governed the universe, he could not allow his calculations to be muddled by a confessed belief in the existence of a creator God, quite apart from the confusion his illness might be creating in his mind. I was quite glad to get away from the tedium of regular Sunday church-going, but was not inclined to abandon my beliefs completely. Even then, possibly under my mother's influence, I was convinced that there had to be more to heaven and earth than was contained in Stephen's cold, impersonal philosophy. Although by this stage I was completely under his spell, bewitched by his clear blue-grey eyes and the broad dimpled smile, I resisted his atheism. Instinctively I knew that I could not allow myself to succumb to such a negative influence, which could offer no consolation, no comfort and no hope for the human condition. Atheism would destroy us both. I needed to cling to whatever rays of hope I could find and maintain sufficient faith for the two of us if any good were to come of our sad plight.

The meetings of the college Christian Union were not well attended, and soon they were to be even less so. The topic for the term's discussions was the nature of divine grace, but it quickly transpired that the leaders of the group, including the young chaplain, whose name we irreverently traduced to the Revd P. Souper, were firmly of the opinion that only baptized, confessed, practising Christians could receive divine grace, salvation or whatever else they liked to call it, and only they had the right qualifications to enter the Kingdom of Heaven. Margaret and I were so indignant that we walked out, furiously compiling lists of all those dearly loved – good people, friends and relations – who did not fulfil all the correct criteria, and held our own long discussions on these topics, which we continued into the vacations, when I went to stay with her and her family in Yorkshire.

Language students nowadays regularly spend a whole year abroad. In the Sixties it was a luxury to be able to spend even a term in the country of one's target language. We Westfield students set out by train and boat in late April to spend the summer on a pre-arranged course at the university of Valencia. We arrived to find that no such course existed and that all the university could offer us was a few classes in Spanish on Shakespeare. The only obligation on us was to collect our certificates of attendance at the end of the term, whether we attended the lectures or not. We went to just one class, which made a travesty of Macbeth, and decided that enough was enough. I had had a lifetime's education in Shakespeare at school and could not bear the thought of having a supplementary dose in Spanish. My companions agreed, so, thereafter, we went to the beach instead.

Only two weeks later, though the others still went to the beach, I was forced to stay at home, confined to my room in the seventh-floor apartment with a blinding headache which at first I thought was sunstroke but which developed into a severe case of chickenpox. I was already feeling wretchedly miserable. I missed Stephen badly: communication by telephone was out of the question in those days, and he did not write to me although I sent him many letters. The only comfort was afforded by my Westfield friends, whose visits kept me in touch with the outside world, and by my landlady, Doña Pilar de Ubeda, and her middle-aged daughter Maribel, who were kindness personified. As I slowly started to regain strength, I wandered into the kitchen, where Doña Pilar gave me lessons in Spanish cookery, a far more useful accomplishment than studying Shakespeare in Spanish. She taught me how to peel an orange tidily in quarters, how to make *gazpacho* and *paella* and she took me shopping with her. Luckily, with a spotty face and in the presence of such an august matron, I was spared the approaches of the men idly lounging around in the streets. Back in the flat, I sat in the living room listening ad nauseam to the two records I had bought myself – Beethoven's *Seventh Symphony* and excerpts from Wagner's *Tristan and Isolde*. The latter reduced me to an exquisitely painful state of woe. At last the longed-for moment came. Setting out by train for Barcelona on the first leg of the journey home, I was glad to leave Valencia behind: despite the succulence of its oranges and the all-pervasive perfume of its citrus groves, it left the nasty taste (of constant sexual harassment and the bitterness) of a repressive regime that thought nothing of flinging students into jail overnight and removing uncomplimentary pages from imported copies of the *Times*.

My parents brought Stephen to meet me, and the initial moment of reunion was happy but short-lived. I soon became aware that in my absence he had changed: his physical condition had not altered markedly, except that he now regularly walked with a stick, but his personality was overshadowed by a deep depression. This revealed itself in a harsh black cynicism, aided and abetted by long hours of Wagnerian opera played at full volume. He was even more terse and uncommunicative, apparently so absorbed in himself that when he offered to teach me to play croquet on the Trinity Hall lawn, for example, he seemed to forget that I was there. Throwing the stick, which had become his constant appendage, to one side, he gave out curt instructions as I aimed my ball towards the first hoop, missing it. He then took up his mallet and, croqueting my ball round the whole course, reached the finishing post before I had even had a second turn. I stood open-mouthed, amused and perturbed at one and the same time. This was indeed an impressive tour de force, in which he scarcely bothered to veil his hostility and frustration, as if he were deliberately trying to deter me from further association with him. It was too late. I was already so deeply involved with him that there was no easy or obvious way out.

It was painful but perhaps beneficial that we were soon to be parted again: Stephen was about to set out for Germany, with his sister Philippa, on a pilgrimage to the Wagnerian shrine, the Festspielhaus in Bayreuth, with tickets for the complete *Ring Cycle*. Thence they were to travel by rail behind the Iron Curtain to Prague. Meanwhile I was to accompany my father to an international governmental conference in Dijon, where I was to stay with a local family, an elderly couple with a highly sophisticated twenty-five-year-old daughter who had a job and a boyfriend. I was not at a loss for diversion however, because Dad's conference, after a day or two of lectures and study sessions, generated its own entertainment in which I was privileged to share. Since we were in Bourgogne, that naturally revolved around the vineyards, the famous *Clos* of the region.

Consequently there began yet another stage, arguably one of the most enjoyable of my education – the cultivation of a discerning palate in the course of which I was pleasurably introduced to the great names and the great bouquets of Bourgogne, Nuits-Saint-Georges, Côtes de Beaune, Clos de Vougeot. The advertising slogan for Nuits-Saint-Georges aroused my innocent curiosity: tantalizingly the deep velvety wine was said to resemble "*la nuit des noces, douce et caressante...*"

From Dijon we drove to Geneva airport to meet my mother and then spent a couple of days in our favourite retreat, high in the Bernese Oberland, at Hohfluh, a tiny village atop the Brenner Pass overlooking the valley of the Aare at Meiringen and enjoying the most spellbinding scenery. Before we left Switzerland for Italy, Dad took us to Lucerne, the medieval city on the edge of the lake, and showed us the sequence of paintings of the Dance of Death, in the roof beams of one of the wooden bridges which spanned the river. He pointed out the white-clad figure of Death, selecting its victim and capturing him in a deadly embrace and then whirling him faster and faster to his doom.

Italy was ravishing, a feast for the mind and the senses. Art, history, music, light and colour met us and pursued us everywhere we went – Como, Florence, San Gimignano, Pisa, Siena, Verona, Padua – in a vertiginous display of florid exuberance. One evening in Florence, after a day in the presence of Michelangelo, Botticelli, Bellini and Leonardo da Vinci, my mother and I were leaning out of the hotel window, looking across the Arno to the Pitti Palace, where we were to attend a concert. It was then, in an expansive moment, that she confided to me her reasons for marrying my father at the beginning of the War. If he were wounded, she said, she wanted to be able to care for him herself. That remark was prescient for, only a few days later, when we arrived at our hotel in Venice, the Hotel Della Salute on a secluded canal behind the church of the same name, the manager produced a postcard addressed to me. It was a view of the castle at Salzburg and it was from Stephen.

I was overjoyed. Could Stephen really have been thinking of me as I had been thinking of him? It gave me grounds for daring to hope that he was looking forward to seeing me at the end of the summer. The postcard was uncharacteristically full of news. He had arrived in Salzburg for the tail end of the Festival, which was quite a contrast to Bayreuth. Czechoslovakia had been wonderful and remarkably cheap, a good advertisement for communism. He did not mention that a bad fall on a train in Germany had deprived him of his front teeth and that many hours of painstaking dentistry by his uncle in Harley Street would be required to replace them. In the glow of romance, albeit conducted at a distance, Venice, its canals, lagoon, palaces, churches, galleries and islands – became even more gloriously scintillating – yet, impatient for the possible opening of a new chapter in my life, I was not sorry to leave it and return to Switzerland. From Basle we were to fly home with the car on board an aeroplane, in a well justified stroke of extravagance after the many thousands of miles my father had driven single-handedly across the Continent over the years.

Stephen was pleased to see me on my return. Intuitively I understood that he had begun to view our relationship in a more positive light and had perhaps decided that all was not lost, that the future did not have to be as black as his worst fears had painted it. Back in Cambridge, one dark wet Saturday evening in October, he hesitantly whispered a proposal of marriage to me. That moment transformed our lives and consigned all my thoughts of a career in the Diplomatic Service to oblivion.

6

Backgrounds

Once the momentous decision had been taken, everything else began to fall into place, if not automatically, then with some determination and effort. We sailed through the next year, carried high on a tide of euphoria. Whatever misgivings my friends and family may have had about Stephen's state of health, they kept them to themselves, and the only comments I received concerned the eccentricity of the Hawking family.

Such comments did not worry me too much, because I liked the Hawkings and regarded their eccentricities with a respectful fascination. They made me welcome, already treating me as one of the family. They may have economized on material goods, preferring the old and tried to the newfangled, and they certainly did compromise on heating to the extent that people who were cold were brusquely told to follow Frank Hawking's example and wear more clothes, a dressing gown for example, even during the day. Moreover, as I had already discovered, there were areas of the house which could be charitably described as distinctly shabby. However, none of this was particularly new to me. It simply indicated that this household had a set of priorities which were not so very different from those I was used to. My own parents had scraped and saved for years. We were not wealthy, and we often had to make do and mend because so much of Dad's income went on our education and on those wonderful summer holidays. We did not have central heating at home, and I was well used to sitting by the fire with my face and toes burning while a freezing draught whistled down the back of my neck. At night in bed I would rest my numbed feet on my hot-water bottle, in the full knowledge that blistering chilblains would be the price of such small comfort the next morning, when an exquisite ice garden of opaque fronds and ferns would cover the window panes. If our house was smarter than the Hawkings', it was both because it was smaller and because Dad had given up all pretensions to any prowess whatsoever as a handyman – and for good reason, since his attempts at repairs usually made matters much worse, bringing ceilings down on his head for example, while his attempts at interior decorating usually sent the paint flying everywhere except on the target – and had long decided that it was cheaper in the long run to pay professionals to do his odd jobs for him.

Rarely when I was present did members of the Hawking family bear out the stories about their habit of bringing books to the table. Mealtimes were generally sociable occasions, calmly presided over by Stephen's mother, who kept remarkably cool in the face of her husband's frequent displays of temper. Although he could be sharp and demanding, Frank Hawking was not hard-hearted. His outbursts were usually directed at the crass inadequacies of some inanimate object, like a blunt carving knife or a spilt glass or a dropped fork, never at people within the family circle. In fact, in handling young Edward, who was given to tantrums particularly at bedtime, he was a model of patience and forbearance. As for Stephen, apparently no longer subject to the savage black moods of the past, his placid, more philosophical nature promised a quieter lifestyle.

The talk at mealtimes was predictably intellectual, ranging over political and international issues. As Philippa had gone up to Oxford to study Chinese, the Cultural Revolution was a frequent topic. I knew little about oriental history or politics and thought it expedient to keep quiet rather than betray my ignorance. Spain and France seemed very parochial and unglamorous by comparison with the Orient, and nobody expressed any interest in them or in their cultures at all. The Hawkings, in any case, knew all there was to know about France, since Isobel had French relatives. They also knew all there was to know about Spain, since she and the children had spent three months living in close proximity to Robert Graves's household in Deià, Majorca, in the winter of 1950, when Frank was away in Africa, engaged on research in tropical medicine. Beryl Graves was a friend of Isobel's from her Oxford days, and Robert Graves was regarded as an icon in the family.

When the supper table was cleared away, we, the younger generation, would settle down to play a board game. A fanatical games player since his early childhood, Stephen had, with his close friend John McClenahan, devised a long and complicated dynastic game, complete with family trees, landed gentry, vast acreages, bishoprics for younger sons and death duties. This game unfortunately had not been preserved, so we were reduced to playing games such as *Cluedo*, *Scrabble* and occasionally the notoriously difficult Chinese game, mah-jong, with its delicately carved ivory tiles. Not only had I already been exposed to Stephen's prowess at croquet but I had also received similar treatment when he offered to teach me to play chess. However, when it came to *Scrabble*, I did not need a mentor as I was confident of being reasonably competent at word games, an art learnt as a very small child from numerous games of *Lexicon* with my loquacious and inventive Great Aunt Effie when we lived in her house in north London.

If there were not a quorum for board games, Stephen and I would sit by the fire after supper while his mother regaled us with episodes of family history. I enjoyed listening to her and admired her as a role model. An Oxford graduate and, before her marriage, an income-tax inspector, she was intelligent and witty, yet totally devoted to her family, appearing to have no ambitions for herself at all. At the time she was teaching history in a private girls' boarding school in St Albans, where her very considerable intellectual qualities were definitely underrated. With a bemused detachment, she took upon herself the task of introducing me to her own past and that of the Hawking family. The second child of seven, she was born in Glasgow, where her father, the son of a wealthy boiler maker, was a doctor. Although her family moved by boat to Plymouth when she was still a young child, she had vivid memories of her grandfather's austere house in Glasgow, where family prayers in the parlour, attended by every member of the household staff, constituted the only form of diversion. On her mother's side, she claimed descent from John Law of Lauriston, who after bankrupting France in the seventeenth century took himself off to Louisiana. In the telling, multifarious and far-reaching family feuds came to light, most of them concerned money, for it appeared that cutting a miscreant out of one's will was considered an automatic and quite acceptable means of expressing profound and puritanical displeasure.

Stephen's father's family were of God-fearing Yorkshire-farming stock. Their claim to distinction had come through an ancestor in the early nine-teenth century who had been steward to the Duke of Devonshire. In recognition of this elevated position he had built himself a sizeable house in Boroughbridge in Yorkshire, and had called it Chatsworth. The family fortunes had fluctuated somewhat since those days, with the consequence that, in the twentieth century, Stephen's grandfather's farming ventures had led to financial ruin and it was left to his grandmother to rescue her family of five children – four boys and a girl – from penury. This she did by opening a school in her house. Its success was said to be a measure of her strength of character. Money, wealth and its creation and loss were prominent elements in Isobel's story-telling, as was her marked tendency to judge others by their intelligence rather than by their integrity or kindness. Charm was regarded as a severe flaw in character, and those unfortunate enough to possess it were to be deeply mistrusted.

As his mother was one of seven children and his father one of five, Stephen naturally had legions of first cousins and a whole army of second cousins. My parents, on the other hand, were both only children, so I had no first cousins: all I possessed were a few second cousins, one in Australia and the rest in rural Norfolk. It therefore came as quite a shock to meet so many people who not only were closely related, but who also bore remarkable facial similarities to each other. On Stephen's mother's side, they characteristically had high cheekbones, close-set blue eyes and wavy, chestnut hair, while the faces of his father's relations were all long and heavily jowled. Only my brother bore any slight resemblance to me, yet here were all of thirty-three cousins who looked like each other, depending on which side of the family they belonged to, and who were all closely connected to Stephen.

Although quite a number lived abroad and divorce had been rather fashionable among them, I met many of them, their friends, husbands, wives and even their former spouses, during the course of that winter's succession of family parties. They treated me in an open and friendly manner, and I began to realize what an advantage a large family network could be: the loss of individuality in appearance was more than compensated by the sense of security which such a network could create. The novelty of this sense of extended family was exhilarating. By comparison my own immediate family circle of parents, brother and one grandmother and two great-aunts seemed a bit limited.

There was however one Hawking who notably lacked the self-assurance of the rest of the family. On hearing of our engagement, Stephen's Aunt Muriel announced that, as she put it, she "just had to come down from Yorkshire to see what sort of girl Stephen was marrying". Muriel was Frank Hawking's only sister. The most timid member of the family, she had stayed at home to look after her ageing parents despite being a gifted musician. Now in her sixties, she wore the marks of frustration in her sad, drooping face and large, soft brown eyes. She was devoted to her brother, Frank, and to his eldest son, and dutifully admired the family's intellectual qualities, although she herself did not share them. Her homely way of speech was often ignored by the other members of the family, though Stephen, who was her Methodist equivalent of a godson, always treated her with a good-natured tolerance. Frequently I would sit and chat to Auntie Muriel, just as I would sometimes escape to Granny Walker's attic, to get away from the competitive intellectual atmosphere of the dining room.

Stephen could be highly critical of people other than his closest relatives. His self-confidence restored, he delighted in bringing his Oxford ways into any conversation, deliberately setting out to shock with his provocative statements. His comment that Norwich cathedral was a very ordinary building profoundly upset my mild-mannered Grandma when I took him to stay with her for a weekend. He considered my friends to be easy victims and had no compunction in monopolizing the conversation at parties with his controversial opinions, often dominating the social scene with vociferous and tenacious arguments.

With me he would argue that artificial flowers were in every way preferable to the real thing and that Brahms, my favourite composer, was second-rate because he was such a poor orchestrator. Rachmaninov was good only for the musical dustbin and Tchaikovsky was primarily a composer of ballet music. So far, my knowledge of composers was embryonic: all I knew about Rachmaninov and Tchaikovsky was that their music had the power to move me profoundly and I knew nothing about Brahms's orchestration. It was only later that I found out, to my silent amusement, that although Wagner had despised Brahms, the feeling was mutual.

While I applauded Stephen's refusal to be drawn into small talk, I was nervously aware that his arrogance was in poor taste and was putting me in danger of losing me my friends, if not my relations. There came a stage when I even feared that he was jeopardizing my chances of any future academic activity. I was content to abandon all my budding hopes of a career in the Foreign Office for his sake, but I was unhappy about letting him destroy whatever opportunity I might have had for pursuing some sort of research. When I took him to meet my supervisor, Alan Deyermond, who was at that time encouraging me to think about doing a PhD in medieval literature, Stephen really excelled himself. Waving his sherry glass around as if the point he was making was so obvious that only a fool could disagree with it, he revelled in the opportunity to tell Alan Deyermond and all my contemporaries that the study of medieval literature was as useful an occupation as studying pebbles on the beach. Fortunately, as Alan Deyermond was also an Oxford graduate, he willingly picked up the gauntlet thus offered and gave Stephen a good run for his money. The argument was inconclusive, and both sides parted on remarkably amiable terms. When I protested on the way home in the car, Stephen shrugged. "You shouldn't take it personally," he said.

Stephen's conviction that intellectual arguments were never to be considered a personal matter was tested during that same year. Professor Fred Hoyle, who had rejected Stephen's postgraduate research application, was at the time pioneering the use of television to popularize science to great effect. He had become a household name and his success was enabling him to put pressure on the government to grant him his own Institute of Astronomy in Cambridge. It was a foregone conclusion that if his demands were not met, he – like so many other British scientists – would join the brain drain to the United States. He had power and popularity, and his recent theories were eagerly followed in the press, especially those which he was developing with his Indian research student, Jayant Narlikar, whose office was near Stephen's on the old Cavendish site in Cambridge.

In advance of publication, Hoyle's latest paper, expounding further aspects of the theory of the steady-state universe which he had developed with Hermann Bondi and Thomas Gold, was presented to a distinguished gathering of scientists at the Royal Society. Then the forum was opened to questions, which on such occasions are usually fairly deferential. Stephen was present and bided his time. At last his raised hand was noticed by the chairman. He, a very junior research student who as yet had no academic research of any note to his credit, struggled to his feet and proceeded to tell Hoyle and his students as well as the rest of the audience that the calculations in the presentation were wrong. The audience was stunned, and Hoyle was ruffled by this piece of effrontery. "How do you know?" he asked, quite sure that Stephen's grounds for disputing his new research could easily be dismissed. He was not expecting Stephen's response. "I've worked it out," he replied, and then added, "in my head." As a result of that intervention, Stephen began to be noticed in scientific circles, and thus he found the subject for his PhD thesis: the properties of expanding universes. Relations between him and Fred Hoyle however never advanced after that incident.

Arguments notwithstanding – scientific, impersonal or otherwise – everything we did in the course of that academic year contributed to a common purpose, our forthcoming marriage, for which a date in July 1965 was set. As it was by no means certain that I should be allowed to stay in Westfield as a married undergraduate, my top priority was to win the consent of the college authorities. Without it, the wedding would probably have to be postponed for another year, because we both knew that the promise my father had demanded of us on our engagement – that I would complete my undergraduate course – was not to be taken lightly. Since a year was a long time in the course of an illness such as Stephen's, as his father persistently reminded me, his survival for that length of time could not be guaranteed. This unpalatable truth was a factor that I should have to bear in mind constantly whenever I looked to the future. In the first instance, it was now up to me to persuade Professor John Varey, the Head of the Spanish Department, and Mrs Matthews, the Principal, that the situation was urgent. Professor Varey's response, when I tentatively broached the matter, was that the situation was most irregular, but that if the Principal gave her blessing, he would not object.

As my previous – and only – encounter with Mrs Matthews had been at the interview in 1962, I was not hopeful of a propitious outcome. At the time appointed by her secretary, six o'clock one evening towards the end of the autumn term of 1964, I knocked with trembling hand at the green baize door which separated her flat in the Regency house from the administrative area of the College. Mrs Matthews evidently sensed my nervousness from the moment I walked through the door. She bade me sit down and thrust a cigarette into one hand and a sherry into the other. "What's the matter?" she began, frowning and looking me straight in the eye with an anxious concern, "don't worry, I'm not going to eat you." I took a deep breath and did my best to explain my relationship with Stephen, his illness, the prognosis and our plans to make the most of whatever time we had left to us. She never took her eyes off me and betrayed very little emotion. When she had heard my tale through without interruption, she came straight to the point. "Well, of course, if you marry, you will have to live out of College, you understand that don't you?" My heart lifted slightly, aware that she had not vetoed our plans outright, and I was able to nod confidently because I had already done my homework on that score. "Yes, I know that," I replied, "I have found out that there is a room available in a private house in Platt's Lane." "Well, then, that's fine," Mrs Matthews replied, staring fixedly at the embers in the grate. "Go ahead and make the most of the chance you have." She paused and then, changing her tone to one of uncharacteristic absent-mindedness, she confided that she herself had been in a similar situation. Her own husband had been severely disabled. She was only too well aware of how important it was to do whatever one knew to be right. Equally she agreed with my father that I must complete my education. She warned me that the future I faced would not be easy. She promised to help in whatever way she could – most significantly, by conveying her agreement to Professor Varey.

Having surmounted that major hurdle, all that remained was to arrange my accommodation in Platt's Lane, which was easily done. Mrs Dunham, the landlady, readily agreed to let the attic room on the third floor to me, and both she and her husband proved to be hospitable and patient landlords. "Patient" because never once did they complain about my monopoly of their telephone in the study downstairs. Stephen had devised a way of ringing me for fourpence, the cost of a local call, via all the intermediate exchanges between Cambridge and London: this meant that there was no time limit on our conversations every evening. Quite apart from the frenzied pleasure of daily communication and love-talk, we had plenty to discuss as we laid our plans for our future. The illness assumed the proportions of a minor background irritant as we talked about job prospects, housing, wedding arrangements and our first trip to the United States, to a summer school at Cornell University in upstate New York, due to start just ten days after the wedding.

7

In Good Faith

Now that my immediate problems had been solved at a stroke, I was confident that in my final year I could finish my degree in London by commuting weekly from Cambridge, especially since current social research suggested that married undergraduates consistently produced better results than frustrated, unmarried students. My father generously continued to pay my allowance to help cover the rail fares, but the responsibility of finding a job and an income to support us both lay with Stephen. For his part, he was now taking his research seriously, realizing that he would have to have a substantial piece of work documented, if not published, to enable him to apply for a Research Fellowship. To this end, he started to expand the ideas which had caused such a stir at Hoyle's Royal Society lecture. He also found by way of compensation for his efforts that his work was actually enjoyable.

Consequently it was with more than just the joyful expectation of a young fiancé awaiting the arrival of his beloved that he greeted me in his rooms, now for convenience in the main body of Trinity Hall, one chilly morning in the February of 1965: he was in fact expecting that I would put my secretarial skills to good use by typing out a job application for him. The look of horrified dismay that spread across his face as I walked into his room with my left arm bulging beneath my coat in a white plaster cast, dashed all my hopes of even the merest display of sympathy. I was not wanting anything more than that, because the circumstances in which the fracture had occurred had been too embarrassing to confess over the telephone.

The truth was that the Westfield hops had livened up considerably with the arrival, the previous year, of male students into the College and the election of a more dynamic entertainments committee on the Students' Union. We now had proper bands playing Sixties' music, the Beatles and the twist. I loved twisting, and at a midweek hop had indulged in an innocent bout of twisting with someone else's boyfriend. The floor was highly polished, my high heels skidded on the slippery surface and down I went, falling heavily onto my outstretched left hand. The searing pain all too obviously indicated another broken wrist, this time from twisting rather than ice skating.

Still rather battered by this ordeal, I did not at first appreciate the reasons for the horror on Stephen's face – not, that is, until he gestured to the borrowed typewriter and the pile of pristine white paper neatly arranged on the table. Dolefully he explained that he had been hoping that I would type out his application for a Research Fellowship at Gonville and Caius College, which had to be submitted by the beginning of the following week. Guilty on account of the twisting, I set to work with a will to write the application out in longhand, using my intact right hand. The exercise took the whole weekend.

To have stayed overnight in Stephen's rooms was unthinkable. On more than one occasion, according to Stephen, the eagle eye of Sam, the surly bedder and guardian of the College morals on Q staircase, must have noticed a scarf or a cardigan of mine carelessly left hanging over the back of a chair in Stephen's study. Scenting the whiff of scandal and a captive prey – for he was no friend to young lady visitors – Sam would put his head round the door of Stephen's bedroom in the early hours, hoping to catch me squeezed illicitly into Stephen's narrow single bed. But his expectations of a juicy scandal to report to the college authorities were constantly disappointed, because many of Stephen's better-established friends regularly offered me hospitality at weekends. Many of these friends already had houses and cars and were now in the process of producing offspring which, for our generation, was the expected progression of events. Ours was the last generation for whom the prime goals were quite straightforward: the ideals of romantic love, marriage, a home and a family. The difference for Stephen and me was that we knew that we had only a brief space of time in which to achieve those goals.

Against all odds, the Fellowship application was actually delivered on time, and Stephen then waited to be called to an interview. It was not however to be quite as simple as that. On the strength of the notoriety of his startling intervention in the Hoyle lecture, Stephen had approached Professor Hermann Bondi at the end of one of the regular fortnightly seminars at King's College, London, to ask him if he would be willing to act as a referee for the Fellowship application. As Hermann Bondi was a neighbour in Hampshire of Stephen's Aunt Loraine and her husband Rus, the Harley Street dentist, a formal letter did not seem necessary. Some weeks later, however, Stephen received an embarrassed message from Gonville and Caius College. In reply to the College's request for a reference for Stephen Hawking, Professor Bondi had disclaimed all knowledge of any candidate of that name. Given the circumstances and the casual nature of Stephen's approach to him, it was perhaps understandable that he should have forgotten. The situation was rectified by means of hasty phone calls, and Stephen was duly summoned for an interview, where he had plenty of scope for impressing the members of the committee with his powers of intellectual argument, the more so since none of them were cosmologists, however eminent their reputations in other disciplines.

The novel idea of admitting a cosmologist to their midst must have appealed to the Fellowship Committee, while for us the appearance of Stephen's name in the list of Fellowship awards was a cause for jubilant celebration. Everything was working out just as we had dared hope, and the date for our wedding could be fixed, as planned, for mid-July. Oblivious to the gloom of medical prognosis and ecstatic in the happiness of love and the promise of success, we glided into that summer through a series of further celebrations, with only a cluster of small bothersome clouds, such as my second-year exams, the question of accommodation and the hitherto unfamiliar evil of income tax, gathering on the horizon.

To our indignation, an unseasonably chill wind of hostile reality blew one of these small clouds all too quickly across our path, temporarily dampening our elation. Flushed with the success of his Fellowship application, Stephen went – within what we in our youthful impatience considered to be a reasonable lapse of time, a fortnight or so – to call on the Bursar of Gonville and Caius (generally pronounced in Cambridge as Keys, the name of the second founder of the College, but written Caius because of the Latinizing tendencies of the Renaissance). The Bursar coldly informed the newly appointed Research Fellow that, as he was not due to take up his post until the following October, it was highly presumptuous of him to seek a consultation six months in advance. As to Stephen's query, a matter which was uppermost in our minds, he certainly was not disposed to tell him how much salary he could expect to earn from the Fellowship. For good measure he decreed categorically that the College did not, furthermore, consider it a duty to provide accommodation for its Research Fellows. Smarting from such high-handed treatment, we were left to surmise roughly what Stephen's income would be and to find somewhere to live. Since there were plenty of married Research Fellows in Cambridge, we assumed that they managed somehow. As for accommodation, we rather liked the look of some new flats which were being built near the market square, and put our name down for one of those with the agent.

So confident were we in ourselves, and so impatient for our future to begin, that we did not allow such mundane problems to bother us for long. Indeed the attitude of the Bursar and those of his ilk simply confirmed Stephen's healthy disrespect for pompous middle-aged authority, a disrespect to which I was becoming a willing convert. We well knew that in our idealism we were deliberately defying common sense and all that was cautious, conventional and ordinary. We were certainly not going to allow our grand schemes to be thwarted or our convictions undermined by petty-minded officialdom. Tilting at such bureaucratic windmills quickly became our personal version of Sixties' rebellion. By contrast, our main battle was with the forces of destiny. In this lofty undertaking, we could afford to ridicule the minor stumbling blocks put in our way by officious college bursars.

When one battles with destiny only the major issues – life, survival and death – are of real significance. So far the forces of destiny seemed to be either dormant or on our side, for in spite of the obstacles our foreseeable future in the Cold War atmosphere of the mid-Sixties was beginning to look as secure as anybody else's. For Stephen, the prospect of marriage meant that he had to get down to work and prove his worth in physics. In my simplicity I believed that faith also had a hand in determining our way forwards. In a sense, we both shared a faith, an existential faith, in our chosen course, but I, encouraged by my mother and by my friends, reached out to a faith in a higher influence – God perhaps – who appeared to be responding to my need for help by strengthening my courage and determination. On the other hand, while I was well aware that the Hawkings, for all their traditional Methodist background, professed themselves to be agnostics if not atheists, I found their tendency to sneer at religious matters unpleasant. Stephen and I spent our first Christmas together just two months after our engagement. The fact that he came to Morning Service with my family produced raised eyebrows and snide comments on our return to 14 Hillside Road. "So do you feel holier now?" Philippa quietly enquired of Stephen in a tone laden with sarcasm, and I sensed a tinge of inexplicable hostility towards me. He laughed in reply while his mother remarked, "He should certainly be holier than thou, because he is now under the influence of a good woman." It was difficult to know how to take these remarks – it was not easy to make light of them, because they smacked of conspiracy and seemed targeted at an essential element, my faith, on which I would depend implicitly in the task before me. This cynicism was very different from the mirth in which I wholeheartedly shared when we analysed the various forms of the marriage service. I was appalled to find that, according to the marriage service of the 1662 Book of Common Prayer, I was expected to become a "follower of godly and sober matrons". I opted instead for the 1928 version, where that ugly phrase did not appear.

Success has a knack of breeding success, and soon we were celebrating again. Another Saturday had been spent in Stephen's rooms writing out another application, this time for a prize, the Gravity Prize, endowed by an American gentleman who in his wisdom believed that the discovery of anti-gravity would cure his gout. It is unlikely that any of the essays submitted ever provided any relief for the poor man's suffering, but his generous prizes provided great financial relief to many a struggling young physicist. Over the years Stephen won the whole range of Gravity Prizes, culminating in the first prize in 1971. Although, to our vexation, Stephen's first entry missed the post that Saturday in 1965, his efforts were nevertheless to be crowned with a very timely degree of success when some weeks later I was urgently called down from my attic in Hampstead to take a call from Stephen. He was ringing from Cambridge – as usual, for fourpence – to tell me that he had been awarded a Commendation Prize, worth £100, in the Gravity competition. I danced round Mrs Dunham's kitchen in raptures. Stephen's hundred pounds – added to the two hundred and fifty pounds which my father had been accumulating for me in National Savings and which he had promised to give me on my twenty-first birthday – would enable us to pay off Stephen's overdraft and buy a car. Later that summer, just before the wedding, Stephen's close friend in Trinity Hall, Rob Donovan, negotiated a very favourable deal for us with his father, a car dealer in Cheshire. We had the choice of two vehicles: one, a gleaming, red-painted, open-topped 1924 Rolls Royce, was tantalizing but quite impractical and rather beyond our means; at the other end of the scale, there was a red Mini on offer. Reluctantly Stephen had to concede that the Mini was better suited to our purse and to our requirements, especially since one of those small clouds looming on my horizon was ominously marked "driving test".

As all my previous attempts had ended in failure, I did not suppose that turning up for the next test in a 1924 Rolls would endear me to the crusty, humourless examiner who, when last I encountered him, had failed me yet again. Drily he had commented, as he clutched his heart, that my driving was not that of a beginner but of a hardened driver; it was alarmingly carefree and much too close to the speed limit. He should have been grateful that, given my recent experiences, I did not exceed the speed limit, overtake on bends or hills and attack dual carriageways from the wrong direction. Ironically, considering his known driving techniques, Stephen still held a valid driving licence, although he was no longer able to drive, so it was within the bounds of the law for me to drive on a provisional licence while he sat beside me. When finally in the autumn of 1965 I passed the dreaded test, it may have been because my bête noire, the chief examiner, was reported to be in hospital.

All those successes and celebrations in the early months of 1965 clearly marked our way forwards, with the result that my concerns became more intensely focused on Cambridge and the wedding. Inevitably a distance was developing between me and my friends and contemporaries, both my student friends in Westfield and my old dancing and tennis friends in St Albans. The last time that I saw many of those early friends was either when we worked together in the sorting office at the Post Office before the Christmas of 1964, or at my twenty-first birthday party: this Stephen's parents kindly agreed to host in their large, rambling house, which was much more spacious than my parents' semi-detached.

It was a glorious day, hot and sunny with bright, clear spring skies, and my happiness was complete. Stephen's present to me, recordings of the late Beethoven Quartets, could only be interpreted as the ultimate expression of our depth of feeling for each other. That birthday was happily very different from the previous year, when Stephen had given me a record of the complete works of Webern and later taken me to a drama about the use of the electric chair in the United States. That afternoon my whole family, including Grandma, had sat in a silent circle in our living room listening to Webern's entire opus. Stephen sat solemnly in an armchair while Dad buried his head in a book, Mum immersed herself in her knitting and Grandma dozed off. With great aplomb my family managed to appear totally unmoved by the assorted atonic clashes, lengthy inconsequential pauses and grating dissonances of the music, while I, sitting on the floor on the verge of hysterics, had to hide my face in a cushion.

In 1965, however, my twenty-first birthday party went with a swing in the warm spring air under the coloured lights on the terrace. It was as magical as a fairy tale, although as in all fairy tales it masked a perceptibly hostile element. Again I sensed an ill-disguised frisson of resentment in Philippa's attitude towards me which I was at a loss to understand. Was it because I had been allowed to take over her home for my party just for one evening? Or was it because she regarded me as intellectually inferior, and "feminine" – a term of abuse in the Hawking lexicon – as well? She clearly found my faith ridiculous. "Don't take it seriously," was Stephen's answer when I told him of my anxieties on that score, but this glib reaction was not sufficient reassurance.

From Mary, the elder of the two sisters, I received a more good-natured response. According to his mother, Stephen had found it hard to forgive his sibling for coming into the world barely seventeen months after his own birth. Mary, shy and gentle by nature, had found herself in an unenviable position in the family, poised between two exceptionally intelligent, determined personalities, Stephen and Philippa. In self-defence, she had forced herself into a fiercely competitive intellectual mould, when really her talents were much more creative and practical. With an intense loyalty to her father, she had taken up medicine, and it was with her father that she communicated most freely. Although my parents had heard first-hand accounts through various friends in St Albans of Frank Hawking's blunt, abrasive behaviour towards his staff in the Medical Research Laboratory at Mill Hill, towards me he was chivalrous and considerate. It was unfortunate that he did not present himself in a better light to the outside world, since he was a sensitive man who possessed generous and honourable qualities. Repeatedly, with endearing Yorkshire directness, he impressed upon me how genuinely delighted he and his family were at our engagement, sincerely promising to help in any way possible. Understandably he was devastated by the diagnosis of his son's illness and, notwithstanding his pleasure at our marriage, his medical background forced him to take a strictly orthodox and pessimistic view. My father had come across information about a Swiss doctor who claimed to be able to treat neurological conditions by means of a controlled diet, and he had offered to pay for Stephen to go to Switzerland for a course of treatment. With the doubtful advantage of superior medical knowledge, Frank Hawking dismissed the Swiss claims as unfounded. He, for his part, was only able to warn me that Stephen's life would be short, as would be his ability to fulfill a marital relationship. Moreover he advised me that if we wanted to have a family, we should not delay, assuring me that Stephen's illness was not genetically inherited.

Stephen's mother, who confided in me that she was convinced that the first symptoms of Stephen's condition had appeared in an unexplained illness when he was thirteen, also thought I should be fully informed of all the horrific developments that could be expected to occur as Stephen's condition degenerated. However, if the only treatments available were to be dismissed, rightly or wrongly, as crank quackery, I did not see much point in having whatever natural optimism I could muster destroyed by a litany of doom-laden prophecies without any palliative advice. I replied that I would prefer not to know the details of the prognosis, because I loved Stephen so much that nothing could deter me from wanting to marry him: I would make a home for him, dismissing all my own previous ambitions which now were insignificant by comparison with the challenge before me. In return, with all the innocence of my twenty-one years, I trusted that Stephen would cherish me and encourage me to fulfil my own interests. I trusted too in the promise that he had made my father when he had asked for my hand: that he would not demand more of me than I could reasonably accomplish, nor would he allow himself to become a millstone round my neck. We had both promised Dad that I would finish my degree course.

The plans for the wedding proceeded apace, attended by much to-ing and fro-ing between St Albans and Cambridge and by the sort of disagreements typical of weddings everywhere: Stephen, supported by his father, refused to wear morning dress, although my father and brother insisted on maintaining a proper sense of style. Similarly Stephen refused to wear a carnation in his buttonhole, since he thought them cheap and vulgar, although for me they were redolent in their colour and perfume of Spain. Roses provided a satisfactory compromise. My father thought that no wedding was complete without a few token speeches, at which Stephen baulked and refused to say anything. The question of bridesmaids came and went unresolved, leaving a gap which on the day was ably filled by nine-year-old Edward as an impromptu pageboy. Happily it was agreed, without audibly dissenting voices, that we should be married in the Chapel of Trinity Hall by the Chaplain, Paul Lucas. The religious service on Thursday 15th July would have to be preceded by a modest civil ceremony in the Shire Hall in Cambridge the day before, as colleges are not licensed for marriages, and the cost of a special licence from the Archbishop of Canterbury at £25 was deemed an unnecessary expense. Having deliberately chosen a small venue, we were then hard-pressed to accommodate all the guests. Some friends and relations had to be axed from the list altogether, while others were consigned to the organ loft.

In the midst of this confusion, I was tussling with Napoleon III, the Paris Commune of 1871 and my final French exams. Shortly before the wedding, Stephen attended his first General Relativity conference, which that year was conveniently held in London. I joined him for the official government reception in Carlton House Terrace, where I met many of the physicists who were subsequently to play significant roles in his career: Kip Thorne, John Wheeler, Charles Misner, George Ellis and two Russian scientists. Many of them were to become lasting friends to both of us. It was at that conference that the world's relativists, including Stephen, were first seized by the fever of excitement at the black-hole research (at that stage known much less graphically by the more pedestrian description of collapsing stars) that was to grip them for decades.

After the civil-marriage ceremony on 14th July, intoned by the Registrar among the filing cabinets and artificial flowers of the Shire Hall, my mother-in-law came up to me and with her wry smile said, "Welcome Mrs 'awkins, because that's how you'll be known from now on." The next day, St Swithin's Day, Stephen's best man Rob Donovan skilfully manoeuvred us and our near and dear through the marriage service and the festivities in the precincts of Trinity Hall without mishap. This was quite a remarkable feat, if only because of the number of elderly relatives present and the immense width of Philippa's hat, to which she had attached a superabundant display of foxgloves, delphiniums and poppies, rivalling the College gardens in their herbaceous exuberance. It was a happy day, despite the grey skies and intermittent drizzle. At last, in the early evening, at the end of the reception in the College hall where my father had publicly thanked Stephen for taking me off his hands, Rob Donovan dropped us off on the outskirts of Cambridge. There in a side street he had parked our recently acquired red Mini, complete with L-plates, well out of the way of my brother's mischievous designs. I settled myself into the driver's seat and, with Stephen beside me, cautiously pulled away from the kerb, heading in the direction of Long Melford in Suffolk and the Bull Inn.

8

An Introduction to Physics

All too soon that first idyllic week of marriage was but a halcyon memory – a memory of winding Suffolk lanes and lush gardens, musty country churches and half-timbered villages. At the end of it, as we sat waiting for take-off to New York, having boarded the plane long in advance of the other passengers, that blissful week with daytime outings to sleepy hamlets, country houses and the coast was quickly superseded by the inexorable advance of science, the synthesized traditions and the pace of the New World.

At Kennedy Airport, we were joining the queue of passengers at passport control when a tall, neatly dressed air hostess approached us, intently examining the file she was carrying. "What are your names?" she asked, looking down a list. "Jane and Stephen Hawking," we answered, not expecting any special messages. "Oh," she said in some surprise, "I don't have your names on my list. How old are you?" Now it was our turn to register some surprise. "I'm twenty-one and he's twenty-three," I replied for both of us. "Gee, I'm so sorry," she gushed, "I thought you were unaccompanied minors!"

Indignant at the insult to our maturity and our married status, we pulled ourselves up to our full height and passed through US customs to the helicopter which was to fly us over New York City to La Guardia airport for the connecting flight to Ithaca in upstate New York. Our first view of New York was depressing. As we flew just above the level of the skyscrapers through a dense smog, the buildings loomed out of the haze like giant javelins poised to spear us on their tips. It was hard to believe that human beings lived and worked down there in that inferno. My suspicions that we had landed in a modern Brobdingnag were confirmed when we were ushered to the limousine that had been sent to collect us from Ithaca airport and take us to Cornell University. Everything – the cars, the roads, the buildings – was ten times larger than anything I had ever seen; even the wide expanse of pleasant green countryside seemed to roll on for ever. Yet for me, a linguist used to the challenge of a foreign language only twenty-three miles away across the Channel, the most baffling aspect was that we had travelled thousands of miles only to find ourselves among people who spoke the same language as we did, even if, like the rest of their country, the language had suffered a bout of inflation on the way.

Our lodgings consisted of student accommodation in a twin-bedded room on the third floor of a new hall of residence on the Cornell campus. As we were both well used to the student way of life, that was not a problem. What really unnerved us was that the third floor had been designated as family accommodation for the duration of the summer school, and we were thrown in to survive as best we could among families with babies and small children who wailed all night or sat out in the corridor protesting while their parents held parties in the lounge area. This unforeseen circumstance spelt an abrupt end to the honeymoon which we had intended to resume on the American side of the Atlantic. Although some of the toddlers were undeniably appealing, a stay in a mammoth nursery was not what we had expected.

The problems were compounded by the logistics of the campus. For the able-bodied these would not have presented any difficulty, but since the hall of residence was the best part of a mile from the lecture theatre and we had no transport, it was a struggle for Stephen to get to the lectures on time. He could walk alone, but progress was slow; he moved much more quickly if he had a helpful arm to lean on, so gladly fulfilling my new role I went everywhere with him. Meals presented another problem. Living, as we still were, on student grants, we could not afford to eat all our meals in the canteen, but as there was not a single utensil in the kitchenette on our floor, we did not have the wherewithal even to make ourselves a cup of tea. Eventually one of the conference secretaries came to the rescue and offered to take me by car down into Ithaca to do some shopping at the nearest Woolworths. As we glided along in her enormous station wagon, I politely asked, by way of conversation, if she had ever been to Europe. She did not mince her words. "No", was her reply. "You see, I don't like going places where they don't have bathrooms."

Duly equipped with a saucepan, cutlery, mugs and plates, plus an electric fan to mitigate the heat – which, unlike Spanish heat, was sticky and humid – I set up an improvised home base, for the first but by no means the only time in my married life, on the third floor of the hall of residence. Brandon Carter, who was a fellow research student with Stephen in Cambridge and had been a guest at our wedding, was an invaluable help: drawing on his childhood experiences in the Australian bush, he taught me how to make tea by the billycan method – in a saucepan, the same saucepan that was used for scrambled eggs, pasta, baked beans and all the other bedsit-type fare on which we depended in those weeks. Versatility was of the essence in this unforeseen introduction to the joys of domesticity.

Much of my day was spent in walking with Stephen to and from the lecture hall and shopping in the nearby campus store. To fill the intervening hours, which were as short as the distances to any other place were long, I resorted to my studies in the library. Then, to vary the monothematic diet of Hispanic studies, I hit upon the idea of borrowing a typewriter and a desk in the secretarial office and began to type out the preliminary draft of the initial chapters of Stephen's doctoral thesis. The universes in question may have been expanding, but they were littered with so many incomprehensible hieroglyphic shapes and forms – as well as conventional numerals and all the normal mathematical signs – dancing above and below the line, that it soon became obvious that this particular enterprise was going to become a typographical nightmare.

Although such a sudden encounter with the nitty-gritty of marriage to a physicist might not have been exactly what I had anticipated from the second week of the honeymoon, I was relieved to have some useful occupation. I was also glad to be able to witness Stephen's intense excitement at moving in international scientific circles where he was already becoming recognized. He was particularly gratified at the increasing collaboration between himself and Roger Penrose, a slightly older British physicist, on a mathematical project known as the theory of singularities or gravitational collapse. The theory proposed that any body undergoing gravitational collapse must form a singularity, a region in space-time where the laws of relativity cease to hold, probably because the curvature of space-time becomes infinite. In the case of a star collapsing under its own gravity when its surface and its volume shrink to zero, Roger conjectured that the singularity would be hidden in what was later to be called a black hole. Inspired by Roger's theory and by the work of the Russians Lifshitz and Khalatnikov, Stephen was confident that these equations could be reversed in time to prove that any expanding model of the universe must have begun with a singularity, thus providing the theoretical basis for the Big Bang. The equations would also provide him with a momentous conclusion to his thesis.

The arrival like a ship in full sail from her family home in Detroit of Roger Penrose's wife, Joan, bearing one small child in a sling on her front and clutching another by the hand, while her elderly mother brought up the rear, afforded some relief from the tedium of life on the third floor. Joan had majored in public speaking, a useful attribute in controlling a family of boys – and an even more essential accomplishment, as I was beginning to realize, for making one's presence felt in the world of physicists where wives – although there were plenty of them with hordes of small children in tow – were scarcely noticed. Some were loud and loquacious, others were inhibited and reserved, others were positively sullen and morose; the handful of wives who themselves had a background in maths or physics tended to adopt a more competitive, masculine style of behaviour, while those whose dormant, half-forgotten talents lay in other areas tended to be prickly and mistrustful. Physics seemed to have taken its toll on all of them and, whether or not they liked each other or got on well with each other, they all had one thing in common: they were already, to all intents and purposes, widows – physics widows.

There were a few memorable diversions. Every day, as we strolled across the campus, I grasped the golden opportunity to chat in Spanish to a Mexican couple who seemed as disoriented in Cornell as I was. Then, one Saturday afternoon, some acquaintances of some friends of Stephen's parents kindly invited us to join them at their summer house by a lake not far from Ithaca. Otherwise, our evenings were spent humming 'Waltzing Matilda' over our single saucepan as it bubbled on the hotplate in the kitchenette on the third floor, while Brandon regaled us with lengthy accounts of his adventures. These often concerned life in the Australian bush, but also touched on his interest in the mathematician James Clerk Maxwell and on a dramatic sailing trip which was to have reached the Mediterranean through the Bay of Biscay but never got further than Cherbourg. When these topics were exhausted, the conversation normally lapsed into a sustained cosmological argument between him and Stephen, while I washed up the saucepan and the plastic plates, wondering whether we were doomed to spend the whole period of the summer school confined to the campus of Cornell University and the third floor of the hall of residence.

Just as I was beginning to resign myself to an unchanging routine, Brian and Susie Burns, an Australian couple who had previously spent some time in Cambridge, offered us a lift in their car to Niagara. Our sudden first sighting of the Falls after the tedious drive through the endless, sulphurous suburbs of the city of Buffalo took our breath away. The might of the immense volume of dark water constantly on the move, relentlessly tumbling over the edge of the precipice, transformed into a mass of white foam and rainbow filaments of cooling spray, was as mesmerizing as the thundering roar was deafening. Our senses numbed, we stumbled across the bridge to the Canadian side to get a better view and stood hypnotized until it was time for us to take the short flight back to Ithaca. Against a threatening sky, we boarded the small plane and took off amid thunder and lightning. For the first time in my life, I was afraid of flying.

The next weekend, Brandon and some friends arranged a sailing trip on Lake Ontario. We set out in a gentle breeze and, once out on the lake, the day slipped by. I swam in the green waters and Stephen sat back deep in thought, enjoying the clear blue skies and the sound of the water gently lapping against the hull. By late afternoon, our companions had long since ceased to share our pleasure at the peaceful conditions and talked anxiously of sending up flares and putting out distress signals – we were becalmed. Brandon helpfully remarked that this was not a situation he had had to deal with in the Bay of Biscay as there you could always rely on the wind. Somehow, much later that evening, we managed to limp back into harbour as in a magnificent blaze the setting sun, sinking from view on the blackened horizon, bathed our weary faces in its amber glow.

It was not until the last week of the summer school that someone – I think it was Ray Sachs, an extrovert Californian physicist, the father of four daughters – had the bright idea of organizing a social event, a picnic in a field, for families. There we were introduced to more wives and more children, but the person who made the greatest impression on us was a quiet American from Texas, Robert Boyer, with whom Stephen had already established a professional rapport. Robert included me in conversation in a natural, friendly manner, and talked about matters other than physics. Indeed, it has to be said that individually many physicists could be quite charming, friendly and down-to-earth. In a group, however, their natural tendency was to slip inexorably into interminable discussions and arguments, almost always about physics. But there was a rival topic of conversation which increasingly exercised the minds, not only of all academics but of all young people: that topic, Vietnam, was liberally aired at that picnic. The growing menace of the war was regarded with fear and loathing; it threatened to cut a swathe through the nation's youth for a cause supported only by the military and the bigoted.

On the last evening, at the end of the summer school, as we sat on the steps of the hall of residence gazing out at a full moon suspended in a translucent sky, I was introduced to Professor Abe Taub, the avuncular mastermind of the summer school, who with his wife Cice was also taking the air and admiring the night sky. We listened in fascination as they talked of their life in California, of the views their house commanded of the Golden Gate bridge, of San Francisco and of the campus and science department at Berkeley where Abe was the leader of the Relativity Group. I detected a tentative invitation from Abe to Stephen and a corresponding eagerness on Stephen's part, though no formal propositions were made.

We wandered back indoors and were about to resume our conversation when, without any warning, Stephen, perhaps affected by a chill in the night air, was seized with a devastating choking fit, the first I had witnessed. The illness, seemingly long-suppressed, suddenly revealed itself in its true terrifying fury. The lurking spectre stepped out of the shadows and grabbed him by the throat, tossed him about, shook him like a doll, trampled him underfoot and hurled his rasping cough round the room till the very air resonated with loud, panic-stricken wheezing. Helpless in the grip of the enemy, Stephen was beyond my reach. I stood by unprepared for this sudden encounter with the dreadful power of motor-neuron disease, the hitherto unseen partner in our marriage. Eventually Stephen managed to gesture to me to thump him on the back. I did so vigorously, determined to expel the invisible monster. At last it receded, as quickly as it had come, leaving us drained and exhausted and the onlookers politely dumbfounded. This onslaught came as a great shock to us both, an ill-omen warning of a hazardous future. Dreams of California disappeared into the mists of the fantasy from which they had begun to emerge.

By the time we returned to New York, the Cornell experience had rapidly turned me – at the age of twenty-one – into a rather confused follower of sober, if not of godly, matrons. The demonic nature of the illness had announced its presence much more dramatically than in lameness, difficulty of movement and lack of coordination. As if that were not enough, I sensed that there was yet another partner lurking in our already overcrowded marriage. The fourth partner first appeared in the form of a trusted and quiescent friend, signalling the way to success and fulfilment for those who followed her. In fact she proved to be a relentless rival, as exacting as any mistress, an inexorable Siren, luring her devotees into deep pools of obsession. She was none other than Physics, cited by Einstein's first wife as the correspondent in divorce proceedings.

New York City provided both a necessary respite from such sombre considerations and the opportunity to restore the balance of our relationship, away from the inveigling companionship of other physicists. A medical colleague of Frank Hawking generously offered us a room in his Manhattan apartment for the weekend. It was ideally situated for our sightseeing excursions to the Metropolitan Museum, the Empire State Building, Time Square and Broadway. Unfortunately Broadway had little to offer in August, so, bizarrely, we spent the Saturday evening in a cinema watching *My Fair Lady*. I had few regrets when we said goodbye to New York. As the bus drove into Kennedy Airport, I looked back over my shoulder to the solid line of clearly etched skyscrapers standing to attention in a grey mass on the horizon, and thought that I had never seen an apparition of such monstrous brutality. I was impatient to return to the manageable, if cramped, proportions and genuinely old-fashioned but less frenzied ways of the Lilliputian world where I belonged. My place was on a continent mellowed by history and a sense of poetic values, where I fondly thought there was greater stability and where people had more time for each other.

9

The Lane

My sentimental illusions about the stability of life on the European side of the Atlantic were quickly dispelled on our return to England, where I found that my parents were about to move to a house only thirty doors up the road from the home where I had lived since the age of six. The break with the past was now irreparably set in bricks and mortar. Although, when last heard of, the flat Stephen and I had reserved over the market place in Cambridge was not yet finished, we had to find a home of our own urgently if only to house all our wedding presents. Loading our luggage and presents into the red Mini, we set off for Cambridge and went straight to the estate agent's. The flats were indeed finished, we were told, but, as the agent had no record of our names or of our booking, they were all already let to other tenants. The Old World was beginning to look distinctly unreliable after all.

We discussed our next move over a despondent lunch. Stephen decided to brave the Bursar of Caius once again in the vain hope that he might be persuaded to help, even temporarily. Together we bearded the ogre in his den. To our surprise, he had changed identity in the previous six months, and the new Bursar was also the lecturer in Tibetan. However that post was a sinecure, since there were never any students in Tibetan, so he had time on his hands in which to oversee the financial affairs of the College. Unlike his predecessor, he did not snap Stephen's head off in indignation but listened gravely, even sympathetically, to his request, and then came up with a brilliant solution, which coaxed a glimmer of a smile from his dour face. "Yes," he mused, "I think we might be able to help – only in the very short term of course, because you know that the College has a policy of not providing housing for Research Fellows, don't you?" We nodded with bated breath. He consulted a list. "There's a room vacant in the Harvey Road hostel: it's twelve shillings and sixpence a night for one man so we will put another bed in and it will be twenty-five shillings a night for the two of you." We had to suppress our outrage at such sharp practice because we had nowhere else to go, hotels being beyond our means, but vowed that we would minimize the amount of time we spent at Harvey Road.

Although the College authorities were harsh and ungenerous, the staff, particularly the housekeeper of the hostel, could not have been kinder. This proved to be characteristic of the college servants, whether cleaning staff, workmen, gardeners, porters or waiters. Unfailingly they revealed qualities of warmth and friendliness often conspicuously absent in the rarified atmosphere of the higher echelons. The housekeeper warmed our room, aired our beds, brought us tea and biscuits that first evening and breakfast in the morning. She even offered to do our washing for us, although that was not necessary as our stay was to be mercifully brief.

In the intervening day, Stephen's supervisor, Dennis Sciama, had come speedily to the rescue by putting us in touch with a Fellow of Peterhouse, who wanted to sublet the house he had been renting from that College. The house was unfurnished, but it was available immediately and moreover it was ideally placed for us, in one of the oldest, most picturesque streets of Cambridge, Little St Mary's Lane, within a hundred yards of Stephen's department, which had recently moved to the building of the old Pitt Press printing works in Mill Lane.

Since number 11 Little St Mary's Lane contained not a stick of furniture, we had to grit our teeth, dip deep into our funds, savings and wedding-present money, and go on a rapid spending spree to buy basic furniture, a bed and an electric ring. While we were waiting for the bed to be delivered, I went out to buy provisions, leaving Stephen propped up against the bare wall of the living room for want of a seat. To my astonishment, when I returned he was comfortably seated on a blue kitchen chair. He explained that a lady from down the road had come to introduce herself and, finding him leaning against the wall, had kindly brought him the chair, which we could borrow until we had more furniture. The lady in question was Thelma Thatcher, the wife of the former Censor, or Master, of Fitzwilliam House, who lived at number 9. Thelma Thatcher was to become one of the most benevolent and most entertaining influences in our lives over the next ten years. That evening we cooked our supper in the Cornell saucepan on the single electric ring, drank sherry from our crystal glasses and, using a box for a table, ate from our bone china, using our gleaming stainless-steel cutlery set. Stephen sat on the Thatchers' kitchen chair while I kneeled on the bare white-tiled floor. No matter that it was somewhat improvised, we celebrated our good luck in having a roof over our heads for the next three months.

Guarded at its entrance by two churches standing sentinel – the Victorian United Reform Church on the right and the medieval Church of Little St Mary on the left – the lane is hidden from the public gaze. Tourists discover it only by chance. These days the lane is closed to through-traffic thanks to a campaign by the residents, including Stephen and me, so visitors to the two big complexes on the river front, the Garden House Hotel and the University Centre, have to gain access via Mill Lane, which is not residential. Number 11 is the last of the main terrace of three-storeyed cottages on the right-hand side of the street, some of which probably date back to the sixteenth century. When we took up residence in 1965, the house had been recently renovated by Peterhouse, a college which, unlike Caius, did provide its Research Fellows with accommodation.

Iron railings on the south side of the lane enclose Little St Mary's churchyard, a wild overgrown garden which, that September, was ablaze with reddening hips and haws and heavy with the scent of autumn roses. The few gravestones which were still standing were so weather-beaten that their inscriptions had become illegible, despite the spreading branches of the towering sycamore trees and the gnarled stems of the wisteria which sheltered them from the worst ravages of the elements. Here Nature had gently absorbed the dead of previous centuries back into her bosom, resurrecting them in a profusion of blossoms which trailed over the railings and reached out to caress the crooked old gas lamp which lit the street at night with its sulphurous glow.

Thelma Thatcher was the self-appointed warden of the lane. She had planted many of the rose bushes in the churchyard, where she exercised Matty, her King Charles spaniel, wrapping each of her paws in plastic bags in wet weather. As a matter of course, she took it upon herself to keep an eye on the well-being of all her neighbours, whatever their age or circumstances. Scarcely had a week gone by than she had lent us more chairs, tables, pots and pans, found us a gas cooker to borrow – from Sister Chalmers, the Peterhouse nurse who was moving into a fully equipped college flat – set about finding us somewhere else to live on the expiry of the present tenancy and served us innumerable glasses of sherry in the elegant, highly polished, antique-filled living room of her fine, whitewashed old house.

In 1965 she must already have been in her seventies, though with her straight back, dark hair and stately figure she could easily have passed for ten years younger. She combined the sparkle of a gifted raconteur with intense practicality: once, she told us, in a moment of inspiration at a Quaker wedding, she stood up and announced that the helpers had forgotten to light the gas under the tea urn. In a manner which would have done justice to Joyce Grenfell, she delighted in playfully deflating the pompous egos of many Cambridge academics. Her style was aristocratic and assertive, but always supported by deeply held and sincere Christian values. A self-professed pillar of the establishment, representing everything that Stephen despised, she found her natural target in woolly-minded liberals. In her, however, Stephen met his match, and he had to respect her for her goodness and generosity even if, politically, she and he were poles apart.

In the next few months, Thelma Thatcher took us under her wing like a mother hen. She kept a kindly eye on Stephen when I was away in London, as well as attending to the needs both of her elderly husband who – according to her, had snatched her out of her cradle – and of her lively, independent daughter Mary, who was assembling a film archive on the domestic lives of the British in India.

All too soon, I had to return to my final year at Westfield. Parting from Stephen each Monday was desperately painful, and the regime was hard for both of us. Stephen was just sufficiently capable of looking after himself to be able to live in the house, but every evening, unless invited out elsewhere, he had to make the long, hazardous trek down King's Parade on his own to eat in College. Our Australian friend, Anne Young, unfailingly kept an eye out for him as he passed her window on the other side of the road, and generally one or other of the younger Fellows would see him home after the meal, when he would ring me to report on the day.

My routine was exhausting. I would leave for London on Monday mornings, spend the week in Westfield and then on Friday afternoons join the commuters once again. In my anxiety to get home to Cambridge, to Stephen – and to Nikolaus Pevsner's

Friday evening course of lectures on Renaissance architecture, which we attended together – I would bite my nails as I watched the minutes tick by on the Underground, wondering how long the train would sit in the tunnel, fearing that I was going to miss the connection from Liverpool Street. For years afterwards, my worst nightmares were dreams of being stuck in a tunnel on the Underground.

During the week, the pressure was on: translations into and from Spanish, essays and seminar papers all had to be submitted within deadlines, and the only time I had for doing them was in the evening. Weekends were taken up with shopping, washing, housework and typing Stephen's thesis, parts of which he would have written out in a scrawly, all but illegible longhand during the week, and parts of which he dictated to me as I sat typing at our shiny new dining table in the otherwise bare living room. The trials of that pre-university secretarial course were now bearing fruit. The shorthand had been moderately useful for taking notes in lectures, but the dreaded typing was proving to be a godsend in tabling the laws of creation, since it saved us a mint of money in professional fees. The thesis first glimpsed at Cornell – with its equations and signs, symbols and coefficients, Greek letterings, numbers above and below the line, and infinite and non-infinite universes – drove me to distraction. However, since it was a scientific thesis, it was blessedly short. Furthermore I derived some small satisfaction from the knowledge that my fingers were consigning the beginnings of the universe to paper. The thought that all these mysteriously coded numbers, letters and signs were penetrating the secrets of that deep, black infinity was awe-inspiring. Dwelling on the poetic immensity of the topic for too long was counterproductive, though, as it distracted concentration from all the little dots and hieroglyphs above and below the line, any of which if misplaced could have thrown the beginnings of the universe into dire disarray and upset the whole order of creation.

I was not a little proud, too, to be able make a contribution of my own, other than the purely mechanical one of typing. Stephen's use of English left much to be desired. His speech was scattered with expressions such as "you know" and "I mean", and his written style showed little concern for the English language. As the daughter of a dedicated civil servant, I had been taught from an early age to use the language precisely, with appreciation for its clarity and its richness. Here was an area where in joining forces with Stephen I could assist him on an intellectual rather than just the physical plane, and also help bridge the gap between the arts and the sciences.

The weekends were also the time for buying more equipment and furnishings, for exploring Cambridgeshire and for seeing friends. We spent the whole of one Saturday afternoon in an electrical shop trying to decide whether we could afford the extra five pounds for a larger fridge than the one we had budgeted for. Considering that Stephen's salary, as we had at last found out, was eleven hundred pounds a year, while our weekly rent and housekeeping when we were both at home – not counting numerous other outgoings – was ten pounds, an extra five pounds on any purchase was a major expenditure. On Sunday afternoons, if the Mini could be extricated from the Caius communal garage, we would tour Cambridgeshire, visiting villages and churches, always looking out for a suitable house or plot of land to buy. Sometimes our expeditions had to be abandoned before they had begun because the Mini was so impossibly hemmed in by ageing Bentleys and Rovers in its corner of the garage that it would have taken a crane to get it out.

One Sunday afternoon, having manoeuvred the Mini out of the garage, we tried to visit the local National Trust property, Anglesey Abbey. As the car park was a good half mile from the house, I drove up along the leafy avenue to the main entrance, expecting a sympathetic welcome for my partially disabled passenger. In fact we were met with rude intolerance and sent away. We went straight home, and I penned my first letter in furious protest, not only at the lack of facilities for the disabled in Britain but also for the scant respect with which they were treated, thus initiating a role for myself as a campaigner for the disabled.

Often, on our Sunday afternoon jaunts, we would happen to be in the vicinity of some of our married friends at teatime and, clinging to the illusion of a spontaneous student lifestyle, we would drop in on them. Slightly older than us, many of these friends had already had their first babies. Consequently we found ourselves drawn more and more into their pattern of domesticity, especially when I became the fascinated and slightly bemused godmother to two of the said babies. Stephen was also being drawn into other circles: those of the Fellowship of

Gonville and Caius. One Saturday evening in early October, I accompanied him as far as the College Chapel for the service for the induction of new Fellows. At the suggestion of the Chaplain, I watched the service from the organ loft and then he invited me, a mere wife dressed in my housecleaning clothes, to dine at High Table. This was an unprecedented break with the past, as it was a long established rule in Cambridge colleges that wives – especially wives – were banned from High Table. High Table was the preserve of the Fellows who cultivated self-importance with the same exquisite care that lesser mortals might be expected to lavish on a prized stamp collection or a breed of racing pigeons. Their conversation revolved around the finer details of the most abstruse subjects – their own subjects naturally, about which they could expatiate at length while avoiding the embarrassment of having to discuss subjects about which they knew little or nothing. Mistresses were preferred to dull, silly wives. Indeed a Fellow might invite any woman to dine provided she was not his wife. It went without saying, of course, that, together with wives, undergraduates were also banned from High Table. Unbeknown to the College authorities, their renegade Chaplain had breached both hallowed rules.

Stephen's induction was soon followed by his first attendance at a meeting of the governing body of the College. Before he had time to understand what was happening that Friday afternoon, he found himself deeply embroiled in College politics. To his confusion, he seemed to have walked right into a re-enactment of the C.P. Snow novel, *The Masters*. The only minor difference was that in the novel the wrangling over the Mastership was deemed to have taken place in Snow's own college, Christ's, whereas the scenes that Stephen was witnessing were taking place in Caius. Here was life imitating art in the most extraordinary manner. As Stephen discovered after the event, the charge against the incumbent Master, Sir Nevill Mott, was that he was using his position to favour his own protégés. At the time it was impossible to tell what was happening. The governing body was in an uproar, tempers were flaring and immoderate accusations were being flung about. As a result of a quick calculation, Stephen had the uncomfortable sensation that the votes of the new Fellows might be decisive – indeed his own vote might be the casting vote – but as they had little idea of what they were voting for, their voting pattern was inevitably arbitrary. Stephen's introduction to college politics came to a dramatic end with the resignation of the Master that very afternoon.

During the course of the next year, the ructions over the Mastership crisis subsided as the new Master, Joseph Needham, tearing himself reluctantly away from his gargantuan task of compiling the history of science in China, guided the College back to stability. Although I found him terse, apart from one memorable occasion when over port in the Combination Room after dinner he expansively warned me never to drink sweet French wine – Barsac and suchlike – because of its high disulphide content, his distinguished wife Dorothy was to give me invaluable help in securing a foothold for myself in Cambridge academic circles. She, notwithstanding all her scientific brilliance, was one of the most modest, likeable academics I ever met.

10

A Winter Break

On the strength of his thesis, Stephen was gaining a reputation for himself as a prodigy in his field. In response to his share in the coveted Adams Prize with Roger Penrose that winter, for an essay in mathematics entitled *Singularities and the Geometry of Space-Time*, his supervisor Dennis Sciama assured me that he was sure Stephen had a career of Newtonian proportions ahead of him and that he would do all he could to encourage its progress. He was as good as his word. For all his ebullience, Dennis Sciama selflessly promoted his students' careers rather than his own. His desire to understand the workings of the universe was more passionate than any personal ambition. By sending his students off to conferences and meetings, whether in London or abroad, and by making them scrutinize and report back on every relevant publication, he dramatically increased his own fund of knowledge as well as theirs, and succeeded in nurturing a generation of exceptional cosmologists, relativists, astrophysicists, applied mathematicians and theoretical physicists. The distinction between these various terms was never quite clear to me, except that the identities changed according to the titles of the conferences: they would all become astrophysicists if the next conference was a conference of the Astrophysical Union or relativists if it was a General Relativity conference, and so on. That autumn the relativists of the July conference in London began, chameleon-like, to adopt the trappings of astrophysicists in preparation for the next conference, in Miami Beach in December.

It was fairly late in the term when Stephen learnt that funds were available for us both to go to Miami. I was doubtful about taking time off from Westfield, even though I would only be missing a couple of days at the end of term, but surprisingly Professor Varey raised no objections, so on a dull December afternoon, after a long wait for the fog to lift at London airport, we took off. It was already dark in Florida when we arrived, so it was not until the next morning that we discovered that our hotel room was right on the beach, looking out over the turquoise waters of the Caribbean. Having just stepped out of cold wet London after a hard term's work, I marvelled at the unreality, the improbability of the situation, as though I had walked into a different dimension, through the looking glass perhaps. This impression was to grow as the stay progressed. The blue skies and sunshine were certainly welcome, especially since Stephen's choking fits were becoming more frequent, and his sister Mary had earnestly advised me to take him away somewhere warm for the winter. At least by a happy chance we had the prospect of a week in the sun.

On the opening day, Stephen, together with his casually dressed colleagues, disappeared into the preliminary sessions of the conference, while I explored the venue. The hotel, built in a curve around the swimming pool, looked remarkably familiar. Was this a sense of déjà vu, I asked myself, for I was sure that I had seen it somewhere before. Suddenly it dawned on me that this was the hotel where the opening shots of *Goldfinger*, the James Bond thriller, were filmed. It was in a room in that hotel that the girl had died of asphyxiation after being covered from head to toe with gold paint! The Hotel Fontainbleau was a modern concrete structure with marble floors, plate glass and huge mirrors covering whole walls. In deference to its name, it was furnished in every nook and cranny with Louis XV-style furniture.

The furnishings were not the least of the incongruities, since the astrophysics conference was a major incongruity in itself. The smartly dressed hotel staff looked distinctly uncomfortable with the delegates, who were by no means models of sartorial elegance in their open-necked shirts, shorts and sandals. One day I ventured into the conference hall, intending to sit in for a while on one of the lectures. At first I was perplexed, not seeing any recognizable faces in the audience, then I noticed that the dress of the delegates bore no relation to the clothing the physicists had been wearing at breakfast, in that these people were all dressed in dark suits with ties, their hair neatly brushed and brilliantined, with not a trace of a beard anywhere. I listened to the speaker only for a moment before realizing that this was a conference of Jewish funeral directors promoting biodegradable plastic coffins.

From the exotic colours and summer sun of Miami we flew into autumn – to Austin, Texas, a small university town which in the mid-Sixties was trumpeted in the press as the home of the brightest and best in cosmology. George Ellis, who travelled with us from Miami, was spending a year in Austin with his wife, Sue, whom I had met briefly at our wedding. As we were to stay with the Ellises for a week, this was my opportunity to get to know them both better and forge the beginning of a lifelong friendship which would survive the vicissitudes of many turbulent episodes in all our lives. Pensive and reserved, George was the son of a much respected former editor of the *Rand Daily Mail*, a paper acclaimed for its resistance to apartheid in South Africa. It was at Cape Town University that Sue, the daughter of a traditional Rhodesian farming family, had met George. Both George and Sue were fierce opponents of apartheid and had become self-imposed political exiles from South Africa, insisting that they could never think of returning to live there. Where George was thoughtful and introverted, Sue was outgoing without being overpowering, vivacious yet sensitive to the needs of others. A talented artist and sculptor, she bubbled with warmth and creativity, qualities which she was putting at the disposal of a school for deprived children near Austin. Among her pupils were not merely the victims of broken homes and physical abuse, some were even tiny black child prostitutes who had been rescued from the Chicago slums and brought to Texas for rehabilitation. It was not hard to imagine what an asset Sue must have been to that particular school, for she had a way of making a fascinating artefact out of the smallest twist of paper, length of wire or handful of matchsticks, and her caring friendliness made her instantly popular among children who from an early age had learnt to mistrust adults.

In creating a structure to her life in Texas, Sue appeared to be the exception rather than the rule among science wives. For them there was little of any interest apart from the Max Beerbohm manuscripts and cartoons in the university library, and the gridlike streets of opulent houses in a landscape dominated by black-billed crane-like oil pumps, nodding up and down as they extracted the liquid gold from the yellow earth. The feeling of remoteness from the rest of civilization was overwhelming in an environment where even radio reception was a chancy thing. This sense of isolation was reinforced by the length of time, all of twenty hours, it took Stephen and me to get back to London via Houston and Chicago, where we were stranded for hours by snow on the runway.

Though Stephen may have harboured ambitions of joining the physics group in Austin, one salutary experience made me more than glad to put America, for all the advantages of its southern climate, behind us once more. We were visiting friends of the Ellises one Sunday afternoon when Stephen had a bad fall, which resulted in his coughing up a spot of blood. As his worst fear was brain damage, he insisted on our hosts calling a doctor. Their consternation was remarkable. They were embarrassed that their guest had had a fall, but it was truly unheard of for doctors to home-visit, especially on a Sunday afternoon, and they doubted very much whether they would be able to persuade any doctor to come. After a long succession of telephone calls, they were finally put in touch with a general practitioner who, as an exception, agreed to come and inspect Stephen. When he arrived he received right royal treatment. As he conducted his tests, which indicated nothing amiss, I concluded that America was a fine place for the healthy and successful, but for the strugglers and the infirm, for the people who, through no fault of their own but through accidents of birth, prejudice or illness were less able to help themselves, it was a harsh society where only the fittest survived.

11

Learning Curves

Our return to England from Texas on Christmas Eve heralded yet another change in our lives. After Christmas in St Albans, we went back to Cambridge to resume residence, not at number 11 Little St Mary's Lane but at number 6. Our tireless supporter, Thelma Thatcher, had rung the absentee owner of the empty house at number 6, a Mrs Teulon-Porter ("such a strange lady, my dears") impressing upon her that it was an absolute disgrace that her house should be vacant at a time of "desperate housing shortage for the young". Mrs Teulon-Porter responded to the urgent call by catching the first bus to Cambridge from her home in Shaftesbury. Despite the misgivings about her strange personality, she was offered generous hospitality at the Thatchers' while she attended to her empty property.

Mrs Teulon Porter was a small, wispy, grey woman, already advanced in years. As Fräulein Teulon, she had come to England in the 1920s, had bought number 6 Little St Mary's Lane and then had married her next-door neighbour, the late Mr Porter. Both she and he were passionate historians of folklore and were closely connected with the Cambridge Folk Museum, which might have accounted for Mrs Thatcher's conviction that they dabbled in the occult. Various items in the house testified to their shared interest: an Anglo-Saxon rune-stone, probably from the churchyard, was incorporated into the fireplace; the door screen was a slice hewn from the trunk of an elm; the offcut wood from a cartwheel had been converted to form a heavy, curved stool; and an eighteenth-century postillion's box, made of oak, had been upended and attached to a wall to form a small cupboard.

Mrs Teulon-Porter seemed harmless enough to us – perhaps because she had been so well tutored by her hostess at number 9, but her house, despite all its quaint additions and its ideal location, struck us as very pokey and gloomy, musty-smelling and sticky with Dickensian grime. The façade in red brick and stuccoed pargeting suggested Edwardian renovations, while the front rooms on all three floors dated from the eighteenth century, charmingly so if one could overlook the dirt. The two flights of stairs were narrow and steep, but did not at that stage present any unsurmountable difficulties. The back of the house – looking out onto a dingy yard enclosed by other houses and a high back wall – appeared to be on the point of collapse, because the foundations had subsided so badly that the floor of the kitchen and, correspondingly, the kitchen ceiling and the floor of the bathroom above, sloped at an alarming angle. Mrs Teulon-Porter did not appear to consider this eccentricity at all hazardous. According to a plaque in the outside wall, John Clarke had masterminded this exemplary piece of engineering in 1770.

It required imagination and Mrs Thatcher's no-nonsense approach to convince us that this really was our dream house. Certainly its situation was perfect. The front rooms, right opposite the old gas lamp, enjoyed a full view of the churchyard, wistfully poetic even in winter, and although the proportions of the ground floor were rather spoilt by the staircase of the house at number 5 butting into the party wall, the two bedrooms were quite sufficient for our requirements. "My dears, all it needs is a coat of paint, you'll be surprised what a coat of paint can do," Thelma Thatcher declared authoritatively, determined not to let her masterly scheme be upset by trivialities.

Thus persuaded, we entered into negotiations with the owner. Stephen boldly made her an offer of £2,000 for her property. Not surprisingly she turned it down, timidly averring with one eye on Mrs Thatcher that she would expect it to fetch at least £4,000 on the open market. She would however agree to let it to us for £4 a week until such time as we could raise the £4,000 needed to buy it. In the meantime we were virtually free to treat the house as our own and redecorate it at will. The arrangement was to everyone's satisfaction. Mrs Thatcher shepherded her guest back to number 9 and there plied her with such liberal quantities of sherry, or possibly gin, that the next we heard was that Mrs Teulon-Porter, before departing for Shaftesbury, had agreed to have the dusty old coal shed and lean-to removed from the back yard and the outside of the house repainted.

Since the house was already vacant, Mrs Teulon-Porter was content to allow us to start redecorating inside before moving in. As Stephen's thesis was now at the bookbinder's, the time which I had previously spent typing it at weekends could now be devoted to my next occupation, that of house-painting. It was rewarding, but bore worryingly little relation to the Spanish studies which I was supposed to be revising for Finals. However, as the house was in a truly depressing state and as we could not afford to have it professionally redecorated, I had no choice but to do it myself. Armed with a collection of brushes and a plentiful supply of white emulsion, I attacked the grimy walls of the living room. My intention was to paint the two most important rooms, the living room and the main bedroom, before moving in, and then tackle the rest – the attic, the two flights of stairs, the kitchen and bathroom – more gradually over the ensuing months.

As I disliked the smell of paint, I usually worked with the front door wide open. The Thatchers were frequent and admiring visitors, plying me with cups of tea and encouraging comments. One day, Mr Thatcher paused as he was passing, bending his military frame slightly to peer in at the open door. "I say," he exclaimed, "you look such a fragile little thing, but, by Jove, you must be tough!" From the top of the stepladder I smiled, flattered by this commendation from a veteran of the First World War who still bore the disfiguring marks of that conflict on his gaunt face. A few days later we were told that the Thatchers had decided to pay their odd-job man to paint the living-room ceiling for us: "Dear Billy's housewarming present to our new neighbours," was Thelma Thatcher's way of describing her husband's extraordinary generosity. The Thatcher's odd-job man, a somewhat portly version of John Gielgud, was a retired artist who filled in his time with larger-scale painting while his wife ran a print shop on King's Parade. He was an amiable man who, I suspected, derived much quiet amusement from my initial attempts at wielding a paintbrush. Indeed, under his benevolent tuition, I soon acquired many of the tricks of his trade, like starting a wall from the top, or applying the brush in a circular motion over an uneven surface, or using a hard edge to paint a window frame.

Stephen's reputation in relativistic circles may have been rapidly ascending the ladder of fame on account of his pursuit of singularities, but my advance in learning was exhibiting an equally dizzying if more erratic series of highs and lows: propelled upwards by intensive doses of medieval and modern languages, philology and literature during the week, and brought to earth by a crash course in the skills of interior decorating on Saturdays. Finally, when I began to find the area of wall and ceiling still to be covered rather more daunting than I had anticipated, we calculated that we could just afford to ask the decorator to paint the kitchen for us, a particularly unpleasant task since the grime and grease were probably as old as the house.

Although my parents had only just moved to their new house, they and my brother Chris came to Cambridge one weekend early in 1966 to redecorate the top-floor bedroom and, in token of his willingness to help, Stephen's father spared a day from his globetrotting to paint the bathroom while I applied a coat of enamel to the old chipped bath. Then, magically, fully justifying Thelma Thatcher's convictions, our tumbledown eighteenth-century cottage acquired the air of a des res, and in the transformation the angles of its floors and ceilings had become simply eccentric curiosities. Our few pieces of furniture, which various colleagues of Stephen's carried the five doors along the lane, fitted in perfectly – although, of course, when we bought them we had not given a moment's thought to the possible proportions of their eventual resting place.

Proud of our restoration of the little house, Stephen and I decided that the new Bursar of Caius was due for another visit, especially as Stephen was by now beginning to feel more sure of his place in the College hierarchy. Early in the New Year, we had braved the annual Ladies' Night, Bishop Shaxton's Solace, when wives were officially welcomed to the College precincts and treated to a banquet, as if in compensation for the contempt in which they were held for the rest of the year. Bishop Shaxton had, in the sixteenth century, bequeathed the munificent sum of twelve shillings and sixpence for the solace of every Fellow who had to spend Christmas at home rather than in the College. The equivalent in modern terms of twelve shillings and sixpence per head was sufficient to provide a lavish five- or six-course dinner with unlimited quantities of the best wines for the Fellowship and their spouses. Typically the meal would consist of soup, a whole lobster, an undefined small game bird each – usually served complete with head and limbs – a substantial creamy pudding, a cheese savoury and then, of course, at dessert, the famous port – or claret – which tradition demanded should only ever be passed clockwise round the table. In theory it was a magnificent spread, but in practice college halls tend to be draughty places, and usually the food was cold before it reached the table. Our first experience of Bishop Shaxton's Solace was a chill one, not only on account of the temperature of the food, the wine and the hall. We were seated on the same table as the former Bursar – the one who had so scathingly dismissed Stephen's perfectly reasonable request for a job description before our marriage. That was bad enough, but our discomfort was compounded by finding ourselves placed out on a limb at the end of the table. After the meal, eaten in a frosty silence, an elderly band appeared from the shadows and struck up antediluvian foxtrots. I had never learnt the foxtrot, as the advent of the Beatles had cut short my brief flirtation with ballroom dancing, and now I could only watch in pensive, glum frustration as our tight-lipped dinner companions deserted us for the dance floor – looking like close-furled black umbrellas, they authoritatively steered their submissive, upholstery-clad wives round the hall, deftly exhibiting a precise, manicured display of ornamental footwork. I was twenty-one: all around me our dining companions were in their forties and fifties, if not their sixties and seventies. It was as if we had been propelled into a geriatric culture where our generation was deliberately snubbed as irrelevant.

The only consolation was that Caius, as one of the richest, most solidly based colleges, could probably afford to lend us a couple of thousand pounds without the loan creating a blip in the college accounts. We were well aware that no building society would even begin to consider the house for a mortgage, but Stephen, undeterred by his previous encounters in the Bursar's office, thought it perfectly reasonable to apply to the College for a loan so that we could improve our offer to Mrs Teulon-Porter. While he was with the Bursar, I sat waiting in the outer office and broached a matter of some delicacy to Mr Clarke, the white-haired bursarial assistant, much more amenable than the Bursar himself. My discussion began in the nature of a complaint. Why, I asked Mr Clarke, had he sent Stephen the application forms for a university pension a few weeks back when it was common knowledge that Stephen's life was going to be so drastically foreshortened that, in all probability, he would not qualify? Was it not a bit heartless of him to have sent the forms? Stephen had taken one look at them and with a weary gesture had pushed them aside, not wanting to contemplate arrangements for a future that others might look forward to, but that was to be denied him.

Mr Clarke did not apologize for any insensitivity; quite the contrary, he shook his head as if unable to comprehend my problem. "Well, young lady, I just follow my instructions," he said, turning his bright blue eyes on me from beneath busy white brows. "My instructions are to send out the forms to all new Fellows, as all new Fellows are by rights entitled to a university pension. Your husband is a new Fellow, so he is entitled to a university pension, just like the rest of them. All he has to do is sign the forms to establish his rights." His words were still ringing in my ears when he added casually as an afterthought, "No need for any medical tests or anything of that sort, if that's what you're thinking."

I could hardly believe what he was saying. This was an area which, in our ignorance, we had tacitly dismissed as inapplicable to us. Now I was being told that it could be resolved with a mere signature and, moreover, that it would assure us of a commodity which neither of us had ever thought about before – that is to say, security. For one afternoon's business we had both been remarkably successful, and through our success had discovered this new goal in life, security, which suddenly assumed a comforting importance. Stephen had persuaded the Bursar to send the College land agent to inspect the house with a view to securing a loan, and I had secured Stephen's rights to a pension. With a loan to buy the house and a pension, our well-being would gain two firm anchors in an otherwise uncertain world.

The College land agent came to survey the house one sunny spring morning, when the churchyard was bursting into a profusion of yellow blossom. Our optimism soon quailed before his dry, unsmiling exterior, and when he issued his verbal summary of his projected report, our hopes were dashed beyond recall. The agent gave us the strong impression that we were wasting his time, calling him out on such a nonsensical errand. Could we not see that the back of the house was falling down? And, as if that were not enough, the third-floor attic was a definite fire hazard. He would not risk sleeping up there, or even using it as a study himself, nor would he advise letting anyone else do so. A two-hundred-year-old house was not, in his opinion, a sensible purchase. In any case, there were so many road-building schemes in the offing that he would not be surprised if the whole lane were demolished to make way for a new access road to the city centre from the west. He could not possibly recommend the property as an investment to the College.

Stephen was infuriated at such a short-sighted verdict, but despite his vociferous protests the Bursar accepted the land agent's report. Some time later, as we were driving past the land agent's office on the other side of the city, Stephen spluttered indignantly as he pointed to the premises. Like our house, the building rose to three floors, but on a larger scale, a good ten feet higher than ours. The third floor was quite obviously, from the discernible lighting, being used as office or study space. Furthermore the whitewashed, gabled, timbered property bulged and leant picturesquely in the manner of a decrepit sixteenth-century building. It made our little eighteenth-century house appear positively modern and well-kept. There was no immediate solution to the problem, except perhaps to save as much money as we could to raise a deposit for a mortgage on a newer house. A system began to evolve whereby Stephen earned the money through salary, teaching and essay competitions, and I, running contrary to the national trend of reckless extravagance encouraged by the Macmillan government, attended to the family finances, paying the bills and saving as much as possible through careful housekeeping. Delicious scraps of streaky bacon came at one shilling and sixpence a pound from the old Sainsbury's, with its marble counters and endless queues; duck livers from Sennit's the poulterer's were nourishing and cheap; the market proved a veritable cornucopia of fresh fruit and vegetables; and the local butcher introduced me to inexpensive cuts of meat – hand of pork and shoulder of lamb never costing more than five shillings – which proved no disgrace on the dinner table when we entertained our new friends from the College and the Department.

The Labour government elected in 1964 inherited from the Conservatives the dubious legacy of a nation engaged in a gigantic spending spree. In the spring of 1966, having exercised my right to vote for the first time, I joined the late-night crowds in the Market Square to greet the success of the Labour candidate in the repeat election, which had been called to increase the government majority. Sadly, our new MP, Robert Davies, died while in office and the Labour government was shackled by its mounting economic problems, frequent strikes and a constant preoccupation with the "balance of payments" crisis, the economic buzz phrase of the Sixties. With a failing currency, Britain was having to relinquish its role as a world power. Home news broadcasts were dominated as never before by economics, while the international background of the war in Vietnam and heightening tensions in the Middle East threatened to give rise to the anticipated superpower confrontation which would unleash the forces of the nuclear arsenals of both sides.

Stephen meanwhile had discovered a way of earning more money and improving himself in the process. He had wanted to study mathematics at Oxford, but his father had been convinced, wrongly as it happened, that there would be no jobs in maths in the future. Aware that he had already disappointed his father by not showing any interest in medicine, Stephen had compromised by agreeing to study physics. When he came to Cambridge as a postgraduate student, therefore, he had only a basic grounding in mathematics. As he was now working with Roger Penrose, an exemplary mathematician, he felt himself at a disadvantage, but he hit upon the happy solution of getting paid for teaching himself the maths course by giving undergraduate supervisions in it for Gonville and Caius College. Thus he steadily worked his way through the syllabus of the Maths Tripos. Needless to say, his progress far outstripped that of his students, whose lack of application he found frustrating, as he pointed out in the end-of-term reports that I wrote down to his dictation. With Brandon Carter, he also attended some of the undergraduate lectures in mathematics, notably the course given by the genial Master of Pembroke College, Sir William Hodge. During the course of the term, the rest of the audience gradually drifted away, leaving Sir William lecturing only to three listeners, Stephen, Brandon and another colleague, Ray McLenaghan. They regretted that they had not taken the opportunity to slip away sooner, but since their absence would have been extremely conspicuous, they felt obliged to stay the course.

It must have been during my final year in London that an uncle of Stephen's by marriage, Herman Hardenberg, a Harley Street psychiatrist, spent a long period in hospital in St John's Wood, just down the road from Westfield, suffering from a heart condition. I used to call on him sometimes of an afternoon when the day's lectures and seminars were over. Herman, the husband of Stephen's aunt Janet, herself a doctor, was a charming, gentle, cultivated man who liked to talk about the subjects that interested me, particularly about the poetry of the Provençal troubadours, the topic of my special paper in Finals. He had been reading C.S. Lewis's *The Allegory of Love*, and naturally approached the tensions of the poetry – where the poet-lover languishes for his unattainable beloved – from the psychological angle. Then our conversation would turn to family topics: I told him about our life in Cambridge and our work on the house. "I hope the Hawkings are treating you well?" he once enquired cautiously, making little secret of his mistrust of that family. I confidently calmed his fears on my account. That the Hawkings were eccentric, even odd, was well known; that they were aloof, convinced of their own intellectual superiority over the rest of the human race, was also widely recognized in St Albans, where they were regarded with a mixture of suspicion and awe. There were upsets and outbursts and there had been tensions in the air at the time of our engagement and the wedding, but these I took as part of the general tenor of family life. I had no substantial reason to complain of the way they treated me. Indeed, as I told Herman, they always seemed delighted to see Stephen and me, and always welcomed us warmly to Hillside Road.

12

An Insignificant Ending

With the approach of summer, the trees and plants in the church-yard competed for the attention of residents and passers-by in a riotous display of colour and perfume. Successive groups of tourists, particularly Americans, would come sauntering down the lane. Many of them would press their noses to our windows in an attempt to peer through the net curtains into our quaint interiors. Not all were susceptible to the beauty of the surroundings: there was the small boy who announced in a loud voice to his parents as they strolled along: "Gee, Momma, I wouldn't like to live here. the Holy Ghost might come up and get yer!" I could not allow myself to dwell on the newly revealed beauties of our surroundings. Apart from a brief celebration for Stephen's PhD in March, my every precious spare moment was spent revising – in London in the College library during the week, in Cambridge with my books spread out around me in the attic at weekends or, that Easter, in St Albans, where we spent the holiday quietly with my parents.

The Hawking household, on the other hand, was in some distress. Stephen's younger sister, Philippa, had recently been taken into hospital in Oxford for reasons which were not disclosed to me. I shared Stephen's concern for her and wanted to visit her, naively hoping that perhaps at last she and I would be able to settle some of those shadowy disturbances which lay between us as sisters-in-law. Because I loved Stephen, I wanted to get on well with his family, to like them and to be liked by them, and I could not understand why this particular relationship should be so difficult. On the day appointed for our visit, however, Stephen's mother told me in no uncertain terms that Philippa wanted to see only Stephen, not me, explaining that no one, least of all Philippa, wanted to upset "this thing (presumably our marriage) between Stephen and you". As Stephen said nothing to mitigate the effect of his mother's bluntness, I was on the point of going home in tears to my parents, but then the old Ford Zephyr would not start and, in a sudden twist of events, I found myself driving Isobel and Stephen to Oxford in our Mini.

While the rest of the party went hospital-visiting, I spent the afternoon in the waiting room, revising the great medieval epic poem based on the exploits in exile of the hero, *el Cantar de Mío Cid*. The time passed quickly as I became absorbed in the sophisticated psychology of the late twelfth-century poem, which deftly interweaves two main thematic strands into its texture: the public image of the invincible warrior and the private face of the devoted husband and father. When the Cid goes into exile, the poet describes his distress at parting from his family as "tearing the nail from the flesh". Later the poet documents how the eponymous hero's many attempts to be generous and encouraging to his cowardly sons-in-law are misconstrued and turned against him. This epic tale, like a distant voice whispering down the centuries, told of the complexity and the unpredictability of the human mind. Even in the twelfth century, the poignant distinction between the hero's private life and his public image was seen as an authentic concept.

On our return from Oxford, no further reference was made to the morning's episode. In the family tradition, it was brushed under the carpet with many other dusty remnants of psychological and emotional detritus, regarded as being too insignificant to merit any consideration in that rarified atmosphere where emotional issues were never discussed because of the threat they might pose to the intellect. It was therefore a surprise, just before the onset of Finals, to receive a letter from Philippa, addressed to me in a minuscule hand. She regretted the differences that there may have been between us but looked forward to a better relationship in the future, assuring me that she respected my desire "to try to love Stephen". Although I responded wholeheartedly to this olive branch, I was as perplexed by that comment as my mother had been some months earlier when the rumour had reached her ears that the Hawkings were thinking of moving to Cambridge to set up a home there for Stephen. Did they not expect the marriage to last, she asked indignantly. I was confused by these undercurrents and wondered why Stephen's family, of all people, seemed so intent on undermining our relationship and our happiness, especially when he was dependent on me for so much of his everyday existence.

As if to confound the doubters, we were closer than ever in the week of Finals. Stephen came to London to give me moral support and stayed in my top-floor room working on the singularity theorems, and occasionally dipping into translations of the great works of Spanish literature – among them Fernando de Rojas's *La Celestina*, the downmarket prototype of Romeo and Juliet with its old procuress, Celestina, one of the most entertaining characters in medieval Spanish literature – while I went out each morning to the examination hall. After the afternoon session, Stephen and I would make off to Hampstead Heath or to the gardens and house of Kenwood in search of respite from writer's cramp and mental constipation. We also visited my much-loved Great Aunt Effie, as irrepressible as ever in her late seventies, still living alone in her large house in Tufnell Park. By the end of the week I was just beginning to get into my stride, but the exams were already nearly over. I felt a huge sense of anticlimax rather than relief. The topics I had revised had proved elusive in the extreme, and I knew that the First which was expected of anyone bearing the name of Hawking would prove just as elusive.

With the last flourish of the pen on the last page of the last Finals paper, I irrevocably signed away my student days. The Beatles record, *Revolver*, which Stephen had given me for my birthday, seemed sadly incongruous. There were no parties, no celebrations, just a few hasty goodbyes before I stepped definitively into my other existence and we set off in the car to meet Roger Penrose, who was to guide us out to his home at Stanmore for dinner with his family. We stopped in the car park of Stanmore station for Roger to collect his car, an elderly blue Volkswagen. Undeterred on finding every tyre flat, Roger drove to a garage round the corner where he pumped them all up. When we reached his single-storey house at the end of a cul-de-sac, tucked away from the stockbroker mansions, we were given an enthusiastic welcome by Joan and by their two small sons, Christopher and Toby, who had been a babe-in-arms at Cornell the previous summer. Now, at eighteen months, he was fully mobile and expressed his infectious *joie de vivre* by racing the length of the living room at full pelt, biscuit in hand, leaving a trail of crumbs across the navy blue carpet. Soon he was hurling his small person into an armchair, clambering onto the arm of the chair and then jumping off, the while declaring, "Don't do that, don't do that!" Blissfully unconcerned by such antics, Roger and Stephen lapsed into the inevitable discussion about the mathematics of physics.

The Finals results were more or less as expected, not brilliant but good enough to allow me to start working for a PhD. From my observations of the dynamics of life in Cambridge, I could see that the role of a wife – and possibly a mother – was a one-way ticket to outer darkness, and that it was essential to preserve my own identity. Even though there were moves afoot to admit women to certain of the more enlightened men's colleges, there were many well-qualified but unhappy wives in Cambridge whose individual talents had been totally disregarded, spurned by a system which refused to acknowledge that wives and mothers might be capable of an intellectual identity of their own.

My weekly commuting to London had come to an end none too soon, for Stephen needed my help more and more. As he had to lean on my arm wherever he went, I walked round to the Department with him every morning, took him home for lunch, which – like every other meal – had to consist of meat and two vegetables to satisfy his enormous appetite, and collected him again in the evening. All thoughts of a career in the Foreign Office had long been consigned to the past, but even a simple job or a teacher-training course was out of the question, as my presence was so obviously constantly required in the small circle of the Department of Applied Mathematics, Little St Mary's Lane and the kitchen. A doctorate seemed to be the ideal solution. I could easily adapt my hours of study in the University Library and my work at home to Stephen's schedule. Furthermore, I was eligible for a student grant, which was a welcome bonus.

The literature of the medieval period attracted me as an area of research, but as our circumstances would not permit me to travel to remote libraries in search of dusty manuscripts, I could not expect to edit a hitherto undiscovered text. My research would have to take the form of a critical study, using texts that were already published, which would not be difficult considering the facilities available in Cambridge. I continued to be registered, however, as a student of London University for various good reasons, the most cogent being that Cambridge PhDs were subject to a fairly strict time limit of three years, whereas there was no such restriction on the London degrees, and it seemed unlikely that I should be able to devote myself uninterruptedly to my thesis.

I did not embark upon my chosen field of research, the medieval lyric poetry of the Iberian Peninsula, straight away because, thanks largely to Stephen, another topic had presented itself as a subject for a preliminary research paper. As a result of reading *La Celestina* while I was doing my exams, Stephen had come up with a bright idea which he put to me as we were driving back to Cambridge at the end of Finals week. Had I not realized, he asked, that the ultimate tragedy of death, destruction and despair in the drama was precipitated by the old bawd Celestina's rejection of a minor character, Parmeno, a youth who has a mother complex about her? The idea was a fascinating one, which won my supervisor's amazed approval: he was even more amazed when I confessed that the idea was Stephen's. I too was astonished at his powers of perception and invention, which could focus on the essence of a problem in any field, my own included. My task was to explore and develop the idea and justify the Freudian concept when applied to a text dating from 1499. The most gratifying aspect of the project was that it was a tribute to the success of our relationship: we were living and working in harmony, supporting each other, participating in each other's interests, despite the disparity of our chosen subjects, despite attempts to divide us and despite the inevitable difficulties of Stephen's worsening disability. We were very happy. We both gained confidence and courage from the strength of our mutual resolve and from our trust in each other. Then in the early autumn we found that I was expecting a baby.

13

Life Cycles

Following close on the confirmation of the pregnancy came the sad fulfilment of one of the inevitable laws of nature: Stephen's paternal grandmother, Mrs Hawking senior, whose acquaintance I had made just a month before, died at the age of ninety-six while Stephen's parents were away in China on an official tour of the country at the height of the Cultural Revolution. That August, on a trip north with Stephen, his mother and Edward to visit ageing relatives, I had been introduced to Isobel's elderly maiden aunts in Edinburgh and, on our return journey, we had stayed overnight in the Hawking ancestral home in Boroughbridge in Yorkshire.

In the early nineteenth century, the ancestor who had been steward to the Duke of Devonshire and built himself the grand mansion had also amended the surname from the vulgar 'awkins to the more genteel Hawking. The Hawking Chatsworth, with its sweeping staircase, high ceilings and bay windows, had seen better days. Poor Aunt Muriel managed the vast house alone, while at the same time attending to her disabled but still imperious mother. Like the house, Mrs Hawking was certainly a shadow of her former self, but it was not hard to discern in her wrinkled features the determination and fortitude of the woman who had raised five children and saved her family from bankruptcy. She lived in the only room in the house which was still warm and habitable, the drawing room. The other rooms, including ours with its half-poster bed, were cold, dark, damp and not a little eerie, in spite of Aunt Muriel's efforts to make them comfortable.

While his parents were away, Stephen's younger brother Edward stayed with my parents. When he came to Cambridge to spend a weekend with us, he found himself, at the tender age of ten, obliged to cook his own Sunday lunch – under his brother's instruction, because I was suddenly laid low with an attack of morning sickness. It lasted all that day and into the next, and the next, and so on for week after week. An experienced friend suggested that the best cure for morning sickness was a cup of tea first thing in the morning before getting up. This was fine in theory, but in practice I could not have a cup of tea without getting up to make it myself. My parents came to the rescue with the gift of a tea-making machine. Thereafter I was troubled by few of the effects of pregnancy and was able to resume my usual routine of study and writing with renewed vigour.

There was no shortage of helpful friends, all of them recent mothers, to advise on the pros and cons of hospitals, nursing homes, health treatments, prophylactic breathing, relaxation classes and breast-feeding. In despair at my ignorance in such matters, they even left their babies with me for practice sessions in changing nappies, but it all seemed highly theoretical since, on the whole, the pregnancy was so straightforward and their babies were so well behaved. I was convinced that babies just ate and slept, whimpering a little from time to time.

My own health was unexceptional by comparison with Stephen's, which was beginning to require some management. Before leaving for China, Frank Hawking had read in a medical journal that a regular intake of vitamin B tablets might benefit the nervous system, which could also be reinforced by a weekly injection of a preparation called hydroxocobalamin. The vitamin tablets could be obtained on prescription from Dr Swan, a Bart's man like Stephen's father, with whom Stephen was registered in Cambridge – but the weekly injections were more of a problem, since the surgery was on the other side of Cambridge and, in Stephen's opinion, a morning spent there waiting for an injection was a morning wasted. We tried it a few times, to Stephen's growing irritation. One morning we arrived back home from the surgery at about midday to find Thelma Thatcher out in the lane, broom in hand, engaged in her daily exercise of sweeping the road and the pavement. Noticing our despondent faces, she called to us, "Dears, dears, what's the matter?" I explained, and she immediately came up with a solution. "Oh, but that's easy! We'll ask Sister Chalmers to call in on her way from Peterhouse!" She hugged us both and then went off to get in touch with Sister Chalmers, who had kindly lent us her gas cooker when we moved into Little St Mary's Lane. At Thelma Thatcher's instigation, she was now commandeered into giving Stephen his injection at home once a week when she had finished her college surgery. This in our household coincided more or less with breakfast time.

A similar problem arose when the medical authorities suggested regular physiotherapy to keep Stephen's joints extended and his muscles active. Already his fingers were beginning to curl, and he could no longer write, except to sign his name. We attended just one physiotherapy session at Addenbrooke's, the new hospital on the outskirts of Cambridge, but by the end of it Stephen was so angry that he declared that he would not squander any more of his precious time waiting around to be treated. It was Dennis Sciama who came to the rescue on this occasion. He persuaded the Institute of Physics to sponsor twice-weekly domiciliary visits by a private physiotherapist from its benevolent fund. This is when Constance Willis entered our lives.

Constance was one of those stalwart English spinster ladies, cast in the same mould as the jolly-hockey-stick Molly Du Cane, the leader of the St Albans Folk Dance and Song Society – open, jovial and straightforward of manner. Before coming to stretch Stephen's muscles at ten o'clock on Tuesday and Thursday mornings, Constance Willis would visit two octogenarian patients in Trinity College: Mr Gow, the eminent classicist, and the Reverend Simpson, formerly Dean of the College – principally to help them put their socks on.

Between them, Sister Chalmers and Miss Willis minimized the inconvenience to Stephen's routine, enabling him to work approximately the same hours as any of his colleagues. In reality, although he might arrive in his office later in the morning than they did, he usually worked later into the evening as well. He would spend long periods deep in thought, and often at weekends would sit silently wrangling with the equations governing the beginning of the universe, training his brain to memorize long, complicated theorems without the aid of pen or paper. "Celestial mechanics," Mr Thatcher called it jokingly. "I suppose your young man is busy with his celestial mechanics?" he would ask if Stephen had passed him in the street without acknowledging him, a common occurrence which, together with Stephen's reluctance to expend any effort on polite small talk, tended to offend some of our more sensitive neighbours, acquaintances and relations, and for which I frequently had to apologize, explaining that Stephen had to put all his concentration into remaining upright.

Bouts of morning sickness had prevented me from attending old Mrs Hawking's funeral in Yorkshire. In fact I had never yet been to a funeral. That omission was sadly soon to be rectified.

Mary Thatcher, the only daughter of our neighbours, was planning an extended study tour of the Middle East, where she would divide her stay of several months between Israel and Jordan. Just before her departure that autumn I saw her walking along the lane hand in hand with her father, whose pace had become slower and more halting. They disappeared from view into the churchyard. This poignant vision of father and daughter struck me forcibly, for it seemed that in those precious moments they were anticipating their final parting. Soon after Mary had left, her father fell ill and was taken into the nursing home, where he died some weeks later.

As dry leaves danced through the streets before the biting December wind, Stephen and I stood hand in hand at the back of the lofty, cold church of the Holy Trinity, the Low Church which William Thatcher had attended in preference to the High Anglicanism of Little St Mary's. The stirring words of the funeral service, intoned as the coffin was carried into the church, sent a chill shiver down my spine. Watching and listening, I was haunted by the paradox that, in one stroke, death had erased all the learning, the experiences, the heroism, the goodness, the achievements, the memories of that life from which we were taking our leave, while within me I was carrying the miraculous beginnings of a new life, a blank page on which the long process of learning, experience, achievements, memories, had still to be written. Beside me stood the child's father, young and vibrant despite the onset of disability. His general health was good, and his determination to enjoy life to the full – and to succeed in physics – was gaining strength by the day. Walking was difficult, buttons were a nuisance, mealtimes took longer and the brain had taken over from pen and paper, but these were mechanical problems which invention and perseverance could overcome. It was unthinkable that he could be a candidate for the sad ceremony we were attending that day. Death was the tragedy of old age, not of youth.

Youth is essential to the very existence of Cambridge, despite the medieval buildings and the fossilized Fellows who come home to roost in their dusty nooks and crannies. The magnetism of the place draws in wave upon wave of young people for three years, or if they are lucky six, and then ejects them into the real world, as if rousing them from an enchantment. Many of our early friends had already gone off to positions in universities all over the globe, and their places were soon filled by new arrivals, some semi-permanent, some transient. One such visitor that autumn was our quiet American friend whom we had met at Cornell, Robert Boyer. He paid only a brief visit to Cambridge, and after a session in the Department came to dinner with us. He talked about his English wife and little daughter, and Vietnam, the main preoccupation of Americans in those days, as well as about singularities and physics.

One day not long after Robert's visit, the radio was blaring out the *News* headlines, while I was preparing lunch and waiting for Stephen to come home. Since his return from Texas, George Ellis had kindly brought Stephen home at lunchtime on his way to eat at the newly opened University Centre on the riverfront at the end of the lane. I listened intently as the main item recounted a sniper attack in Austin, Texas. A madman had climbed to the top of the university tower, from where he had shot at the lecturers and students crossing the square below. One of the victims had been shot dead. The report was all the more horrific on account of the familiarity of the scene. I could picture it in my mind's eye and realized at once that the sniper's targets could well have included some of our acquaintances. Later that day we heard that it was Robert Boyer who was the victim of the sniper's bullet. This was not death from old age, or from natural catastrophe like the recent Aberfan disaster in Wales, or from premature illness, it was death at the brutal hand of man. There was a sober truth in those stark words of the funeral service: "…by man came death…" Shocked and bewildered at such a cruel trick of fate, we searched for a lasting way of expressing our sorrow and our admiration for Robert Boyer.

14

An Imperfect World

Robert George was born, weighing six pounds five ounces, at ten o'clock at night on Sunday 28th May 1967, just as Francis Chichester, the lone yachtsman, sailed into Plymouth harbour to be met by cheering crowds on his return from his round-the-world voyage. Robert's birth was received with private rejoicing of such intensity that when Stephen went the next morning to impart the good news to Peck and How Ghee Ang, our neighbours from Singapore who had taken over the house at number 11 from us, he was so overcome with emotion that Peck feared that I had died in childbirth.

Robert, in his eagerness to come into the world two weeks early, had taken me by surprise. In March, Stephen's sister Mary, his cousin Julian and I, together with thousands of other graduates, had all received our BA degrees at the mammoth London University degree ceremony in the Albert Hall, the occasion marred only by the absence of the Chancellor of the University, the Queen Mother, on account of illness. Afterwards our parents treated us to a memorable party in a splendid venue, the Royal Society of Tropical Medicine, obtained for our use by my father-in-law.

Earlier in the academic year, Dr Dorothy Needham, the distinguished wife of the Master of Caius, had taken me under her wing and introduced me to a fledgling academic society, Lucy Cavendish College, pioneered by two scientists, Dr Anna Bidder and Dr Kate Bertram; their aim was to promote academic opportunities for mature women students in Cambridge. Association with Lucy Cavendish College allowed me to acquire MA status in the University, and this in turn, most importantly, allowed me to borrow books from the University Library. By late spring, the Celestina paper inspired by Stephen, 'Madre Celestina', was at the printer's, and I saw no reason to suppose that I would not be able to combine motherhood with research. On the last Friday in May, true to my usual routine, I spent most of the day blithely working in the University Library, assembling material for the thesis. I did not suspect that this was to be my last visit to the Library for quite a long time.

That evening, disregarding the strange tightening sensations in my thighs, I went with Sue Ellis, who was also pregnant, to a party for wives given by Wilma Batchelor, the wife of the Head of the Department. On the Saturday morning, after an uncomfortable night, the tightening sensations became stronger and more frequent, so I dashed into town to do a copious amount of shopping for Stephen before I was out of action. Feeling rather ill as I heaved it all home, I called in at the butcher's for a few final purchases. Chris the butcher took one look at me and insisted on serving me ahead of the queue. "Jane," he said, "I think you had better go straight home!" I gladly followed his advice.

Later that day, at the height of a thunderstorm, How Ghee, who was the father of two little daughters, drove Stephen and me to the nursing home, but I soon wished that I had stayed at home or applied for a bed at the maternity hospital – which, in those days, admitted only women from deprived backgrounds or those with complications. The ageing midwives were every bit as crusty as the spinster school ma'ams of my teenage years. As I walked down the corridor with Stephen leaning on my arm, I felt the onset of a strong contraction, like the tentacles of an octopus embracing and squeezing my abdomen. Assiduously following the techniques acquired in the newly introduced antenatal classes, I leant against a door post and focused my attention on the much-practised breathing exercises.

"What on earth's the matter with you?" the steely-eyed Sister enquired harshly. She was much younger than the rest of her staff and should have known better. There, after the procedure came to a standstill for the next twenty-four hours, the baby was finally delivered, not by one of the midwives but by John Owens, a cheerful young doctor from the surgery where I was registered. Meanwhile Stephen was my faithful companion, sitting at my bedside for long hours and even sneaking in on his mother's arm by the garden entrance at six o'clock the next morning.

I lay in bed, bored and frustrated, transported only by the magnificent, overpowering themes of the Brahms double concerto for violin and cello which I had memorized as my mantra, the music on which I had learnt to concentrate to distract my mind from the pain. The music took me back to the week's holiday arranged for us by my parents that Easter, just two months before the birth. The cottage they had rented was down on the edge of the cove at Port St Isaac in Cornwall, a very long way from Cambridge. They probably thought, mistakenly as it happened, that this would be my last opportunity to travel for a long time. During that week Stephen, in concession to my tastes, had given me the recording of the Brahms concerto for a birthday present.

As Stephen's self-confidence had grown, so he had gained in fierce determination. During our stay in Port St Isaac, an afternoon's drive took us to Tintagel, one of the reputed homes of the Arthurian legend, perched remotely on the north coast of Cornwall. Disappointingly, the ruined castle was not visible from the village and, according to the postmistress, the only approach was down the steep rocky gully, the Vale of Avalon. Stephen insisted on seeing the castle and – unable to deny him anything, so conscious were we of his shortened life expectancy – my mother and I, one on each side, guided, lifted, bore him down the wild, uneven descent, stumbling over the stones in our path with the wind blowing off the sea into our faces. The sapphire band of sea at the end of the path seemed to recede, and the castle proved elusive. After we had struggled on for about three-quarters of an hour, my mother was getting short of breath and was worrying about me in my advanced state of pregnancy, but Stephen refused to give up. By a happy chance, a Land Rover appeared from nowhere, climbing the rough track back up to the village, so we hailed the driver. He was reluctant to stop, but paused to tell us that the castle was still a long way off, round a headland. The castle was evidently beyond our reach, but we pleaded with him to take us back to the village. Finally with brusque impatience he agreed to take just one passenger. There was no question but that that passenger had to be Stephen. With similar single-mindedness, Stephen was pursuing plans to attend a summer school at the Battelle Memorial Institute in Seattle that July. With never a moment's hesitation, I agreed to the plans, seeing no reason why the three of us, Stephen, myself and the baby, should not enjoy seven weeks on the Pacific coast. After all, babies just ate and slept.

The joy the baby brought was intoxicating. Within minutes of his birth he was lodged in the crook of my arm, looking slightly purple but observing his surroundings with consummate lack of concern as if he had seen it all before. "A future professor" was my mother-in-law's predictable verdict on her first grandchild.

When he was next brought to me, he had recovered from the birthing experience and had gained a healthy colour. His eyes were of the deepest, brightest blue, set in a neat elfin face with rosy cheeks and pointed ears. He had no hair, only an incipient blond down in a whorl on the crown of his head and on the tips of his ears. The minute fingers, each equipped with its own tiny nail, clasped my own outstretched finger.

This beautiful little creature, the miraculous embodiment of perfection, had come into a painfully imperfect world. In the week after his birth, the Six Day War erupted in the Middle East with violent consequences which were to last throughout the decades of the child's upbringing and long into his adulthood. In my simple, post-natal frame of mind, I was convinced that if the world were to be run by the mothers of newborn babies rather than hardened old men inciting brash youths to violence, wars would cease overnight.

Gradually in the days following Robert's birth we acclimatized to a new reality. Grandparents helped out for a couple of weeks, and then we were on our own, evolving a dramatically changed lifestyle. Henceforth expeditions – to the Department or into town – involved three people plus a pram and a walking stick. Luckily George Ellis came to the rescue. Not only did he bring Stephen home at lunchtime, he also collected him after lunch and brought him home in the evening. One afternoon, after a couple of weeks, when we had begun to achieve some faint semblance of normality, I considered that the time had come to return to my books and my growing card index of the language of the medieval love poetry of the Iberian Peninsula. The baby was fed and changed and placed in his pram out in the backyard under the blue sky. He looked comfortable and drowsy in the warm afternoon air. I expected him to sleep for at least an hour. Stifling my own tendency to yawn, I crept upstairs to my books and cards in the attic and spread them out on the table. No sooner had I found my place than a raucous cry came from below. I hurried down to Robert, picked him up, fed him and changed his nappy again. He did not really appear to be very hungry. I laid him down gently in his carrycot-pram and went back upstairs, only to be followed by the same cry. This little scene was re-enacted many times that afternoon until finally I realized that this tiny baby was neither hungry nor sleepy: he just wanted to be sociable. So at the age of one month he started work on a PhD thesis, helping me by wriggling on my knee and gurgling while I tried to write. That single afternoon completely destroyed whatever illusions I might have held about combining motherhood with some sort of intellectual occupation. Nor did I have any notion of the demands on the body of the birth process. I fully counted on being up and about my normal business within a week, little realizing that the nine-month gestation and the trauma of the long birth would take their toll of my strength. I had no idea that feeding the baby would be such an exhausting and time-consuming commitment which, combined with the topsy-turvy schedule of infant demands, day and night, would mean that I would often slip into a doze when eventually he went to sleep.

As July approached, I began to have severe qualms about the Seattle trip, especially as the arrangements were becoming more and more complicated. Charlie Misner, an American visitor to the Department who had become Robert's godfather at the christening in Caius Chapel in June, wanted Stephen to visit him at the University of Maryland after the Seattle summer school, to talk about singularities. Both he and his Danish wife, Susanne, assured us that we would be welcome to stay with them and their four young children in their large house in the suburbs of Washington DC. I could not allow myself to appear half-hearted, but I was not sure how we were going to get to Seattle in one piece, let alone further afield. The tiredness I felt as I tried to pack for Stephen, myself and our six-week-old baby was devastating. I had not expected anything like this, nor had I expected that my own body, previously so utterly reliable, would let me down so catastrophically.

Somehow, assisted by a posse of anxious parents, none more so than my mother, we managed to check in at London Airport on time on the morning of 17th July, 1967. Our goodbyes were hasty, because the airline promptly provided a wheelchair for Stephen, who found himself obliged to sit in it and be wheeled directly through customs and passport control to the departure lounge. Laden with Robert and with assorted bags of provisions for the flight, I hurried along behind. The ventilation system at Terminal Three had broken down that day, the hottest day of the summer, with the result that hot air was being sucked into the building but none was being let out, making a veritable inferno of the departure lounge. We had just reached the lounge when the loudspeaker announced that our flight was delayed.

While we sat waiting in the stifling heat, Robert eagerly gulped down the entire contents of the bottle of diluted rose-hip syrup which was supposed to last him all the way to Seattle. The first announcement was soon followed by another, inviting Pan American passengers to collect complimentary refreshments from the bar. I deposited Robert on Stephen's knee and went over to join the queue for our free sandwiches. When I returned, I froze in absolute horror at the sight that met my eyes. Robert was still safely sitting on his father's knee, smiling beatifically and leaning comfortably back against Stephen's chest, with Stephen's arm around him. Stephen's face wore an agonized expression. Down his new trousers there flowed a vast yellow river. He sat helplessly trapped as the yellow tide streamed into his shoes. For the only time in my life, I screamed – I dropped the sandwiches and screamed.

Screaming sounds a pretty irrational reaction, but surprisingly it was the most sensible in the circumstances. My screams summoned much-needed help with amazing alacrity. A portly, green-clad nurse appeared from nowhere and took charge. One severely critical glance at me was enough to convince her, quite rightly, that I was hopelessly unequal to the situation. She commandeered the wheelchair and pushed it and its occupants, father and son, back through passport and customs, disregarding the officials in our path, to a nursery where she cleaned up the baby, leaving me the task of rubbing Stephen down. While we were in the nursery, the last call for our flight was announced over the tannoy. Unmoved, the nurse rang through to central control and told them that the flight would have to wait for us. Thus at the age of seven weeks, Robert acquired the distinction of having delayed the departure of an international flight.

Stephen had to sit in those trousers for the whole nine-hour length of that spectacular flight. He sat in them over Iceland, which was etched in the sea like a jewel in a satin case, over the ice floes of the North Atlantic, over Greenland's snow-capped mountains and glistening glaciers, over the frozen waters of Hudson Bay and the arid wastes of northern Canada. Then at last, signalling the end of Stephen's ordeal, Mount Rainier loomed on the horizon as we came in to land at Tacoma airport. A day or two later, I took the trousers to the dry-cleaner's, but Stephen refused to wear them ever again.

Part Two

1

Sleepless in Seattle

The provisions made for us in Seattle in 1967 by the Battelle Memorial Institute were very generous. As well as a spacious single-storey house, lavishly equipped with all mod cons – including a dishwasher and a tumbler-dryer – and an enormous car with automatic controls, they provided a twice-weekly deposit of clean nappies and the corresponding collection of the dirty ones by that singularly American institution, the diaper service. If such arrangements did not altogether fill me with confidence, it was not because I was unappreciative, but that I was overwhelmed by being washed-up on an alien shore, albeit in luxurious isolation, deprived so soon after giving birth of the support and help of my mother, family and friends at home. Here I was solely responsible both for my ailing husband and for my new baby, and there was no George Ellis to give Stephen a helping hand round the corner to work.

The Battelle Institute, the secretary assured me, was very close at hand, only two miles or so away – but two miles or twenty, it did not make much difference: Stephen had to be taken there by car, and to take Stephen by car, I also had to take Robert. This meant helping Stephen dress and eat in the early morning, and then feeding and bathing Robert – in that order or in reverse – depending on whose needs were the most pressing. Then the monstrous car – a Ford Mercury Comet – had to be backed round to the front of the house, and my two charges, tiny but voracious Robert in his carrycot, and then Stephen on my arm, taken one by one down the steps of the long path and settled, the one on the backseat and the other in the front. Methodically carried out, this routine could have been tolerable. As it was, although we tried our hardest to minimize the number of morning sessions that Stephen missed, the system was reduced to breaking point – our darling baby, who had just learnt to sleep through the night in England, was now, in Seattle with an eight-hour time change, sleeping soundly all day and wide-awake and full of sociable intentions all night. In addition Seattle was enjoying – or suffering – its most intense heatwave ever.

For some time, in a spirit of nervous self-preservation, I restricted my excursions only to the Battelle Institute and the corner stores – notably, of course, the dry-cleaner's. I drove the massive car with such trepidation that eventually, despite the heat, I decided to do what no American mother would have dreamt of doing: I walked down to the stores pushing my carrycot-pram and loaded the shopping into it beside the baby.

With the jubilation of a shipwrecked sailor sighting a rescue boat, I greeted the arrival of the Penrose family. Eric, the latest addition to the family, was somewhat more mobile than Robert, but frequently recumbent. When the two prams stood side by side, or the two babies were placed down together on a rug, Joan would remark that they were continuing the Hawking-Penrose dialogue. Thanks to Joan, my social scene brightened considerably. She introduced me to some of the other wives of the delegates and took me on various excursions to downtown Seattle, where I browsed in the department stores and bought baby clothes. Under her influence, my confidence grew as I began to find my way up and down the north-south axis of the freeway through the centre of Seattle, even managing to locate an old childhood playmate from Norwich, who had married a Boeing engineer.

Then one Sunday, even more adventurously, Stephen's map-reading guided us to a ferry port, and we crossed Puget Sound to the Olympic Peninsula, where I took Robert down to the water's edge and dipped his toes in the shimmering but icy waters of the Pacific Ocean. Another weekend, with Robert propped up between us asleep on the bench-seat in the front of the car, we drove the hundred and fifty miles north, across the border to Vancouver, to visit our Australian friends from Cambridge, the Youngs, who had come to rest in the University of British Columbia. Vancouver was as cold and misty as Seattle was hot and dry, and had the Canadian charm of being more relaxed than its American neighbour.

Back in Seattle, we assembled with the rest of the group one hot Saturday morning down on the Waterfront for one of the few excursions organized by the Battelle Institute – a ferry ride to the Indian reservation on Blake Island. While waiting for the ferry, Jeannette Wheeler, the wife of a leading American physicist, came up to introduce herself. That very year, in a flash of inspiration worthy of Archimedes, John Wheeler had lighted upon the name *black hole* for the phenomenon that Stephen and many others were studying, while he was having a bath. Down on the Seattle Waterfront, Jeannette – a regal, grey-haired lady who, by all accounts, was a member of that select group, the Daughters of the American Revolution – took charge of Robert's pram while Stephen leant on my arm. Two little old ladies peered lovingly into the pram, and one of them reached out to tickle the toes of the sleeping infant, uncovered in the heat of the day. Horrified, Jeannette Wheeler barked at her not to disturb the sleeping baby. The poor little lady jumped out of her skin and, with her companion, edged away nervously into the crowd. Personally, I thought a bit of tickling of Robert's toes to wake him up during the day might be a very good idea. Then I might get some sleep at night. As it was, he slept for most of that day, waking only to gaze angelically into the weather-beaten face of the elderly Indian squaw who rocked him on her knee while I ate dinner at the long communal table in a big old-fashioned barn.

At least on this particular excursion, my only responsibility, apart from attending to the baby's needs, was to push the pram with one hand and support Stephen with the other. The other interesting excursions where I had to drive long distances left me so tired and so strained that I was on my knees with exhaustion by the time Gillian, my school friend, came over to Seattle from Vancouver Island, where her husband Geoffrey, an engineer, had a two-year appointment. Gillian – and Geoffrey, who was able only to spend a weekend with us – were my salvation. Geoffrey took over the driving, taking us on long journeys – not least a day trip to Mount Rainier – collected shopping and helped Stephen in and out of the car, while Gill willingly gave a hand in the running of the kitchen. For one week, I could relax a little.

While Gill was still with us, an incident occurred which we both still remember with distaste. The token monument which Seattle retained from the World Fair of 1962 was the Space Needle, a concrete pylon some three hundred feet high, topped by a viewing platform in the shape of a flying saucer. On Gill's last Saturday with us, we went up the Space Needle in the express lift and admired the views – over the sparkling green waters of Puget Sound and the white crests of the Olympic Peninsula to the west, the rugged Cascade range of mountains to the east, and to the south Mount Rainier, the massive dormant volcano. The views were majestic, but with Gill carrying Robert and Stephen leaning on my arm we soon wilted in the sweltering sun and returned to the lift to join the queue for the descent. Near us there stood a couple of girls, teenagers perhaps, but not so very much younger than Gill and me. They watched us, nudging each other; then, as we were all standing together in the lift, they started making spiteful, rude remarks about Stephen's appearance, as he leant languidly against the wall, in temperatures that were enough to make anyone look bedraggled. As they laughed and giggled, my anguish grew. I wanted to slap their faces and make them apologize. I wanted to shout at them that this was my courageous, dearly loved husband and the father of the beautiful baby, and a great scientist, but in my English reticence I neither did nor said any of these things: I simply looked away, busying myself with Robert, trying to pretend that they were not there. Never did an express lift, travelling at four feet per second, take so long to reach the ground. As we emerged from the lift, one of the girls glanced over Gill's shoulder at Robert. "Is that your baby?" she asked me in perplexed admiration. "Of course!" I snapped. She and her companion hurried away, I hoped in shame. Gill remarked, "What strange people!" understating what she and I both felt. Fortunately Gill and I had stationed ourselves between Stephen and those girls, so he was unaware of what had happened.

After this episode I was ready to go home forthwith. Nonetheless, one evening towards the end of the summer school, at the Battelle cocktail hour, Stephen was offered the tantalizing possibility of a two-week stay at the University of California in Berkeley, and immediately a Brazilian participant in the Battelle summer school offered us the empty flat of an absent friend. The offer was attractive in financial terms and, since we had already come so far, another two weeks on the West Coast, in California of all places, did not seem a great hardship. I had not entirely lost the spirit of adventure which had taken me round southern Spain in my student days, and this would be our opportunity to discover for ourselves that Utopia with which Abe and Cice Taub had tempted us in Cornell in 1965.

Encumbered by masses of paraphernalia – the pram and inordinate amounts of luggage – we flew down to San Francisco, where I was required to master yet another enormous car and negotiate yet another maze of freeways. Fortunately Stephen was a better navigator than he had been a driver – except on those occasions when he would spot an exit at the last minute and yell at me to cross four lanes immediately. After swerving a few times and bumping over a few kerbs in good Keystone-Cop style, we at last found the address of our absent landlords, a homely two-room flat in an old wooden house with a distant view, through the haze and the mist, of the Golden Gate bridge. The accommodation, though much more in keeping with our style and age than the sumptuous middle-class, middle-aged house in Seattle, posed a fearsome logistical problem as it was on the top floor of the house, on the second storey. The routine which we had hoped to leave behind in Seattle had to come into play again, except that every outing now required not two but three trips up and down – not one but two flights of stairs. Robert, at fourteen weeks, was too heavy to be carried in the carrycot, so that had to be taken down to the car first, then Stephen – leaving Robert on a rug on the floor – then Robert himself. In compensation for all this inconvenience, we maximized the use of the car and often, of an evening or exceptionally of a late afternoon, we would drive up into the parched hills behind Berkeley, or sometimes, more adventurously, north along the San Andreas Fault – a deserted, marshy area where the cracks in the road testified to the tremendous natural forces lying beneath the surface. Once we drove down to a desolate cove on a coastline not unlike Cornwall, where, defying the American way of life, hippies lived free of the constraints of a materialistic society in shacks on the beach.

Abe Taub, the Head of the Relativity Group in Berkeley, secured a temporary appointment for Stephen in his department, and one evening he and Cice invited us to dinner in their house high up in the hills overlooking the bay. It was further away than we expected, and by the time we arrived the evening was already drawing in. Unable to see where to park, I drove into a gully by the side of the road. The wheels locked and the car was stuck. After trying unsuccessfully to heave the car out of the ditch on my own, I went to seek help from the Taubs and their distinguished guests, among them a highly sophisticated and influential Parisian mathematician, Professor Lichnerowicz. The men took off their smart jackets, rolled up their sleeves and set to the task with chivalrous gusto. When at last we were extricated from the ditch and shown into the house – embarrassingly late and very dishevelled – Robert started to whimper. He had played this trick on us once before in Seattle. Sleeping soundly until the very moment when his carrycot was put gently down in a darkened side-room, he would suddenly start to protest, as though sensing that there was a party elsewhere from which he was being excluded. The only remedy was to allow him to spend the evening on my knee at the table, alongside all the other guests. Cice Taub remained unflustered by so many disruptions to her genteel gathering and, perhaps taking pity on my haggard appearance, invited me to accompany her and Mme Lichnerowicz to the Berkeley Rose Garden the next day.

The Rose Garden became my haven of peace and solitude in the frenzied environment of the Bay area, and a respite from the strenuous routine demanded by our living arrangements. It had a calming effect on Robert, who would lie in his pram under the pergolas watching the patterns of light on the roses and the leaves above his head. I sat by him in the shade, breathing in the perfume of the roses, immersed in my book, Stendhal's *The Charterhouse of Parma*, and gazing out over the Bay from time to time. My thoughts were drawn to Spain – to the gardens of the Generalife above Granada where, only a few short years before, I had tried to imagine a future for myself with Stephen. That future had become a reality, and had exceeded our wildest hopes. I was tired but resilient, and my happiness far outweighed my tiredness. Stephen was already recognized and sought after in scientific circles for his intuitive grasp of complicated concepts, his ability to visualize mathematical structures in many dimensions and for his phenomenal powers of memory. The future stretched ahead of us, now physically embodied in the small, thriving person of our baby son.

If the future had acquired a reassuring aura of certainty, the key to it lay in managing the present. Living each day as it came, rather than projecting some fanciful mirage on to the distant future, was becoming a way of life. From that perspective, the general outline of the future was fairly clear-cut: in the short term our star was in the ascendant. In the long term, the huge question mark that hung over the whole human race might well obliterate us all. The Vietnam war had escalated – to use the coinage then current – into the ugliest of conflicts in which the horrors of modern chemical science were being cynically unleashed on a simple peasant population, propelled by the uncontrolled military industrial complexes of both East and West. A mere spark somewhere else on our troubled planet could ignite a global conflagration.

We lived for the present, but even that had an annoying way of tripping us up with unforeseen obstacles. For example, the Brazilian couple who had, with the best of intentions, found us the flat, offered to take us on a tour of the sights of San Francisco. For once, I looked forward to sitting back and enjoying a day out. They arrived early one Saturday morning, bringing with them a Brazilian friend who spoke no English. I helped Stephen down the stairs, expecting to install him in the Brazilians' car first before going back up for Robert, who would travel on my knee. As we excitedly emerged into the street, we looked around for their car. Apart from our own Plymouth, there was only a decrepit grey Volkswagen parked in front of the house. "Where's your car?" I asked our Brazilian host for the day. He looked at me in surprise. "No, no, we are no going in our car, it too small for all of us. We take your car." With sinking heart I unlocked our car. Stephen sat in the back with the Brazilian ladies and our "host" settled himself in the passenger seat in the front, directing me, the chauffeur, while holding Robert on his knee. One look at him was enough to make Robert bawl as he never had before. He bawled all day – across the Oakland Bridge, all through the hours of torrid, nose-to-tail traffic jams in which we sat roasting, all through Haight-Ashbury, up and down all the steep streets of central San Francisco. I would gladly have bawled my head off too. Desperately wanting to comfort my frantic, hot, uncomfortable baby, there I was, trapped in the driving seat in a senseless situation, not of our own making.

There was a lull when at last we reached Golden Gate Park. Distancing ourselves from our passengers, we joined a large hippy peace gathering and sat on the grass with the flower-power people, swaying to the beat of the music. Around the lawns were people of my own age, yet somehow I was already much older than them. Stephen and I shared their idealism and hatred of violence. We, too, had asserted a comparable freedom against a rigid society in our fight against bureaucracy and narrow-mindedness – yet, to maintain our difficult course, we were constrained to follow a routine as organized and as rigid as any imposed by the society against which they were rebelling. The Vietnam war, though we shared their antagonism to it, was not our main target. Our efforts were directed against illness and ignorance.

After that day, I decided that never again would I depend on other people. However, putting that resolution into practice was easier said than done, for Stephen had already accepted a pressing invitation to spend time in Charlie Misner's department at the University of Maryland. Washington DC was on the way home, we reasoned, so another few weeks would not make much difference. Indeed breaking the journey halfway would help us all, including Robert, to cope with the jet lag. We also looked forward to seeing Stephen's sister Mary, now a qualified doctor, who was working on the East Coast, and to visiting Stephen's old friend John McClenahan and his lively Spanish-speaking American wife and her family in Philadelphia.

On the flight east, we sat in the same row as a middle-aged lady who sobbed for the whole journey. Since she occasionally cast longing glances at Robert, I passed him to her to cuddle for a while. A pale smile flickered across her face as he beguiled her with his tinkling laughter. Her companion leant across the aisle to tell me that she was returning home from Vietnam, where her only son had been killed. The hippies were right to protest at being used as cannon fodder when many of them had neither the right to vote, nor even the right to buy themselves a drink, since the age of majority was still twenty-one. Many of them were lucky in that, as students, their military call-up would be deferred and then their college professors would try to help the most able of them avoid the draft, while others would escape abroad, to Canada perhaps. The son of the mother on the plane had not been so fortunate.

Our visit to the Misners in Maryland was evidently not best timed, because Susanne was engaged in a stressful daily battle with the school authorities who were rejecting Francis, their eldest son, on account of his mild autism. We saw Stephen's sister, Mary, and spent a weekend with the McClenahans, but I was exhausted and depressed, especially because I had had to resort to feeding Robert with baby formula. I sat on the bed in the basement guest apartment of the Misners' luxury home in Silver Spring tearful at the breaking of that first bond with my baby.

If the recourse to bottles had unhappy psychological repercussions for me, it had even worse physical consequences for the Misners. One evening, Charlie and Susanne, who was beginning to relax a little from her daily struggle, put on a splendid dinner party to introduce us to some of their friends. All the children were asleep and we sat round the table eating and drinking, talking and laughing. Later we sank drowsily into comfortable armchairs while Charlie put on a slide show of charming family photos. In my semi-somnolent state of idle contentment, I suddenly became conscious of a very nasty smell coming from the kitchen. The horrible truth was soon revealed when other people began to frown and cough, as they too detected the poisonous odour, and I realized that I was responsible for it. Before dinner I had put Robert's plastic bottles and their rubber teats on the stove to boil, and in the convivial atmosphere I had forgotten all about them. The contents of the saucepan had evaporated completely, filling the kitchen with an evil black smoke which was quickly penetrating every corner of the spotlessly clean house. Utterly mortified, I would not have been surprised if we had been turned out into the street, baby and all, there and then. To Charlie and Susanne's lasting credit, they did no such thing and the next day, summoning a prodigious degree of charity, they even managed somehow to make light of the shameful episode. They must have been heartily glad to see the back of us some days later when they cheerily waved us and our four-month-old baby goodbye. Their relief at seeing us go could not have been greater than mine at the prospect of going home.

2

Terra Firma

That trip to Seattle – and beyond – changed our lives, in some ways for better, in others for worse. The money Stephen had earned in lecture fees during those long months across the Atlantic had a healthy effect on our bank balance. On the strength of it we were able to go out and buy a badly needed automatic washing machine and, in good American style, a tumbler-dryer as well. This would have been an extraordinary supply of consumer goods for any British household in the Sixties, but Stephen decided – after one searing exposure to domestic reality – that our lifestyle demanded even more electrical aids. That domestic reality arose one Friday evening later that winter of 1967, when we gave a large dinner party for an eminent Russian scientist, Vitaly Ginzburg, who had come to Cambridge from Moscow on a three-month visit. Not only was the length of his visit exceptional in the repressive climate of the Cold War, but he had also been allowed to bring his glamorous blonde wife with him. The amount of crockery and cutlery piled in the kitchen afterwards indicated the success of the dinner party. Leaning himself against the kitchen wall, Stephen picked up a tea towel, but so disgusted was he by the waste of time occasioned by so much washing-up that the following day he enlisted George Ellis's help and went off into town to buy a dishwasher.

There were other less tangible effects of the American trip. It was well established that the phenomenon that Stephen was researching had an inspired, easily identifiable name, the *black hole*, which was much less cumbersome than *gravitational collapse of a massive star*, the process predicted in the mathematics of the singularity theorems, and it lent unity to scientific research. It was, too, a name which caught the imagination of the media. As a result of the Seattle summer school Stephen had firmly consolidated his international position as a pioneer in this research, and we had widely enlarged our circle of friends. Stephen calculated that, by the time we returned to England in

October, Robert had flown such a vast distance in relation to his age that, even in his sleep, he was in theory still moving. Luckily Robert himself did not appear to be disturbed by this particular consequence of his first visit to America. I too had travelled far, but unlike Robert I suffered long-lasting and tormenting results from these travels. They had sown the seeds of a paralysing fear of flying, which grew like a giant weed in my mind in the months and years after our return home. By comparison with my carefree attitude to flying as a student only two years previously, this fear was both frustrating and incomprehensible. It was not until some time later that the reason for the phobia emerged. When I reviewed the events of those four months in America, I realized that the problem lay not with flying – since we had flown in many different aeroplanes over vast distances without incident – but with the attendant circumstances, the stresses and strains of being wholly responsible, a mere seven weeks after giving birth, for two other fragile but very demanding lives. That onerous and exhausting responsibility slowly crystallized into a fear of flying for want of any other outlet. The simple fact of being able to rationalize the fear did not make dealing with it any easier, because I was ashamed to admit to such a weakness, especially when our lives were strictly governed by Stephen's laudably brave maxim – that if there was physical illness in the home, there was no room for psychological problems as well.

Despite Stephen's excitement at the marked success of his research and his determination to avail himself of every conference, seminar or lecturing opportunity across the globe, the question of further travels luckily did not arise that winter, a winter which we spent in a comfortably stationary state, readjusting to the familiar routine of academic life. Stephen's Research Fellowship had been renewed for a further two years, and now that Rob Donovan, his former best man, was also a Research Fellow of Gonville and Caius College, Stephen could regularly count on his help for going into College to dine once a week. My routine was rather less predictable and consisted of a constant struggle to reconcile the needs of the baby with the demands of my thesis. When I played with Robert, my conscience told me that I ought to be working on the thesis. When I worked on the thesis, my natural instincts encouraged me to want to play with the baby. It was not a very satisfactory state of affairs – nevertheless it was the only way I could maintain my intellectual self-esteem in an environment where babies were disdained and regarded only as necessary facts of life. Theses, on the other hand, were respected. In the late Sixties, the university offered no crèche facilities – though, true to its male chauvinist instincts, it had for many years boasted a rifle range.

The fact that I was able to persevere with my research at all was largely thanks to my mother and to the succession of nannies employed to care for Inigo Shaffer, the baby son of neighbours in the lane. My mother would often come over to Cambridge by train early on a Friday, arriving just as I was taking Stephen to work, and would look after Robert so that I could spend the best part of the day in the University Library collecting books and other material to study at home during the next week. Sometimes Inigo's nanny would take Robert over for an hour or so, or – as the boys grew older – invite him to play with Inigo for an afternoon, leaving me free to return to the Library. This system also allowed me occasionally to attend and give seminars in London, confident that Robert was being well looked after and that Stephen, helped by George Ellis, was able to have lunch with the rest of the Relativity Group in the newly opened University Centre.

Thus I was able to pursue my project, an investigation of the linguistic and thematic similarities and discrepancies of the three main periods and areas of popular love poetry in medieval Spain. While Stephen mentally roamed the universe, I travelled in time – back to the *kharjas*, the earliest flowering of popular poetry in the Romance languages. I began my research by documenting the Mozarabic vocabulary – an early dialect of Spanish from Muslim Spain – used in the *kharjas*, which consisted of little more than poetic fragments incorporated as refrains in longer Hebrew and classical Arabic odes and elegies. I intended then to extend the exercise to the Galician-Portuguese *Cantigas de Amigo* of the thirteenth century, and finally to the fifteenth-century Castilian popular lyrics or *villancicos*. These three areas of lyric flowering, disparate in time as well as in place, shared many common features: the love songs were all sung by a girl, either looking forward to meeting her lover at dawn or lamenting his absence or illness. Often the girl would confide her joy or her grief spontaneously to her mother or her sisters, yet in many instances the imagery of these seemingly fresh and unsophisticated lyrics was derived from the language of the Christian religious background.

There were many conflicting theories, not to say contentions, attendant upon the provenance and interpretation of the poetry, especially of the *kharjas*, and it was through this maze that I had to find my way as a novice research student in the University Library. My time was spent scanning the huge green-jacketed catalogue volumes, pursuing arcane articles in unfamiliar journals, seeking out cryptic references in footnotes and searching the stacks and the shelves for the numerous works of literary criticism on which I would write notes at home during the course of the following week. Just occasionally I actually came into contact with original medieval manuscripts, an unforgettable experience, but not one which advanced my research very efficiently, because the temptation to marvel over the beauties of the illustrated initials and the precision of the script was far too distracting.

Though the prospect of having to plough my way through reams of critical material was daunting, I relished those hours in the Library. I loved the curiously deferential effect that that shrine of erudition produced on its worshippers as, like shadows, they flitted through its vast silent halls. Each student, whether young or old, was wrapped in his own small capsule of scholarship, assured of the freedom of being able to read and write without interruption. An even greater compensation for the tedium which some aspects of the research entailed was to be found in the poetry itself, particularly in the *kharjas*. The *kharjas* had first been interpreted, edited and published by Samuel Stern, an Oxford Scholar who in 1948, in Cairo, had discovered their bare bones, written in apparently nonsensical Arabic or Hebrew script. He found that by transcribing the fragments into Roman script and then adding vowels, the enigmatic Arabic and Hebrew texts could be made to spring into being as tiny snatches of Romance love poetry, breathing a pulsating life. For example, Stern had transcribed one group of Hebrew letters into Roman consonants thus: *gryd bs 'y yrmnl's km kntnyr 'mw m'ly sn 'lhbyb nn bbr' yw 'dbl'ry dmnd'ry.* With the addition of vowels, the text reads as follows: *Garid vos ay yermanellas com contenir a meu male Sin al-habib non vivireyu advolarey demandare.* Apart from one archaic form, and one Arabic expression, *al-habib*, the poem is now perfectly intelligible, even to a modern Spanish speaker:

Tell me little sisters,
How to contain my grief.

I shall not live without my lover
I shall fly away to look for him.

In another *kharja*, in a clear reference to her Christian background, she cries forlornly:

Venid la pasca ayun sin ellu...
...meu corajon por ellu

Easter comes still without him...
...my heart for him

When the lover does return, he comes like the sun with the glory of the dawn, for in these poems the lovers meet at dawn – and will meet at dawn down the ages of Spanish popular lyric poetry, unlike the sophisticated Provençal tradition, where aristocratic lovers part at dawn:

non dormiray mamma
a rayo de mañana
Bon Abu 'l-Qasim
la faj de matrana

I shall not sleep, mother,
in the morning light
Good Abu 'l-Qasim
the face of the morning

But for me, the most poignant fragments were those heart-rending lyrics in which the girl weeps in despair at her lover's illness:

Vaisse meu corajon de mib
ya rabbi si se me tornerad
Tan mal me doled li 'l-habib
enfermo yed cuand sanarad

My heart leaves my body
will it ever return?
My grief for my lover is so great
He is ill – when will he recover?

In one *kharja*, the only decipherable word is *enfermad* – ill – and in another the girl herself falls ill with the cares of loving:

> *Tan t'amaray tan t'amaray*
> *habib tan t'amaray*
> *Enfermaron welyos cuidas*
> *ya dolen tan male*

> I shall love you always,
> I shall love you always, my love,
> My eyes are ill with weeping,
> they hurt so much!

3

Heavenly Spheres

Although in tactical terms it was sensible for me to be registered as a London student, in reality it meant that I was very isolated in Cambridge. London seminars and supervisions under the auspices of my supervisor, Alan Deyermond, were always stimulating, but my opportunities for going down to London were infrequent. In Cambridge, where I read in the Library and wrote at home, I had no forum for discussion. Thanks to Dr Dorothy Needham, I had become an affiliated student of Lucy Cavendish College, a newly founded Collegiate Society for mature women students, and, by dint of careful organization – which involved having Robert fed, bathed and tucked up in his cot, and Stephen's meal ready for him on the table – I managed to go out a couple of times a term to the Lucy Cavendish dining nights which took place in Churchill College.

A solution to my problem of academic isolation came in a most unexpected form – through Robert's growing friendship with our neighbours' child, Inigo Shaffer. One of the guests at Inigo's first birthday party was a vivacious, auburn-haired six-year-old girl, Cressida Dronke, who, peering out from behind a hideous pair of multicoloured reflecting sunglasses, regaled the company of very small boys and their astounded mothers and nannies with a long and fascinating account of a production of *Romeo and Juliet* to which her parents had just taken her. There was apparently nothing unusual in this early introduction to Shakespeare, for Cressida had been a hardened theatre-goer since babyhood.

I already knew of Peter Dronke, who lectured in Medieval Latin, from his awesome reputation as one of the most gifted intellects in Cambridge, not confining himself simply to medieval Latin but ranging over the whole gamut of medieval literary studies, including my own. The happy chance meeting with the Dronkes led to my acquiring an unofficial, surrogate supervisor in Cambridge. Peter was always ready to share his vast fund of knowledge and to pass on helpful suggestions, constructive criticisms and useful references, while his wife Ursula, herself a scholar of old Norse and Icelandic sagas, was a constant source of kindly encouragement. Another important consequence of meeting Peter and Ursula was that they invited me to join the coveted, informal seminars which they hosted in their own home on Thursday evenings during term time. Only Peter could truly be said to be the master of all those sometimes abstruse topics expounded in the seminars, for their range was eclectic, covering most of late classical and medieval European thought and literature. We, the students, sat respectfully on the mustard-coloured carpet, literally at the feet of some of the greatest scholars of the day.

I was surprised and amused to find how close those seminars brought me in philosophical terms to the study of cosmology, albeit medieval cosmology. Inevitably many discussions dwelt on the twelfth-century intellectual expansion which emanated from Paris, particularly from the cathedral school of Chartres, where it was believed that God, the universe and mankind could be examined and comprehended by means of numbers, weights and geometrical symbols, effectively turning theology into mathematics. The new universities of both Paris and Oxford were at the heart of a continued, intense intellectual debate, in which primarily the nature of God, creation and the origins of the universe exercised the minds of scholars and theologians. The vigorous renaissance which took place in the twelfth century owed much to the innovative ideas coming from Spain, where in the year 1085 the Christian forces had recaptured Toledo from the Moors, with the result that that mixed, multilingual city had become one of the richest cultural centres in Europe, renowned as a thriving school of translation on account of its heritage of Arabic literature and supposedly lost works of classical antiquity.

In the thirteenth century, Alfonso the Wise of Castile expanded the role of Toledo as a major centre for translation and scholarship by participating in its activities himself, pioneering the use of Spanish rather than Latin for all documents and attempting various historical projects in that language. The translations produced at his court were even more significant than Alfonso's other projects and included a book on chess, the scientific theories on the nature of light of Alhazen, the foremost Arab scientist of the eleventh century – thus laying down the foundations of perspective on which Leonardo da Vinci would build in northern Italy in the fifteenth century – and, most importantly, the *Almagest*, the great work of Ptolemy, the Alexandrian mathematician and astronomer of the second century AD.

Originally written in Greek, the *Almagest* existed only in an Arabic version until Alfonso commissioned its translation in Toledo. Ptolemy's cosmological model of the universe was based on the Aristotelian concept of a stationary earth, orbited by the sun, the moon, the planets and the stars. In the Ptolemaic, or geocentric model, the earth is fixed at the centre of the universe while the heavenly bodies, the sun, the moon and the planets each move around the earth along the paths of their own fixed spheres. A system of smaller circular motions or epicycles is introduced to account for recognized inequalities in the motions of the bodies. Beyond the sphere of Saturn is the sphere on which the fixed stars are carried across the sky, and beyond that is the primum mobile, the mysterious divine force behind the cyclical movement of the spheres. This perfect, circular movement which propelled the planets on their course created a celestial music, the harmony of the spheres. The Ptolemaic model did not actually coincide with the scriptural view of the universe as being made up of the heavens, a flat earth and hell beneath, but since it could be made to match up with it without drastically upsetting previously held views of God's place in the heavens and of hell in the depths of the earth, it became a tenet of religious dogma in Christendom until it was questioned by the Polish astronomer Copernicus in the sixteenth century. For the Christian church the most important implication of this geocentric model was that Man, the inhabitant of the earth, was at the centre of the universe and that divine attention was focused solely on him and his behaviour.

Stephen came to one of these seminars about early cosmological models in the Dronkes' living room with a colleague from the Department, Nigel Weiss, whose wife, Judy, was a member of the seminar. The two scientists were forced to concede that the thinking of the twelfth-century philosophers, Thierry of Chartres, Alan of Lille and, in the thirteenth century, Robert Grosseteste and Roger Bacon among many others, was extraordinarily far-sighted, accurate and perceptive. Included in the ranks of the philosophers was a woman, the strong-minded

German abbess Hildegard of Bingen, who devised her own version of cosmology in which the universe took the shape of an egg. Hildegard of Bingen was far in advance of her times. Not only was she an early cosmonaut, she also proposed that women must make good the social and religious failings caused by the weaknesses of men and, to that end, should follow her example by undertaking missionary journeys along the Rhine, preaching, condemning heretics and righting social wrongs.

Several ironies struck me in the course of these seminars, particularly during the one that Stephen and Nigel Weiss attended. The most glaring one, of course, was that in the second half of the twentieth century the position of women in society, especially in science, had progressed at a snail's pace since the twelfth, despite Hildegard's brisk and frequent affirmations of the strength and glory of women. As far as the cosmologies were concerned, I was amused by the reflection that though advances in science may be revolutionary in the twentieth century, certain conceptual links with older theories die hard. The Ptolemaic system, which had gained ready acceptance in the thirteenth century but had later been supplanted by the Copernican solar system, still had a point of contact, however implausible, with an important cosmological principle of the twentieth century: the anthropic principle.

This was one of those subjects on which, during that period at the end of the Sixties and the early Seventies, Stephen spent long hours in concentrated argument with Brandon Carter, usually on Saturday afternoons when we drove out of Cambridge to the pastoral bliss of the country cottage which Brandon and his Belgian wife, Lucette, had been renovating since their recent marriage. Lucette and I would take Robert for long walks across the fields, conversing in French about our favourite authors, painters and composers, prepare tea and supper – and still Brandon and Stephen would be engaged in an intellectual contest over the fine detail of the principle, with neither prepared to concede.

The anthropic principle, as far as I understood it from Stephen's explanations in those rare moments when we discussed his work together, left me wondering at its close philosophical affinity to the medieval universe. As in the medieval, Ptolemaic universe, Man is once again placed at the centre of creation by the anthropic principle, or more precisely by what is known as its "strong" version. The proponents of the "strong" anthropic principle claim that the universe in which we exist is the only possible kind of universe in which we could exist, because from the time of the Big Bang some fifteen thousand million years ago, it has expanded according to the precise conditions, often involving chance chemical coincidences and very fine physical tuning, which are required for the development of intelligent life. Intelligent life is then able to ask why the universe is as it is observed to be, but this is a tautological question, the answer to which is: if our universe were any different, intelligent life would not exist to pose the question. In a real sense therefore, mankind could still be said to occupy a special place at the centre of the universe, just as he had in the Ptolemaic system. Whereas for medieval man, this special position was a strong statement of the unique relationship between human beings and their Creator, modern scientists appeared to be irritated or merely amused by any such inferences being drawn from the anthropic principle.

Although the modern universe is most certainly not bounded by the medieval concepts of heaven or hell, it is in many respects a more hostile environment than its neatly organized medieval counterpart, if only on account of its extremes of temperature and its vast expanses of space and time in which the human race appears to live in solitary isolation. In 1968 for a fleeting moment it seemed as if we might not be alone in the dark immensity of space after all. One afternoon in February of that year, when I called in at the Department, the tea room was buzzing with excitement. A research student in radio astronomy, Jocelyn Bell, and her supervisor Antony Hewish, had picked up regular, pulsating radio signals from outer space through the row of radio telescopes positioned on the disused Cambridge to Oxford railway line at Lord's Bridge, some three miles out of Cambridge. Could these signals be our first contact with extra-terrestrial life – little green men perhaps? Jokingly they named the first sources of these radio waves LGMs. The excitement died down when the sources of the radio pulses were identified as neutron stars, tiny remnants of stars, possibly only twenty miles across, with massive densities of hundreds of millions of tons per cubic inch. There was no chance that neutron stars could be supporting life.

While twentieth-century cosmologists might still retain some tenuous conceptual common ground with the Ptolemaic system through the anthropic principle, and might respect the intellects of the earlier twelfth-century philosophers of Chartres, Oxford and even Bingen on the Rhine, the Dronkes' medieval seminars served to bring into clear perspective the vastly divergent modern approach to the subject of creation. The main intent of the twelfth-century philosophers was directed towards reconciling the existence of God with the rigours of the laws of science, thus unifying the image of the Creator with the scientific complexity of his creation. To this end, Alan of Lille attempted to reconstruct theology as a mathematical science, and another student of Chartres, Nicholas of Amiens, tried to make it conform to Euclidean geometry, using geometrical symbols to explain the Trinity. However eccentric these notions may appear nowadays, they were undoubtedly genuine attempts to introduce a scientific objectivity to the teachings of theology and to explore and explain divine mystery through numbers and mathematical structures.

Conversely, their intellectual heirs, some eight hundred years later, seemed intent on distancing science as far as possible from religion and on excluding God from any role in Creation. The suggestion of the presence of a Creator-God was an awkward obstacle for an atheistic scientist whose aim was to reduce the origins of the universe to a unified package of scientific laws, expressed in equations and symbols. To the uninitiated, these equations and symbols were far more difficult to comprehend than the notion of God as the prime mover, the motivating force behind creation. Strangely, to the happy band of the initiated, the equations were said to reveal a miraculous, breathtaking mathematical beauty. This revelation, reflecting the hidden wonders of the universe, was almost a modern version of Plato's heavenly world of Forms. In the fifth century BC, Plato, Aristotle's teacher and a major influence on medieval thought, described a theory of Forms, or perfect heavenly Ideas, unrelated to the senses, discernible only to the mind. Each perfect Form or Idea had its counterpart in the tangible, corruptible, imperfect forms manifest on earth. The reverence with which modern scientists treated the mathematics of the universe suggested similar intimations of sublime perfection, but unfortunately these intimations of perfection were not easily accessible to those who were not fluent with mathematical jargon and for whom equations were impenetrable. Another difficulty, which apparently was a direct result of their obsession with mathematics, was the irrelevance for these scientists of the concept of a personal God. If through their calculations they were diminishing any possible scope for a Creator, it was logical that they could not envisage any other place or role for God in the physical universe.

In the face of dogmatic rational arguments, there was no point in raising questions of spirituality and religious faith, questions of the soul and of a God who was prepared to suffer for the sake of humanity – questions which ran completely counter to the selfish reality of genetic theory. Issues of morality, conscience, the appreciation of the arts, were best kept out of the arena lest they too became victims of the positivist approach. Still reacting against the organized religion of my childhood, I did not attend either of the two churches at the end of the lane regularly, but I sought sanctity in the garden of Little St Mary's, where Thelma Thatcher assigned a small patch of ground by the railings opposite our house for me to tend. There, under the rambling roses, I could weed, rake, hoe and plant bulbs for the spring and roses for the summer while pondering mysteries, theories and realities. Robert and Inigo played running along the winding paths and clambering over the mossy tombs while I worked. The ancient, sacred garden sprang to life with the music of their bright young voices, and our strip of ground blossomed with the pink-and-white striped rose that Stephen had given me for my birthday. It was the famous *Rosa gallica*, named Rosamundi after Henry II's mistress, Fair Rosamund.

4

Dangerous Dynamics

Since the churchyard garden was enclosed, Robert and Inigo could play there safe from harm, letting off their inordinate amounts of energy. From early infancy it was quite apparent that Robert was blessed with at least twice the normal fund of energy of a small boy. Quite apart from overturning all my notions regarding the sleep patterns of a newborn infant, he discovered, at about eight weeks, that his feet and legs were meant for standing on. Thereafter, he would not sit down, insisting on being held upright on my knee. Even when in Seattle we had been invited to take advantage of a free photographic session by courtesy of the diaper service, Robert resisted all attempts to make him lie gurgling on a rug or peep out coyly from under a blanket draped over his head, and reduced the photographer to a state of apoplexy when grudgingly he had to allow my arms to appear in the shot, in discreet support of the twelve-week-old baby who was firmly planted on his two small feet.

By the age of seven months, this inventive child had found out how to dismantle his cot so that all the joins, catches and hinges had to be tightly tied together with string to stop him falling out. Nevertheless, no sooner had Stephen and I turned our backs each evening and crept away downstairs, yawning and fondly trusting that repetitive readings of *Thomas the Tank Engine* had at last softly lulled our audience into the realms of sleep, than we would hear the tiny feet coming busily down the stairs to join us for our supper and whatever concert we might be listening to on the radio. Since he could no longer dismantle his cot, Robert learnt to vault over the bar and then drop onto the floor beneath. At about eleven o'clock we would all fall into bed together.

Even before he had perfected that degree of agility, Robert's dynamism had given us a quite a scare. In the spring of 1968, my parents took us to Cornwall once again with my brother Chris. Happily Robert was prepared to sit quite contentedly in the car, strapped in his seat, no matter how long the journey – but when at last in the early evening we adults sank drowsily into the comfortable armchairs in our rented cottage, Robert, already able at ten months old to walk nimbly round the furniture, set off on a tour of the ground floor. A sudden high-pitched scream from behind my back roused us precipitately. To steady himself, Robert had placed one small hand, his right, against an electric storage heater, which, unbeknown to us, was turned to its maximum setting, and the heat had seared off the skin of his palm. Thanks to my brother's medical training, Robert was pacified with a fraction of an aspirin – the only painkiller available – the hand gently treated and bandaged in a clean handkerchief, and we all, though shocked, managed to get a good night's sleep. Robert, Chris and I spent the best part of the next day searching out a doctor, because overnight the infant hand had swollen into one huge blister. The doctor, impressed at the quality of the first aid administered by a mere dental student, simply provided a pediatric painkilling prescription and more substantial dressings and thereafter commissioned Chris to continue to care for his small patient.

In the summer of that same year, the year of Robert's first birthday, How Ghee and Peck Ang with their small daughters left the house at number 11 to return home to Singapore. In true Little St Mary's Lane style, the Thatchers gave an informal farewell party for them, to which we and Inigo and his parents were invited, together with half a dozen or so other guests. Inigo and Robert were by this stage completely at home in the Thatcher household. They adored Thelma, and she reciprocated with a grandmotherly affection. They would call on her every morning, peering through her letter box, calling "Tatch, Tatch!" in the hope of being invited in to play with the collection of bright marbles on her solitaire table. They were frequent teatime visitors, sitting at her elegant Regency table on her elegant Regency chairs – though as a precautionary measure she did apologetically cover the yellow-striped damask seats with plastic sheeting. At the Angs' party no one took much notice of the small boys who were happily amusing themselves, until Thelma called for a toast to the Angs – How Ghee, Peck, Susan and demure little Ming – and their future happiness. We all turned to pick up our glasses of champagne from the occasional tables only to find that they were all drained dry. From upstairs, there came the sound of running water, of much flushing and splashing and peals of laughter. Two rather tipsy one-year-olds were having their own, much more entertaining party well out of sight in the Thatchers' bathroom.

Later that summer Stephen and I took Robert on his first bucket-and-spade holiday to the north Norfolk coast, where I encountered the unforeseen dilemma of needing to be in two places at once. As Stephen's speed of movement slowed down, so Robert's accelerated. Stephen found it difficult to walk across the soft, yielding sand, and so did I, as I supported him on one arm and carried bags, bucket and spade, towels and a folding chair on the other. Robert, in the meantime, would be racing away, heading for the open sea. Luckily, on that coast, the tide goes out as far as the eye can see, and that week was a week of low tides by day, so we managed to avoid undue mishap.

On the final morning I went upstairs to pack our bags, leaving Stephen and Robert downstairs in the main room at the front of the house. At the back, a sun room with an open mezzanine half-loft approached by a rickety ladder had been added to the cottage. For obvious reasons we did not use this room and kept the door to it firmly closed. After half an hour of packing I came downstairs to find Stephen sitting alone in the front room. "Where's Robert?" I asked in bewilderment. Stephen gestured towards the back room. "He opened that door," he said, "went through it and closed it behind him. There was nothing I could do, and you didn't hear when I tried to call you."

Momentarily I glanced at the door in horror, then burst into the room. There was no sign of Robert. My eyes travelled upwards, and there, to my astonishment, was my little son in his blue T-shirt and checked trousers, sitting at the top of the ladder on the open mezzanine floor, cross-legged like an infant Buddha, blissfully unconcerned by the drop beneath. I raced up the ladder and grabbed him before he had time to move.

If on that first visit to the coast, Robert did not succeed in hurling himself into the sea, it was only because his legs were too short for him to get to the water's edge before I caught up with him. After depositing his father on the folding chair on the firmer sand midway between the dunes and the shore, I would sprint over the beach at speeds which could well have won me an Olympic medal. Over the course of the next two or three years, Robert regularly threw himself headlong into any available stretch of water, be it sea, pond or swimming pool, as soon as my eye was distracted for a second. On a later visit to Norfolk with the Ellises and their little daughter – dark-haired, blue-eyed Maggie – Sue plunged into the sea like lightning to rescue Robert, who had run straight into the water and disappeared. When we visited the Cleghorns – the parents of Stephen's school friend Bill – out in the country, Robert made a beeline for their pond and fell in, amongst the weed, the mud and the frogs. And in the summer of 1969, when we spent the month of July at the University of Warwick at a summer school appropriately enough on Catastrophe Theory, Robert excelled himself by jumping into the deep end of the nearby swimming pool at every opportunity. Happily on those occasions, as his father was in lectures and not dependent on my supporting arm, Robert had the full benefit of my undivided attention.

That summer school coincided with that "great leap for mankind", the Moonwalk, which we watched on television in the student Common Room. Giant leaps, small steps and all-too-real catastrophes narrowly averted, these sonorous terms seemed to sum up the essence of our day-to-day lives. Giant leaps were needed to keep up with Robert's mercurial movements, while Stephen's steps were becoming smaller, slower and more unsteady. Each morning I would drive Stephen from the student hostel where we were lodging to the lecture hall on the other side of the new campus. At Stephen's pace, the lecture hall was some five minutes' walk away from the car park, across courtyards and through a maze of passages. Robert, just two years old, would shoot out of the car as soon as it came to a standstill, and hare away ahead of his father and me. The only consolation was that he had an unerring sense of direction which led him through the tortuous route to the lecture hall, where he would install himself in the front row. It became a standing joke among the other delegates that Robert's appearance in the early morning always heralded Stephen's arrival five minutes later. The lecturer would then adjust the order of his lecture notes, deferring any important results until Stephen arrived.

At home, we had to barricade the house to prevent Robert from escaping and throwing himself in the river. On our afternoon walks I was hard-pressed to find a means of expending all his energy without exhausting myself, especially as he would never turn round to go back home until he was on the point of collapse, and then he had to be carried or taken in the pushchair.

Generally I left the pushchair at home, because on our outward journeys, when speed of reflex was all-important, it tended to interfere with the swiftness of my reactions. "Put reins on him," my parents urged sensibly, worried by my haggard appearance. "You don't understand, he won't walk with reins on," I insisted, to their disbelief. "Nonsense," they said, thinking that this was just another example of my crackpot theories about personal freedoms. "All right, you try," I replied defiantly, handing them back the set of pale-blue, leather reins they had just given me. They picked up their cherubic, blond, blue-eyed grandson, and carried him and the reins down to the broad path along the river bank, away from the traffic. In no time at all, they were back at the house asking for the pushchair. "You were right," my mother sighed, "when we put the reins on him, he sat down and refused to move. When Dad tried tugging on the reins, he kept his legs firmly crossed and when Dad lifted the reins, he just left the ground, and there he was, dangling in mid-air on the end of the strap!"

Never in all the long years of my education and, unsurprisingly, nowhere in all those reams of medieval literature, had I encountered one jot of advice on bringing up children. Apparently through the ages, children had just happened, and it had never been thought necessary to teach their parents how to look after them. If this was an example of the workings of the geneticists' selfish gene, the selfish gene was intent on self-destruction. From six o'clock in the morning till eleven at night, Robert was full of golden smiles – cheerful, loving and utterly adorable – but his boundless energy brought me to my knees. I thumbed through my only guide, the already well-worn pages of Dr Spock's *Baby and Child Care*, searching for help and reassurance. Comfortingly, Dr Spock seemed to recognize the problem, but his solution – putting a netting over the cot – was not one that I could bring myself to adopt for fear that Robert might strangle himself. Then I turned to my doctor, Dr Wilson, who sympathetically recommended a glass of sherry – for me – in the evening "at about six o'clock, when Robert has gone to bed", and also prescribed a tonic.

Early one morning in the September of 1969, I was aroused from my slumbers not by a sound or by a light but by a smell – a sweet sticky smell which subconsciously I knew to be wrong. I opened my eyes to find Robert standing by my side of the bed with a broad grin all over his face and a viscous, pinkish liquid dribbling down the front of his blue sleeping suit. I jumped out of bed and stumbled down the stairs to the kitchen. A chair stood by the fridge and the floor was littered with empty bottles, all of them medicine bottles. One of the bottles had contained the sweet, syrupy antihistamine which the doctor had prescribed for Robert for a recent cold and earache, and which had a conveniently soporific effect; another had contained the stimulant which I had been taking to pep me up. At two years of age, Robert had pushed a chair into the kitchen, climbed up onto the fridge and reached up to the shelf where, for want of a medicine cupboard, the bottles were stored. He had swigged the lot.

Leaving Stephen to fend for himself as best he could, I dressed in haste and ran with Robert in his pushchair to the doctor's surgery. The surgery, only a couple of hundred yards away, was just opening, and we were given priority. As Robert was already starting to show signs of drowsiness, Dr Wilson sent us immediately to hospital, half a mile away in the other direction, by taxi. There the nightmare really began, as the seriousness of the situation became evident. Robert, his arms and legs jerking and flailing out in all directions, was taken from me and held down while his stomach was pumped out. At first, the nurses were terse, only asking what medicines he had taken, then, when they had tried all the interventionary methods at their disposal to rid the child's system of the poisonous cocktail, one of them turned to me and said: "He is extremely ill, you realize – there is nothing more we can do, we shall just have to wait and see what happens."

Only once before had Robert's health given cause for anxiety. The previous winter we had gone with the Ellises to Majorca for a week's holiday over the New Year. We had barely arrived when Robert fell seriously ill with a virulent strain of Spanish tummy which confined us to the hotel room for the whole duration of the stay. Unable to digest even plain water he wasted away before our eyes like the innocent child victims of the Biafran war in Nigeria, while the local doctor debated whether to take him into hospital or send us back home in advance of the rest of the party. As soon as the plane touched down at Gatwick, Robert began to make a miraculous recovery. By the time we reached my parents' house in St Albans, he was ready to play his favourite game of emptying all the tins from the cupboard and rolling them across the kitchen floor. That episode had been harrowing but this was far worse; the worst agony imaginable, the agony of watching one's child die.

They tied Robert down in a cot in a partitioned room on the children's ward and beckoned me to a chair in a corner. He tossed violently under the restraints placed across the cot to prevent him hurting himself. Mechanically I sat down, too numbed to speak or think or weep. Life drained away from my own body as our beautiful, darling child, our most precious possession, sank into a deep coma. This child had astounded everyone with his beauty, his happy nature and his liveliness. He was the living personification of all that was good and positive in our world and our relationship. I, and Stephen too, loved him more than anything else. We had created him out of love, I had given birth to him and we had nurtured him with passionate love and care. Now we seemed to be losing him through a combination of circumstances – my tiredness, his energy and the inadequacy of the precautions that we had taken for his safety. If he died, I should die too. My brain was capable of formulating only a single thought expressed in half a dozen words. They revolved round and round in my head, stuck in a single groove, to the exclusion of all else: "Please God, don't let him die. Please God, don't let him die. Please God…"

Every so often a nurse would come in to check Robert's breathing and his pulse. Pursing her lips, she would tiptoe away again while I, blankly staring into cold, empty space, stayed in my corner clinging to my formula, repeating it over and over again. Some hours later, the Ward Sister came in. She went through the customary procedures and then, instead of tiptoeing away, pronounced that Robert was in a relatively stable though still critical condition. His state was not hopeful, all that could be said was that it was not deteriorating further. Coming to my senses at this slightest of changes, I was shocked to remember that I had left Stephen alone in the house, scarcely able to look after himself. Where was I most needed – here in the hospital with my comatose infant son, or at home with my disabled husband who, without my help, might fall or hurt himself or choke? I must have mumbled a few intelligible words to the sister because she sent me out to check up on Stephen. I ran down the road through the fine grey drizzle to look for him.

Thankfully George had come in to help him get up and had taken him to work. By this stage he was having lunch in the University Centre, desperate for news but not knowing where to find us. I sat with him for a short while. There was nothing we could say to comfort each other, because there was no comfort to be had in our situation, except that we both shared the same sense of utter, bleak devastation, enveloped in an unremitting pall of greyness. I watched as Stephen ate his lunch. I could not even bring myself to drink a glass of water. It seemed pointless to try. There was no reason to stay alive. How could I live with such grief? We were crossing the threshold into that dark chasm where all hope is abandoned.

Scarcely daring to return to the hospital, I left Stephen in George's care. I entered the ward fearful of what I might find. All was silent. A young nurse followed me as I tiptoed into Robert's room. He was there in the cot, still alive. He was asleep, lying quietly on his back, as beatific as a Bellini cherub. To my surprise the nurse's face lit up with a smile as she pointed to the sleeping child. "Look, he's breathing normally now. He's sleeping it off, and soon he'll come out of the coma, he's past the worse," she said. Only tears, not words, could describe my feelings, tears of gratitude and relief. "You'll be able to take him home when he wakes up," the nurse continued – in a matter of fact fashion, as if this was just one more crisis in her busy routine, now thankfully resolved. I rang Stephen to tell him the good news, and at half-past three Robert began to wake up. "You can take him home now," they said. Within ten minutes he was discharged and we stepped out into the vivid reality of our everyday lives. Once back home, we sent word to our neighbours to come and join us for a celebration. They all came and we watched silently as if in a trance while Robert and Inigo pushed their toy cars round the floor, unconcerned and totally unaware of the day's drama.

That day Robert survived, but a little bit of me died. Some, though not all, of that extravagant youthful optimism which had fired me with so much enthusiasm now lay buried beneath a heavy burden of anxiety, that dull care in its ravelled sleave, which once it infects the mind is never banished. I had come so dangerously close to the worst catastrophe that a mother can bear – the loss of her child – that I became neurotically protective, often perhaps irritating Robert and his siblings by my concern for their safety.

Luckily the experience seemed to have left Robert unscathed. Nor did it reduce in any way his fund of energy, as our visit to a conference in Switzerland the following spring aptly demonstrated. While Stephen spent his days plunged into the murky past of the universe in the conference centre at Gwatt on the shores of Lake Thun, Robert and I went walking. This was where Robert discovered his passion for the mountains, the true outlet for his climbing instincts. When, later that week, we and the Ellises spent a few days in the family hotel at Hohfluh, high above the Aare valley where I used to stay with my parents, Robert was in his element. More than once, at less than three years old, he insisted on scrambling up as far as the snowline while I, several months pregnant again, plodded along behind.

5

Universal Expansion

A less dramatic crisis than Robert's calamitous encounter with the medicines loomed over us as the 1960s drew to a close: Stephen's Research Fellowship – which had already been renewed for a further term of two years in 1967 – was in 1969 about to expire. There was no mechanism for renewing it yet again, but because Stephen was unable to lecture, he could not follow the normal course of most other Research Fellows and apply for a university teaching post. Nor was there any point in expecting a full Fellowship, since College Fellowships, as opposed to Research Fellowships, are not salaried appointments but simply offer membership of an exclusive dining club, albeit a highly intellectual one, founded – it goes without saying – on the most estimable educational principles.

In 1968 Stephen had become a member of the newly opened Institute of Astronomy, a long single-storeyed building, luxuriously fitted out and set among trees in green fields in the grounds of the Observatory, on the Madingley Road outside Cambridge. This accorded him an office, which he shared with Brandon, and a desk – but it did not provide him with a salary, and it was unlikely to do so for as long as Fred Hoyle remained its director, since he had never forgiven Stephen for his notorious intervention at the Royal Society lecture some years before. Unlike in America, paid research posts in Britain were few and far between.

Such was the excitement generated by black-hole research over the past four years, however, that Stephen did not lack powerful advocates: Dennis Sciama willingly took up the challenge, as did Hermann Bondi, whose help my father enlisted on our behalf. It was rumoured that King's College had a salaried Senior Research Fellowship, which the governing body were prepared to offer Stephen. The authorities of Gonville and Caius bridled at these rumours and stepped in with a special category of Fellowship, a six-year Fellowship for Distinction in Science, before King's had a chance to make their offer.

With a secure job and a steady income, it was time for us to review our living arrangements. Although we drove out to the villages at weekends prospecting for suitable properties, we constantly came up against the intractable problem of transport: if we bought a new house in a village, even the closest village, I should have to drive Stephen to work every morning and collect him every evening, and such pressure could become irksome, especially with two small children in tow. It was impossible to better our situation in Little St Mary's Lane. With help, Stephen could still walk to work in the Department in the mornings, though occasionally he would get a lift out to the Institute in the afternoons for seminars and discussions with Brandon. For Robert there was a delightfully old-fashioned playgroup close at hand in the Quaker Meeting House, just across the fen, and the University Library – as and when I managed to find the time and the energy to work there – was within five minutes' cycling distance. We were within a stone's throw of the centre of the city, and the churchyard not only catered perfectly for Robert's outdoor needs but also fulfilled my gardening aspirations. The only drawback was that the house was so small and decrepit, despite my attempts to redecorate it.

Our enterprising friends, George and Sue Ellis, had bought and renovated a house at Cottenham, a fen village outside Cambridge, and Brandon and Lucette had done the same to their dream cottage out in the heart of the country soon after their marriage in 1969. Even in Little St Mary's Lane, various neighbours had cleverly enlarged and renovated their previously ramshackle dwellings, making sizeable, attractive townhouses of them, and at number 5 the author and biographer of Rose Macaulay, Constance Babington-Smith, had imaginatively adapted the limited space in her narrow house to meet her bookish requirements. Having seen, with a tinge of envy, how versatile the houses could be, we realized that ours was no exception. However, we were caught in the proverbial catch-22 situation. We had saved enough money for a deposit on a mortgage for a new property, and council grants were available for the renovation of old properties, but because of its age our house did not qualify for a mortgage and, of course, the College on the advice of its land agent had dismissed the property as a bad investment.

As we were mulling over this dilemma, a change of policy on the part of our building society removed the problem altogether, and mortgages – at a higher rate of interest – became available on older properties. An agreed mortgage from a building society had the added advantage that it would qualify us for an extra loan – at a low rate of interest – from the university. Quite suddenly, everything started to fall into place, though Stephen was sceptical. It seemed to me, as I pored with pencil and ruler over scraps of paper, that some of the ideas used by our neighbours along the lane could well be incorporated into our house to enlarge and renovate it. On the ground floor there could be an elegant through-room from front to back by making two rooms into one, with a new kitchen out at one side of the yard, while the first and second floors could be remodelled to provide a new bathroom, bedrooms and a roof garden. A retired surveyor, the aptly named Mr Thrift, who proved to be a true and also genial master of his profession, drew up detailed plans which enlarged the house seemingly beyond the bounds of probability, exploiting every inch of space.

He and I investigated grants – both improvement grants and grants for the disabled – and as soon as we had our draft plans ready laid, we were able to apply to a building society for a mortgage. Unlike the odious college land agent, the building society surveyor cheerfully inspected the house and, glancing at the proposed plans, nodded. "It'll be quite charming, won't it?" he said, indicating that he would readily approve the property for a mortgage. We were now able to approach our landlady again with a more realistic offer for the house, and this time she accepted. It really seemed that all things were possible. But we had scant opportunity to enjoy being householders: shortly after we had signed the completion, all the furniture had to be stored away in the front bedrooms, and we ourselves had to move out to allow the builders to invade our property. Further loans, including a generous one from Stephen's parents, and improvement grants were enabling us to embark on a major rebuilding programme.

George and Sue Ellis, with Maggie and one-year-old Andy, had gone to spend six months in Chicago, the home of the highly respected Indian theoretical physicist and Nobel Prize winner, Professor Subrahmanyan Chandrasekhar and his wife, Lola. Chandrasekhar, though a Fellow of Trinity College, had been forced to seek a post in America after being humiliated by his close friend Arthur Eddington at the Royal Astronomical Society in 1933. Chandrasekhar had anticipated black-hole research by predicting the ultimate collapse of massive stars under their own weight, only to have his theory scathingly ridiculed by Eddington and the astronomy establishment. In Chicago, the Chandrasekhars lived in the sort of style which only a childless couple can maintain. Everything in their quietly secluded flat was as white as snow: a thick-piled white carpet, a white sofa and chairs, white curtains – all in all, a white nightmare for a visiting mother, like Sue, with very small children whose fingers were permanently smeared in sticky chocolate.

Meanwhile, we gratefully took over the Ellises' eminently practical, child-oriented, converted country cottage in Cottenham for the duration of the renovations to 6 Little St Mary's Lane. It was only through living in the country that I fully understood the convenience of living in town. The house was delightful but the isolation was distressing, particularly because I felt sick all day throughout the pregnancy. Stephen had to be driven into Cambridge to the department each morning and collected in the evening, except on those occasions when he was ready in time to catch a lift with other Cottenham commuter neighbours. Robert was unsettled, missing both Inigo and his playgroup, while I sorely missed my friends in the lane, especially the Thatchers, and all attempts to work on my thesis were quite futile. My depression was not eased by the constant pounding of the news reports from the Middle East, which suggested that another confrontation between the Egyptians and the Israelis – and consequently between the superpowers – was imminent. Not only were the two countries regularly raiding each other's territory, but also a new aspect of war had reared its ugly head in the hijacking of civilian airliners. I became tense and irritable, and, I am ashamed to say, short-tempered with my nearest and dearest: with Stephen, with Robert and, to my lasting regret, with my dearly loved, but very slow-moving grandmother, who came from Norwich to stay with us for one very hot, enervating week.

At last, against all expectation, the house, which for months had looked like a bomb site, while what was left of it was held up by a solitary metal pole, was in a sufficiently habitable state for us to return to it in mid-October. It was not yet finished and each day brought a succession of different craftsmen, plumbers, plasterers, painters, electricians, all uncomfortably aware of the protruding deadline – or rather lifeline – to which they had to conform. Once back at home, Stephen and Robert could resume their normal routines and I could get on with scrubbing floors, rearranging furniture, hanging curtains and preparing the new back bedroom for the baby. This bedroom and a minuscule new bathroom alongside it occupied the space of the old sloping bathroom on the first floor. They overlooked a roof garden above the kitchen, which had been built out as planned into the yard at the side of the house. The area of the old kitchen was now the dining area of the through-room which extended from front to back, supported in the middle by a solid girder, mysteriously referred to as an RSJ. In the rear wall, constructed of mottled pink, black and yellow old Cambridge bricks, Mr Thrift had reinstated the John Clark's eighteenth-century plaque.

At the top of the house on the third floor behind Robert's attic, there was a new room which on the plans had to be labelled a storeroom, because the ceiling was a few inches below the statutory height for a habitable room, on account of a side window in the neighbouring property. However when the building inspector made his final survey, he cast his eyes round the room and impassively commented, "This could be quite a nice bedroom, couldn't it?" I hastened to point out to him, in no uncertain terms, that the room was full of boxes and suitcases in recognition of its expressed purpose. Soon afterwards, the so-called storeroom found its true function as a magnificent playroom – safe, out of sight, out of earshot and out of mind.

A fortnight later, on 31st October, when the workmen had left, we gave a party and invited forty of our friends to squeeze into our house – a happy combination of old at the front and brand new at the back. The excitement and the effort of putting on the party produced positive results, and the next day found me languishing in a state of some discomfort on the chaise longue which I had just finished upholstering. That night I went into hospital, having decided that I would never again put myself and a new baby at the mercy of the crabby old midwives in the nursing home, and insisting that this birth should take place attended by our serene, ever-smiling local midwife, in the maternity hospital.

In an unprecedented display of early-morning activity, I gave birth to a daughter, Lucy, at 8 a.m. on Monday 2nd November. Our midwife gave me all proper attention and then, naturally enough after being on duty all night, went home, leaving the baby and me in the care of the hospital nurses. But 8 a.m. on a Monday morning was an unfortunate time to be born. As soon as the nurses in attendance at the birth had washed and dressed the baby, they went off duty, leaving me stranded on the delivery table while the poor little creature – in the cot beside me but just out of my reach – screamed until her face turned bright red. I longed to comfort her, but I had been instructed not to move and, in any case, in my postnatal daze, I feared I might drop her. I lay cold and helpless on the hard table, distressed that the tiny red-faced infant in the cot was receiving such a rude introduction to life.

After two days in hospital I was ready and longing to go home – so ready that I had put my coat on and had wrapped my pretty little pink-faced doll, now much calmer, in warm lacy shawls – when a doctor appeared and ordered me back into bed, explaining that he was going to attach me to a drip containing iron rations to replenish my own failing supplies before letting me go home. Regretfully I obeyed and, instead of returning home to Stephen and Robert, I sadly took refuge in my book, *Buddenbrooks*, Thomas Mann's saga of a Prussian family at the end of the nineteenth century. My patience in the maternity hospital was rewarded the next day when Lucy and I went home, probably in much better shape thanks to the iron supplements that had been pumped into me. It was good to be back in the lane, where in early November the last roses, sweeter and more intense than any roses in summer, were coming into bloom in the garden. Robert arrived home from nursery school with Inigo, soon after midday. He flapped at the letter box, peering through it in excitement, and then rushed into the house, demanding, "Where's the baby, where's the baby?" As soon as he saw his tiny sister lying on a rug on the floor, he went straight over to her and gave her a kiss. Thereafter, although Lucy, once she had acquired the power of speech, hardly allowed him to get a word in edgeways, this fraternal relationship was one area where Dr Spock's good advice was never called for as Robert showed not the least sign of sibling rivalry.

Although Stephen's father and brother, Edward, had gone to Louisiana for the academic year in the cause of tropical medicine, his mother had stayed in England to be in Cambridge over the immediate period of Lucy's birth, because Stephen was beginning to need much more help with his daily needs. He could still pull himself up the stairs, but his walking was so slow and unsteady that he had recently, with the greatest distaste, at last taken to a wheelchair. In the four days of my absence in hospital, my substitute on the home front needed to be someone with patience, understanding and stamina, whom Stephen could trust implicitly. George was his stalwart helper in the Department, but he had his own young family to go home to in the evenings, so naturally Stephen preferred to have his mother look after him when I was out of action. She stayed on for a few days after my return home and was kind, good-humoured and energetic, if detached. The routine was exacting: the shopping and the washing had to be done, the house cleaned, meals prepared and Robert and Stephen looked after single-handedly. The days since that one occasion when Stephen had picked up a tea towel to help with the washing-up were long gone. His illness made it impossible for him to help with the running of the house, because there was nothing of a practical nature that he could do. The advantage for him of this practical inability was that it allowed him unlimited time to indulge his driving passion for physics, which I accepted, because I knew that he would never have willingly been distracted from it by the mundane considerations of cookery, housework and nappies, whatever his circumstances.

After my return home, my own mother took over from Isobel to enable her to join her family in America, where her restraining presence was urgently needed. In his detestation of reptiles, Stephen's father had disobeyed all local advice and had tackled a deadly cottonmouth snake with a broom handle in a fight to the death. Stephen was to visit his family in Louisiana in December on his way to a conference in Texas, six weeks after Lucy's birth, but it was agreed to my immense relief that he should go with George, and I should stay at home with the two children.

When all the grandparents had left, our routine changed again, revolving around the baby and Stephen, with a great deal of willing help from three-year-old Robert, Inigo's nanny and Thelma Thatcher. I felt myself very blessed in my two thriving children. Stephen, however, was worried about Lucy. She slept for long periods during the day and, at night, was positively angelic, so much so that he was convinced that there was something wrong with her. He expected all babies to be like Robert, active and energetic at all hours of the day and the night. I did not share this anxiety. I thoroughly revelled in the blissfully quiet period after her birth which was one of the most stable, contented periods in our lives, especially welcome after the activity of the rebuilding work.

The house was a delight in its brightly painted cleanliness and comparative spaciousness, and the baby a source of great joy; she was so tiny that I could hold her in the palm of one hand, and so quiet that when the health visitor came to call, she did not even notice her lying beside me on the bed. Little Lucy observed conventional bedtimes, allowing me to run a fairly well-ordered household, care for Stephen and Robert and sleep regular hours. At night I was also able to resume reading novels while Stephen was getting ready for bed. We agreed tacitly – since all reference to his illness was offensive to him – that it was important for him to continue to do as much for himself as he could, even if that took time. He could undress himself once I had loosened his shoelaces and undone his buttons, and then he would struggle out of his clothes and into his pyjamas while I lay reading, a precious luxury at the end of each long day. Stephen's night-time routine was a slow one, not only because of the physical constraints but also because his concentration was always directed elsewhere, usually onto a relativistic problem. One evening, he took even longer than usual to get into bed, but it was not until the next morning that I found out why. That night, while putting his pyjamas on and visualizing the geometry of black holes in his head, he had solved one of the major problems in black-hole research. The solution stated that if two black holes collide and form one, the surface area of the two combined cannot be smaller, and must nearly always be larger, than the sum of the two initial black holes – or more concisely, whatever happens to a black hole, its surface area can never decrease in size. This solution was to make Stephen, at the age of twenty-eight, the dominant figure in black-hole theory. As black holes had become a topic of general conversation, it was also to make him a recognized figure of some fascination to the population at large. In Seattle we had been orbiting the newly named phenomenon, the black hole; now we had definitely crossed its event horizon, that boundary from which there is no escape. The theory predicted that, once sucked across the event horizon, the unlucky traveller would be stretched and elongated like a piece of spaghetti, never to have any hope of emerging or of leaving any indications as to his fate.

6

On Campaign

1970, the year of Lucy's birth, saw the passing of the Chronically Sick and Disabled Persons' Act. Though it was hailed across the world as a historic breakthrough in asserting the rights of the disabled, the government refused to implement it fully for many years, leaving already hard-pressed individuals to conduct their own campaigns for its enforcement locally. However it did give substance to our many complaints against the various public bodies whose buildings did not allow easy access to disabled people.

Carrying a small baby in a sling on my front while pushing Stephen in his wheelchair, with three-year-old Robert trotting alongside, I was in the vanguard of protesters, campaigning on behalf of the disabled and their carers. A high kerb or a badly placed step, let alone a flight of steps, presented the sort of obstacle which could turn an otherwise manageable family outing into a disaster. Not robust enough – at only seven-and-a-half stones – to surmount the obstacle unaided, I would have to lie in wait, hopefully scanning the vicinity for a male passer-by from whom I could solicit help. Then I would have to hand my baby over to any kindly lady who happened to be around. Together, the accosted male, Robert and I would heave the chair and its occupant up or over the hurdle, always wary lest the helper should lift the wrong part of the chair – the armrest or the footrest – which might come away in his hand. Finally I would shower the helper with gushing thanks before we continued on our way. Often to my relief, the helpers would volunteer before I had to importune them. Often, as they lifted the chair with Stephen in it, they would ask in amazement, "What do you feed him on? He weighs a ton for such a slight chap." "It's all in his brain," I would reply.

Our letters of protest to the City Surveyor were met with a superior disdain, reminiscent of Stephen's early encounters with the bursars of Gonville and Caius. The City Surveyor had never before heard of disabled people wanting to cross the city as far as Marks & Spencer to buy their own underwear, so he failed to see the need for such an expedition – as if disabled people and their families had no right to venture that far. Injustice spurred us into action. Why should Stephen have to suffer restraints on his lifestyle other than those inflicted by an unkind Nature? Why should short-sighted bureaucrats be allowed to make life doubly difficult for him, when he, unlike those smug officials, the scourge of Seventies' Britain, was using his restricted allowance of life to abundant advantage every day?

After many battles we succeeded in persuading the Arts Theatre and the cinema to make seating areas available for wheelchairs. The University began slowly to revise its provisions for access, as did a few of the more liberal colleges. We took our campaign further afield – to the English National Opera at the Coliseum, where our needs were immediately acknowledged, and to the Royal Opera House at Covent Garden, where help consisted of offloading the responsibility for wheelchair access to two elderly front-of-house attendants who, poor things, while struggling with Stephen up the stairs to the stalls, dropped him. By a curious coincidence, the attitude of the City Council towards access for the disabled mellowed rapidly as Stephen's fame grew, but that was long after those strenuous years during which I pushed the wheelchair with two tiny children in tow.

Most of the colleges were slower to make adjustments, pleading poverty or the impracticality of adapting historic build-ings without contravening conservation laws. Often, college dining halls would be accessible only via the kitchens, with their treacherous obstacle courses of steaming vats, sizzling grills and laden trolleys, and creaking, smelly service lifts already laden with stacks of crockery, trays of hors d'oeuvre and cases of wine. Then our late arrival at High Table would be greeted with pompous disdain, as if such disruptions were too frightfully embarrassing and boring. Our battle with one college, so advanced in its eagerness to admit women but distinctly tardy in its attention to the requirements of the disabled, continued late into the Eighties.

Quite apart from steps and kerbs, there were many unforeseen hazards in the course of everyday life. Once, when taking Stephen with Lucy on his knee out for a walk across the fen, the front castor of the wheelchair stuck in a rut, jolting the frightened occupants out of the chair on to the muddy path. On another occasion, when Lucy was slightly older, we avoided the ruts but came across a rather different obstacle in our path. To cut down on baggage, I had left the house with only my door key and no money in my pocket. As we turned through the wrought-iron gates into King's College, Lucy inevitably spotted an ice-cream van parked on the verge. She had begun to acquire language at ten months' old, when, lying on our bed, she had looked up at the light fitting and announced, "lat, lat," so demanding an ice cream at the age of one was well within her capabilities. Refusing to take my apologetic "no" for an answer, she slid off her father's knee to the ground at his feet, and staged a furious infant sit-down demonstration on the pathway. I could not carry her and push Stephen at the same time so Robert and I tried to cajole the agitated little ball of royal blue garments and auburn curls, but to no avail. The King's Choristers paused on their way from the choir school to evensong in the chapel and stood wonderingly round her in a circle, perturbed at the spectacle of so much anguish in such a tiny person. After an eternity an acquaintance of Stephen's from another group in the Department appeared on the scene and came to the rescue. While I pushed Stephen, he carried Lucy, still loudly proclaiming her indignation, home – without an ice cream.

As we had no time to read newspapers, we relied on my parents for useful snippets of information culled from theirs. Often they would send us bundles of cuttings, sometimes about discoveries in astrophysics, sometimes about benefits for the disabled. Since in one of the latter it was suggested that disabled people could reclaim the cost of the motor-vehicle licence, we approached Stephen's doctor for clarification. It transpired that the information in the article was ahead of its time: in 1971 there was no mechanism yet in place for reclaiming the licence fee – that was to follow some years later – but Dr Swan suggested that Stephen might like to apply for a disabled vehicle.

This amazing possibility began to open up exciting horizons. If he could manage the joystick controls of an electric car, Stephen would have a new, mechanical mobility in compensation for his diminishing personal movement. An application was accepted, the bureaucratic formalities completed, but just one hitch remained: the vehicle had to be parked under cover near an electric socket to charge its batteries overnight. As so often happened, a solution came from an entirely unexpected source when Hugh Corbett, the Warden of the University Centre at the river end of the lane, responded to our need and unhesitatingly offered Stephen a parking space under cover by a plug.

Although disabled vehicles were criticized for their instability, the electric car – which travelled at the speed of a fast bicycle – enabled Stephen once again to be master of his own routine, driving where he wanted and dividing his working day between the Department in the morning and the Institute of Astronomy in the afternoon. On his return home in the early evening, he would draw up outside the house, hooting the horn, and Robert would rush out excitedly and clamber onto a ledge beside him for the final fifty yards of the journey down to the University Centre, while I would follow on with the wheelchair to bring Stephen back home. As ever no system was completely trouble-free. The car was subject to frequent breakdowns, and often we found it hemmed in its parking place by other vehicles. Once it overturned, giving Stephen a nasty fright, though fortunately no injuries.

In summer the children and I would sometimes take a picnic out into the grounds of the Observatory and visit Stephen in his office in the Institute of Astronomy. The children's high-pitched voices would race ahead of them along the plush carpeted corridors, like gusts of fresh spring air, announcing their presence to their delighted father. The expressions on Stephen's face were always a much more powerful measure of his emotions than his spoken words, and on these occasions it was the smile on his face that conveyed his unmistakable joy in his children. The Observatory, purpose-built in 1823 with a dome in the centre and residential wings for the astronomers, had the appearance of an unusual but imposing country house, set in carefully tended orchards and gardens, where we acquired a small patch in which to grow our own produce. While the churchyard was ideal for growing roses and lilies, I baulked at the thought of growing vegetables in its soil. Out at the Observatory the children set to with a will, chatting incessantly while they dug, planted seeds and watched them grow. Then at the end of the day we would proudly take our armfuls of beans and carrots and lettuces into the Institute to show Stephen, before setting off for home ahead of him.

Those carefree afternoons spent on the verge of the country proved to be a respite from the increasing trials of life in Little St Mary's Lane. When we had chanced upon it in 1965, the lane was a haven of tranquillity. By the early Seventies, it was becoming a busy and dangerous thoroughfare to the University Centre, Peterhouse College and the Garden House Hotel on the river bank. Not infrequently a ten-ton lorry would misguidedly come down the lane intending to deliver its load to the Centre or the hotel, only to find itself stuck halfway where the road narrowed. The lorry would then have to back up to Trumpington Street, narrowly missing the façades of our houses and filling our front rooms with fumes.

If this was the main problem by day, by night our ears were assaulted by a barrage of thudding pop music from the Peterhouse so-called music room. The Fellows of Peterhouse had cleverly situated their music room – where regular pop sessions were held – as far away from the main body of the College as possible, in a room overlooking the churchyard. Perhaps they thought that it did not matter if the slumbers of the dead were disturbed. Unfortunately they gave little thought to the living of the neighbourhood – especially the very elderly and the very young – for whom the nocturnal wailings, poundings and crashings were intolerable. Advance warning of an imminent session could be detected in the afternoon with the whistling of speakers, the occasional chord on a guitar, the crash of a lone cymbal. On one such afternoon, Thatcher nodded in the direction of Peterhouse, "Isn't it lovely, dear," she said, "I think they're having a *thé dansant*."

More campaigning – this time not about disabled issues – was an urgent necessity. A succession of letters to the Governing Body of Peterhouse, anguished telephone calls in the middle of the night to the porters and even, on one occasion, to the Master himself, eventually produced a compromise, curtailing the hours for full-decibel power and reducing the volume after midnight.

The traffic, a real danger for the three small children, Robert, Lucy and Inigo, who liked to ride their tricycles up and down the road and pay social calls on the neighbours, was a more intractable problem and one which demanded a more organized campaign of meetings and many more letters, most of which did not meet with an encouraging response. However the complexion of the issue changed dramatically on account of a devastating fire which struck the Garden House Hotel in 1972, a couple of years after it had been targeted in a student protest for appearing to support the military regime in Greece.

By the end of the day of the fire, the scene of so many happy family gatherings was nothing more than a charred smoking shell, from which there soon arose ambitious plans for greatly enlarged premises. Architectural considerations apart, a horrendous volume of traffic would certainly ensue, so we, the residents of the lane, opposed the plans unanimously. Just as both sides were heading for a confrontation, we realized that the two apparently conflicting aims were not as incompatible as they had seemed. The managers wanted a new hotel, and we wanted the lane closed and its peace and safety restored; by joining forces instead of opposing each other, both objectives could be achieved, and this was in effect the final result of a tense meeting of residents and managers expertly chaired by the Thatchers at number 9.

If in Cambridge Stephen and I had begun to find ways of adapting and controlling our environment, elsewhere it was more difficult. On their return from Louisiana late in 1970, Stephen's parents decided to buy a country cottage. I hopefully suggested that a cottage on the east coast would be a wonderful asset for our family. In both Norfolk and Suffolk, though the sand was soft, the terrain was level and manageable, allowing Stephen to be pushed to the very edge of the beach from where he could watch the children at play. My idea was curtly dismissed. "The east coast is much too cold for Father; he would hate having a cottage there," Isobel remarked. This was puzzling, since Frank Hawking spent most of his time working in the garden in all seasons and all weathers – just like the hardy Mr McGregor in *Peter Rabbit* – and indoors he wrapped himself in a dressing gown for warmth rather than install more heating appliances, leaving everyone else to freeze in the sub-arctic conditions.

Isobel went prospecting for a cottage with Philippa, who had come back from a two-year period of study in Japan, and returned rapturously enthusing over their find – a stone-built cottage overlooking a bend in the river Wye above a village called Llandogo in Monmouthshire – a place of lovely walks and views, with streams and woods for the children to play in and explore. I had never been to Wales and was easily infected by their enthusiasm, the more so because in April 1971 we had acquired a large, shiny new car, a replacement for the ailing Mini, financed by Stephen's First Prize in the annual Gravity Competition for an essay which he had run off just after Christmas.

Despite its size – about three times larger than the Mini – even the new car was barely adequate for all our luggage, as I found when I experimented with various ways of loading it for the exploratory trip to Wales in the autumn of 1971. Once the wheelchair, the pushchair and the travel cot were stowed away in the capacious rear section, there was little room for the suitcases. The next expedient was a roof rack, but that created its own set of the problems: by the time I had packed for the four of us, closed the house, eased Stephen into the front seat of the car, folded the wheelchair and lifted it into the back, strapped the children into their seats, loaded their luggage, including the travel cot and the pushchair, and then heaved four heavy cases onto the roof rack, I was so exhausted that the 220-mile journey, three times as far as the distance to the Suffolk or the Norfolk coasts, became an ordeal rather than an adventure. Even when the M4 opened just shortly after our first trip, the distance still proved to be a major drawback.

Nevertheless, when we stopped across the Welsh border for a tea break and saw the road signs in a foreign language and smelt the tingling damp air, our sense of excitement returned. At last we could truthfully tell Robert, who had been asking how much further ever since we left Cambridge, that we were nearly there. Some miles of open hill roads and then winding, leafy lanes brought us at last to our destination. The description we had been given of the cottage was undeniably accurate. Its position above the river Wye was breathtakingly beautiful, commanding an uninterrupted view of the river, the valley and the tree-covered hills on the opposite bank, where in a glow of radiant colour, autumn reigned in all its glory. A stream ran down the hillside beside the house, and a path through the beech woods at the back climbed up over damp peaty undergrowth to the waterfalls at Cleddon. Not so very far away, on the Black Mountains and the Brecon Beacons, a chill wind raged incessantly, testing the stamina of even the toughest hillwalker. The house itself was certainly picturesque – whitewashed, slate-roofed, set into the green hillside, blue wood smoke curling gently upwards from its chimney – and its attractions were undeniable.

This faithful description had omitted several important details, however, such as the fact that the hillside was little short of vertical, so that the only possible movement was up or down, and the only stretch of horizontal surface suitable for a wheelchair was a track a mere hundred yards long to the blackberry thicket at the edge of the wood. Moreover the house itself was reached by a flight of a dozen steep stone steps, slippery with moss and lichen, while inside a long, steep staircase led up to the bedrooms and the only bathroom. It could not have been more inappropriate for Stephen. Although his father stood by, it took him ten minutes to get up or down the stairs to the bathroom and more than ten minutes to get up or down the treacherous steps to the road. All excursions had to be made by car because there was nowhere else for him to go.

The children loved the place and a part of me shared their enjoyment. The changing colours were mesmerizing and the clear air refreshing. I relished my mother-in-law's meals. She was an excellent cook, except on those occasions when she chose to economize by serving us fresh-ground elder or brackish nettles from the garden. Unlike Stephen, who would wrinkle his nose in disgust, I also enjoyed my father-in-law's home-made wine, especially the luscious, golden mead which he fermented from the honey produced by his own bees. After supper we would spend long, lazy evenings in front of the open fire, playing board games until the children's heads started to loll sleepily. But on those occasions when I went out walking or climbing with Robert, I felt very unhappy at leaving Stephen behind, sitting sadly indoors or out on the terrace. Nowhere could more effectively or more cruelly have emphasized the limitations of his disability. I was upset and baffled. It seemed that the Hawkings considered themselves free of all basic responsibility for Stephen. If we visited them, they would be prepared to help, but otherwise they appeared to disregard the inconveniences of motor-neuron disease.

7

Upward Mobility

Llandogo with all its obstacles in 1971 turned out to be a useful rehearsal for the next summer's excursion – to the annual summer school in physics at Les Houches in the French Alps on the lower slopes of Mont Blanc – which was the brainchild of Cecile de Witt and her American husband Bryce. The mother of four daughters and an outstanding physicist at a time when women physicists were rare, Cecile was one of those capable women – not unlike some of the Fellows of Lucy Cavendish – of whom I stood in awe. From her home in America she organized the conferences in her native France and invited her own hand-picked participants. At Les Houches she supervised all the arrangements, led the sessions and climbed the mountains. For Stephen, she commissioned a labour force, brought in bulldozers to construct a ramp up to the chalet where we were to stay for six weeks, and made every possible provision for our comfort. She could hardly be blamed for the weather in the Alps that summer.

Stephen flew out to Geneva with his colleagues while my parents and I drove the rest of the family to Paris for the over-night Motorail to Saint-Gervais, some twenty miles from Les Houches. We happened to arrive in Paris on the chaotic weekend of *le grand rush* in late July, when the whole of France goes on holiday, but somehow Dad managed to find the Motorail depot and somehow, with our small charges, we managed to fight our way through the massed hordes of travellers on to the train at the Gare de Lyon. The next morning, with the nightmarish journey behind us, the sun shone as we relaxed over breakfast of coffee and croissants outside the station at Saint-Gervais, and it still shone, bathing the white peaks in glistening magnificence, as we excitedly embarked on the winding journey up the Chamonix valley to the very heart of the mountains.

Scarcely had we climbed the steep track to the summer school, a cluster of chalets and lecture halls set among meadows and pine trees, than the sun disappeared, a mist descended and it began to rain. It rained and it rained and it was cold. Water dripped from every roof, every gutter, every branch and every blade of grass, and Cecile's carefully constructed ramp soon turned into a mud slide. In the middle of July, Dad and I had to resort to feeding the woodburning stove an endless supply of logs to keep the chalet warm and to dry the nappies with which every corner was festooned. Dear little Lucy did her best to help by spontaneously potty-training herself at the age of twenty months.

In these circumstances, despite the elevation and the vertical nature of all expeditions, Stephen was happy. From morning till night he was surrounded by colleagues from all over the world whose driving passion was the study of black holes. Occasionally some of them went off in groups for the day, weather permitting, to climb Mont Blanc, but that only added to the excitement and the tension and lent an additional aura of superiority to their overall image. Nothing was too difficult for this breed of superhumans who were capable of mastering the secrets of the Universe and also of conquering any physical challenge on earth. Stephen of course was included in this category, since obviously he was fighting his own physical challenges with the gritty courage of a hardened mountaineer. The rest of us – the hangers-on, the wives, mothers, grandparents and babies – were left to our own devices, to shop and cook and find our own entertainment. Raids on the local supermarket for its somewhat limited range of supplies provided eggs for a staple diet of omelettes cooked over a bottled-gas stove. Although there was a restaurant which catered for the delegates, it was too expensive for the whole family to eat there all the time, and in any case the conversation at table inevitably veered, in the friendliest possible way, towards the rarefied subjects of black holes or alpine mountaineering in which we – that is the family – were not able to participate constructively.

As and when the rain eased off we would set out for a walk, under the dripping branches, up the mountainside at the back of the chalet, past the lecture hall into the wood to search for wild raspberries and blueberries. Then we encountered another unexpected challenge. While Robert, true to form, would charge ahead, Lucy adamantly refused to walk more than a couple of yards at a time and would then put her arms up, wanting to be carried. Because Robert's limitless energy now seemed quite normal, Lucy's reluctance to move perplexed me, just as her sleepiness when new-born had perplexed Stephen. Our progress up the mountain track was slow, and rarely did we reach the clearing where the raspberries and blueberries grew before it started to rain again. On one of these expeditions, an extraordinary thing happened.

For once Lucy was actually walking on her own two feet with Robert, ten yards or so ahead of her grandparents and me. Bringing up the rear I was enjoying an unaccustomed freedom of movement, unencumbered by any other person, small or large, when suddenly I saw the children stop in their tracks. They stood stock-still, whispering to each other very quietly and, beckoning to us to lower our voices, pointed to the ground. There, wending its way across the path from one side to the other was the smallest, most perfectly formed adder, the white diamond markings on its body standing out clearly against the grey. It took no notice of us as it slithered into the undergrowth. It was beautiful to watch, but even more striking were the children's reactions, as if some primitive instinct had warned them to stand quiet and still.

However high-powered their physics and impressive their mountaineering feats, the American participants at Les Houches brought a carefree atmosphere to the centre which helped to mitigate the effects of the rain. There was nothing superficial about their relaxed friendliness. Kip Thorne and his botanist wife, Linda, had made the break from the constraints of their Mormon background to search for broader truths unshackled by religious dogma. Whatever their private thoughts, they never voiced any criticism of the rigours of their background, but brought the positive aspects of Mormonism, a deep caring and concern for their fellow beings, to a wider world.

Jim Bardeen, the quietest, most self-effacing physicist imaginable, was working closely with Stephen and Brandon Carter on the painstaking task of constructing the laws of black-hole mechanics from the basis of Einstein's equations of general relativity. The new set of laws detailing the physics of black holes had caused a hubbub of excitement when their similarity to the second law of thermodynamics had become apparent, and it was this similarity which was driving cosmologists to attempt to narrow the gap between thermodynamics and black holes by putting the theory of black holes into the language of thermodynamics. The laws of thermodynamics govern microcosmic operations; they dictate the behaviour of atoms and molecules, including their eventual decay into heat, which they exchange with the objects around them. However the conundrum that now faced physicists was that the laws of thermodynamics, although similar, could not work in the case of black holes, because the predictions were that nothing, not even heat, could escape from a black hole.

Stephen, Jim and Brandon were attempting to unravel this major enigma when, one afternoon, unable to endure another drop of rain, I bundled the children and their grandparents into the car and set off over the pass beyond Chamonix to Switzerland, convinced that the sun must be shining somewhere. Somewhere there must be a welcome transfer of heat from one celestial body to another, even if heat did signify decay, or "entropy" in scientific terminology. Jim's wife, Nancy, came with us and enthralled the children, singing to them, telling them stories, sharing jokes and reciting poems all the way to Martigny – where indeed the sun was shining – and back. Through the infectious gaiety which shone from her big brown eyes, Nancy concealed the deep pain of the recent loss of both her parents.

It was also in Les Houches that Bernard Carr, Stephen's new research student, came bounding into our lives one wet afternoon. Bernard was certainly different from the expected run of research students. He was talkative, sociable, unselfconscious, the result perhaps of being sent to boarding school at the age of six. His conversation ranged widely over many topics, often coming to rest on his other main interest, parapsychology, a subject which physicists, including Stephen, tended to regard with derision. For Bernard however, coincidences and telepathic communication were significant. Indeed he was astounded to find that his impromptu visit from Geneva – where he was staying – to Les Houches, was actually expected by Stephen, his new supervisor, who had already summoned him in an undelivered word-of-mouth invitation through a third party. Bernard's early ambition had been to become a spaceman. As a child, to his mother's consternation, he had once spent a whole day preparing for this objective by standing on his head in the cupboard under the stairs while his younger brother sat outside the door acting as mission control. His mother must have been grateful that his intellect destined him for the theory rather than the practice of space exploration.

When at last the sun consented to shine in France as well as Switzerland, and the mountains appeared from behind the clouds,

Kip and Linda offered to take Robert and me on a mountain walk, up towards one of the glaciers, the Glacier de Bionnassay on the west face of Mont Blanc. Leaving Lucy and Stephen with my parents, we took the cable car from Les Houches up to a ridge from where we could look down to the toy chalets and villages dotted about the valley. The summer school down to our left was just out of sight behind the dark trees, while to our right a steep path ascended the mountainside, following the track of the funicular railway which crawled laboriously up from Saint-Gervais to the top station at the Nid de l'Aigle, the Eagle's Nest. The dazzling whiteness of the mountain against the deep blue sky was intoxicating, leading us on, up and up, pausing now and then to share Linda's ecstatic delight at the wide range of alpine plants and flowers opening in the afternoon sun. We continued our climb, higher and higher, beyond the end of the railway line in the direction of the massive blue-grey expanse of the glacier, still searching for more specimens for Linda.

It was not until we reached the first of the climbers' refuges in the lee of the Dôme du Goûter that, as one, we realized that we were alone on the mountain. Far below, the trains had ceased to run and all the other walkers had melted away although the sun was still high. Eagles wheeled silently overhead, a distant stream trickled down the rocks; otherwise there was little movement: an eerie quietness prevailed. None of us had thought of checking the time of the last cable car down to the village. At a brisk pace, almost a run, we set off back down the track to the cable-car station, more than an hour's walk away. Against all expectation, there in the station was a cable car with an attendant standing beside it. We ran to him smiling with relief, but he turned a dour face towards us, barring our way. Implacably indifferent, he announced that the last cable car had gone at five-thirty and it was now nearly six o'clock. We pleaded with him breathlessly, pointing to our five-year-old, who was – for once – beginning to tire. The man was impervious, hard as flint. We turned away, anxious and angry. On the ridge above the station there was a hostel from where we tried to call the summer school, but there was no reply. We dared not wait any longer, as the sun was now lower in the sky, so we left money with the hostel keeper asking her to try to ring again and leave a message.

There was nothing for it but to head straight down the mountainside as fast as possible, taking the path when we could find it, scrambling through bracken and long grass when we could not. A patriarchal figure, like St Christopher in a medieval painting, Kip carried Robert, whose legs had borne him well for more than four hours, but were now aching with weariness. Fighting our way through the undergrowth, we watched in disbelief as the cable car, carrying the same disobliging attendant, sailed over our heads on its homeward run down to Les Houches. The air grew chill as the sun sank behind the mountains, and the sky darkened. We persevered, thankful at least that we were walking down the mountain not up it.

The village of Les Houches was by no means the end of the road. The summer-school enclave was another three quarters of an hour away, up the hillside further west. It must have been well after nine when we stumbled blindly into the brightly lit refectory where everyone was anxiously waiting for news of us. No message had come from the hostel and the worried group of family – my parents and Stephen – colleagues and students were fearing the worst. Tearful with tiredness and relief, we fell into each other's arms.

At the end of August, as we dodged the showers at the last social function of the summer school – a barbecue where a whole lamb was being roasted over a pit – Kip suggested that Stephen might like to visit Moscow for talks with those many Russian scientists whose freedom to travel was severely restricted. He promised to make all the arrangements for a private visit which could be timed to follow on from the Copernicus Conference in Poland in the summer of 1973. Kip's well-meaning suggestions made my blood run cold. While Lucy was a baby, Stephen had travelled abroad to conferences either with George Ellis or Gary Gibbons, his first research student, or with his mother. Now that Robert was five and Lucy one and a half, my period of respite from international travel seemed to be drawing to a close. Frequently Stephen would ask if I would go with him to conferences in far-flung places; just as frequently I would reply that I could not bear to leave the children.

Divided loyalties were beginning to tear me apart. Stephen was pursuing his career with an iron will, and conferences gave him the chance to assert his presence on the international scene. It had been my genuine aim to help him achieve all possible success, but since making that commitment, I had become the mother of his children, and to them I owed an equal responsibility. Although

Stephen obviously required my help for many of his personal needs, the children needed my help for all of theirs. They were small enough still to need a constant presence. If their future was insecure on account of the health of their father, then I, their mother, had to compensate for that by not abandoning them more than necessary. Although they would be in excellent hands with their grandparents, I found the prospect of being thousands of miles apart from them for any length of time excruciating.

The scenario was set for a grim, recurring competition. Stephen would ask if I would like to go with him to a conference in, say, New York and tensely I would decline. Tacitly ignoring my reluctance, he would repeat the same question week after week until I was reduced to a frenzy, overwhelmed with guilt at letting him down, yet saddened by his lack of understanding. This pressure exacerbated the fear of flying which had pursued me since the tour of America in 1967, hovering over me like a great black bird at the mere mention of air travel. I had flown only twice since then, once on the winter holiday to Majorca when Robert fell sick, and the second time to Switzerland in May 1970. There had been a trip planned to Tbilisi in Georgia in September 1968, but to my silent relief, many British scientists, including Stephen, refused to attend in protest against the Russian invasion of Czechoslovakia that August. My fear of air travel was not completely unjustified: in the late Sixties and Seventies, not only did aeroplanes fall out of the sky with chilling regularity, they were also the favourite targets for hijackings by the growing bands of international terrorists.

The sum total of all the conflicting pressures doomed me to years of misery and travel by the longest, most roundabout means. In 1971, when Stephen was invited to attend a conference in Trieste, he went by air while Robert and I took the train, leaving seven-month-old Lucy with my parents. After the long, hot journey across Europe, we stopped in Venice, where Robert, bewitched by the view from the top of the Campanile, refused to descend – until the sudden clang of the heavy bells at midday sent him running for the lift. He then insisted on sitting down at a table in St Mark's Square outside Florian's, which proved to be an expensive lesson – the equivalent of £6 for a tiny cup of coffee – so the next time we passed Florian's by and sat down on the steps around the porticoed square – only to become targets for the local pigeons.

Two years later, the proposed trip to Moscow via Warsaw was a very different undertaking: travel by air was indispensable and applications for visas had to be sent months in advance. There was no choice; I would be away from the children for nearly a month, as in those repressive days after the fall of Khrushchev, nobody other than me would be granted a visa to accompany Stephen. The prospect haunted me but the plans were laid, the tickets were booked – paid for, as always by some scientific organization or other – and, with some difficulty, the visas extracted from the Russian embassy. It was very dispiriting to think that in the space of a few short years, I had become a pale shadow of the student who had travelled alone round Spain, blithely disregarding all parental concerns, revelling in the spirit of adventure, and relishing air travel, even in clapped-out propeller aircraft. Bound for Warsaw and Moscow but wan with care, I slipped away from the children as they played happily in their grandparents' house in St Albans in August 1973.

8

Intellect and Ignorance

Astronomers were flocking to Poland in 1973 to celebrate the 500th anniversary of the birth of Nicolaus Copernicus, the Polish astronomer whose dissatisfaction with the complicated mathematics needed to account for the movement of the planets in the earth-centred universe of Ptolemy's theory compelled him to develop a new theory of the universe in 1514. Still considering myself as something of a medievalist, but a medievalist with more than a passing interest in cosmology, I was fascinated by the iconoclastic effect of the Copernican theory, which postulated that the earth and other planets revolved around the sun, and thus superseded the Ptolemaic theory which had become tantamount to an article of faith, both scientific and religious, though in fact it bore little relation to the biblical concept of a flat earth, above which was heaven and below which was hell. On my first visit behind the Iron Curtain – apart from a day trip to Yugoslavia from Trieste in 1971 – I also found in Poland a lesson in the nature of tragedy: the tragedy of history in a country which bore the scars of oppression and division, the philosophical tragedy for mankind of the schism between science and religion which resulted from Copernicus' theory, and the tragedy of genius.

Although Copernicus did not live to see how his theory was developed by Galileo in the seventeenth century, he must have been well aware of its dangerously controversial nature. He might be seen as the first scientist to open the Pandora's box of science, with its dual potential of advancing human knowledge and yet of posing uncomfortable dilemmas which would test man's moral integrity. The theory well deserved the term by which it came to be known: the "Copernican Revolution". Since, according to Copernicus, the earth was no longer at the centre of the universe, man was not at the centre of creation. Man, therefore, could no longer be said to have a special relationship with the Creator. This fundamental change in perspective was to liberate man from the oppressive medieval obsession with the divine image, enabling him to expand his intellectual capabilities and value his own physical attributes – and it was one of the powerful influences behind the philosophy of the European Renaissance, when architects built palaces rather than cathedrals, and artists and sculptors replaced the religious image with the human form, depicted for its own sake, for its beauty and strength. In scientific terms, the Copernican theory paved the way for the discoveries of Newton in seventeenth-century England, where a positive after-effect of an otherwise fanatical Puritanism had been the release of rational thought from the grip of religious superstition. Within Catholicism, however, the Copernican theory was to produce an ugly, anti-scientific reaction, the repercussions of which are still felt throughout society.

Perhaps wary of its implications, Copernicus did not permit his work *Concerning the Revolution of the Heavenly Spheres* to be published until just before he died; a copy of the printed work was reputedly brought to him on his deathbed on 24th May 1543. Nonetheless he had not sought to hide its contents, for the theory had been widely disseminated over a long period, and he himself had lectured to the Pope Clement VII on the subject in Rome in 1533. Perhaps the Pope did not fully understand the implications of the lecture because it was presented to him merely as a simplification of the cumbersome Ptolemaic mathematics, or perhaps he did not take it seriously, because it was not until some time later – in the seventeenth century – that it fell to Galileo Galilei to bear the full brunt of the Church's ire for his support and publicizing of the new system.

A charming popular account of the spyglass ascribes its invention to children who were playing around with bits of glass and lenses in the workshop of a Flemish spectacle-maker and found that by putting two lenses together they could see distant objects plainly. The spectacle-maker saw the potential of the gadget for the toy market, but when in 1609 Galileo heard of it, he worked out the underlying theory in one night and developed his own improved version, the telescope, which he demonstrated to that city's incredulous merchants from the Campanile in Venice. To their astonishment, they could see in detail the markings on a sailing ship on the horizon, two hours from port. Galileo then realized that his revolutionary navigational aid could be turned on the heavens. He built a telescope in Padua, discovered four new planets – in fact the satellites of Jupiter – and published his own watercolour maps of the moon. His observations, which showed that not all heavenly bodies necessarily orbited the earth, convinced him of the accuracy of the Copernican theory. In 1610 he somewhat naively publicized his proof of the theory obtained from his observations, and in the next few years found himself in conflict with the Church, for whom the earth was theologically fixed at the centre of the universe.

In 1600, Giordano Bruno had been burnt at the stake for daring to speculate about astronomical matters, yet Galileo was undeterred by Bruno's fate. Innocently supposing that no one would want to contradict visible evidence, he went on to become the main and most successful proponent of the Copernican theory, especially because he published his findings in the vernacular language, Italian, instead of Latin. The attack this represented on the traditional Judeo-Christian view of a conveniently earth-centred universe posed an unacceptable threat from within to a church already struggling to contain the forces of Protestantism from without, and in 1616 the Church authorities issued an admonition requiring Galileo not to hold or defend the Copernican doctrine.

The election in 1623 of Maffeo Barberini to the Papacy as Urban VIII alleviated Galileo's uncomfortable situation temporarily. Barberini was a highly cultured man and a lover of the arts, but he was also proud, extravagant and autocratic – he reputedly had all the birds in the Vatican garden killed because they disturbed him. He was however a friend of Galileo's and helped to bring about a limited relaxation of the 1616 injunction by commissioning Galileo to write a discourse – *Dialogo sopra i due massimi sistemi del mondo, tolemaico e copernicano* – giving the arguments for and against the two competing systems, on condition that the discourse should be completely neutral. Inevitably the book, when it appeared in 1632, was seen as a categorical statement of the force of the Copernican argument and led to Galileo's arrest and trial by the Inquisition. He was sentenced to house arrest in his villa at Arcetri where, old, blind and captive, the king of infinite space bounded in a nutshell, he eloquently lamented the disparity between the vastness of his area of research and the limitations of his physical condition, a situation with which it was all too easy for us to sympathize: "This universe is now shrivelled up for me into such a narrow compass as is filled by my own bodily sensations."

Despite the life sentence of house arrest, his creative powers were not dulled. A new manuscript, *Concerning Two New Sciences*, was smuggled out of Italy to Holland where it was published in 1638. With this manuscript, Galileo is said to have laid the foundations of modern experimental and theoretical physics, and with it the scientific tradition moved north, away from the repressions of southern Europe.

Although Galileo was a devout Catholic, it was his conflict with the Vatican, sadly mismanaged on both sides, that lay at the basis of the running battle between science and religion, a tragic and confusing schism which persists unresolved. More than ever today, religion finds its revelatory truths threatened by scientific theory, and retreats into a defensive corner, while scientists go into the attack insisting that rational argument is the only valid criterion for an understanding of the workings of the universe. Maybe both sides have misunderstood the nature of their respective roles. Scientists are equipped to answer the mechanical question of *how* the universe and everything in it, including life, came about. But since their modes of thought are dictated by purely rational, materialistic criteria, physicists cannot claim to answer the questions of *why* the universe exists, and *why* we human beings are here to observe it, any more than molecular biologists can satisfactorily explain *why* – if our actions are determined by the workings of a selfish genetic coding – we occasionally listen to the voice of conscience and behave with altruism, compassion and generosity. Even these human qualities have come under attack from evolutionary psychologists who have ascribed altruism to a crude genetic theory by which familial cooperation is said to favour the survival of the species. Likewise the spiritual sophistication of musical, artistic and poetic activity is regarded as just a highly advanced function of primitive origins.

Frequently over the decades of our marriage, stimulated by a scientific article or television programme, I found my mind exercised by questions of this nature and would try to discuss them with Stephen. In the early days our arguments on the topics rehearsed above were playful and fairly light-hearted. Increasingly in later years, they became more personal, divisive and hurtful. The damaging schism between religion and science seemed to have extended its reach into our very lives: Stephen would adamantly assert the blunt positivist stance which I found too depressing and too limiting to my view of the world, because I fervently needed to believe that there was more to life than the bald facts of the laws of physics and the day-to-day struggle for survival. Compromise was anathema to Stephen however, because it admitted an unacceptable degree of uncertainty, when he dealt only in the certainties of mathematics.

Galileo died on 8th January 1642, the year in which Newton was born and three hundred years to the day before Stephen was born. It was therefore not surprising that Stephen adopted Galileo as his hero. When in 1975 he received a medal from the Pope, he took the opportunity to launch a personal campaign for Galileo's rehabilitation. The campaign was eventually successful but was nevertheless seen as a victory for the rational advance of science over the hidebound antiquated forces of religion, a theological capitulation, rather than as a reconciliation of science with religion.

In the sixteenth century, Nicolaus Copernicus had led the life of a true Renaissance man, untroubled by the crises that Galileo was to suffer in the next century. Copernicus enjoyed all the advantages, breadth of education and experience of that period of intellectual expansion and travelled widely, as far as Bologna, Padua and Rome. He studied medicine as well as mathematics and astronomy. He made translations from Greek into Latin, fulfilled a number of diplomatic functions and presented proposals for the reform of various Polish currencies. Ironically, five hundred years later, such broad possibilities were denied to Copernicus' modern compatriots as they celebrated his quincentenary.

From the scientific point of view, the great advantage of the Polish setting for the commemorative conference was that it provided a meeting place for all the great minds from both West and East, since Russian physicists were able to travel to Poland, if not further field, with relative freedom. For Westerners, Poland was certainly more accessible than the Soviet Union: our Polish visas came through automatically, whereas the Russians were much less welcoming. The only inconvenience of entry into Poland, as a number of male delegates found, was that the bearer of a passport was expected to resemble his photograph down to the last detail. Since the year was 1973, many of the younger delegates and students were sporting long hair and fine bushy growths of beard, bearing little resemblance to their passport photos which could have been taken nearly ten years earlier when they were but whining schoolboys with satchel and shining faces. The only means of persuading the Polish authorities that they really were who they purported to be, and not decadent hippies intent on undermining the purity of communist culture, was to shave off their beards and cut their hair at the border post. They arrived in Warsaw looking like sheep from the shearer. Stephen was probably the only one among them whose hair was actually shorter than on his photo and did not have to subject himself to an urgent trim.

The Poland we witnessed in 1973 was a sad country, ravaged by Germany and dominated by Russia. It was hardly surprising that the Poles regarded all foreigners, ourselves included, with suspicion. We were all tarred with the same brush: if we were not German, we must be Russian. Protesting our Britishness was of no avail because we and the Americans came from the envied affluent societies to which the Poles would like to belong but from which they were barred. Plate-glass shopfronts bore ample evidence of western aspirations, but inside the shops the shelves were either bare or the goods they displayed were shoddy and prohibitively expensive.

Everywhere Poland showed signs of a country ill at ease with itself, caught on the horns of a dilemma between old and new, East and West. Torn apart throughout its history by both its neighbours, Russia and Germany, it had painstakingly reconstructed much that it had lost in the Second World War – especially, in fine detail, the old town of Warsaw. In contrast, Stalin's unwelcome post-war gift to the Polish people was a megalithic municipal building of which it was said that the best views of Warsaw could be seen from it – meaning that only by viewing Warsaw from the Stalin monument could one avoid seeing the monument itself. In that building the Copernicus conference took place. It was approached from without by means of a long flight of steps. Another long flight of steps led down inside the building from the foyer to the conference area. Each morning, Stephen's student Bernard Carr and I would carry Stephen to the top of the steps, sit him down on a chair and then bring up the wheelchair. Inside, for want of a lift, we would then take the wheelchair down the corresponding inner flight of stairs before carrying Stephen down to it. This process was repeated in reverse sequence at the end of the day, possibly also several times during the course of the day, subject to variations in the programme and the venue. Those steps did not impress us with Stalin's generosity to the Polish people: they impressed us only with his megalomania.

A repressive Communism, imposed by Russia, which condemned peasant farmers to appear as lean as the emaciated cows we saw them herding along the country roads or the teams of scrawny oxen they drove across the fields, had produced a defiant reaction in the people. Poland was the most devoutly Catholic country in Europe: the Polish Church had become a symbol of national independence and nobly fulfilled its role as the defender of liberty, producing martyrs from among its priesthood. Nonetheless, I was perplexed to find strong reminiscences in Polish churches of the Church in Spain, so unlike the refreshing simplicity of English Catholicism which had resulted from the reforms of John XXIII's inspired papacy. As in Spain, churches in Poland were ornate, darkly lit, incense-filled, full of extravagant plaster saints and virgins, imbued with that distasteful air of superstition. Clusters of little old crones, draped in black, crowded round the porches and genuflected at the altars just as they did in Francoist Spain. Polish independence as manifested through the Catholic church was a very conservative force, competing against a hostile political system with its own traditional opiate, whereas in Spain the attitude of the Catholic church was equally conservative but was generally one of political compliance with the repressive regime.

Cracow, to which the conference adjourned for the second session, was more assured of its identity than Warsaw, since its monuments – Wawel Castle and the church of St Mary – had survived the war intact, but the vicinity of Cracow was tainted with the chilling notoriety of Auschwitz. There was no official excursion to Auschwitz, but some Jewish participants organized their own outing and came back communicating to the rest of us their devastation at what they had witnessed.

The only place in that unhappy country where I detected any sense of peace and integrity was at Chopin's birthplace, a single-storeyed thatched house, set in a tangle of greenery at Żelazowa Wola in the country outside Warsaw. Although Chopin's family moved to Warsaw when he was a baby, he spent summer holidays at Żelazowa Wola, the country seat of his mother's aristocratic relations, the Skarbeks, and it was there that he put the finishing touches to his E-minor piano concerto. He also spent holidays with school friends in the country. On one such holiday, he and his friends went on an excursion to Torum and found the house where Copernicus was born. Shocked by the condition of the house, Chopin complained that the room where Copernicus was born was occupied by "some German who stuffs himself with potatoes and then probably passes foul winds".

The old house at Żelazowa Wola, with its sparse furnishings, polished floors, family portraits and collection of instruments, modestly conjured up the atmosphere of life in a cultured Polish family in the early nineteenth century. It was not just the aura of unworldliness that held me enthralled, but also the evocative silence. Mazurkas and waltzes hung on the air as though the main living room were still echoing with the strains of a family party. Nocturnes wafted in on a scented breeze from the shady garden. The setting lent a visual, tangible dimension to that powerfully emotive music. Above all, the house spoke of peace, the peace of a devoted family which had nurtured that most seductive of Romantic geniuses, the genius for whom, according to his good friend Delacroix, "heaven was jealous of the earth". Like Copernicus, Chopin lived abroad for much of his life. He left Poland in 1830 never to return to his beloved homeland. His requited love for the young Polish girl Maria Wodzi´nska, whom he met in Dresden, was thwarted by her parents, who disapproved of the match on the grounds of Chopin's ill health. Marriage to Maria might have taken him back to Poland. Instead he settled in his father's native country, France, where he formed a tempestuous liaison with the volatile female novelist of licentious repute, George Sand, and died of consumption in 1849 at the age of thirty-nine.

The tragic experience seemed to be the hallmark of that stay in Poland, where so many resonances seemed to touch familiar chords and reveal points of similarity with our own lives. The tragic experience pursued us to the very end, for it was in the scientific company of Claudio Teitelbaum, a young Chilean delegate to the conference, and his wife that strange fleeting poetic memories from my own past resurfaced. Although they were living in Princeton, the Teitelbaums had close connections with the government of President Allende – the newly elected socialist government of Chile – through Claudio's father, who was one of Allende's ambassadors. They were part of the circle of dedicated left-wing reformers which included Pablo

Neruda, the inspired poet at whose feet I had worshipped as an undergraduate. In 1964 Neruda had come to read his poetry at a gathering in King's College, London, and I still carried in my mind the sensual sonority – as rich and evocative as Chopin's music – that he brought to his love poems, caressing and emphasizing their lush strain of natural imagery. Neruda, a communist, was so deeply involved in Chilean politics that the presidency was within his grasp, but he relinquished his ambitions in favour of his friend, Salvador Allende. It was in Cracow, in the bare lounge of the hotel on the last day of the Copernicus meeting, that news reached us of the right-wing military coup against the legitimate Chilean government, allegedly with CIA support. Allende had died in the defence of the Presidential Palace. The Teitelbaums were stunned not only at the death of their much admired President but also at the death of their dreams of reforming the impoverished lives of the oppressed peasants of Chile. They with thousands of others were destined to spend many years in exile. Their destiny was fortunate by comparison with those who did not manage to flee the vicious reprisals exacted by the right-wing Pinochet regime. Two weeks later Pablo Neruda, a Spanish-speaking poet of genius like Lorca before him, died in the aftermath of right-wing revolution.

9

Chekhovian Footfalls

If the impressions I carried from Poland were confusing, Moscow was perversely reassuring in that there was no room for doubt among its citizens about their own political identity or about ours. We knew – and everyone else knew – that the Soviet Union was a totalitarian police state and that there was little to be gained by hankering after a liberal democracy. The Muscovites politely recognized that we came from a privileged society without holding that against us. On the flight between Warsaw and Moscow, Kip warned us to behave as though our hotel room were bugged, not just for our own safety, but for all the colleagues we would be meeting. Stephen had visited Moscow once before, as a student, with a group of Baptists – strange company for one of such forceful atheistic opinions. Even stranger was the fact that he had helped them to smuggle Bibles into Russia in his shoes.

Such reminiscences were hardly appropriate on the present occasion, which had acquired the importance of a high-level official exchange, with all the concomitant VIP treatment. On arrival at the Hotel Rossiya, a massive square block between Red Square and the Moskva River, we glanced round our suite, equipped with samovar and fridge, half-expecting to uncover a microphone strategically placed to record our private thoughts. We did not however resort to the lengths of the diplomat in a joke then circulating: he was said to have pulled up the carpet and snipped at the wires he found beneath it. A loud crash and a horrified shout came from the room below where the chandelier had fallen to the ground.

We had already noticed that the lift bypassed the first floor of the hotel; this was out of bounds and was said to be reserved on all four sides of the hotel, each a quarter of a mile long, for "administration", for which we read "listening devices". Moreover, many of the Russians who had come to meet us at the airport, bearing welcoming bouquets of roses and carnations, were reluctant to enter the hotel beyond the lobby. Significantly in the light of their reticence, Dr Ivanenko, an elderly scientist of modest reputation, was only too pleased to sit in Kip's room for hours at a time, precisely enunciating, as if to hidden ears, all that he had achieved for Soviet science. It was Ivanenko who always accompanied groups of younger Russian astrophysicists to conferences in the West. We generally supposed that he was their minder, especially because they were forever inventing schemes for evading him. His own behaviour could be mysteriously unpredictable. In 1970, while we were at the conference centre at Gwatt in Switzerland, he had disappeared during the course of a boat trip along the shores of Lake Thun, not to be seen again until he turned up sometime later in Moscow.

The purpose of Stephen's visit to Moscow was twofold. Primarily a theoretician, he had begun to dabble in the practical question of black-hole detection. In this he was following the example of an American physicist, Joseph Weber, who had been conducting a solitary struggle to build a machine for catching the minuscule vibrations of the gravitational waves which were predicted to come from stars as they collapsed into black holes. We had spent several afternoons scouring rubbish tips in Cambridge for disused vacuum chambers which might be fitted up, in somewhat Heath-Robinson fashion, with detector bars immersed in liquid nitrogen, to complement Weber's work in Europe. This aspect of black-hole research had also been taken up in Moscow, at the university, by Vladimir Braginsky, an experimental physicist who showed us his laboratory and cheerfully gave me the remnants of a stick of synthetic ruby which he had used in his experiment. He was blessed with an extrovert nature which concealed the extent of his scientific foresight and revealed itself in his penchant for risqué political jokes, even in a semi-public setting. It was Braginsky who at dinner one night kept the company captivated with a torrent of jokes, interspersed with a succession of toasts in vodka and Georgian champagne. Not all his jokes were hysterically funny. Most had a political edge, as for example the joke about transport: an American, an Englishman and a Russian were comparing methods of transport. The American said, "Well of course, we need three cars, one for me, one for my wife and a motorhome for holidays." The Englishman said modestly, "Well, we have a runabout for town-driving and a family car for holidays." The Russian said, "Well, the public transport is very good in Moscow so we don't need a car in town and, when we go on holiday, we go in tanks..."

Stephen had also come to Moscow for conversations with those Russians, many of them Jewish, whose freedom to travel had been severely curtailed. Yakov Borisovich Zel'dovich, a fiery, impetuous character, had been in the forefront of the development of the Soviet atom bomb in the Forties and Fifties. In the late Fifties and early Sixties, like his American counterpart, John Wheeler, he turned his attention to astrophysics, where the conditions inside an imploding star mirrored those of the hydrogen bomb. In consequence Zel'dovich became a foremost authority in black-hole research. However, because of the secrecy surrounding his earlier work, he never expected to be able to emerge from behind the Iron Curtain and come to the West to share fully the international excitement aroused by black holes. The seminal research in imploding stars which his group generated was broadcast to the outside world on his behalf by a rather shy and rather tense younger colleague, Igor Novikov, with whom Stephen developed a strong working relationship.

Like Zel'dovich, Evgeny Lifshitz, also a Jewish physicist in the group, suffered travel restrictions, as did the many gifted students who knew that they would have to wait years before receiving the coveted first travel permit, itself a passport to the rubber-stamping of further permits. Some were voci-ferous and intense, others reserved and pensive. However extrovert some of their personalities might appear to be, it was obvious that they lived under extreme tension in an undercurrent of fear. All were seriously concerned at the restrictions placed on their creativity by incompetent officialdom, and all were afraid of the power of the KGB if they tried to improve their situation.

Kip had many conversations on this theme with his Russian friends, while Stephen and I provided a useful front of social activity. One evening this previously successful ploy backfired. Throughout our stay, our hosts showered us with tickets for the Bolshoi: for the opera, *Boris Godunov*, *Prince Igor*, and for the ballet, *Sleeping Beauty* and *The Nutcracker*. Though Stephen was eager to attend the opera, he was very reluctant about the ballet. Indeed, on the only previous occasion when we had been to the ballet together, to a production of *Giselle* at the Arts Theatre in Cambridge, he complained of a headache in the first act and I had to take him home in the interval, only to find that he made an immediate and miraculous recovery. In Moscow we were consistently in our seats in good time for the opera, but when we arrived at the Bolshoi for *The Nutcracker* the doors were already closing. We were hurriedly ushered into a side aisle and the doors closed smartly behind us. Kip, who had been intending to use the cover of the ballet to escape with a colleague, Vladimir Belinsky, into the streets of Moscow for surreptitious discussions on matters political as well as scientific, found himself trapped. He had come into the theatre to help us settle in, and when the doors closed, he had no option but to sit patiently through the first act of *The Nutcracker* till the interval, while Belinsky waited for him outside in the foyer. At least Stephen had a companion in adversity.

Although we were well aware of these cloak-and-dagger operations lurking in the background, we began to realize that Stephen's scientific colleagues enjoyed in a limited fashion a freedom denied to the rest of the people, the freedom of thought. In its ignorance, Communist officialdom was unable to measure the significance of abstruse scientific research. Consequently it tended to leave scientists in peace as long as they behaved with caution and towed the party line – unless, that is, like Andrei Sakharov, they spoke out openly against the regime on overtly political grounds. Indeed, in his book *Black Holes and Time Warps*, Kip Thorne refers to the unnecessary fear he felt for the Russians, Lifshitz and Khalatnikov, when they courageously wanted to acknowledge the error of their claim that a star cannot create a singularity when it implodes to form a black hole:

> For a theoretical physicist it is more than embarrassing to admit a major error in a published result. It is ego-shattering... Though errors can be shattering for an American or European physicist, in the Soviet Union they were far worse. One's position in the pecking order of scientists was particularly important in the Soviet Union; it determined such things as possibilities for travel abroad and election to the Academy of Sciences, which in turn brought privileges such as near doubling of one's salary and a chauffeured limousine at one's beck and call...

Lifshitz's freedom to travel had already been long curtailed when, to his immense credit and with the greatest urgency, he had persuaded Kip on an earlier visit to Moscow in 1969 to smuggle out a paper retracting the claim and admitting the mistake. The paper was published in the West. As Kip thankfully remarks, "The Soviet authorities never noticed."

Stephen got on well with his Russian colleagues because they shared his intuitive approach to physics. Like him they were concerned only with the crux of any problem; the fine detail did not interest them, and for Stephen, who carried all his theories in his head, fine detail was a hindrance to clarity of thought. Effectively, like him, they discarded all dead wood for a clearer view of the trees. They adapted this approach to whatever subject was under discussion, whether physics or literature. They gave the impression of having stepped out of the past, from the pages of Turgenev, Tolstoy or Chekhov. They talked about art and literature – their own Russian masters and Shakespeare, Molière, Cervantes and Lorca as well. Like my student acquaintances in Franco's Spain, they recited poetry and composed verses for any occasion – including poems in Stephen's honour. To them, it seemed, one more repressive regime meant little, because their country had always been governed by totalitarian regimes and had no experience of democracy, so, like generations of Russians before them, they found their solace in art, music and literature. In a society dominated by *Soviet* materialism, culture was their spiritual resource. Through them, I felt I could touch the soul of the country, the mournful soul of Mother Russia, who always draws her exiled children back to her lonely rolling landscapes of rivers and birch forests. Their personalities shone out of the background of their bleak lives like the golden domes of the well-preserved though no longer functioning churches which would suddenly appear from behind the gaunt concrete blocks of modern Moscow, illuminating the grey dreariness with their gleaming brilliance.

These colleagues seemed just as happy to take us on cultural expeditions as to talk about science. Often our days were a combination of the two: scientific discussions would accompany our sightseeing. We wandered through the golden-domed cathedrals of the Kremlin, purged of their religious function by an officious Communism which nevertheless had not managed to eradicate their air of sanctity. We stood enraptured before the altar walls of icons, and we examined floors of semi-precious stone. We ambled through the art galleries, the Tretyakov and the Pushkin, and made the pilgrimage to Tolstoy's homely wooden house, with its stuffed bear standing on the creaky landing ready to receive visiting cards, and its little room at the back where the great man applied himself to his other passion, shoemaking. From Tolstoy's garden I picked up a handful of fallen maple leaves, rich brown, orange and yellow.

I asked to see a functioning church and was taken both to the extravagantly decorative, red, green and white church of St Nicholas in Moscow and to the Novodevichy Monastery on the outskirts. Despite the wailing chants and the mumbling icon-kissing of the elderly devotees, neither place could convey the essence of holiness with the power of the two decommissioned, empty little churches which stood abandoned outside our window, dwarfed by the bulk of the hotel. One was brick-built, topped by a gold cross; the other was little more than a golden dome. It seemed that in banning organized religion, the Communist regime had actually encouraged the growth of an inner spirituality, which was ever present for those who were receptive to it and alien to those who were not.

In the age of space travel, we were drawn back into the past through the lives of the dignified, poetic individuals with whom we were associating. There were few cars on their roads, their material possessions were scarce and their clothing was drab. Health care was available to them free of charge, but what we saw of it suggested that Soviet hospitals and doctors were to be avoided at all costs. During the second week Stephen needed a dose of hydroxocobalamin, the fortifying vitamin injection which, in Cambridge, Sister Chalmers came to give him every fortnight. With some difficulty, his colleagues persuaded a doctor to come to the hotel. At first glance, I thought that it was Miss Meiklejohn, the terrifying, doughty games mistress from St Albans High School, who had walked into our room. She produced her equipment from a black bag: a steel kidney-shaped bowl, a metal syringe and a selection of reusable needles. We both winced. Stoical as ever, Stephen sat quietly while she jabbed the bluntest of her needles into his thin flesh. Squeamish as ever, I turned away.

The endless, grey-raincoated queues in the shops where our friends bought their food brought back childhood memories of post-war London. Whether in GUM, the state department store on Red Square, or in neighbourhood shops, the system seemed expressly designed to discourage its customers from making any purchases whatsoever. First they had to queue to find out whether the desired items were available on the shelves, then they had to queue to pay for them in advance at the cash desk, and finally, clutching their receipts, they had to return to the original queue to claim their purchases. As privileged foreigners we could shop at the tourist shops, the Berioska shops, which were greedy for our pounds and dollars. There, wooden toys, brightly coloured shawls, amber beads and painted trays abounded. I assumed that all the goods were produced in the Soviet Union until I chanced upon a pair of black leather gloves which bore the label "made by the Co-op, Blackburn, Lancs".

In other Berioska shops, foreign visitors could buy fresh and imported foodstuffs such as grapes, oranges and tomatoes, which for the average Russian were luxuries. If the food produced in the hotel, supposedly a first-class hotel, was any yardstick, the average Russian lived on an erratic subsistence diet of yogurt, ice cream, hard-boiled eggs, black bread and cucumber. Such meat as the hotel managed to provide was usually concealed in minute quantities in floury rissoles, or was so tough and tasteless as to be good only for shoe leather. My smattering of Russian, learnt in an evening class some years previously, was not much help in choosing from the numerous pages of the menu, because once we had made our selection, we would be told that it was "off".

For the first few days, we despaired of getting an edible square meal until one evening we discovered a restaurant, secreted away on the top floor of the hotel, looking out over the red stars on the towers of the Kremlin. We found ourselves sitting near a Frenchman and watched in amazement as his meal was served. With the suave confidence of a Parisian dining in one of the best restaurants in his native city, he embarked on his first course, which consisted of a dish of caviar, smoked fish and cold meats, with a small glass of vodka. Then, while we pushed a flattened piece of chicken swimming in grease around our plates, his main course came to the table. Crisp brown slices of roast potato enveloped a steaming, succulent, baked sturgeon. Enviously we watched him eat, savouring the aromas which wafted in our direction. It was not until he leant back in his chair with a Gallic sigh and a gesture of deep satisfaction that it occured to me that here was somebody with whom I could actually communicate. All I had to do was ask him in French where to find sturgeon and caviar on the menu. Obligingly, he indicated items 32 and 54, thus holding out the delectable promise of an acceptable diet for the rest of our stay. It was our bad luck that the very next day, the top-floor restaurant closed down, and items 32 and 54 never featured on the menus of the other less classy restaurants.

Mistrust of the next meal became a constant preoccupation. However, with some anticipation we looked forward optimistically to one of the supposed highlights of our stay, dinner in the Seventh Heaven revolving restaurant of the Ostankino Tower, a radio tower on the outskirts of the city. The tower, a space-age status symbol, was closely guarded – supposedly because of its strategic importance – and only special guests were allowed to dine there. Even they were not permitted to approach the tower directly, but were frisked at the perimeter fence some fifty yards away, and then led along an underground tunnel to the lift. Cameras were forbidden, we were told, since during the course of its heavenly revolutions, the restaurant passed by a milk factory. For "milk", read "armaments", Kip said. The milk factory came round with disconcerting frequency as we tucked into our first good meal in weeks. Nor was the ride a smooth one – the tower lurched drunkenly halfway through each cycle – which may explain why Stephen and I spent the next twenty-four hours competing for occupation of the bathroom.

It was no surprise to us that our Russian hosts were not at liberty to invite us into their own homes, but there was one notable exception. On our last evening in Moscow we were invited to dinner at the home of Professor Isaac Khalatnikov. Khalatnikov was a beaming, expansive character whom we had first met at the General Relativity Conference in London just before our marriage in 1965. The taxi delivered us to an imposing block of flats, close to the river in the centre of Moscow. We had heard from contemporaries of the difficulties of family life in Moscow. Apartments were scarce. Entitlement to housing depended on one's standing in the Party. Newly-weds frequently had to live with their parents in two-bedroom flats. Later, families would often take in surviving members of the older generation, particularly the babushka, whose presence was well-nigh essential, even in such cramped conditions, because she would generally run the household and care for the children while her daughter or daughter-in-law was out at work. We were astonished therefore to find that the Khalatnikovs' apartment was exceptionally large, consisting of several spacious, well-furnished rooms complete with television and hi-fi. Furthermore the food on the table was a veritable banquet which would not have been out of place at a Western dinner party. The servings of caviar, meat, vegetables, salads and fruit were lavish and tastefully presented. Stephen and I were appreciative but mystified. Why, in a society which trumpeted its equality, did this family enjoy such an ostentatiously indulgent lifestyle? As usual Kip provided the answer: it had nothing whatsoever to do with Isaac Khalatnikov's distinguished scientific status. It was the consequence of his wife's connections. Valentina Nikolaevna, a rather sturdy blonde lady for whom my gift of delicate costume jewellery was singularly inappropriate, was none other than the daughter of a Hero of the Revolution. In a nation where all were said to be equal, some were more equal than others. By virtue of her birth, Valentina Nikolaevna was entitled to all the prerogatives of the new aristocracy, including preferential housing and the right to buy her food in the Berioska shops.

The maple leaves that I had collected from Tolstoy's garden proved to be an eloquent metaphor of the Moscow we saw in those weeks of our visit. It was with genuine relief that we joined in the cheers of the passengers when the London-bound plane took off in a swirling snowstorm in mid-September. Like the snow, the autumn leaves were harbingers of winter in a country where all those freedoms of speech, expression, thought, movement which we took for granted were permanently frozen. Yet their vivid colours sang of our irrepressible friends, those courageous people stranded in that political wasteland. As winter approached in Cambridge, we realized that together with the leaves and the souvenirs, the wooden dancing bears and hand-painted china, we had brought back with us an unwelcome legacy of Soviet oppression. For several weeks after our return, we were unable to communicate freely in our own home for fear that the walls might be listening to us. If this was a measure of the psychological pressure that our friends lived under all the time, our admiration for them could only increase. Thrilled as we were to be back with our children, such a realization was sobering. How, we asked, would we cope in those circumstances?

At Christmas time that year, my mother and I took the children to see the London version of *The Nutcracker* ballet at the Festival Hall. Lucy was entranced by the spectacle and thereafter insisted on being called Clara, like the child heroine of the ballet. She spent every spare minute dancing to a well-worn record and devised her own version of the Cossack dance by running the length of the living room and kicking one small leg in the air before turning and racing back to the other end. Like father, like son, Robert was less enchanted by the performance and would have preferred his father's favourite Christmas-time treat, the pantomime. He fidgeted his way through the first half of the ballet, and no sooner had the second half begun than he dragged his grandma out of the auditorium on the irrefutable pretext of having drunk too much orange squash in the interval. They were not allowed to return to their seats so my mother had to make do with a closed-circuit screening of the rest of the performance in the foyer, while Robert contentedly watched the barges plying up and down the Thames.

10

A Chill Wind

That winter in Cambridge we faced our own set of pressures, though not of a political nature. The conference in Poland and the visit to Moscow, combined with the previous year's discoveries at Les Houches, had opened up new possibilities and new problems for black-hole research. The secret aim of all physicists was to uncover the philosopher's stone, the as yet unformulated unified field theory, which would unite all the branches of physics. It would reconcile the large-scale structure of the universe – about which Stephen and George Ellis had written a book – with the small-scale structures of quantum mechanics or elementary particle physics, and the theory of electromagnetism. Black holes held out the tantalizing prospect that they might be the key to the first stage of this particular quest – in the enigmatic resemblance between general relativity and thermodynamics contained in their laws.

Such was the lure of this goal that not only was Stephen intent on following up his Moscow discussions with consultations worldwide at every available conference, he increasingly spent his every waking hour immersed in such deliberations. The question of travels abroad came up with disturbing regularity. I repeated the canon of my excuses, but it sounded feeble to claim that the strain of leaving the children was too great when the future of physics was at stake.

At the same time, I was confused by Stephen's tendency to spend quite so many hours in the evenings and at weekends, like Rodin's *Thinker* with his head bent low resting on his right hand, transported to another dimension, lost to me and to the children playing around him. However compelling the intellectual challenge of black-hole physics, I could not fathom such depths of self-absorption. I would at first suppose that he was engrossed in a mathematical problem, so I would cheerfully ask him what was on his mind, but often he would not reply, and I would quickly become anxious. Perhaps he was uncomfortable in his wheelchair or not feeling well, I would enquire. Had I upset him perhaps by refusing to go to the next conference? As he still would not reply, or merely gave an unconvincing shake of the head, my imagination would run riot as I began to suspect that all these factors and many more, not least dejection at his deteriorating condition, were oppressing him unbearably. The position he adopted was, after all, one traditionally used by artists to depict depression.

Undeniably his speech was becoming indistinct, necessitating boring sessions with a speech therapist to try and redress the slur. Some people, whom we preferred to think of as deaf or stupid, could not understand him at all. He required my help with the minutiae of every personal need, dressing and bathing, as well as with larger movements. He had to be lifted bodily in and out of the wheelchair, the car, the bath and the bed. Food had to be cut into small morsels so that he could eat with a spoon, and mealtimes were protracted. The stairs in our house were now a major obstacle. He could still pull himself up – that in itself was recommended exercise – but he needed to have someone standing behind him for reassurance. It was natural that when away from home, he wanted to have me with him all the time. Pent-up guilt at my own reluctance to take advantage of all those opportunities to travel the globe, and frustration at the lack of communication, would tie me in knots of anxiety and despair. I felt like that traveller who had fallen into a black hole: stretched, tugged and pulled like a piece of spaghetti by uncontrollable forces.

A couple of days later, Stephen would emerge from his isolation. With a triumphant smile, he would announce that he had solved yet another major problem in physics. It was only after the event that these episodes became a joke. As each new situation was marginally different from the previous one, I never learnt to recognize the symptoms. At the time I always worried that Stephen might really be feeling unwell. Each time I would compliment him on his success, but secretly I realized that the children and I had joined battle with that irresistible goddess, first encountered in America in 1965, the goddess of Physics, who deprived children of their fathers and wives of their husbands. After all, I remembered that Mrs Einstein had cited Physics as the third party in her divorce proceedings.

For Stephen those periods of intense concentration may have been useful exercises in cultivating that silent, inner strength which would enable him to think in eleven dimensions. Unable to tell whether it was oblivion or indifference to my need to talk that sealed him off so hermetically, I found those periods sheer torture, especially when, as sometimes happened, they were accompanied by long sessions of Wagnerian opera, particularly *The Ring Cycle*, played at full volume on the radio or the record player. It was then, as I felt my own voice stifled and my own spontaneity suppressed inside me, that I grew to hate Wagner. The music was powerful, so powerful that I was irresistibly drawn into the sensual luxury of those hypnotizing chords and thrilling modulations, but my daily round did not allow me a single moment's respite from the unending demands of shopping, cooking, housework, childcare and Stephencare. From the kitchen or the bathroom, or even the playroom on the top floor, I would be all too conscious of the inveigling power of the music, insinuating itself through enthralling harmonies and discords. I would try to disregard its beckoning, ambiguous strains, knowing it to be far too manipulative for my confused state of mind. The open clarity of Mediterranean culture was my touchstone, not the dark menace of northern myth, where all heroes were doomed to premature death and chaos and evil triumphed. Stephen might be as bewitched by this force as he was by physics – since both for him had become a religion – but I had to keep my feet on the ground. If I allowed myself to yield to the sombre tyranny of that music, the structure I had built around me would collapse and crumble to dust. Wagner came to represent an evil genius, the philosopher of the master race, the demon behind Auschwitz, and potentially an alienating force. I was simply too young to be able to cope with so much emotional pressure.

Thankfully our diet of entertainment was not limited to Wagner, but was vastly eclectic. It ranged from Wagner, inescapably, and Verdi and Mozart in the opera houses, through performances of the Elgar oratorios in King's College Chapel and Monteverdi Vespers in St Albans Abbey, to *Princess Ida* at the Arts Theatre – since, truly broad in his tastes, Stephen was a Gilbert and Sullivan fan as well as a Wagnerian. Apart from Wagner, his favourite entertainments however were the Footlights, the university review in summer, and the pantomime in winter. For both of these he suspended his usually acerbic critical judgement. I often found the Footlights tedious, since the standard of humour never quite matched up to the unrealistic expectations aroused by the *Beyond the Fringe* generation, and as for the pantomime, the smutty jokes wore thin through constant sniggering repetition.

To occupy those other solitary evenings at home when Stephen was immersed in thought but Wagner was mercifully suppressed, when the trappings of the day were cleared away and the children finally in bed, I bought a very compact piano on the pretext that Robert should start having lessons. In an environment where everyone was so naturally accomplished, it was embarrassing to admit that I really wanted to have lessons myself. I took some lessons with a retired schoolteacher who, sympathizing with my ambitions, sensitively refrained from telling me that I was too old to learn to play. Rising to the challenge, he trained me in the basics of theory and harmony and, to my satisfaction, allowed me to choose my own repertoire. Robert also had lessons – with a young teacher who drew pictures for him of fairies dancing in the treble clef and giants stomping about in the bass.

Since he had started school, Robert, previously so happy and lively, was becoming much quieter and more reserved. He was only four and a quarter when, in line with local education policy, he was obliged to start school. I was convinced that this was too early. Some time later I read that the psychological difference between a four-year-old and a five-year-old is the same as the difference between a seven-year-old and an eleven-year-old, and that starting school at such a young age is actually damaging to a child's development. Robert was a shy little boy and, when asked what he did in the lunch hour his reply, casually delivered, made me very sad. "Oh," he said with a shrug, "I just sit on the steps." His primary school had an excellent reputation for bringing out the best in fast-learning children from academic backgrounds, and was essentially a literary school where those children who could read quickly made rapid progress. Some years later Lucy, bubbling with creative and literary talent, flourished there. Robert however had great difficulty in reading. I feared that this might be a delayed effect of the medicine-swallowing episode, but my mother-in-law's comments were comforting. It was obvious that Robert was just a chip off the old block, she said, because Stephen had not learnt to read until he was seven or eight years old. I then fully understood why the winter spent by the Hawkings with the Graves family in Majorca had left such an unhappy impression on Stephen. If at the age of nine he had only just learnt to read, the daily sessions spent analysing the Book of Genesis under the eagle eye of Robert Graves must have been grim. Stephen wisely maintained that it did not matter what Robert read so long as he learnt to read, whereupon we plied Robert with the *Beano* and every imaginable joke book, so that each mealtime was accompanied with interminable jokes of the "Knock, knock", "Who's there?" variety and Robert's reading improved dramatically.

Dyslexia was not a condition that was recognized in educational circles in the early Seventies. Nowadays it is claimed that both Leonardo da Vinci and Einstein were probably dyslexic. We suspected that Stephen was dyslexic and were fairly sure that Robert was too, but, apart from a remedial reading class, there was no specific help for dyslexics in the state system. They were classed at best as lazy, at worst as backward, slow learners, already at the age of five, consigned to a second-rate future. I knew that Robert was not backward: this was the child who at the age of four, when we were gardening one afternoon, had asked quite seriously, "Mummy, who was God born inside?" This was the child who, at five, had sat down at the piano to explain the concept of minus numbers to me. "Look, Mummy," he said, "all these notes going up from middle C are plus numbers and all the ones going down from middle C are minus numbers."

I was sure that the emphasis that the school placed on literary rather than numerical skills was wrong for Robert. A new teacher who came to the school when he was just six announced that she was going to start an advanced maths group. I pleaded with her to let him join the group. She clearly found it hard to not to laugh. "But he can't read!" she remonstrated, "How can he possibly do maths?" I persevered, "Please just let him try." With the greatest scepticism, she agreed to let him join the class for three weeks. During those three weeks Robert did not appear to be having any trouble with the advanced maths and he seemed much less tense. At the end of the three weeks, he brought a message home from the new teacher, saying that she would like to talk to me after school. She came out to meet me at the school gate. "Mrs Hawking, I owe you an apology," she began fulsomely, "I really didn't think that Robert would be able to cope with the advanced maths when you asked me to let him come into the class, but I really must apologize because I was so wrong. He is extraordinarily good at maths, and is way ahead of all the others." But the maths class came to an untimely end after only two terms when the teacher left to have a baby, and then Robert was back at square one. As Stephen and I had blithely assumed that, in accordance with our socialist principles, our children would be educated in state schools, we were now presented with a resounding clash of loyalties because the needs of our child were not compatible with our political principles. The state system had not served Robert well so far. He needed to be praised for the subjects he could do well, particularly maths, and he needed encouragement, not castigation, in those he found difficult, particularly reading and writing. Only in the private sector could we be sure that the classes would be small enough for him to receive proper attention. The sonorously entitled Fellowship for Distinction in Science did not pay a large enough salary for us to be able to afford private education, nor did the Research Assistantships to which Stephen was subsequently appointed – at the Institute of Astronomy in 1972 after Fred Hoyle's departure, and also at the Department of Applied Mathematics in 1973. But by another of those ironic twists of fate, the finance became available – in a way that we regretted.

In 1970, shortly after Lucy's birth, Stephen's lonely Aunt Muriel had died. Instead of enjoying her new-found freedom after her mother's death, she had simply wasted away. The money she might have spent on herself, by going off on a round-the-world trip for instance, she saved cautiously to provide for the uncertainties of the future. The future never came and the money was left to some of her great-nephews and nieces, among them Robert on whom she particularly doted. Of itself, the inheritance was not sufficient to finance long years of education, but when set to work with an equal share from Stephen's father, it amounted to enough to buy a small house which could be let out quite profitably. Half the rent went to Stephen's parents while the other half contributed substantially to Robert's school fees. Cambridge was a good place for such a venture, because properties were still fairly cheap and the floating population of visiting scholars meant that there was a constant demand for rented properties. With my experience of renovating our own house, I was put in charge of the project. Buying and renovating another house and then letting it became an additional burden when my hands and my time were already full. The insight it gave me into the squalor of other people's lives was disheartening, but since I was all too conscious of the need to save money for the ever-mounting school fees, I had no option but to take up the paintbrush for an intensive week of solo decorating once or twice a year. Sometimes this exercise had to be carried out even more frequently to satisfy summer visitors.

Such taxing activity and wearing preoccupations left less and less time and energy for the thesis. I had succeeded in assembling material for the first chapter and had come up with a few original ideas of my own. I traced some close verbal reminiscences between the *kharjas* and the *Song of Solomon*, and I detected striking similarities between the *kharjas* and the Mozarabic hymns, the hymns of the native Christian populace under Moorish domination. With luck, all other things being equal, I might be able to snatch an hour for the thesis in the morning, while Lucy was at nursery school after I had taken Stephen to the Department. Keeping up with my own research stretched me to the limit. There was no longer any chance of broadening my grasp of other areas of medieval research, let alone investigating the other fields and topics which came up for discussion at the Lucy Cavendish dinners. I was out of touch with the political and international scene and had scant time for reading. I had little to offer and little to gain, other than a depressing awareness of my own inadequacy, from either Lucy Cavendish or the Dronkes' medieval seminars. When I did attend one or the other, I had to bluff my way through discussions and conversations or else maintain a dull silence. It was an uncomfortable situation in which I felt a fraud, and my attendance at both lapsed.

In Lucy Cavendish, I had just one friend, Hanna Scolnicov, with whom I felt at ease. Hanna, an Elizabethan scholar from Jerusalem, was enjoying the respite which she found in Cambridge from the tensions of her war-torn homeland. Hanna and I discovered that we had much in common. Although our circumstances were inevitably disparate, we were both trying to live normal lives and bring up our three-year-olds, Robert and Anat, against a background of tension and uncertainty. When we met, I had just given birth to Lucy and Hanna was expecting her second child. By the time Ariel was born the following summer, we had become friends for life. Moreover, in Hanna's husband, Shmuel, a classical philosopher, Stephen had found an intellectual sparring partner. Both Hanna and Shmuel were so much more intuitive and perceptive than many people who had known us longer and supposedly better. When Shmuel's sabbatical year came to an end and they nervously returned to Israel with their young family, there was even less incentive for me to attend Lucy Cavendish, and I became even more isolated and out of touch.

It did not matter much. Stephen's career was so obviously more important than mine. He was bound to make a big splash in the pond of physics, whereas I would be lucky to make the smallest ripple on the surface of language studies. And, as I reminded myself often, I did have the consolation of the children, both of them lively and funny, loving and adorable. Many people who might well have stared cruelly at Stephen, absorbed by the freakishness of disability – the same people who would have called him a cripple – were visibly nonplussed by the sight of a seriously handicapped father with such strikingly beautiful children, each one a miracle of lucid perfection. Stephen gained confidence through his pride in them. He could confound those doubting onlookers by announcing, "These are my children." The acute joy that we shared in their purity and innocence, their quaint sayings and their sense of wonder, gave us in turn moments of profound tenderness. In those moments, the bond between us strengthened till it embraced not just ourselves but our home and our family, reaching out to include all those people we valued most. The family, our family, had become my *raison d'être*.

I comforted myself that no amount of academic recognition could have equalled the creative fulfilment I derived from my family. If sometimes the long hours of childcare and baby talk seemed unremitting, I was well compensated by the privilege of rediscovering the world, its wonders and inconsistencies, through the eyes of small children. Happily my parents also delighted in this pleasure. Never were grandparents so keen to enjoy their grandchildren, and never were grandchildren so indulged by their grandparents. The children brought my parents some light relief from their own anxieties, which were focused on my grandmother, whose health and memory were failing fast. When eventually she moved to St Albans from her home in Norwich, it was too late for her to settle with confidence anywhere else, and all too soon, in her disorientation, she fell and broke an arm. I already knew when I waved goodbye to her one Sunday afternoon in early December 1973, that I should never see her again. I wept all week for that brave, gentle spirit whom I loved so much. It came as a great sorrow but no surprise when my mother rang the following Friday, 7th December, to tell me that she had died in her sleep.

11

Balancing Act

The gradual disappearance of close friends from our social scene did nothing to alleviate my flagging spirits. My school friends and college friends I saw rarely; either they had gone abroad or were raising families in other cities. The friends of the past few years were branching out, leaving Cambridge to climb the career ladder wherever the jobs happened to be. Rob Donovan, who had been Stephen's best man at our wedding, had with his wife Marian and their little daughter Jane left Cambridge for Edinburgh. Thereafter our contact with them was sporadic, though when we were able to meet, the strength of our friendship resumed in as lively and stimulating a manner as ever. We stayed with them outside Edinburgh in the summer of 1973, just before the planned trip to Moscow. As always in the company of old friends, our conversations ranged far and wide, recalling those Sunday afternoon visits soon after our marriage. We would gossip about the Cambridge scene, the latest convulsions in Gonville and Caius, developments in science, the complexity of grant applications and friends dispersed across the globe.

When we spoke of the Moscow trip, Rob insisted that we should not be lulled by lack of media coverage into supposing that in the post-Cuban Missile Crisis era the arms race had disappeared into the attic of history. Surreptitiously, both superpowers were developing a huge array of ever more sophisticated weaponry. Although the threat of nuclear warfare still hung over us all each time the superpowers, like snarling dragons, caught a whiff of each other's presence in some contested corner of the world, the fact that they were actually enlarging and refining their already enormous nuclear arsenals was not widely publicized. Rob's remarks worried and angered me. Now that we had children it was not enough to say that there would be consolation in all being blown up together. I was not prepared to stand back and let that monstrous apocalypse destroy the lives of my precious offspring. But what could I – or we – do? There was little use in appealing to the scientists who had developed these weapons in the Forties and Fifties – many of whom were known to us on both sides of the Iron Curtain – because the decisions were now in the hands of untrustworthy politicians, the devious Nixon in the United States and the inscrutable Brezhnev in the Soviet Union. It was almost harder to digest these unpalatable truths against the pristine background of Scotland's purple-headed mountains, where the honey-laden air sang of biblical simplicity, than in any man-made urban setting.

The Carters, Brandon and Lucette, with whom we also used to spend so many weekend afternoons, had moved to France with their baby daughter, Catherine. Brandon had taken up a research post at the Observatoire de Paris at Meudon. The Observatoire was set in the grounds of a château, rather like its Cambridge counterpart, and commanded magnificent views over Paris. I missed Lucette greatly for many reasons, quite apart from the fact that she was the only person I knew in Cambridge with whom I could speak French. A respected mathematician, she was clever and articulate without ever being pretentious. Her sincere interest in people and her enthusiastic sense of family were not typical of the Cambridge academics with whom she had mixed. She was musical, imaginative and blessed with a delicate sense of poetry. It was Lucette who through her rhapsodic delight in the trees and flowers, colours and perfumes of the churchyard, introduced me to Proust.

The greatest shock came with the loss of the Ellises. Their departure was especially distressing because they were not leaving Cambridge simply to go to another job, but because their marriage had ended. We identified so closely with them that when George and Sue separated, our own family seemed to be under threat. Our two families, each with two small children, had shared so much that we had become part of each other's support system. Sue was Lucy's godmother. We had bought and renovated our houses, had our babies, gone on holiday and attended conferences, almost in tandem. On the one hand, George and Stephen had written a book together, *The Large-Scale Structure of Space-Time*, and on the other, Sue and I had conferred and confided in each other over many of the crises of motherhood and the struggle to compete with the goddess Physics. George and Stephen were alike in that they could cut themselves off from the basic realities of the outside world, plunging out of the reach of their families deep into the realms of the theoretical universe. The many shared and parallel experiences had built an interdependence into our marriages, and when theirs failed, the solidity of ours was shaken.

All those friendships with couples who had now left Cambridge had been formed in special circumstances. They were the product of Stephen's contacts in the Department or in one or other of the colleges. He had shared interests, usually scientific, with the husbands while I discovered common interests with their wives. On the departure of the Ellises, our very close, foursome friendships petered out. Although we were on good terms with many of the younger Fellows of Caius and their wives and had made new friends among the more recent postgraduates in the Department, a subtle change occurred. I made many female friends through the children, but the husbands and fathers of those families did not necessarily have much in common with Stephen, and they were understandably deterred by the difficulties of communication. Moreover I tended to make friends among people with whom there was a perceptible bond of sympathy. They either had cause for sorrow in their own lives or they had some special knowledge of the needs of the disabled. Of all those several valuable friendships, two in particular, the most loyal and the most lasting, had very relevant points of contact with Stephen.

Among Constance Willis's team of assistants – "Daddy's exercisers" as Robert called them – there was a slim, fair-haired girl of about my own age, Caroline Chamberlain. In the summer of 1970 Caroline ceased to practise as a physiotherapist because she was expecting a baby at the same time as I was expecting Lucy. As she lived nearby in the Leys School – the local boys' public school where her husband taught geography – we kept in touch and were brought into closer friendship after our daughters were born. My mind was focused ever more intensely on the problems of disability, for it sometimes seemed that a trap was closing over all of us, over the children and me as well as over Stephen. Information was pretty well non-existent and I began to depend on Caroline's fund of professional knowledge for guidance. At once practical and cheerful yet very sensitive, she was well aware of the array of difficulties we faced at every turn and, despite all the pressures of being a housemaster's wife, would do her best to come up with an answer, be it a more comfortable posture, an item of equipment – such as a wheelchair cushion or a caliper – or the address of some useful pioneering organization.

At the school gate, that traditional meeting place for mothers, I found another stalwart friend in Joy Cadbury, whose children, Thomas and Lucy, were the same age as Robert and our Lucy. Joy's retiring gentleness confounded my perceived image of an Oxford graduate. Far from vaunting her intellectual prowess at the expense of others, she played it down as if it were of absolutely no relevance to her present lifestyle. The daughter of a Devon doctor, she had fulfilled her real ambition – to become a pediatric nurse – after graduating from Oxford. Joy took our situation deeply to heart, always ready to take the children off my hands in times of crisis, always ready to give an unobtrusive hand when the strain was overwhelming. She was not unfamiliar with motor-neuron disease, the incurable degenerative illness about which so little was known, because two hundred and fifty miles away her own elderly father was suffering its terminal stages.

In Devon, not far from Joy's family home, I had other allies in my brother and his wife Penelope. After Chris's first temporary job in Brighton, they had moved to Devon when Chris joined a dental practice in Tiverton. Artistic by nature and interested in character and relationships, Penelope understood my need to talk about personalities, influences and emotions and the ways people communicated with each other – subjects which in the Hawking family were virtually proscribed. In Chris and his wife I found a deep well of understanding and support; the drawback was that they lived so far away.

Not all new acquaintances could afford to bring me the encouragement which I found in Caroline, Joy and my relations. Some of my new friends were as marginalized as I was, though in different ways. Often they themselves needed support and turned to me for help. From the vantage point of the physical illness which dominated our lives and which was so immediately obvious and clearly defined, I had only occasionally in the past glimpsed other tragedies. With greater maturity I began to awaken to the many causes and complications of suffering. Some people were struggling with their emotions and with poverty after a traumatic divorce, others were alienated from their families, others were simply a long way from home. These situations and many others I could regard with a certain objectivity, and I tried to give some sort of sensible encouragement to the people experiencing them. Ironically the situations which were closer to my own were much harder to deal with.

Some well-intentioned friends promised to introduce me to a nurse whose husband was suffering from multiple sclerosis. I looked forward to this meeting, hoping that we might be able to bring each other the consolation of shared experience. It was hard even to mention the problems – the crushing responsibility, the emotional strain, the aching fatigue of bringing up two small children unaided at the same time as caring for a seriously disabled person who was wasting away before one's very eyes – without pangs of disloyalty. Stephen never talked about the illness, but nor did he ever complain. His heroic stoicism increased my sense of guilt at even giving voice to the slightest misgivings. But it was the very lack of communication that was hardest to bear, sometimes harder than all the physical stresses and strains combined. Whereas I had originally hoped that there would be fulfilment in unity of purpose, in fighting together against the odds stacked so heavily against us, it seemed that now I was little more than a drudge, effectively reduced to that role which in Cambridge academic circles epitomized a woman's place. Fundamentally I knew that I needed help – physical help and emotional support – in keeping my beloved family going.

Just once I summoned the courage to broach my woes – with the utmost caution – to Thelma Thatcher. Her response, if not a rebuff, was decisive in its severity. "Jane," she said, "I say to you what I always say when things cannot be altered: count your blessings." Her answer was honest and she was right. I had much to be thankful for – not least, my family and Stephen's dedicated hard work and courage. I was not destitute and I had no alternative but to accept my chosen lot, keep faith, work hard and make the best of it – as, I found out, Thelma herself had to do on losing her two infant sons. After all I was not unhappy: I derived intense happiness from the two most beautiful and enchanting children anybody could wish for – Robert with his silvery blond hair, neat round face and wide enquiring eyes, and Lucy, auburn-haired with a pink and white skin as soft as swansdown. I was just tired, exhausted from broken nights, back-breaking physical strain and the constant nagging sense of worry and responsibility. I was ashamed at having even attempted to unburden myself, and slunk away to count my blessings.

Practical as ever, Thelma called by the next day. "I've been thinking, dear, you must have more help. I'm just going to call on Constance Babington-Smith, shall I ask her to send her cleaning woman along to you?" Constance Babington-Smith's cleaning lady, bustling Mrs Teversham, was a treasure of the first order, as was her successor a year or so later, tall, angular Winnie Brown. Once a week, cleanliness and order were restored to our household. However, the housework was but a part of the problem. I still needed a sympathetic listener, someone who would patiently listen to my intimate anxieties with understanding and without reprimand. I was not expecting the flourish of a magic wand suddenly to put everything to rights, but I did cherish the hope that perhaps the new contact, the woman with the disabled husband, would be the person who would listen and respond with more understanding than anyone else, and possibly might be able to suggest ways of dealing with some of the practical difficulties of caring more or less single-handedly with severe disability. It was not to be. By the time we met she was on the point of departure for the USA with a new partner, leaving her husband in a home for the disabled.

Thelma Thatcher's stark philosophy of counting one's blessings was the only valid course open to me. I had pledged myself to Stephen. In so doing I had committed myself to trying to provide him with a normal life. It was beginning to appear that that pledge meant keeping up a façade of normality, however abnormal life might become for the rest of us in the process. I had no intention of reneging on my pledge, but isolated glimpses into the lives of others – such as the one I had just experienced – served to emphasize rather than alleviate my consuming isolation. Long ago we had discovered that there was no organization, no medical authority to whom we could turn for enlightened advice and assistance. Now, since there was no one to whom I could turn for personal support in finding a path through the maze of problems, I resolved to trust my own counsel, steering well clear of unsettling people and situations, pretending more than ever that ours was just a normal family, beset with a difficulty which was best kept confined to the background.

12

Event Horizons

One dark, windy evening – 14th February 1974 – I drove Stephen over to Oxford to a conference at the Rutherford Laboratory on the site of the Atomic Energy Research Establishment at Harwell. We stayed in the Cozener's House at Abingdon, an old country house on the banks of the Thames, which that winter was in flood. The rain pouring from heavy skies did not dampen our spirits, for Stephen and I – and a handful of his students – were tense with excitement, anticipating a momentous occasion: Stephen was about to produce a new theory. At last he had reached a resolution of the black-hole mechanics versus thermodynamics paradox which had been troubling him since the summer school at Les Houches. He had been spurred into obsessive calculation by the vexatious doubts cast on his earlier conclusions by a Princeton student of John Wheeler's – who had been so struck by the similarity between the laws of thermodynamics and Stephen's 1971 black-hole result that he claimed that the laws of thermodynamics and the laws governing black holes were actually the same laws. In Stephen's opinion, this claim was absurd, since to obey the laws of thermodynamics, black holes would have to have a finite temperature and would have to radiate; that is to say, the two sets of laws would have to coincide in all aspects, not just one. In his resolution of the question, Stephen's elaboration was innovative beyond all expectation.

Those intense periods of total concentration, which the children and I had witnessed, had led him to the conclusion that, contrary to all previously held theories on black holes, a black hole could radiate energy. As the hole radiates, it evaporates, losing mass and energy. Proportionately its temperature and surface gravity increase as it shrinks to the size of a nucleus, still weighing between a thousand and 100 million tons. Finally, at an unimaginable temperature, it disappears in a massive explosion. Thus black holes were no longer to be considered impenetrably black and their activity could be seen to obey, rather than conflict with, the laws of thermodynamics. The long gestation of this particular infant had been cloaked in secrecy. For my part, I felt a certain vested interest in attending its birth since its rivalry for Stephen's attentions had already caused me much heartache. Bernard Carr was to act as assistant midwife, projecting a transcript of Stephen's lecture on slides to the audience.

On the morning of the lecture, I sat outside the lecture hall in the tea room, idly flicking through a newspaper while waiting for Stephen's session to begin at 11 a.m. My concentration was interrupted by the raucous chatter of a gaggle of charladies in the far corner. Their spoons clinked noisily against the side of their cups as they stirred their coffee, and their cigarettes filled the room with smoke. Irritatingly their gossip was as pervasive as the smoke from their cigarettes, and I found myself compelled to listen as they mulled over the conference and the delegates. To my bewilderment, one of them observed to her two companions, "And there's one of them there, that young chap, he's living on borrowed time, isn't he?" Momentarily I could not think whom they meant. "Oh, yes," one of her companions agreed, "a right state he's in, looks as if he's falling apart at the seams, can hardly hold his head up." She laughed a light callous laugh, amused at her own comic invention. It reminded me of a comment Frank Hawking, already white-haired and seventy years old, had once made in my hearing to the effect that Stephen was likely to die before he did. That had shaken my sense of security and then as now, the offhand condemnation of Stephen behind his back and the dismissal of our vision for the future had made me smart in silence.

When Stephen came rolling out of the lecture hall in his wheelchair, ready for a quick coffee before embarking on his lecture, I scrutinized him carefully from head to foot. He was alive certainly – alive with excitement and anticipation – but I had to ask myself if he really looked as if he were living on borrowed time, and if he were really falling apart at the seams. I had to concede that, to a casual observer, he probably did, and that concession to outside perceptions made me very sad. Fortunately such concerns could not have been further from his mind. Firmly rooted in the physical world and as unaware as Don Quixote of unkind scepticism at his appearance and purpose, he was ready to charge into battle accompanied by his faithful Sancho Panza, Bernard Carr. Still shaken, I followed them into the lecture hall. I comforted myself with the reflection that those cleaning women had only seen the pitiable state of the frail body and were ignorant of the power of the mind and the strength of the spirit, conveyed so eloquently in that imperious cranium and those fine, intelligent eyes. My conviction that Stephen was immortal was nonetheless reeling from yet another blow.

With exquisite irony, Stephen reaffirmed his immortality in that very lecture, although at the time the chairman and some of the audience gave the impression that they thought that he had taken leave of his senses. I sat on the edge of my seat as I listened to Stephen, hunched in his chair under the lights on the stage, and read the slides which Bernard brought up on the overhead projector, clarifying the substance of Stephen's faint whispering speech. In effect the lecture was given twice, once by Stephen himself and again by the slides, so there was not the slightest doubt about the message: black holes were not as black as they seemed.

Despite the clarity of the presentation, silence reigned as the lecture came to an end. The audience seemed to be having difficulty digesting that simple message. The chairman, Professor John G. Taylor, of King's College, London, did not remain silent for long however. Aghast at this heretical attack on the gospel of the black hole, he sprang to his feet, blustering, "Well, this is quite preposterous! I have never heard anything like it. I have no alternative but to bring this session to an immediate close!" His behaviour seemed to *me* to be quite preposterous, reminiscent in fact of Eddington's attack on Chandrasekhar in 1933, except that Eddington had used "absurd" rather than "preposterous" to describe Chandrasekhar's theory. Not only is it usual for a chairman to allow time for questions after a lecture, it is also a commonly accepted courtesy that he should thank the speaker for his "extremely stimulating talk". J.G. Taylor (not to be confused with Professor J.C. Taylor, the particle physicist who, with his wife Mary, was to become a close friend some years later) extended neither of these courtesies to Stephen; rather he gave the impression that he would willingly have had him burnt at the stake for heresy. This conscious insult to Stephen was as intolerable as the cleaning ladies' mindless remarks. It implied a deliberate attempt to belittle him, suggesting that he had now proven himself to be incapacitated mentally as well as physically.

Whereas in the lecture hall one could have heard a pin drop, in the refectory after the lecture there was uproar. It was as if particles from radiating black holes were spinning in all directions, knocking the delegates sideways like skittles. Bernard settled Stephen quietly at a corner table while I went to queue at the counter for food. Still blustering and indignantly muttering to his students, J.G. Taylor stood behind me in the queue, unaware of my identity. I was rehearsing a few cutting remarks in Stephen's defence when I heard him splutter, "We must get that paper out straight away!" I thought better of drawing attention to myself and went to report what I had heard to Stephen. Although he shrugged in a good-humoured way, he sent his own paper off to *Nature* immediately on our return to Cambridge. Since it was reviewed for the magazine by none other than J.G. Taylor, it was no surprise that it was rejected. Stephen then requested that it should be sent to an independent referee and, on the second time of asking, it was accepted. J.G. Taylor's paper was also accepted but died a natural death, while Stephen's marked the first step along the road towards the unification of physics, the reconciliation of the large-scale structure of the universe with the small-scale structure of the atom – through the medium of the black hole. Undoubtedly the Rutherford experience served also to reinforce Stephen's determination to fight against all odds, whether physical or in physics. The same experience left me proud but perturbed by the many hidden undercurrents it had revealed. The theory of the evaporation of black holes paved the way for Stephen's election to the Royal Society the following spring at the unprecedentedly early age of thirty-two. In the seventeenth century Fellows had been elected as young as twelve years old, but that was in the days when privilege rather than merit ensured election. In the more recent past a Fellowship was an honour to which scientists aspired towards the end rather than the beginning of their careers, usually after acquiring a handful of honorary doctorates and serving on a few advisory scientific committees along the way. It is the crowning glory of a scientific career, second only in prestige to a Nobel Prize.

We were informed of the election in mid-March, a couple of weeks in advance of the official announcement, giving me time to arrange a surprise celebration. I planned a champagne reception in the dignified setting of the Senior Parlour in Caius, to which Stephen's family, friends and colleagues were invited, and I prepared a buffet dinner for a smaller, more intimate group of family and friends at home afterwards. There was no more fitting occasion on which to open the two bottles of Château Lafitte 1945 which had appeared a couple of years back on the Caius Fellows' wine list at the remarkable – though erroneous – price of forty-five shillings a bottle. The number of guests for the dinner party was limited therefore not by the capacity of the house nor by the amount of crockery we possessed, but by the quantity of extremely rare old claret in the two bottles, just enough for everyone to have a taste.

On the evening of 22nd March 1974, Stephen's students diplomatically steered him in the direction of the College where he was cheered as a conquering hero by friends and family, students and colleagues. The children did their best to pass round plates of canapés, caviar toasts, vol-au-vents and the miniature smoked salmon and asparagus rolls in which the Caius catering department excelled. Dennis Sciama agreed to propose the toast to Stephen and this he did very generously, listing all Stephen's many scientific achievements which, he said, would have more than justified his faith in him without this culminating honour of the Fellowship of the Royal Society. The children and I stood together in a glow of pride.

It was Stephen's turn to reply. It was a measure of the change in him since our marriage that he was well accustomed to making speeches in public these days but, of course, on this occasion the party had come as a surprise and he had had no chance to prepare what he was going to say. He actually made quite a long speech, speaking slowly and clearly, though faintly. He talked about the course of his research and the unexpected way in which it had developed over the past ten years or so, since coming to Cambridge. He thanked Dennis Sciama for his support and inspiration, and he thanked his friends for coming to the party, talking as was his habit always in terms of "I" not "we". With my arms round each of the children, I waited at the side of the room for him to turn towards us with a smile, a nod, just a brief word of recognition for the domestic achievements of the nine years of our marriage. It may have been a mere oversight in the excitement of the moment that he did not mention us at all. He finished speaking to general applause, while I bit my lip to conceal my disappointment.

In the very week of the publication of the Royal Society Fellowship list, Stephen received an approach – no doubt instigated by Kip Thorne – from Caltech, the California Institute of Technology in Pasadena, inviting him to take up the offer of a visiting Fellowship for the following academic year. The offer was lavish in the extreme. Quite apart from a salary on an American scale, it included a large, fully furnished house rent-free, the use of a car and all possible aids and appurtenances, including an electrically powered wheelchair to allow Stephen maximum independence. Physiotherapy and medical care would be arranged for him, and schooling for the children. Stephen's students, Bernard Carr and Peter De'Ath, were also invited to accompany him. We needed a change, a change that would bring us a renewal of commitment, a new perspective and a fresh impetus. A change would be good for the children, too, and this was an appropriate time to make it. Lucy had not yet started school and Robert would be moving out of the state system the following year. The offer from the Americans, who espoused our cause with generosity and imagination, was even more opportune – and our situation in Cambridge much more precarious – than we realized. Years later a close friend reported to me a scene witnessed at a somewhat frosty dinner party in Cambridge in that period in the early Seventies. To the surprise of that dinner guest, Stephen's likely fate was indicated in a remark delivered with consummate indifference by a senior don. "As long as Stephen Hawking pulls his weight, he can stay in this university," the speaker announced, "but as soon as he ceases to do that, he will have to go..." Luckily for us we were able to go of our own volition, not quite sure of what the future would hold, but in the event, we were actually to be invited back a year later.

If an opportunity to exchange the icy chill of the fen winds for the warm deserts of southern California was to be welcomed, the obstacles associated with such an enterprise could not be lightly dismissed. Weighing up the advantages against the disadvantages preoccupied me most. Whereas Stephen might well have mastered the fifteen-thousand-million-year history of the universe, my vision of the future had become restricted only to the foreseeable perspective of the next few days. I had learnt not to speculate on a more distant future, or plan for two, five, ten or twenty years hence. However the next eighteen months demanded careful consideration, especially in the light of my past chaotic experiences on the west coast of America. I steeled myself to confront my personal problem, the fear of flying. At least this time I should not have to abandon my children because they, of course, would be coming with us – but that, in a changed perspective, was the least of my anxieties. Far more worrying was the question of how I was going to manage to travel a third of the way across the world, solely responsible for Stephen in his very debilitated state, as well as for the children. Secondly how should I cope for a whole year, entirely alone, with neither parents nor neighbours on hand to help in time of crisis? Frequently in the past couple of years when I had been laid low with flu, headaches, backache and even pleurisy, I had been able to rely on my mother or the Thatchers to come and help. No such help would be forthcoming in California.

In addition, one of the most perplexing stumbling blocks for some time had been Stephen's absolute rejection of any outside help with his care. He staunchly refused to accept any help, apart from snippets of advice from his father, which might suggest either an acknowledgement of his condition per se or of the fact that it was deteriorating. This attitude, together with his refusal to mention the illness, was one of the props which underpinned his courage and was part of his defence mechanism. I well understood that if once he admitted the gravity of his condition his courage might fail him. I well understood, too, that the mere struggle to get out of bed in the morning might defeat him if he gave any thought to his plight. How I wished that he, for his part, could understand that just a little help to relieve me of some of the severe grinding physical strain which was stifling my true optimistic self might contribute to an improvement in our relationship.

My doctor had listened to my troubles and had conferred with Stephen's doctor. Together they had tried to initiate a rota of domiciliary male nurses to lift Stephen in and out of the bath at least a couple of times a week. This embryonic plan was aborted soon after it was conceived, because the pleasant but elderly male nurse was able to come only at five o'clock in the afternoon, and such an abrupt interruption or conclusion to his working day was, understandably, anathema to Stephen. Only a miracle could resolve the problems we faced. However, that Easter a miracle of an idea floated into my mind like a thistledown seed gliding to earth. It lightened my step and removed my anxieties at the impracticability of well-meaning attempts from the other side of the world to offer us a welcome change of scene. The idea was quite simple: we should invite Stephen's students to live with us in our large Californian house. We could offer them free accommodation in return for help with the mechanics of lifting, dressing and bathing. This was all the more essential since Stephen was no longer able to feed himself at all and needed a constantly watchful eye. With assistance from Bernard, he would not be humiliated by the unmentionable indignity of having to receive help from nurses – which he considered a detrimental step, an acceptance of the deterioration in his condition – but would be assisted by people from his own circle, if not family then at least friends, part of the household. Stephen's first reaction to the idea was automatic rejection, but when he had had time to think about it and realized that the fate of the Californian venture might hang on his decision, he changed his mind. I broached the idea to Bernard Carr and then to Peter De'Ath who, after due consideration, agreed that it would suit all parties very nicely.

There remained one major function to be fulfilled that summer: Stephen's admission to the Fellowship of the Royal Society on Thursday 2nd May. We set off from Cambridge in good time for lunch at Carlton House Terrace, the fine eighteenth-century headquarters of the Royal Society overlooking the Mall. As we approached north London, the car began to lurch uncontrollably and the steering became heavier and heavier. We had no alternative but to press on with the journey, hoping against hope that we would be able to reach our destination. At last, tugging the resistant steering wheel round, I turned with relief into the forecourt of Carlton House Terrace, there to embark on the well-rehearsed sequence of searching out the usual bevy of elderly porters, heaving the various parts of the wheelchair out of the car, assembling them, stationing the chair by the passenger seat and then lifting Stephen under the arms and swinging him round from his car seat into the chair. Then the porters had to be instructed in the careful lifting of the chair up the inevitable flight of steps to the main entrance. This time the sequence was more complicated because the car as well as Stephen needed attention: the front nearside tyre was flat.

As on many occasions, help came from the least expected quarter. It was the secretary of the Royal Society himself – a man of few words, flustered with the demands of the important guests and the significance of the occasion, for all of which he was responsible – who got down on his hands and knees, dressed in his smart dark grey suit, and changed the wheel for us while, unawares, we were being regally entertained to a formal luncheon by another Cambridge scientist, the President of the Royal Society, Sir Alan Hodgkin. The admission took place in the early afternoon amid much ceremonial in the lecture theatre. Speeches were made introducing each new Fellow who then stepped onto the platform to sign the admissions book. When Stephen's turn came, a hush descended on the audience and the book was brought down from the podium for his signature. He inscribed his name slowly and carefully to a tense silence. His final flourish was greeted by a burst of rapturous applause, which brought a jubilant smile to his face and tears to my eyes.

Stephen was not the only Cambridge scientist to be honoured that year, nor yet the only physicist from the Department. John Polkinghorne, the Professor of Particle Physics, was also being admitted to the Fellowship of the Royal Society on the same occasion. Having reached the apogee of his career in science, he was on the point of giving up physics to take up theology; that is to say, from being Professor Polkinghorne FRS, he was about to become an undergraduate again, embarking on the long haul of study for ordination, curacy and parish, with the particular motivation of healing the schism between science and religion which had originated with Galileo. In his opinion, science and religion were not in opposition but were two complementary aspects of one reality. This thesis would become the theme of his writings as a priest-scientist. Although we did not know him well, I admired his conviction and was greatly encouraged to find that atheism was not an essential prerequisite of science, and not all scientists were as atheistic as they seemed.

Part Three

1

Letter from America

"Oh, hi! My name is Mary Lou and I live in Sierra Madre. And who are you? Where are you from?" The speaker, a slight, tanned figure, invited our reply with a broad smile. As we had only just arrived at the party, hosted by some English expatriates, a week or so after landing in Los Angeles, we were not yet accustomed to such directness. There was a long pause while we overcame our surprise and realized that an equally spontaneous reply was expected. After all, it had taken the best part of ten years for us to be recognized at parties in Cambridge, and even then the approach was always tinged with a certain diffidence. Of late some of the senior Fellows – and more especially their wives – had regularly shown a benevolent interest in us, but over the years we had become used to sitting trapped at the ends of tables, or in corners on our own, never really expecting anyone to speak to us, always pleasantly surprised if during the course of the evening we happened to encounter a friendly face. Indeed one of the kitchen managers had once confided in me that it was difficult to place us at table at College feasts because no one really wanted to sit with us. Small wonder, then, that we were unprepared for Mary Lou's initiative. Her exuberance was infectious and I attempted to convey our elation at all things Californian in my letters home to our families and friends, as for instance in my first letter to my parents, written in the days before regular phone contact was financially feasible:

535 South Wilson Avenue
30th August, 1974   *Pasadena, CA 91106*
USA

Dear Mum and Dad,
This is so exciting! The flight was very long, but very straight-forward by comparison with the last time we flew over the Pole when Robert was a small baby. Like a born traveller retracing his steps, Robert was entranced by the scenery, black peaks

growing out of snowfields, mountains rising out of a frozen sea where occasional waterholes glowed deep emerald in the ice, white specks of icebergs in Hudson Bay, then the deserts of America, the Salt Lake and finally the coastal mountains. In contrast, when we were high over the Atlantic, Lucy, quite unimpressed by the adventure, asked if we were on the ground yet…

We all revived on landing, although it was about 2 a.m. (your time), and were wide-eyed at the sight of so much that was new and unfamiliar – palm trees, huge cars, our own gleaming station wagon in which Kip came to meet us, freeways weaving in and out of the city in all directions, skyscrapers and, ultimately, the house with its white weatherboarding, looking much prettier than in the photos. It was dusk when we arrived and there was a light in every window – a Disney fantasy come true! It is as elegant inside as it is pretty out. And so comfortable! Huge sofas that you just sink into and bathrooms everywhere, all colour-coordinated, of course! Everything is brand new, all the imitation-antique furniture, the towels, the china, even the saucepans! These people must think that we are used to an astronomical standard of living. If only they knew! From the kitchen sink I can look out onto mountains, while Stephen is actually closer to his office than in Cambridge because the house is right opposite the campus. Like a small boy with a new toy, he is excitedly learning to manoeuvre his electric wheelchair, the same as the one he has at the Institute only much faster. It's years since he has had such freedom of movement, though the chair has to be lifted over kerbs and steps, which is a bit of a problem since kerbs are very high here as no one ever walks out in the street and the frame is very heavy. The two solid gel batteries each weigh a ton, not to mention the occupant. We have had engineers here all day attending to the wheelchair and making adjustments to all the other appliances. Nothing it seems is too much trouble.

The garden is rather bare and is tended by a team of gardeners, who came with shears, brooms and a vacuum cleaner. They cut back, tidy up and hoover the lawn, but would never recognize a weed if it stared them in the face. The grass needs a great deal of water, which comes up from an underground irrigation system – no need for hosepipes or watering cans. It's all so exotic! The first morning we stepped out onto the patio to find a hummingbird hovering by a weird-looking plant, with spiky orange and blue flowers. All around the house are camellia bushes the size of trees and by the patio there is a huge Californian dry oak, just waiting to be climbed. Round the edge of the garden we have an orange tree in bloom and in fruit at one and the same time, two avocados, a fir tree and a small palm. So far, as it is so hot, we have eaten all our meals on the patio – just as well since the dining room is so beautiful with its plush red carpet and its mahogany table, we hardly dare step inside the door, let alone eat there.

The children and I went for a bathe in the Caltech pool this afternoon. Lucy fell in and did not like it at all. She is regarded as terribly backward since at three she cannot swim, but Robert will be swimming within the week; at present he swims underwater. We are all so dazed with healthy, happy tiredness that Lucy has gone to sleep in front of the television, (novelty though it is, we hardly ever watch it because of the interminable adverts) and even Robert shows signs of dozing off. I think I may be asleep before him even so.

Much love, Jane

My father was due to retire from the Ministry of Agriculture on his sixtieth birthday in December 1974 after a long and dedicated career, and he and my mother planned to celebrate his retirement by coming out to stay with us in California. In the meantime we had a constant stream of visitors, some of whom stayed for a weekend or so while others, like Peter De'Ath, Stephen's PhD student, took up residence and helped Bernard with Stephen's care, until he found his own accommodation. I grew more confident at driving and did not find shopping for so many visitors a strain, because all the purchases were neatly packed into brown paper (not plastic) sacks and carried out to the car for me by smiling assistants. Moreover Robert – aged seven – was a brilliant navigator: he seemed to carry the freeway map in his head and, unlike his father, told me where to turn off well in advance.

On the children's first morning at the Pasadena Town and Country School, I delivered them somewhat apprehensively to the school gate, then at noon I returned to pick up Lucy from the nursery department and joined the car queue of waiting mothers, sidling round the block in their automobiles. As I edged to the school gate, I gave her name to the teacher standing guard on the pavement and he hailed her over the loudspeaker: "Loossee Hokking, Loossee Hokking!" he bellowed. No one came forwards and there was no sign of Loossee Hokking among the crowd of small children waiting patiently inside. A great commotion ensued. Could Loossee Hokking have been kidnapped – the worst fear of the school – on her first day? The place was in chaos. I parked the car and went in. The Principal came running out of her office and a bevy of middle-aged ladies scattered in all directions in frantic search of the lost infant. Loossee Hokking was not hard to find. She had liked school so much that she had taken herself off to lunch and was intending to stay until two-thirty. Thereafter she came out of school, sometimes temperamentally, a bit the worse for wear, as it was a long day for a three-year-old.

The children found a new friend in Shu, the eight-year-old son of our Japanese neighbours, Ken and Hiroko Naka, who had lived for some time in Cambridge before moving to the United States. Ken was a biologist, specializing in catfish eyes, some sort of scientific oddity closely resembling the human eye. The Nakas not only took Robert and Lucy to school every morning after that first day, they also planned all sorts of expeditions to fun parks and beaches for the three children. As I found out when I collected the children from school in the afternoon, Shu's conversation was peppered with computer jargon. While Lucy babbled on irrepressibly, Shu conducted his own monologue at which Robert nodded knowingly; doubtless attracted by this, his first introduction to information technology, the science that would eventually become his career. Delighting in his new-found independence, Stephen also secretly rejoiced in being the star of the campus – where he sat in an air-conditioned office all day. Ramps appeared everywhere on campus as well as in the driveway to the house. He had his own secretary, Polly Grandmontagne, and a regular physiotherapist, Sylvie Teschke, whose husband, a Swiss watchmaker, was anxiously anticipating the end of his livelihood with the advent of quartz watches. Bernard Carr, Stephen's student, began to settle into the routine of our household, unfailingly cheerful despite his somewhat erratic regime, which consisted of helping me put Stephen to bed at night then going out to parties, after which he would sit up till the early hours watching horror movies on account, he said, of his insomnia – and then he would sleep till lunchtime. Once I went upstairs to rouse him in the middle of the morning and found him sleeping soundly with his body in the bed and his head on the floor!

That autumn Mary Thatcher came on a tour of the United States, to lecture on her newly released film archive of the lives of the British in India. Like all our visitors we took her to the local attraction, the Huntington Gardens and Gallery, founded by Mr Huntington who had made his money on the railways and married his aunt to keep it in the family. Her portrait suggests that he paid a rather heavy price for the privilege, but the accumulation of wealth enabled him to purchase Constable's *View on the Stour*, various Chaucerian manuscripts and the Gutenberg Bible among other notable works for his Gallery, as well as establishing a beautiful garden. The garden was divided into fascinating specialized geographical and botanical areas: a viciously prickly desert-cactus garden, an Australian area with eucalyptus trees but no kangaroos, a jungle area, row upon row of camellias, a Shakespearean knot garden, a classical Japanese garden complete with bridge, tea house, and gongs, and a mysteriously philosophical Zen garden – mostly raked gravel dotted about with a few significantly sited rocks. In fact some of the best of European art was to be found within easy reach. If it were not in the Huntington Gallery, it would be in the Pasadena Museum of California Art, the J. Paul Getty Museum at Malibu, or Hearst Castle on the way up to San Francisco. Sometimes I felt quite sentimental if not a little homesick on seeing European art, particular the Constable, in the brash brightness of California. There was little room for those subtleties of life that we knew so well, the grey skies, the respectable shabbiness, the crumbling buildings, the diffidence, the snobbery. The Californian skies, the colours, the landscape, the people, their behaviour and their use of language I found starkly well-defined, honest and devoid of nuance. As for the food, it was gargantuan, but so stuffed with additives that we were glad to be able to grow some of our own fruit. Fifty-two avocado pears fell off the tree one weekend in October when we were away in Santa Barbara. We hurriedly picked them all up on our return and stored them in the bottom of the fridge to save them from the weekly cleansing operation by the gardeners.

That November I wrote to warn Mum and Dad what to expect.

Dear Mum and Dad,

We are so much looking forward to seeing you in just a couple of weeks but I hope you will be able to stand the pace here. Don't come to California for a rest! We live in a constant social whirl. As our house is the largest and closest to the campus, it has become the venue for the Relativity Group's entertaining this year. Kip and Linda have a lovely old Spanish-style villa up in Altadena but that is some way out of town and the area around them is so thick with thieves that as soon as they buy anything new, it disappears. The same goes for any cars parked in the street. So we have some of the parties here instead, cocktail parties, dinner parties, evening drinks parties – not to mention Lucy's birthday party to which she insisted on inviting the whole class plus teachers… Soon we shall be cooking a turkey for Thanksgiving. I don't know how many people will be coming but I'm leaving the traditional trimmings like pumpkin pie to the Americans who know how to do those things. There's no accounting for some of their tastes anyhow. Some people came to dinner last week and I served them a beef casserole. To my amazement they added autumn strawberries from a bowl on the table to their plates of stew!

You will meet our new friends too, especially the other Fairchild Fellows in Stephen's field, the Dickes and the Israels. Bob and Annie Dicke from Princeton are very much like you. He is intellectual and an excellent pianist, and she is warm and grandmotherly. The children and I often go to tea with her and swim in the pool at their block of flats, grandly known here as "condominiums". Did you meet the Israels from Edmonton when they came to Cambridge with their ten-year-old son Mark in 1971? They are very cosmopolitan in outlook but gentle, humorous and immensely knowledgeable, without a trace of affectation.

A special message for Chris: Robert developed toothache last week, although I had taken him to the school dentist just before we came out here, so on Thursday we went to see a dentist. California style. Potted plants, plush carpets, soft sofas and piped music greeted us. The dentist came out to talk to me after he had inspected Robert's teeth. "Well, Mrs Hokking," *he began, then paused for his words to take effect, "this will be quite an investment… those young molars need remedial dentistry, stainless-steel crowns… around one hundred and eighty dollars, I would estimate...*" I can imagine Chris's reaction but what choice do I have except to pay up?!

The children and I have joined the local library. Robert took out a book on the British Empire, which struck me as rather excessively patriotic, but not bad for a child who only a year ago was accused of being backward. I also have an addictive new interest thanks to another Caltech wife, Tricia Holmes. Tricia, who is Irish, has introduced me to the evening choral class at Pasadena City College. Once a week we sight-sing our way through a major choral work. I'm not a good sight-singer but it is very exciting. Last week it was Brahms's German Requiem, this week the Mozart Requiem and so on. Later in the year we shall be doing the St Matthew Passion over two weeks. The approach reminds me of the way Americans travel in Europe, a day in Paris, a day in London, two days in Venice, perhaps.

Lucy also has a special activity thanks also to Tricia Holmes, whose little girl, Lizzie, is more or less Lucy's age. Lizzie and Lucy go to ballet together, so the ballet shoes are in use again, and this time it's the real thing, no messing around with nursery rhymes and free expression, but no tears either. The teacher is young and rather seriously American. Her reservation is that she might be teaching Lucy by the wrong method... Since I last wrote we have taken in another migrant to fill up some of the space in this house. Anna Zytkov, a young Polish astrophysicist, has moved in until she can find somewhere to rent. No sooner had she arrived than I suggested a game of tennis, although I have not played in years. We had just begun to play when Anna fell over, and broke her ankle. Since then, in her immobilized state, she has built the most beautiful, fully furnished doll's house out of a large cardboard box for Lucy for her birthday. It is a real work of art, so delicately and imaginatively crafted that it makes the garish plastic artefacts that one sees in the shops look monstrously vulgar and clumsy.

We shall have a full house at Christmas. I think Anna will have left by then, but in addition to the six of us plus Bernard, George Ellis will be coming to stay for a couple of days when he and Stephen return from a conference in Dallas on the 21st, and on the 23rd, Philippa Hawking will be coming over from New York where she is working at present. We will be at the airport at 5 a.m. on the 16th to meet you! Be prepared for

all the usual end-of-term activities at the school – Robert is
reciting from the Battle of Bunker Hill – and for a huge party
here on the 21st.

Much love till 16th
December, Jane

In early December, Stephen went off with his entourage to the
conference in Dallas. While the children and I were alone in the
house, I awoke one night to find the bed and the floor shaking
beneath me. Our instructions were that we should run to the
porch in the event of an earthquake, but I was too terrified to
move, literally petrified. When finally I recovered my senses, I ran
upstairs to see if the children were all right and was astonished
to find them both sound asleep. I went back to bed, turned out
the light and then it happened again. Even the aftershock was
tremendous, quite unlike the little tremors that rattled windows
regularly each afternoon. However, had there been earthquakes
at Christmas, we probably should not have noticed them (just
as Stephen failed to notice a major earthquake in Persia in 1962
because he was travelling cross-country on a bus at the time and
was suffering from dysentery). Mum and Dad, George Ellis and
Stephen on their return from Dallas, and Stephen's sister Philippa
arrived in the middle of consecutive nights, and then we gave a party
for forty or so friends and colleagues, who enjoyed themselves so
much that they stayed till after 2 a.m. To prove it, we have a photo
of a very distinguished elderly physicist, Willy Fowler, practising
yoga on the living-room floor at 2 a.m. precisely!

Sixteen people came to Christmas dinner, which meant that
the children had a ready-made audience for their conjuring
show. Robert was given a conjuring set and he, with his ebullient
assistant, regaled us with a winningly innocent first attempt at
sleight of hand – a change from the constant diet of riddles and
jokes which bemused us and kept the children in ecstasies of
laughter. The contrast between his quasi-professional opening
gambit – "If you want to ask questions, please ask them after the
show and not before it" – and the disarray in his box of tricks,
his pleasure when a trick actually worked and his suppressed
irritation at his show-stealing assistant, not to mention his
gaping toothless smile, were very endearing.

After Christmas and the Pasadena Parade on New Year's Day,
we summoned the energy to take the family to Disneyland for a

day. The queues were long and the children managed to ride on only two attractions each. We did have a good vantage point for the lavishly produced Disneyland parade though, but even that was a bit of a disaster because it was Lucy's misfortune to be offered an apple by the Wicked Witch in the Snow White section. She was so terrified that she hid behind my skirts. Then early in the New Year we drove over to Death Valley, the desert park, 300 miles to the north-east. It was a great relief to have my parents with me to share the driving, to help with loading Stephen and the wheelchair – not to mention the batteries – into the car, and to keep the children entertained while I attended to Stephen. We were awed by the weird primeval landscape, a giants' playground where the Valley floor is littered with sand dunes here, volcanic craters there, and scree and sand-coloured rock protuberances everywhere. Vast salt flats below sea level are all that remain of a deep ice-age lake. On all sides the Valley is enclosed by rugged snowcapped mountains, which in their many-hued stratifications bear witness to enormous geological upheavals in the dawn of time. In summer Death Valley is said to be the hottest desert in the world and is almost barren of vegetation: only cacti, desert holly and the creosote plant survive among its hostile rocks and stones, and only the tiny, prehistoric pupfish can withstand the extreme saltiness of its few shallow creeks. Constantly changing colour with the movement of the sun, the landscape is magnificent but not beautiful. The sorry tales of the pioneers who tried to cross the Valley in 1849 and the ghost-town remnants of the gold prospectors' dreams, together with the sterility and silence of the place, invest it with a menacing and forbidding atmosphere. My mother remarked how dynamic, tough and persevering those pioneers must have been and added that we shouldn't be surprised to find those same qualities in modern Californians, especially the women, the descendants of those pioneers.

We came home to a nice surprise. We had already organized a small farewell party for my parents, so it was a happy coincidence that on the same occasion we could celebrate the award, to Stephen and Roger Penrose, of the Eddington Medal by the Royal Astronomical Society. It was all very prestigious but we were not really sure what it signified, as the announcement came as a complete surprise. Nevertheless, it did have the effect of reminding Stephen to pay his overdue subscription. Lucy was determined to go back to England with her grandparents and packed her suitcase specially. She was so indignant when the plane took off without her that we had to make a quick dash to the nearest Kentucky Fried Chicken outlet to calm her down.

Martin Rees – now President of the Royal Society and Master of Trinity College, Cambridge, but back in 1975 simply one of our best, most unpretentious and kindest friends – had agreed to cast our votes that spring in the referendum on British entry to the Common Market. It was probably a complete waste of his time as Stephen's vote most certainly cancelled out mine. (Stephen had a habit of doing this in elections.) To my way of thinking, from California Britain appeared as a small offshore European island, which would do well to settle down to its rightful place within the Common Market instead of dwelling on past glories and lost greatness. Fortunately this is just what happened, despite Stephen's attempt to sabotage my vote.

Stephen meanwhile was getting up to all sorts of mischief. As a sort of insurance policy, he bet Kip Thorne that the constellation Cygnus X-1 did *not* contain a black hole, because he felt he would need some consolation in the form of four years' subscription to *Private Eye* if that actually proved to be the case. Kip for his part was content with just one year's subscription to *Penthouse* magazine if, as seemed likely, Cygnus X-1 did contain a black hole. Otherwise, Stephen was making contacts with particle physicists, which meant that his interests were moving way beyond the event horizon into the heart of the black hole. He was attending lectures by two eminent particle physicists, Richard Feynman and Murray Gell-Mann, whose gentlemanly behaviour towards each other concealed an arch rivalry. Stephen was present when Feynman turned up at the first of a course of lectures by Gell-Mann. Noticing Feynman in the audience, Gell-Mann announced that he would be using his lecture series to conduct a survey of current research in particle physics and proceeded to read from his notes in a monotone. After ten minutes, Feynman got up and left. To Stephen's great amusement, Gell-Mann then heaved a sigh and declared, "Ah, good, now we can get on with the real stuff!" and proceeded to talk about his own recent research at the cutting edge of particle physics.

Winter was scarcely noticeable, though it rained hard, sometimes for two or three days at a time. Then the sun would shine again in an azure sky and the clouds would clear from the mountains, revealing the splendour of the peaks sparkling with fresh snow.

The rain suddenly brought spring to the canyons which, so brown when we first arrived, were now green and lush, while the roadsides and cliffs by the beach rippled with wild flowers: orange poppies, blue lupines, sunflowers and daisies. We did not let the rain interfere with our activities. On George Washington's birthday in February, we went out for a drive and came back several hours later having driven 350 miles, the longest distance I have ever driven in one day. We climbed up through the swirling icy mists of Palomar Mountain to the world's largest telescope, and then crossed the scorching dryness of the Anza-Borrego Desert, where masses of flowers were coming into bloom. When Stephen's mother and his Aunt Janet came to stay in March, we piled into the car and went off to the Joshua Tree National Park, a high desert area above 3000 feet, where the Joshua Tree produces its lily-like flowers. At a lower elevation, there is a forest of cacti appropriately called "jumping chollas". One of them jumped at me, implanting its barbs in my leg, a rather mean thing to do on my birthday I thought, especially as the children had already sat on my birthday cake in the back of the car. Aunt Janet's medical expertise came to the rescue – of my leg, not the cake.

In April, Stephen received the Pope Pius XI Gold Medal for science at a full session of the Pontifical Academy. It seemed that the notion of the Big Bang as the point of creation appealed to the Vatican, and at last Galileo had found a champion when Stephen in his address to the assembly made a special plea for the rehabilitation of Galileo's memory – three hundred and thirty three years after his death.

While Stephen was away in Europe, the children, Annie Dicke and I took the boat across a very choppy sea to Catalina Island. In those days the island was a gem, unspoilt and free of traffic, but what impressed us most was the trip we took in a glass-bottomed boat. The sight of the tranquil, gleaming world of the seabed, where seaweed grew to a height of twenty feet and fish, unaware of our presence, darted with a quicksilver grace between its branches, held us spellbound. I wondered how we could be so ignorant of the silent beauty and mystery of that other world which was literally at our feet and on our shores. When I revisited Catalina Island in 1996, the island had lost its pristine beauty and was as polluted under the surface of the ocean as it was on land. That change was to be a potent image of the way our lives had changed in the interim.

As that year in California drew to a close, I sensed that although it had been positive and exhilarating in so many ways, it had begun to define a widening fault line between our shining public image and our darkening private face. It also brought me sharply up against my own limitations. At three years old, Lucy might have been a backward swimmer, but apparently I was a really retarded mother. In America in the early days of women's lib, a woman who did not have a job by the time her child was two was regarded as a miserable failure, inevitably lacking in "personal fulfilment". So I threw myself headlong into a crazy round of activity. The endless stream of visitors, the frantic socializing, books from the library and, of course, the children, kept me more or less occupied, distracting my mind from the dispiriting effect that life on the edge of the Caltech vortex had on anyone who was not an international scientific genius. Caltech, the temple where devotees came to worship at the altar of science, particularly physics, excluded all else. The Wives' Club struggled valiantly to entertain spouses with trips to places like the J. Paul Getty Museum and the occasional concert or play in the theatre, but there were quite a lot of unhappy, disaffected wives, demoralized by their husbands' total obsession with science.

I managed to avoid being swallowed up by the Caltech abyss, but nevertheless it caused me to question my own situation. One weekend in Santa Barbara, while Stephen was engaged in endless discussions with his colleague Jim Hartle, I sat on the beach, wrapped up against the icy wind, gazing out to sea while the children played. As I ran the loose sand through my fingers, I asked myself where my life was going. What did I have to show for my thirty years? I had the children, "my blessings" as dear Thelma Thatcher would say, and Stephen. Certainly proud of his extraordinary achievements, I didn't really feel that I shared in his success – yet everything that happened to him was crucial to me, whether an honour, sparkling with fame and glory, or one of those life-threatening choking fits seizing him unawares. I loved him for his courage, his wit, his sense of the ridiculous and the absurd, and that wicked charisma which enabled him – and still enables him – to twist most people, including me, round his little finger. So I was achieving what I set out to do – to devote myself to Stephen, giving him the chance of fulfilling his genius. But in the process I was beginning to lose my own identity. I could no longer count myself a Hispanist or even a linguist, and I felt that I did not command respect anywhere, in California or in Cambridge. Perhaps all the frenzied socializing and entertaining was really just my Freudian way of saying, "Please notice me too!"

It was in California that for the first time ever we met a family in similar circumstances to our own. The Irelands, David, Joyce and John, lived over in Arcadia, only a few miles from Pasadena. Like Stephen, David was a scientist by training. He studied and taught maths. Confined to a wheelchair, he was also severely disabled with a neurological illness and could do little for himself. Very positive in attitude, Joyce was an organized, energetic person and had married David in the full knowledge of his illness. Stephen was very nervous about meeting the Irelands and I felt for him in his anxiety, wanting to protect him – but though he was clearly shaken by David's condition, he managed to put on a cheerful smile and together we kept up the bright façade of normality. I wondered what the Irelands thought of us. They may have admired our determination but the façade would not have fooled them. They knew too much about the battles and the struggles.

In many respects their battles mirrored ours, but there was a fundamental difference between us. The difference was that their approach to David's illness was quite open – open with themselves and open to the outside world, not concealing the difficulties and the pain behind a brave smile. David consigned that spirit of frankness to a book, written to introduce himself to his son, John, in case he died before John was born or before John was old enough to know him. *Letters to an Unborn Child* is a very honest self-portrait and a moving account of the battles that David and Joyce underwent. It also recounts a journey in self-awareness, as David's confronts his major failing, the concealment of his true self behind a popular, jovial exterior. Through his eventual work as a counsellor, David discovered an enhanced faith in the love of God, a personal, unconditional love, outside the realms of time and space, and through this he could face the future without fear or bitterness. David's book taught me that my tearful frustrations, even the bouts of anger I felt at thoughtlessness and lack of consideration, usually when I was tired beyond endurance, were all valid emotions since, in David's words, "they release the poisons which sicken or kill us". Conversely, according to David, imperturbable self-control, bottling up powerful emotions and suppressing the emotions of others, is unhealthy and dangerous. I was struck by the irony of discovering these truths through the words of someone who was, if anything, even more disabled than Stephen, someone who, through his own suffering, had learnt to reach out and help other people.

One person who also reached out to other people was Ruth Hughes, the voluntary organiser at Caltech of the visitors' pound of toys and children's bikes. A refugee from the Nazis, Ruth was remarkably perceptive and concerned for me as well as for the children. She astounded me when I was introduced to her by saying that she had first seen Stephen in the Athenaeum, the Caltech Faculty Club, and while everyone else was praising his courage and brilliance – in a land where success is adored and failure deplored – she had said to herself that there must be someone equally courageous behind him or he simply would not be there. Nobody had ever said anything like that to me before and it quite threw me off my stride. Later when Stephen was awarded the Papal medal, Ruth presented me with a pearl brooch because, she said, I should be given something too.

2

Establishments

Before we left Cambridge for California in the summer of 1974, I knew that we would not return to 6 Little St Mary's Lane because the house was too small for our growing family and the stairs too perilous for Stephen. But Cambridge has very few residential properties within easy reach of the town centre, so the question of where we might move to was not easily resolved. Although our house might fetch a very reasonable price on the open market, we would never be able to afford to buy a larger, more suitable house anywhere near the Department, certainly not in the Grange Road area, where, before our marriage, Stephen had lodgings. This time however I had no qualms about approaching Gonville and Caius College, which was lapping up the reflected glory of Stephen's repeated successes and would be unlikely to treat us with the same harsh indifference that it had shown in the Sixties when we were young, unknown and struggling to make ends meet.

It transpired that the Bursar no longer dealt with the letting of College property. Luckily it had been taken over by the Revd John Sturdy, who had been appointed Dean shortly before Stephen's induction as a Research Fellow in October 1965, and who with his wife had befriended us from that time onwards, always supportive, always concerned for the children, always deeply caring. John, a studious, other-worldly Hebrew scholar of saintly appearance, was well complemented by his bustling, intensely practical wife Jill. In those early years, the Sturdys already had two children and were expecting their third baby at the same time as I was expecting Robert. Over the next fifteen years they adopted nine more from all backgrounds, colours and creeds. Jill took a degree in English, did a teacher-training course and then founded her own school to support and educate her family. At Christmas the Sturdys instituted a party in the College for the children of all members and employees, whether Fellows, kitchen staff or cleaners. John Sturdy or their eldest son, John

Christian, would dress up as Father Christmas and the children had a fine time boisterously playing musical chairs round High Table.

I was sure that I could count on John's sympathy. Even so, his speed of response was surprising. "Have you thought about where you would like to live?" he asked – as if the range of choice was unlimited – when we met to discuss the prospects in June 1974. Thinking my request to be rather hopeless, I sighed, "Somewhere in the Grange Road area, I suppose." "Well," he replied calmly, "let's go and look at the properties in that area and see if there is anything suitable for you." We looked at half-a-dozen houses, formerly family homes that now belonged to the College, on the west side of Cambridge, on the fringes of the Victorian village of Newnham. Some were too distant from the Department for Stephen, some were too close to noisy main roads and others were not spacious enough on the ground floor for a wheelchair. There was one house however, in West Road just off the Backs, which immediately caught my attention. Solid and extensive, with a Victorian self-assurance, it stood in large gardens next door to Harvey Court, the monstrous development which had featured in *Cambridge New Architecture* way back in the Sixties. We were already well acquainted with those gardens since they had been the venue every summer for Robert's birthday parties. My mother would arrive bearing a lavishly decorated birthday cake – sometimes in the shape of a train, sometimes a car, sometimes a fort – and my father and I would organize enough games and entertainments to keep upwards of a dozen small children amused for two hours, the most taxing two hours of the entire social calendar, apart from those dedicated to Lucy's birthday party, which being in the winter was, if anything, even more challenging.

With a few modifications, the ground floor at 5 West Road could be made very suitable for us, especially because it consisted of a sufficient number of large, well-lit rooms to accommodate the whole family, plus all the other necessary facilities, still leaving space to spare for parties for all ages. It was further from the Department than Little St Mary's Lane, but not inconveniently far, and was about the same distance from the primary school that Lucy would be attending. The gardens offered scope for parties and games of all descriptions – particularly cricket, practised with the greatest reluctance at St Albans High School, but now vital to the proper upbringing of my son. The house had been vaguely threatened with demolition in the early Seventies, I remembered, when the land on which it stood had been earmarked as the possible location for a new college, Robinson College. However, the site was too small and the house was spared. And only five years or so previously 5 West Road had been a thriving family hotel, the West House Hotel, but when its lease ran out the College had taken it over for use as undergraduate accommodation. The students had been given free rein to choose their own colour schemes, and the once fine Victorian dining room now had a black ceiling and scarlet walls. This did not upset me unduly as paint was superficial and easily changed. I was much more impressed by the dimensions of the house, so at the end of our tour I opted for the West House without hesitation – and, incidentally, effectively silenced the faction in the College which wanted to demolish any building, including that house, which had been built before 1960. Negotiations proceeded without a hitch and it was agreed that, on our return from California in 1975, we would occupy the ground floor. In part exchange for the rent, the College would have the use of our own house in Little St Mary's Lane for Fellows, since the College had relaxed its rules to allow Fellows to rent accommodation.

During our absence, partition walls were erected on the stair-case to screen the ground floor from the undergraduates upstairs; the newly created flat was redecorated throughout, and ramps were built at the front and at the garden doors. In directing these operations from California, I enlisted the support of a courageous young man, Toby Church, who as a student had been struck down by a paralysing illness which had deprived him of the power of speech and the use of his legs. Toby had employed his engineering expertise to adapt his environment to his needs so that he could look after himself – with a little help from nurses – and also to build his own invention, the Lightwriter, a small, laptop keyboard with a digital screen into which he could type his speech. Unfortunately, the invention was not of much help to Stephen since operating the keyboard required too much dexterity, and Toby was not particularly interested in electric wheelchairs since he was concerned to keep his arm muscles in good shape by propelling himself around under his own steam. But as my intermediary, Toby propelled himself round to West Road many times in the course of the summer of 1975. On our return from California, it was a pleasure to move into such lovely surroundings. For all the sixteen years of our occupancy, we were conscious of our good fortune in being able to live in that house. The rooms were vast and high-ceilinged, with decorative plaster cornices and delicately embossed central roses around the light fittings. The tall sash windows gave onto a true English lawn, framed with carefully chosen conifers and deciduous trees: dark, forbidding yew mingled with the light fronds of willow. A giant sequoia – a Californian redwood, evidently a sapling newly introduced to Europe when the house was built – towered above the tumbledown conservatory at one corner of the building, communing with its partner, a *Thuja plicata* or western red cedar of comparable height at the far end of the lawn. The gnarled old apple tree faithfully produced its blossoms and its crop with such abundance that every two years the ground beneath would be carpeted with an excess of cooking apples from October to December. "Not stewed apple again!" the children would chorus at the supper table while their father would grin in mischievous collusion. Eventually he decided that he was allergic to stewed fruit, but that was not an excuse that the children were allowed to get away with.

In summer we would hang a hammock, swings and climbing ropes from the branches of the apple tree and listen to the twittering of the fledgling blackbirds inside its hollow trunk. To the left of the apple tree, in full view of the living-room window, lay the gracefully curving herbaceous border with its backdrop of flowering trees and bushes, lilac, almond and hawthorn. Even in the depths of the harshest winter, the beauty of the garden was still magical. Late one night after a persistent snowfall, I peered out through the heavy curtains and shivered in wonder at the transformation of the dank, brown winter garden outside. The full moon in a cloudless sky illuminated a glistening blanket of snow, covering lawn and trees with an enchanted, dazzling purity.

In its prime, the garden must have been a splendid sight. Despite the rampant goosegrass and pervasive ground elder, it still conveyed hints of its former glory in its myriad collection of perennials. Like the trees, they must have been planted as part of an overall scheme, perhaps as much as a century ago when the house was built. I tried to supplement the efforts of the hard-pressed College gardeners with a little weeding and planting in an attempt to subdue the goosegrass. Jeremy Prynne, a colleague of Stephen's in the Fellowship and College librarian, applauded my efforts and proposed that I should be elected to the College gardening committee since, as he remarked, many of its members could not distinguish a dandelion from a daffodil. However his proposal was rejected out-of-hand because it was inconceivable that a non-Fellow, let alone a wife, should be elected to a College committee.

From the time of our arrival in the autumn of 1975, the house, like the garden, was to lend itself enthusiastically to countless parties. There were the family celebrations, the birthday parties and the Christmas dinners. There were also the duty occasions – fundraising events as I became drawn into charity work, coffee mornings and musical evenings, departmental parties, parties for the beginning and the end of the academic year, conference receptions and dinners. In summer, there were tea parties (again usually for conferences, mostly of visiting American and Russian scientists) on the lawn with cucumber sandwiches and croquet, and there were the folk-dance evenings, barbecue suppers and firework parties. Such occasions were fun and they were usually appreciated, but it was hard work since I did not receive any help with the catering until years later. It was scarcely surprising that sometimes the unofficial companions of the official guests, the hangers-on, mistook me in my working apron for a college servant, and condescendingly demanded another glass of wine or another sandwich with scant respect, not realizing that I was the hostess.

We appeared to live in privileged surroundings, but there were disadvantages. Despite our occupancy, the house remained under threat of demolition. After the completion of the renovations carried out for our benefit, only minimal maintenance work was authorized. In winter, the central heating system, based on the original Victorian radiators, was scarcely adequate when the north wind blew snow through the gaps in the ill-fitting doors and windows. At one stage the gas fires, used to supplement the radiators, were found to be emitting more fumes into the rooms than they were sending up the chimneys. The wiring consisted of an eccentric combination of modern sockets fitted onto old wires of which no one knew the provenance.

Much more alarmingly, ceilings tended to crash to the ground with disturbing regularity, even though my father, with his catastrophic history of provoking the gravitational collapse of many a ceiling, was nowhere in the vicinity. By the grace of God, the damage was never more than material. One July night in 1978 the living-room ceiling lost its key and descended with an almighty thud amid a cloud of grime and plaster dust, smashing the stereo system to smithereens in the room beneath and sending the chandelier into a spin. Fortunately we had just gone to bed and the children were sleeping safely in their rooms. Equally luckily, no one was in the bath when a little later the bathroom ceiling also came down.

Outside, the roof regularly shed its tiles. This latter hazard was rectified thanks to a timely visit by His Royal Highness the Duke of Edinburgh, Chancellor of the University of Cambridge, who came to pay Stephen a private visit in June 1982. So afraid were we that a tile might crash onto the royal pate as His Highness entered the front door that I asked for a protective screen of netting to be put round the guttering. The point was taken and, some months later, the building was reroofed. Thanks to the royal visit we also acquired new bathroom fittings.

We were not the sole residents of the house since we occupied only the ground floor. Students, who had a separate entrance, lived on the upper floors, and mice lived in the dark depths of the cellar among the equipment belonging to the University Caving Club. The mice kept their distance after Lucy acquired a predatory cat, but it was less easy to attain a satisfactory modus vivendi with the students. As individuals they were as delightfully a friendly bunch as one could hope to meet, as we discovered on those occasions when we invited them in for a drink, or met them on the lawn in the middle of the night when the intermittent fault in the fire alarm roused the whole house for no good reason. But inevitably, the students' lifestyle, their routine and their habits were often at odds with ours. At times their presence made itself felt in a more tangible form than just loud noises and bumps in the night. About once a year someone would leave the bathwater running in the student bathroom upstairs, just above our kitchen. The last time this happened, I arrived home at lunchtime with a quarter of an hour to spare before the expected arrival of some cousins of Stephen's from New Zealand. I could hear the rush of flowing water the moment I turned my key in the door and smelt a musty dankness as I crossed the hall to the kitchen. The floor was already under a layer of water and the best plates and bowls, put out ready on the worktop, were collecting dirty puddles. The cheese, tomatoes, lettuce and bread swam in warm, grey pools, as more water poured through the ceiling and trickled down the light fitting...

Such drawbacks had not yet come to our notice however when, in September 1975, my mother and I cleaned out 6 Little St Mary's Lane before handing it over to the College, and I arranged the removal of our possessions to 5 West Road. Post-California our circumstances changed dramatically. We had come back to England to living quarters which were more akin to a mini-stately home, or a Master's Lodge, and Stephen was assured of his first official post in the University, a Readership, since while we were away a rumour had circulated in Cambridge that we were considering staying in California for good. Immediately the old biblical adage about a prophet being without honour in his own country proved itself and the Readership, later to be superseded by a personal Chair, materialized. Far from wanting Stephen to go, as had been predicted once by a senior don, the University had actually been impatient for his return.

The Readership brought with it the much-needed services of a secretary – in the form of Judy Fella, who introduced a fresh vitality and an unaccustomed glamour to the drab realms of the Department of Applied Mathematics and Theoretical Physics. Judy worked for Stephen for many years with tireless loyalty and efficiency. At last there was someone to take over the administration of his official life in England, just as Polly Grandmontagne had done in California. She typed his papers, including the hieroglyphs, dealt with his correspondence, organized his conferences, arranged his travels and applied for his visas, all of which amounted to a full-time occupation since he was now much in demand with celebrity status.

America was not unique in its adulation of success. In a more discreet fashion, cloaked in a diffident respectability, the same attitude prevailed in Britain. Afraid of being outdone in the scramble to acknowledge the brilliant scientific star blazing across their horizons, successive scientific institutions took their lead from each other and awarded Stephen their most prestigious medals. On many an occasion over the course of the next few years, my parents would come over to Cambridge in time to meet the children from school while I picked Stephen up from the Department, loaded him and the wheelchair into the car, and then set off for some smart London hotel – the Savoy, the Dorchester or the Grosvenor – where the evening's presentation dinner was to take place. Sometimes we were given overnight accommodation and that eased the strain on me since I was chauffeur, nurse, valet, cup-bearer and interpreter, as well as companion-wife, all at once. When finally all the intervening hurdles between the customary tenor of life in Cambridge and the glitzy London social scene had been surmounted, we would appear, always late, decked out in evening dress – complete with the hand-tied bow tie on which Stephen insisted – in a sparkling ballroom or dining room to be greeted by the assembled ranks of the scientific intelligentsia, peers of the realm and assorted dignitaries. They were all very charming and their wives were often kindly, but to me they all seemed so old, older than my parents: they were not the sort of people I was likely to meet in the street or at the school gate where my real friends were. The same people, along with the most affected members of London's glitterati, also turned up at other notable social occasions in the scientific calendar, particularly the *Conversazioni,* the evening gatherings in summer at the Royal Society, where the rich and famous mercilessly elbowed each other out of the way in the scrum for drinks and canapés, while the exhibitors, guarding their carefully prepared displays, patiently waited for the chattering assembly to show some interest in their painstaking research.

The artificial glamour of these occasions was simultaneously entertaining and irritating. While I enjoyed myself, I was inevitably aware of the hours ahead. There would be no coachman to drive us home from London after midnight or to help get Stephen ready for bed, and the next morning we would be back in our routine. I would be dressing Stephen, feeding him his breakfast, his pills and his tea, then I would clean the house and put two or three loads of washing into the machine before peeling the onions and potatoes for the next meal. Across the road, the tower of the University Library would loom accusingly, a silent but eloquent reminder of my neglected thesis. There would be no glass slipper either, even though there might be a glistening gold medal, set on a bed of satin and velvet, to remind us that the previous evening had not been just a passing dream. Even the medals disappeared from view after a day or two. Since the house was subject to occasional, opportunistic petty theft – handbags stolen from the hall, bicycles stolen from the porch – the medals had to be consigned to the bank vault, rarely to be seen again.

3

Buried Treasure

The reality of everyday life always began the night before, when, after giving Stephen his medications and putting him to bed, I would lay out the breakfast things for the children. At long last, Robert's enthusiasm for early rising found its true purpose, since he could be trusted to get his own breakfast and supervise Lucy's as well. In the morning I would get Stephen out of bed, dress him and give him a cup of tea and his early-morning vitamins, before taking Lucy to school on the back of my bike. On my return, usually laden with shopping, I would give Stephen his breakfast and attend to his personal needs before he went to work. After the freedom he had enjoyed in California, Stephen was in no mind to put up with the frustrations of a push wheelchair and applied to the Department of Health for an electric model, the fast one, since, according to the propaganda, such appliances were available free of charge. However, the truth did not conform to the promise of the advertising. All the force of Stephen's considerable persistence and doggedness were not enough to shift the grey officials of that particular governmental department into granting his application, for fear of setting a precedent which would open the floodgates to similar applicants. They told him that he could submit another application for the three-wheeler battery-driven car, which he now lacked the strength to control, or, indeed, for an electric wheelchair – but only the slow model, designed for indoor use like the one, purchased by a philanthropic fund, he already had at the Institute. We wasted hours arguing our case for the faster chair unsuccessfully. So much for the Welfare State. It had contributed so very little to our welfare that one might suppose that its purpose was actually to prevent the disabled from working to their full capacity and, consequently, from contributing as taxpayers to the National Exchequer. A handful of vitamin pills on prescription seemed to be the best it could offer with only minimal physical, practical, moral or financial support.

We became even more dependent on family, students and friends in the daily battle to function as a family. Stephen did acquire the wheelchair he wanted – from philanthropic funds, not through the National Health Service – and, discreetly accompanied by a student, rode to work in it every morning. His route took him along the path through King's College, where aconites and snowdrops bloom in winter and daffodils in spring, across the river over the humpbacked bridge and out of the College by a side entrance, to his office in the Department on the opposite side of Silver Street. That Stephen was at last able to enjoy the basic human right to move about freely, as and when and where he chose, was not a result of any government provision or benefit, it was the result only of his own hard work and of his own success in physics.

Transport for the children was another problem. I took Lucy to school on the back of my bike every morning, but Robert's school was some distance away. Thanks to a relative newcomer to Cambridge, John Stark, Robert got to school on time. Jean and John Stark and their two children had come to Cambridge from London in the early Seventies when John took up the post of chest consultant at Addenbrooke's Hospital; they had moved into the house that Fred Hoyle had built for himself a decade earlier. John kindly picked Robert up on his way to work, and dropped him together with his own son Dan, off at the Perse Preparatory School. I returned the Starks' help by collecting the boys in the afternoon and taking Dan home. I would occasionally stay and talk to Jean while the children played. A graduate of the London School of Economics, she found the male-chauvinist attitudes prevalent in Cambridge, and the domination of all walks of life by the University, cramping and discouraging. We shared our frustration at a system which had educated us to compete with men until the age of twenty-one or twenty-two, and then had summarily consigned us to second-class status. Not for one moment did we regret our roles as wives and mothers, but we did resent the low esteem which society, particularly Cambridge society, accorded those essential roles.

It was Jean who insisted that I should take up the thesis again, though I thought it foolish even to contemplate such a hopeless enterprise. It had been a presence in my life, sometimes welcome, sometimes much resented, for nearly ten years. I had completed only one third of the whole project, although I had amassed a vast amount of material, and I could not envisage ever finishing it. The only free time at my disposal was the sparse intervening period between Stephen's departure at midday and a quick round of the shops in the early afternoon, before picking Lucy up from school at a quarter past three – two and a half hours at the most. Nevertheless, thanks to Jean's insistence – and to the extraordinary example of Henry Button, one of my father's old Civil Service colleagues who had begun his research on the German *Minnesänger* in 1934 and finished it on retirement forty years later – the prospect began to appear less ludicrous.

As the three areas and periods of my research were so clearly defined, the return to it was less challenging than I had feared. I had already documented my ideas on the earliest lyrics, the Mozarabic *kharjas*, and could now turn my attention to the second area of medieval lyrical flowering – Galicia, the north-western corner of the Iberian Peninsula. There the language was more akin to Portuguese than Castilian, and the city of Santiago de Compostela had attained international renown and commercial success on account of the shrine of St James, whose coffin, according to one local legend, was said to have been washed up on the Galician coastline in 824. By the thirteenth century the songs of the Galician troubadours had ousted the waning poetry of Provence as the favourite amusement at the Castilian court, and their composition developed into yet another of the full-scale industries of that remarkable king, Alfonso the Wise. Among many widely disparate compositions is a large group, the *cantigas de amigo,* which consist of love songs voiced by women and which contain many of the themes and features of the *kharjas* – the lovers often meet at dawn, the girl confides in a mother figure or her sisters, the lover is often absent. They also exhibit folkloric elements in their style and language, which appear to hark back to traditional antecedents. In those few hours at my disposal each day, it was my task to sift out the traditional elements from the five hundred and twelve *cantigas de amigo*, evaluate any salient stylistic and linguistic features which they shared with the *kharjas*, compare their language with that of learned classical or biblical precedents and situate them against a more general European background.

I found many similarities between the *kharjas* and the *cantigas de amigo*, which were possibly the result of Mozarabic migrations northwards, away from later waves of fanatical Arab oppression. I also found striking differences, in that the *cantigas* do not contain any of the clear-cut radiance of *kharja* imagery or any sense of urgent anticipation. The imagery derives from the natural background of the mountains and streams of the north-western corner of the Peninsula, exposed to the turbulence of the Atlantic winds, and is identified with the emotions of the protagonists. Cultured poets would have read classical and biblical allusions into this imagery of wind and waves, trees, mountains and streams, where stags come to trouble the waters. But much more persuasive in the search for the origins of this poetry is the influence of a distant pagan past, veiled in the mists of a much earlier time than the confident Christian certainties of the *kharjas*.

A girl, closely identified with the beauty and whiteness of the dawn, gets up early and goes to wash tunics in the stream, a stream dedicated perhaps to one of the ancient Celtic fertility gods or goddesses of Galicia whose stones and inscriptions still survive:

> *Levantou-s' a velida,*
> *levantou-s' alva,*
> *e vai lavar camisas*
> *em o alto:*
> *vai-las lavar alva.*

> The lovely girl arose,
> the dawn arose,
> and goes to wash tunics
> in the stream:
> the dawn goes to wash them.

In some of these dawn poems she is interrupted by the playful antics of the wind – in pagan terms, the vehicle of evil spirits – in others by the mountain stag. The stag stirring up the water is symbolic both of the lover's presence and of their passionate activity, yet conceals any explicit reference to sexuality:

> *Passa seu amigo*
> *que a muit' ama;*
> *o cervo do monte*
> *volvia a augua*

The Sixth Form at St Albans High School. I am standing second
from the right in the back row, next to Gillian Phillips on my left
and Diana King on my right.

Wedding in Trinity Hall, Cambridge, 15th July 1965. From left to right:
my grandmother, Stephen's father, my mother, my brother Chris, Stephen, me,
Rob Donovan, Stephen's mother, Stephen's grandmother, my father.

Little St Mary's Lane

Stephen with Robert,
29th May 1967.

Robert aged nine months sitting between
Stephen and my father.

Lucy's christening, December 1970.

Family excursion,
Little St Mary's Lane, 1971.

Stephen turning back the waves,
Brancaster, summer 1971.

Picnic on the Cam with my parents, Kip Thorne, Brandon, Lucette and Catherine Carter, John and Suzanne McClenahan and unidentified scientist with back to camera.

Robert, Lucy and Inigo Schaffer at play
in Little St Mary's Churchyard 1972.

FRS, May 1974.

Christmas 1975 at West Road with Mary and Thelma Thatcher, my parents, Aunt Effie and Uncle Jack.

Croquet party at 5 West Road, summer 1980 – with Alan Lapedes and girlfriend (end 2nd row left); next to him Gary Gibbons. Front row: Don Page on Robert's right, Nick Warner on his left and, next to him, Bernard Carr; Bernard Whiting behind Lucy and Mary Whiting seated in front of me.

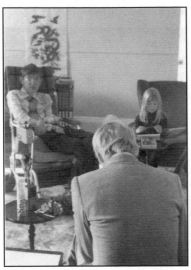

David Hockney drawing Stephen and Lucy
drawing Hockney, Cambridge, March 1978.

Visit of the Duke of Edinburgh,
June 10th 1981.

PhD, Albert Hall, March 1981.

Stephen, Tim and me in audience
with the Pope, Rome 1986
(courtesy of Fotografia Felici)..

Family party in 1986 with Jonathan – bottle in hand – and my Uncle Jack sitting between my parents and Don Page..

Madrid, October 1987. From left to right (seated around the table): Pam Benson (nurse), Stephen, Pedro Gonzalez Diaz, Elaine Mason (nurse), Raymond LaFlamme (student), Tim, me, Carmen Sigüenza González.

The Moulin at first sight.

Companion of Honour, Buckingham Palace, July 1989.

In the new house with the children and my parents, November 1994.

At Wimpole Hall, 4th July 1997.

Robert, Lucy, Tim and me, 4th July 1997.

With Jonathan and Bill Loveless, 4th July 1997.

Lucy and Robert at Lucy's christening.

Tim, aged two and a half.

My brother Chris and his wife Penelope with their children,
Calendula, Celeste, Peter and William.

Tim, Lucy and me with Stephen after the presentation of the Copley Medal
at the Royal Society, 30th November 2006.

leda dos amores'
dos amores leda.

Her lover passes by
who loves her a lot;
the mountain stag
stirs the water
happy in love,
happy in love.

The appearance of the stag at the fountain as a biblical reminiscence recalls the Song of Songs and the Psalms, but, at the
popular level, it could well be a vestige of the persistent pagan
fertility rites condemned by several scandalized bishops in the
fourth and fifth centuries
   Many of the poems conveyed a bleakness and a melancholy
which set them apart from the bright immediacy of the *kharjas*.
Here the obstacles to true love are fickleness, unfaithfulness and
rejection, as well as the practical realities of warfare or social
convention, and they find expression through the medium of
trees, birds and fountains. Surveying the emotional wasteland
that her life has become, the lovelorn girl calls to her negligent
lover, reminding him how the birds used to sing of their love. She
accuses him of destroying the landscape of their love through
his cruelty. The repeated refrain, *leda m' and' eu*, expresses her
longing for the happiness she has lost.

Vós lhi tolhestes os ramos en que siian
e lhi secastes as fontes en que bevian;
leda m' and' eu.

You took away the branches where they [the birds] perched
and dried up the springs where they drank;
Let me be happy.

Although the return to the thesis revived my intellectual morale,
it was lonely work, sitting at a desk in the library, surrounded
by yellowing tomes, trying to evaluate the relative importance
of each of the numerous influences which had contributed to
the composition of these poems. Stephen's attitude to medieval
studies had not mellowed with the years. In his opinion they

were still as worthless as gathering pebbles on a beach. The medieval seminar, formerly such a source of encouragement and enthusiasm, had been disbanded; my links with the Cambridge Spanish Department had never been more than tenuous, and although my mother still loyally came to look after the children on Friday afternoons, I felt out of touch with the London seminars.

The plangent voices of the *cantigas* filled my inner world and accompanied me in my solitary activities. They were with me as I went about my household chores, they occupied my mind while I sat feeding Stephen his interminable meals – diced to small morsels, spoonful by spoonful, mouthful by mouthful – and whenever an opportune moment, however brief, presented itself, I would dash to my table in the bay window of the living room and jot down a few notes, a few ideas, a few references. Yet, studying those songs, annotating them, analysing them was not enough. I passionately wanted to be able to express those emotions myself, through song, the song of any period. After my introduction to vocal music in California, I longed to be able to sing well. Vocal technique was portable, unlike the piano, and could be practised anywhere at any time, even at the kitchen sink.

Although Stephen's contempt for medieval studies was un-relenting and his devotion to grand opera, especially Wagner, continued unabated, he did, nevertheless, encourage my new interest. Just once a week he and a student would come home early to babysit, so that I could go out for an hour to an evening class in vocal technique, which was taken by a distinguished baritone, Nigel Wickens, who was both a singing teacher and a performer. His tall, erect figure was made all the more imposing by his domed cranium, and on initial acquaintance he was not a little intimidating, particularly on account of the exaggerated precision of his diction. This, however, was but one of the features of his expansive personality. Well-versed in the arts of performance, he could hold his class in awed subjection one minute – and the next send them into convulsive laughter. A veritable musical magician, Nigel would open his box of tricks every week and reveal a wealth of glittering gemstones, displaying all the shades and colours of the emotional spectrum and encapsulating the rich legacy of a succession of musical geniuses, Schubert, Schumann, Brahms, Fauré, Mozart… geniuses whose songs touched the inner self, reaching in to tap the core of the soul, expressing hopes and fears, sadness and a sense of tragedy for which words alone were inadequate. Sometimes the sadness of the songs and the ill-defined sense of longing that they evoked were so painful as to be unbearable. After a couple of classes, I knew that I wanted to learn to sing properly, to train my voice from scratch and create my own instrument.

4

A Board Game

Well-settled in the new surroundings and secure in his employment in the university, Stephen was changing direction in physics, turning his back on the macrocosmic laws of general relativity and immersing himself more and more in quantum mechanics – the laws which operate at the microcosmic level of the elementary particle, the physics of the quanta, the building blocks of matter. This change, which was a consequence both of his black-hole research and of his contacts with particle physicists in California, was beckoning him to a further quest, the search for a theory of quantum gravity which, he hoped, would reconcile Einstein's laws of general relativity with the physics of quantum mechanics. Einstein had been deeply suspicious of the theory of quantum mechanics, developed by Werner Heisenberg and Niels Bohr in the 1920s. He mistrusted the elements of uncertainty and randomness implied in that scientific breakthrough because they undermined his belief in the beautifully well-ordered nature of the universe. He voiced this dislike forcibly to Niels Bohr, telling him that "God does not play dice with the universe".

The origins of the universe had held my imagination for the whole extent of my married life and before. My mother used to point out the constellations, sparkling against the bright, unpolluted clarity of the Norfolk night sky when Chris and I were children. Still in the Seventies, terrestrial lighting was dim enough for Robert and Lucy and me to be able to look up at the night sky and marvel at the remote, spangled beauty of the glittering stars in the darkness. We could speculate about immeasurable distances and incomprehensible time spans and wonder at the genius, their father and my husband, who could transform that infinite space and time into mathematical equations and then carry those equations in his head – as if, according to Werner Israel, he was composing a whole Mozart symphony in his head. Those equations held the key to many questions about our origins and our position in the universe, not least the all-important question of the nature of our role as the minuscule inhabitants of an insignificant planet revolving round an ordinary star on the outer reaches of an unremarkable galaxy. These questions appealed to my imagination, even if my knowledge of the physics and the maths was only rudimentary. In contrast, the collisions of invisible particles, especially when those particles were not only invisible but imaginary as well, did not fire my interest with the same passion as the extraordinary mental journey through billions of light years to the beginning of space and time. Nor, I have to confess, did the set of scientists with whom Stephen was now associating attract me in the least. On the whole, particle physicists were a dry, obsessive bunch of boffins, little concerned with personal contact but very concerned with their own scientific reputations. They were much more aggressively competitive than the relaxed, friendly relativists with whom we had associated in the past. They attended conferences and came to the social functions arranged on their behalf, but, apart from a handful of ebulliently jovial Russians, their personalities made very little lasting impression. In among that grey morass it was an occasional pleasure to see the faces of those cultured, articulate, charming old friends from the relativity days – the Israels, the Hartles, Kip Thorne, George Ellis, the Carters and the Bardeens.

At least the most famous quantum physicist of them all left a long lasting impression, though he was certainly taciturn. Paul Dirac, a Cambridge physicist who in the 1920s had reconciled quantum mechanics with Einstein's theory of special relativity and in 1933 had won the Nobel Prize, was regarded as a legendary figure in physics. Stephen and Brandon considered themselves as Dirac's scientific grandchildren, since their supervisor, Dennis Sciama, had himself been supervised by Dirac. I had been introduced to Dirac and his wife, Margit Wigner, the sister of a distinguished Hungarian physicist, in Trieste in 1971. It was said of Dirac that when he introduced Margit to a colleague soon after their marriage, he did not say "This is my wife" but "This is Wigner's sister". After Paul's retirement in 1968 from the Lucasian chair – Newton's chair – the Diracs had moved from Cambridge to Florida, where he became an emeritus professor. The story was told that Dirac had once watched his wife knitting a garment. When she reached the end of the "knit" row, her husband, having worked out the mathematical theory of the craft of knitting, immediately instructed her how to turn the needles and "purl" the next row.

The Diracs visited us one afternoon in Cambridge. Margit was not dissimilar to Thelma Thatcher in her aristocratic bearing. If anything, though, with her flowing auburn hair, hers was an even more irrepressible personality, unselfconscious and gifted with a natural ease of conversation which contrasted strikingly with her husband's silence. As we sat having tea on the lawn, she talked about their travels, their family and their home in Florida, and she admired the children, chatting with them freely and openly, while her husband listened and watched. Margit more than compensated for his periods of taciturnity, attributed to the pressure put upon him by his Swiss schoolteacher father, who would only allow him to speak in impeccable French as a child at home in Bristol. She often spoke for her husband, just as I often found myself acting as Stephen's mouthpiece, especially when the talk did not concern physics. Stephen and Paul Dirac were not unalike in that they were both men of few words and preferred to put their well-considered utterances either to the service of physics or to trumping an otherwise meandering discussion. But in one particular respect they differed drastically.

In the week of their stay in Cambridge, Margit Dirac rang with an invitation to the ballet at the Arts Theatre. I hesitated, knowing only too well that Stephen would not be best pleased to spend an evening watching *Coppélia* even in the company of one of the world's most famous scientists. "No, no, my dear, it's not him we are inviting!" Margit exclaimed emphatically in response to my excuses on Stephen's behalf. "Paul wants you to come with us!" Paul's wishes brooked no further hesitation. A couple of evenings later I joined them at the theatre, slightly surprised to find that Paul really was there too, for I suspected that he would share Stephen's contempt for the dance that I loved so much. I was wrong: he seemed to enjoy the performance as much as anyone else. Despite his taciturnity, he and Margit exuded a comforting reassurance, making me very welcome, and for one evening I was not obliged to do anything at all, least of all worry about whether my companions were enjoying themselves.

At home, the routine was eased when a new postgraduate student of Stephen's, Alan Lapedes from Princeton, agreed to come and live in our spare room and, like Bernard in California, help with the more onerous tasks, especially the lifting. Reserved and self-contained, Alan was an uncomplaining helper, but I was wary of exploiting his willingness, since with other colleagues he often contributed to Stephen's daily care in the Department too.

Indeed problems with Stephen's bodily comfort were now considerable, because, true to form, he refused to resort to any palliative measures and often kept us tied to the house at weekends. During the week it was a perpetual source of anxiety and frustration, despite the efforts of Constance Willis's latest assistant, Sue Smith; she tried to make him take more regular exercise, by straightening his body and helping him to walk the length of the hall, supported by one helper on each side. However much Sue, with her engaging northern sense of humour, amused Stephen by telling him all the latest gossip in her own entertaining fashion, she could never persuade him to devote any more than those two hours of her visits to his exercises each week. "Now, you will do them, won't you, just for me?" she would plead, but he would simply regale her with one of his most beguiling, sphinxlike smiles.

The fact was that since Stephen was sedentary for all his waking hours, his limbs were much wasted through illness and lack of exercise. To outsiders, the mechanical advantages of the electric wheelchair, and the independence it conferred, hid the true extent of the ravages of motor-neuron disease because he was able to get about quite freely, flitting back and forth across the river, to and from the department. Any obstacle in the way of this revolutionary vehicle, however, required the assistance, not just of one able-bodied man but two or three to lift its 120 kilograms over a steep step or up a flight of stairs. If, on the way to an evening out together, we encountered a single step, we were in trouble.

Unlike me, Stephen, surprisingly, was not usually prey to the numerous minor ailments which the children brought home from school. He maintained a healthy appetite and a robust constitution, priding himself on never missing a day's work. Outsiders could have no concept, though, of how painfully emaciated his body had become, nor did they generally witness those horrendous choking fits which would come on at supper time and last well into the night, when I would cradle him in my arms like a frightened child, till the wheezings subsided and his breathing slipped into the easy rhythm of sleep. We tried to avoid these fits by experimenting with different diets, at first eliminating sugar, and then dairy products and finally gluten, the sticky protein in flour which binds bread and cakes. They were all suspected of irritating the hypersensitive lining of the throat. Although the children and I continued to eat bread and cakes, and cooking without sugar was not difficult, the challenge of gluten-free cookery in the 1970s – long before the advent of "free from" products on supermarket shelves – required some major adjustments in the kitchen since gluten-free flour in those days was a culinary nightmare. Even so, that challenge was infinitely preferable to those terrible life-threatening attacks of choking.

Just as we thought that we had escaped the worst of the winter's ills, the spring of 1976 lay in wait with a series of cruel tricks which made of it an obstacle course akin to a snakes-and-ladders board, though with many more snakes than ladders and with the dice weighted to land on the snakes. On 20th March the first small snake on the board snapped us up when Lucy fell ill with chickenpox. This unremarkable though uncomfortable ailment was certainly better disposed of in early childhood than at the age of twenty, as I knew from my own experience as a student in Valencia. By the following Monday, 22nd March, poor little Lucy was miserably red with spots, crying for all the attention I could give her by day and by night. As far as the chickenpox was concerned, we were no different from any other family with young children, but there the similarity ended. It was fortunate that Lucy made a speedy recovery during the course of that week, since the next throw of the dice was to send us hurtling down a much more precipitous snake.

On the Saturday morning at the end of that week, we all awoke with sore throats, and the next day both Alan and Stephen were distinctly unwell. The inflamed throats were accompanied by a high fever. Inherently mistrustful of the medical profession, still resentful of their shabby treatment of him in 1963 at the time of diagnosis, and as phobic about hospitals as I was about flying, Stephen forbade me to call a doctor even though he was neither able to eat nor drink and was coughing on every breath. Later the next day, in desperation, I called the duty doctor, but Stephen shook his head in furious rejection of all her suggestions for palliative measures, such as cough syrup or any sort of cough suppressant, because he had formulated a theory that such measures, in suppressing his natural reflexes, could be more dangerous than the cough itself. Effectively he had become his own doctor and was convinced that he knew more about his condition than any member of the medical profession. Stephen's mother, who had come over for tea on the Sunday afternoon, stayed on, and between us we nursed Stephen through a very disturbed night. The next day – my birthday – though very ill, pale, gaunt and racked by the choking, Stephen still refused to allow me to fetch help until late in the day when – as a major concession to me on my birthday – he let me call the doctor. When finally Dr Swan was permitted to set foot in the house at 7.30 p.m., his reaction was pragmatically straightforward: he called an ambulance at once, reassuring Stephen that he would be home again in a couple of days.

It was surely providential that at that blackest of moments when we arrived at the admissions unit – with Stephen thinking that he was about to be confined to a condemned cell and I, in an anguish of uncertainty, helplessly stroking his arm – the sound of a familiar voice, confident and authoritative, emerged from the doctors' office. It belonged to John Stark, the chest consultant who drove Robert to school every day. Stephen could not fail to respect John as a friend, whatever his opinion of doctors in general, and I was overjoyed to encounter someone in authority who could take charge of the situation without demanding lengthy explanations, someone with the medical expertise to relieve me of the impossible responsibility of caring for a very sick patient unaided. Nevertheless, because Stephen was so helpless in his inability to communicate with more than a handful of people, and because of his terror of being fed either a medicine or a food which could have harmful effects, I stayed in the hospital at his bedside all night. The next day showed a slight improvement in his condition – which had been diagnosed as an acute chest infection – as he gradually began to climb the first rungs on the ladder towards recovery, and two days later he was so much more cheerful that he seemed well enough to come home.

In the meantime, life at home had resumed a semblance of its usual pace. My parents had come to look after the children, Lucy had gone back to school and Robert went on a school day trip to York. When Alan and I collected Stephen from the hospital on 1st April, we entertained the foolishly optimistic hope that we were going to be able to get back to normal straight away. No sooner had we arrived home, so full of eager anticipation, than Stephen began to choke violently and incessantly and almost immediately slipped back into a desperate state. There was nothing that could be done to help him in his suffering, despite all the advice of the medical experts. He choked whatever position he adopted, whether sitting up or lying down. He could neither eat nor drink and was too weak to endure physiotherapy. My mother, Bernard Carr, Alan and I operated a rota system. One or two of us sat with Stephen all day and all night while the others slept. There was little doubt that the situation was extremely critical. I hardly needed the doctors to tell me that I should prepare myself for the worst.

Where medical science had admitted defeat, the concern shown by friends brought an unexpected revival of strength, inspiring a spontaneous renewal of hope. John Sturdy, the Dean of Caius, and his wife Jill came one evening, quietly and unobtrusively, to offer support through their prayers. Stephen's students and colleagues were unwavering in their devotion, visiting regularly and helping with his care, often through the night. Gradually, though still very frail and prone to choking attacks, Stephen began to improve until on Sunday 4th April he spent the whole day without choking at all and managed to eat a little pureed food. But that night his condition deteriorated again, and the following day saw us sliding back to square one. Robert awoke that morning with a high temperature, covered from head to foot in chickenpox blisters, and during the day he became delirious.

As my father was himself on the point of going into hospital in St Albans for an operation, my parents had returned home when Stephen first began to show signs of recovery. In their absence I had to throw myself on my good friends for help with the children, especially on Joy Cadbury, who for several years had hovered in the background, always ready to help with the utmost sensitivity when the need arose. In 1973 Robert had stayed with the Cadburys while we were in Russia and both he and Lucy always felt very much at home with their children, Thomas and Lucy Grace. They had already spent a couple of nights with the Cadburys when Stephen was in intensive care and I was with him at the hospital. The magnanimity with which Joy offered to nurse Robert, bespeckled with red blisters as he was, was quite beyond any call of friendship, *since* it was a foregone conclusion that both her own children would develop chickenpox within the next three weeks. I had no option but to let Robert go as the demands on me were so great, and my own resources were so depleted, that I could scarcely register what was happening to us.

In Joy's tender care Robert bounced back to health, though, of course, her children succumbed. My father came through his operation, and when, a day later, I managed to snatch an afternoon for a flying visit to St Albans, I was glad to find him up and about, walking round the ward. Stephen's recovery was slower and less predictable, mostly because he refused to take the penicillin he had been prescribed. He sat silently in his chair, resting his head on his hand, in the same melancholy posture he had first adopted in the Sixties. He did not speak, he choked frequently, and ate and drank in small, careful sips. He was not strong enough to go out, so the Department came to him and held its seminars in our living room. At last over the Easter weekend, he began to show signs of gaining strength. Only then could we begin to sleep at nights and I could relax my guard a little. The children came home, and in the one remaining week of the school holidays we looked forward to catching up on some holiday activities.

Stephen had other ideas. That Easter Monday, still in the early stages of convalescence, he summoned his students, commandeered the car and set off for a five-day conference in Oxford. As I stood in the doorway watching them go, my disbelief at such recklessness condensed into a desperate urge to escape – as far away as possible. Dennis and Lydia Sciama, who were aghast at Stephen's foolhardiness, recommended a hotel in St Ives in Cornwall. In a daze of miserable incomprehension, scarcely knowing where we were going or why, driven by a manic desire to get away from Cambridge, the children and I fled to London and boarded a train at Paddington for the West Country. The train whisked us further and further south. After Exeter it slowed down, crawling along at a snail's pace, snaking along winding branch lines. Oblivious to the slow passing of time, to the children's games, to their laughter and chatter, I gazed blankly out of the window, staring at the primrose-spattered fields of Cornwall without really seeing them, plunged into a stupor of exhausted dejection.

5

Celtic Woodland

It was obvious: we were living on the edge of a precipice. Yet it is possible even on the edge of a precipice to put down roots that penetrate rock and stone, roots that insinuate themselves into even the most meagre soils to form a sufficiently secure foundation for the branches above, stunted though they be, to produce foliage, flowers and fruit. At the end of April, on our return from Cornwall and Stephen's from Oxford, the children went back to school as if the nightmare of the Easter holidays had never happened. Quietly philosophical and undemanding, Robert had always taken his father's illness and disability in his stride, and fortunately he now went to a school which provided plenty of scope for doing all those physical activities that he and his father could not do together. Since Lucy followed her brother's lead in everything, she showed few signs of disturbance at the unconventional nature of her background. Our lives appeared to have taken up their usual rhythms, though perhaps with an even greater determination to focus on each moment of each day. As Stephen and the children settled back into their routines, I grasped every spare second to jot down a few thoughts on the thesis; I redecorated, yet again, the rented house owned jointly by Robert and his grandparents, upon which we depended for paying part of his school fees; I attended the singing class whenever possible; and I cooked for dinner parties for the advancing hordes of summer visitors to the Department.

In midsummer, a BBC television crew came to make a film about Stephen, as part of a two-hour documentary on the origins of the universe. By chance, the producer, Vivienne King, had been a student at Westfield in the same year as me. Although she had studied maths, she did not adopt a hardline scientific approach to the filming but wanted to present Stephen sympathetically, as a rounded figure set against the background of his family life. This image appealed to me because I feared that a hardline scientific approach could well present him as a sinister character,

259

like the malevolent wheelchair-bound Dr Strangelove in Stanley Kubrick's film. The finished product, the first and best of its kind, contained the elements of a poetic idyll – albeit in a scientific context. Stephen was, of course, seen at work in the Department, interacting with his students, conducting seminars, expounding his latest theories. He was also interviewed at home against the backdrop of the two children playing in the summer sun among the flowers in the garden. When the film was broadcast worldwide the following winter as part of a major BBC documentary – *The Key to the Universe* – a school friend of Lucy's, the daughter of a visiting scholar, watched it back home in Japan. The mother wrote to tell us that her daughter had stood transfixed in front of the television screen when she saw Lucy sitting on her swing under the apple tree. "Lucy, Lucy..." was all that she could say as the tears poured down her cheeks.

This was certainly the image of self-sufficiency to which we continued to aspire, though that image and the sweet illusion of success were becoming less easy to sustain. Alan Lapedes was so exhausted on his return from the Oxford conference after Easter, that he had to go away for a couple of weeks to recover. After all, he had been ill with a chest infection too, but no one had given a moment's thought to his state of health, because his help had been urgently required in caring for Stephen. He had unstintingly helped throughout the critical period – and beyond, because when Stephen decided to go to Oxford, he had had no choice but to go with him.

Stephen's valiant attempts to appear fit and well may have stood him in good stead in the Department, but at home his spirits were alarmingly low and his constitution was dangerously weakened. He spoke only to voice his demands, and no sooner had one need been met, one command fulfilled, than another would arise, stretching me to the limit of my endurance. We needed help more than ever but no help was forthcoming, in spite of our doctors' concerted appeals to the National Health Service. In any case, Stephen still absolutely refused to accept any outside nursing help. My doctor applied to the local authority for a home help to assist with the domestic chores, since all our spare income was spent on augmenting Robert's school fees and did not run to the luxury of a daily help. No help materialized, however, because when the social worker came to assess us, one glance at our surroundings was enough to disqualify us from any benefits. She was only one in a long line of people who failed to distinguish between the gilded illusion that we struggled to maintain and the brutal reality at the core of our situation.

Help, when it came, assumed a form which, in its innocence, was so precious that although it eased the physical strain, it increased a hundred times my guilt at being unable to cope on my own. Robert, at nearly nine years old, stepped out of his childhood and began to fetch and carry, lift and heave, feed and wash, and even take his father to the bathroom when I was overwhelmed with the weight of other chores, or just too exhausted to respond. In Stephen's pragmatic philosophy of survival, Robert's arms and legs were as good a substitute for his own as anyone else's, and certainly better than having a nurse in the house, even temporarily. It disturbed me greatly that Robert's childhood, that unrepeatable period of freedom, was being brought to such an abrupt conclusion.

For the week of half-term at the end of May, I arranged the family holiday that we had not had at Easter – five relaxing days in our favourite hotel, the Anchor at Walberswick, only two and a half hours' drive from Cambridge. Despite all the efforts of the hotel staff to cater for all our needs, including the diet, the holiday was a disaster. Stephen choked from beginning to end, but took umbrage at the suggestion that he might prefer to eat his meals in the privacy of our own chalet. Consequently every mealtime was an ordeal, as his convulsive wheezings ricocheted off the walls and distracted the other guests from their food. He subsided into a depressed lethargy and built a wall around himself, communicating only to express his needs in a morbid game of "Simon says...". Robert's help was called for again and again when I reached breaking point – as I did often since this situation demanded more stamina and courage than I possessed.

I was desperate for help and asked myself frequently where I could find it, almost always drawing a blank. Our friends were all keen enough to help in the short term, but they had their own families, their own lives to lead. There was no one who could spare the time or the energy to give us the undertaking, the dedication we needed so badly – above all to relieve Robert of the premature burdens and responsibilities that were being placed on his young shoulders. In my despair I approached Stephen's parents, since they were the only people I could turn to. My own parents had given us huge amounts of help throughout our marriage and were wonderful grandparents, but there was little that they could do in this extreme situation where medical intervention was often required, nor did I feel that it was fair to ask them. Stephen's father had promised to help in any way possible in that euphoric period before our wedding in 1965. Indeed Frank Hawking had painted the bathroom for us when we first moved into Little St Mary's Lane; he and Isobel had paid for my stay in the nursing home when Robert was born, and they had also paid for us to have a cleaner once a week when Robert was a small baby. They had given us quite a large sum of money to help us buy our house, and had generously handed on a couple of family antiques to grace our living room. Isobel had come to look after Stephen when the children were born, and she had also been prepared to fly off with him to conferences across the world when small children and flying phobia kept me grounded. On our annual trip to the cottage in Wales, she and Frank could be relied upon to help with Stephen's care; she, with controlled good nature, often calming her husband's impatience, for clearly it took a considerable emotional effort and self-discipline for him to reconcile himself to the time-consuming restraints of Stephen's severe disability. Although their own property was so dauntingly unsuitable for a disabled person in a wheelchair, they were curiously meticulous about reconnoitring castles and beauty spots for excursions, counting steps and registering any other hurdles in advance of our arrival.

Their visits to Cambridge however were always much more formal than my parents'. Mum and Dad were demonstrative and passionate grandparents, involving themselves in every aspect of the children's lives and our own, whereas Stephen's parents behaved like guests rather than close relations – and of late I had begun to sense a distancing in their attitude, as if the veneer of normality we struggled to maintain was so convincing that no more involvement was required on their part. On our return from Walberswick, I wrote a despairing letter to them, begging them to bring their minds and their medical knowledge to bear on the situation to help ease the overwhelming difficulties which were threatening us. My promise to Stephen had not altered, but, with the best will in the world, it was becoming much more difficult to sustain, particularly in the face of the unrelenting stress, all day and every day and much of the night as well. If anything the pace of life had accelerated since Stephen's recent chest infection, with a major conference in Cambridge, more dinners, more sherry parties and more receptions. I was at breaking point, but still Stephen rejected any proposals to relieve either the children – especially Robert – or me, of the strain. His constant rejection of our need for more help was an alienating force, wearing away the empathy with which I had shared every dispiriting stage in the development of his condition. In his reply to my letter, Frank Hawking promised to confer with Stephen's doctor about the medical aspects of the case and said that there would be ample opportunity to discuss other matters at greater length during our forthcoming summer holiday in Llandogo.

There was actually very little opportunity to discuss these matters in Wales because of the characteristic Hawking reluctance to discuss anything of a personal nature. Dutifully Frank helped with Stephen's care every morning and then, usually clad in boots, waterproofs and a sou'wester, he disappeared into the wilderness to attack the weeds which were making a mockery of his attempts to grow vegetables in the rainforest conditions of the steep east-facing hillside. Isobel valiantly did her best to organize interesting excursions for us, dodging the showers in the afternoons – a teddy bears' picnic, a visit to Goodrich Castle, a hunt for four-leaf clover – all pleasant, sociable family outings, conducted without any reference to the underlying problems and tensions. One morning she came to me and in a tone of flustered defiance said, "If you want to talk to Father, you had better see him now." She pointed outside to where Frank stood in the pouring rain. I donned my raincoat and joined him under the dripping trees. We walked along the road, not speaking, splashing across the rivulets that were rushing straight down the hill to swell the river in the valley below. My thoughts and emotions were churning in such a chaotic whirlpool that they would not be so easily channelled into a coherent flow. I was afraid of appearing disloyal to Stephen, yet I had to persuade his family that all was not well, that ways and means had to be sought, and if necessary imposed, to lighten the burdens. If nothing else, it was essential to relieve Robert of the tasks that were oppressing him.

I succeeded in none of my aims. The merest hint of dis-satisfaction with our situation was quickly identified as disloyalty to Stephen, summarily dismissed with the implication that it was a symptom of my own inadequacy. Frank did at least offer to discuss the situation with Stephen, but doubted that his words would have any effect. In any case, he asserted, there could be no question of forcing Stephen to accept more help. His only other comments were that Stephen was very courageous, that he drew his courage from his determination, and that he, Frank, was sure that Stephen was doing his best for his family. He was providing well for us, we had two lovely children and we were very fortunate in the position we occupied. I did not dispute the truth of all this, and by comparison with many disabled families we were no doubt well off, but there was little comfort in the repetition of such truisms. These were the blessings that I had conditioned myself to count for so many years. I knew well enough that Stephen's determination was his defence against the illness, but I did not understand why he had to use it as a weapon against his family. As for Robert, Frank expressed his concern for him by turning my argument on its head: Robert was too introverted, he said; he should be brought out of his shell so that, in the future, social ineptitude would not damage his career as Frank believed it had damaged his own, depriving him of recognition for his important work in tropical medicine.

There was no use in arguing. Though robust and in sterling health, Frank was old, a good ten years older than my father. Perhaps he was too old to understand how I felt and too old to adjust to what was being asked of him. For all his genuine concern for Stephen, he evidently found it difficult to see what was before his very eyes. To try and explain the obvious, to repeat the contents of my letter – that Robert's introversion was mainly a result of the home situation – would have been hopeless; the more so, considering that my purely practical suggestion that perhaps Frank and Isobel might begin to participate in the running of the rented house in Cambridge, especially when so much redecoration and refurbishing were required between tenancies, had been quashed outright on account of the distance – some fifty miles – between St Albans and Cambridge. The conversation petered out and we returned to the house.

Later the sky cleared. I was sitting on the terrace shelling peas for lunch when Isobel came and sat beside me. "So I gather you have talked to Father?" she enquired, eyeing me intently. "Not really," I replied. She pursed her lips and with the same defiance that she had shown earlier, she announced fiercely. "You do know, don't you, that Father will never allow Stephen to be put into a residential home?" So saying she stood up, turned on her heel and marched into the house. Her remarks stung me to the quick. I had never so much as thought about a residential home for Stephen, let alone mentioned such a preposterous idea. I had simply asked for help to protect my own young son from the psychological ravages of the physical disease which was afflicting theirs. Humiliated and even more despondent, I stood up. Abandoning the half-filled saucepan of peas, I walked slowly away from the house into Cleddon wood and there, in utter desolation, sat down on a broad, flat stone, scarcely conscious of the noise of the falls resounding in my ears. Never had I been so alone – alone there in the forest, on the hillside by the fast flowing stream. There was sympathy in nature when human beings could offer none, but nature was powerless to influence intellectual beings whose sole criterion was rational thought, who refused to recognize reality when it stood, bared before them, pleading for help.

In the second week of the holiday, when the sun shone dependably out of a clear sky, it appeared that I might have misjudged Stephen's mother. She took us to a hotel at the seaside on the coast and shared in Stephen's care for much of the time, sometimes feeding him his meals, helping to dress him and sitting by him on the path above the beach so that I could play with the children on the sands below and bathe in the sea. My spirits rose as my energies began to revive. It seemed that Isobel was responding to my pleas, after all, and was genuinely making an effort to help. I was grateful, but I smiled in puzzlement at some of the remarks she made. "Looking after Stephen is not really that difficult, you know," she observed breezily. "Robert doesn't seem to mind helping his father at all; in fact, I think it's good for them both," was her next cheerful remark. I was prepared to view such remarks as kindly meant, since the holiday that she had generously provided had been such fun and so beneficial to us all. However the persistent harping on the ease with which all my responsibilities could be accomplished, and the implication that my cries for help were not to be taken seriously, dampened my reawakening confidence in her. She did not seem to understand that, whereas my childhood naivety had long since died and my inherent youthful optimism had vanished, the thought that that was already happening to Robert at less than ten years of age was intolerable. "Really the wheelchair is not as heavy as you might think," she announced airily at the end of the week. "Lucy helped me to put it and the batteries in the car and between us we managed perfectly well." Lucy was five years old; the weight of the chair and its solid gel batteries had already made many a strapping student blanch.

Sad news greeted us in Cambridge at the end of August. During our absence Thelma Thatcher had been taken into hospital for an operation from which she did not recover. The ten years that we had known her, though a large proportion of our lives, were only a small proportion of hers, yet she treated us as if we were part of her family. Her soul was large, all-embracing, caring and practical, always ready to come to the rescue in times of crisis, always ready to help those worse off than herself, always ready with her quick sense of humour to pinpoint the ridiculous or the absurd. The children adored her and she adored them as their adoptive granny. For me she was a true friend and a staunch ally, whose judgement, I knew, was always sound, even though sometimes it might have been hard to digest. I had seen her just before we went to Wales. She was philosophical, dismissing her own health problems as insignificant, although she already knew that they were serious. Typically she was more concerned to talk about us. "I wish old Thatcher were stronger and could help her brave girl more," she said as she hugged me for the last time.

6

A Backwards Glance

That autumn, many scientists joined us for family meals at the end of long days filled with all the usual bustle associated with children and schools, clubs and after-school activities, as well as Stephen's requirements. Not much had changed in our circumstances – and Robert's help was still often called upon at home – but that week by the sea, the second week of the holiday in Wales, had restored both my stamina and my resolve, and I was better able to cope. Stephen was also in better health and spirits, although his recovery from the spring's bout of pneumonia did not mean that motor-neuron disease, which continued to exact its implacable toll of muscle degeneration, eating difficulties, choking fits and respiratory problems, had retreated.

In the Department the latest academic exercise to gain popularity was the symposium, a sort of protracted conference which extended over a whole year. This exercise held great attractions for Stephen since, with the increased funding now at his disposal, he could bring scientists to Cambridge from all over the world and work with them at leisure on lengthy projects such as books and papers – something which would have been an impossible undertaking in the hurried atmosphere of the customary four- or five-day conference. Although he was still wavering in his interests between general relativity and quantum mechanics, most of the visitors to the Relativity Group in the early part of the academic year were the old familiar faces, and most of them came from North America.

From my standpoint, the most formidable of them were the modest, amiable Chandrasekhars – not because of any clashes of personality, but because, just before they arrived for a dinner party, I learnt that they were vegan. I had supposed that they were vegetarian after mistakenly serving them a fish sandwich at a tea party, but had not suspected further complications. A last-minute revision of the menu was called for. Out went my planned recipes, and the search was on for meat-free, fish-free and dairy-free dishes – that were also gluten-free and sugar-free. My old Spanish stand-by, gazpacho, lent a touch of distinction to a meal of mushroom and onion risotto. It was really more appropriate to the Sunday supper table than to a dinner party for such distinguished guests.

In the middle of the term, the Cambridge coterie decamped to Oxford, where Dennis Sciama had moved to take up a Fellowship at All Souls College. Roger Penrose had been appointed Professor of Mathematics there, and he and Dennis regularly organized one-, two- and three-day conferences. While Stephen and his colleagues gave their seminars, I took the opportunity to get to know the museums and monuments of Oxford better. Over the past few years we had made six-monthly visits to the meetings in Oxford, even when the children were very small, and I too had begun to appreciate the charm of the place, at once more cosmopolitan and animated than its fenland counterpart. Stephen loved being back in Oxford. He carried the layout of the city in his head and, with a hint of pride, could direct me infallibly to any location, negotiating lanes and back streets with an easy confidence. He would nostalgically point out the wall he had once climbed over, only to fall into the arms of a policeman, and the bridge he and some friends were daubing with a ban-the-bomb slogan in the middle of the night, when a policeman sauntered by and arrested the friends, who left Stephen dangling in a cage beneath the bridge. These and other similar yarns had a somewhat apocryphal ring to them, though there were plenty of photos to attest to Stephen's disastrous antics on the river. There was little doubt, too, that he had been an eager participant in the sconce – a sort of beer-drinking contest, imposed as a fine for a breach of behaviour. Stephen's delight in those memories was touching: they provided a tantalizing glimpse of the old carefree rebel with whom I had fallen in love. They related, of course, to the days of his hedonistic youth, before the diagnosis of motor-neuron disease, which was, in chronological terms, a Cambridge phenomenon.

For conferences and trips further afield there were now plenty of colleagues and students who were glad of the opportunity to travel and to meet the famous names in physics. This was a great relief to me as I was still terrified both of aeroplanes and of leaving my children. I tried to be both father and mother to each of them and did not want them to suffer from having a severely disabled father, though of course I encouraged them to love and respect him. Unbeknown to Stephen, I shared my concerns with their teachers in the vain hope of protecting them against teasing in the playground. Occasionally, as in December 1976, when Stephen flew off with his students to Boston for a pre-Christmas conference, I could devote myself to my maternal role, attend the nativity plays, ballet shows and school carol services and take the children to the College Christmas party.

That December, Alan Lapedes, who had given us so much quietly dedicated help throughout the period of crisis, returned to his home in Princeton. I then spring-cleaned the spare room, our one room in the upstairs part of the house, for the arrival of our new resident physicist, Don Page, whom we had met in California where he was a former graduate student of Kip Thorne's. He and his mother had come to Cambridge on a tour of inspection. Naturally, they wanted to see whether the arrangement we were offering was suitable – and, I suspected, to judge whether I was a sufficiently respectable landlady. Evidently we passed the test, for Don bounced energetically into our household, like A.A. Milne's Tigger. He arrived with Stephen on his return from Boston on 18th December, and eagerly joined in all our Christmas festivities.

I had moved among physicists for long enough to know that they mostly come from somewhat unusual backgrounds. Don Page's background was so unusual that it was exceptional even among physicists. Born of missionary-teacher parents, he was brought up in isolation in a remote part of Alaska, where his parents provided his early schooling. He later attended a Christian college in Missouri, his parents' home state, and from there graduated to Caltech where he joined Kip's group as a postgraduate student. His fundamentalist beliefs were so firmly ingrained that the apparent clash between them and his field of study, gravitational physics and the origins of the universe, while paradoxical to many onlookers, did not appear to disturb him unduly, because he was able to compartmentalize his activities. On the one hand, his Christianity was devout, principled according to absolute values which, as yet unchallenged in their rigidity, could seem to lack sensitivity; on the other, those very evangelical convictions required of him a tireless zeal in all his endeavours.

While I respected his fervour – he attended church twice on Sundays, with additional midweek bible-study classes – and welcomed the supportive religious influence he brought to our lives, I sided with Stephen in refusing to be evangelized, particularly at breakfast time. Doubtless well-meaning, Don cherished the hope of making a spectacular conversion – comparable to that of Saul on the road to Damascus – through his early-morning bible readings and prayers. I could have told him that he was doomed to failure, for his broad, floodlit highway of biblical certainties was even less likely to meet with success than my own path, a quiet, unpretentious amble along the meandering lanes of simple trust in faith and deeds. Stephen had no patience with anything other than the rational power of physics, so I very much doubted that Don's earnest readings and literal sermons – at 8.30 in the morning when I came back from taking Lucy to school – were going to illuminate the way forwards. In any case Stephen always hid behind the newspaper, which was propped up on a wooden frame for want of an electronic page-turner, at breakfast. The upright newspaper was a barrier that the laden spoon had to negotiate when delivering his substantial breakfast of pills, laxative, boiled eggs, pork chops, rice and tea, and it was also a barrier to conversation.

This was not a barrier that Don had anticipated when he came down to breakfast in the early days, armed with Bible and edifying tracts. I said nothing, leaving him to address his invisible congregation as best he could. Shielded by the *Times*, Stephen would not be distracted from his perusal of current affairs, essential for a Fellow who prided himself on having the last word in high-table discussions – whether about Britain's precarious financial position shorn up by loans from the United States, or about the test runs of the Space Shuttle. I usually managed little more than a quick glance at the headlines, whereas Stephen read slowly, mentally photographing and digesting every snippet of information, every fact and figure, for regurgitation on some later occasion, probably at High Table.

As Don was finding his task heavy-going, it occurred to me that a distraction was needed, so I invited him to help himself to cornflakes, muesli, boiled eggs and toast, and asked if he had ever tried Marmite. He picked up the round, brown jar with its yellow lid. "No, no, we don't have this in the US; I guess it's some kinda chocolate," he replied, avidly ladling thick spoonfuls of the dark, treacly substance onto his slice of toast. "Try it and see," I said, whereupon he took a large bite. His open, childlike expression creased into wrinkles of repulsion at the pungent, salty assault on his taste buds. Even Stephen looked up from the newspaper, his broad grin revealing those alluring dimples in his cheeks. Good-humouredly, after a moment's puzzlement, Don was able to take the joke in good part, and never again did he bring his proselytizing zeal to the breakfast table.

The great advantage of having an American from Caltech in residence was that whenever Stephen wanted to go to Los Angeles – or anywhere else in the United States for that matter – in the interests of science, the American would want to go too. So although the following summer Stephen pressed me to accompany him to America for three weeks, Don was all too ready to go instead. This unexpectedly easy solution to a previously intractable problem cleared the way for me to fulfil a longing which had lain dormant for many years. It was in fact thirteen years since I had set foot on the Spanish mainland, and I longed to renew my contact with that country and its civilization, which had played such a significant role in my education before all my modest pretensions and aspirations were swallowed up. Pleasantries exchanged on dining nights with the Spanish butler of Caius had scarcely sufficed to maintain my once fluent command of the spoken language, and over the years that skill had dwindled pitifully to a handful of insubstantial polite formulae. The thesis was suffering from a serious lack of inspiration and motivation, partly on account of its length which had become unwieldy, partly because of the huge quantities of scrappy notes which remained to be incorporated into some sort of order, and partly because the topics were so remote that I was losing touch with them.

As always, my parents jumped at any suggestion of a holiday with their grandchildren, and together Dad and I planned an extensive tour through northern Spain and Portugal, coinciding here and there with the *camino francés*, the old pilgrim route to Santiago de Compostela. The mere exercise of planning brought back memories of those wonderful European holidays of old – especially because my father, with his historian's nose, had lost none of his talent for scenting out singular historical treasures which the ordinary tourist would have passed by.

Once all the summer activities were out of the way – dinner parties for a mini-conference, barbecues, lunch parties, children's tea parties, school sports days, college functions, mundane but necessary considerations such as servicing the car and cleaning out the rented house for reletting, and, ultimately, a vicious attack of measles which put Lucy to bed just before the end of term – Stephen left for California and we finally set sail for Bilbao. Although that grimy, industrial city on Spain's northern coast gave us a damp, cloudy reception, my heart leapt when I set foot on Spanish soil again. It continued to leap throughout that holiday, not only at the rediscovery of Spain, a liberated country where fascism was dead and democracy was tentatively establishing itself, but also at perceptible glimpses of my former self, the once hopeful, adventurous teenager, long buried under a heap of exacting burdens and more urgent priorities. By degrees I regained my grasp of the Spanish language, its grammar, syntax and vocabulary, for that too was part of my rediscovery. With its vitality the language reawakened my linguistic voice, so long reduced to a timid silence by the oppressive weight of intellectual prejudice in Cambridge, where one soon learnt to keep quiet rather than make a fool of oneself.

Cities with sonorous names – Burgos, Salamanca, Santiago, León, Coimbra and Oporto – and extravagant cathedrals, medieval monasteries, Mozarabic chapels, pilgrimage processions, sun-baked plains and gnarled olive groves blazed a trail of dazzling light and torrid heat into the chill drabness of our northern lives. In the rocky inlets, streams, pine trees and mountains, I discovered the landscape and the living traditions of the *cantigas de amigo*. The sensation that the ponderous weight of scholarship that I was trying to mould into a thesis had some basis in reality, that medieval studies were after all a more relevant, productive activity than collecting pebbles on the beach, gave me a tremendous boost. I promised myself that I would finish the thesis, come what may, even though it might not lead anywhere, even though it might simply be an end in itself. I felt impatient to record all that I had seen and relate it to the texts, but not so much so that I wanted to rush back to Cambridge before we had all squeezed every ounce of benefit from those weeks in Spain and Portugal. The children after all needed some compensation, in the form of a few days by the sea, for all the hours they had spent uncomplainingly in the back of the car. Lucy, whose imagination was so fertile that she could keep herself and everyone else amused no matter how long the journeys or how searing the heat, was fascinated by the cockle-shell motif of the pilgrim route to the tomb of St James at Santiago. She kept her eyes open for the shell on buildings, statues and signs, letting out a yell of triumph whenever she spied one. Perhaps not surprisingly after so many religious monuments, she and Robert became pretty confused in their grasp of the lives of the saints, with the result that, when we came down to the sea at Ofir in Portugal, they devised a crazy game in which Lucy played the part of John the Baptist, drenching her brother with sea water – while he, wrapped in a towel, played the part of a stoical pilgrim en route to the tomb of St James. Any religious connotations to this game were, needless to say, entirely spurious. While the children were engaged in this heretical and obstreperous pursuit, the one near-disaster of the holiday occurred when Dad found himself unwittingly shut in his room by a faulty door lock. There was no telephone in the room and the only possible exit was via the balcony: the only way to get off his balcony was to leap across a seventy foot drop onto ours and escape through our room. He joined us on the beach, bursting with pride at this daredevil achievement – which we all had to agree, with astonished amusement, was no mean feat for a sixty-three-year-old.

7

Impasse

In that autumn of 1977, with my mind once more fired with the glowing impressions of the Iberian Peninsula, I was determined to attack the thesis with fresh insight and vigour, although the organization of the material remained daunting and time was still a crucial factor. Stephen returned from California to promotion – to a personal chair in gravitational physics. His elevation to a professorship had implications beyond that of a modest salary increase, since the title and position assured him of enhanced respect and recognition wherever he went – with a few exceptions, one of them within his own Department. His promotion coincided with the redecoration and refurbishment of the Department, and for some time he waited for the carpet – to which as a professor he was entitled – to be laid in his office. After some months of waiting in vain, he decided to broach the matter with the Head of the Department, who tut-tutted peevishly at his request. "Only professors are entitled to carpets," he said. "But I am a professor!" Stephen remonstrated. Eventually, in somewhat belated confirmation of his status, his professorial carpet arrived.

Carpets notwithstanding, Stephen was afraid that the appointment might put a distance between him and his students, but he took comfort in the fact that the physical help he required of them disarmed any diffidence created by his lofty reputation. Although an undisputed intellectual potentate, he shuddered at the thought of conforming to the image of an establishment professor, aloof from students and colleagues. He preferred the image of the eternal youth with the boyish grin, poking fun at the very authority of which he himself was now a part.

While Stephen's physical condition may have been an effective equalizer in the sphere of the Department, his promotion, although welcome, created subtle problems for me in our dealings with the world at large, not least because his growing reputation so totally exceeded our circumstances. Only our very closest friends realized that on the home scene the struggle for daily survival continued unabated as before. Despite the piti-less onslaughts of motor-neuron disease, Stephen had become a national figure, the youngest Fellow of the Royal Society, the recipient of umpteen awards and medals, Einstein's successor and a professor at the University of Cambridge. The very paradox of his situation had made him the darling of the media. Not only in the popular perception but also, I began to suspect, in the eyes of his own family, his success was proof that he had conquered motor-neuron disease and therefore the battle was won: we could not possibly be in need of help. It was the most cruel irony that we had become the innocent victims of our own success. There was not simply a schism between the public face and the private image, they were actually in conflict with each other. Certainly the public functions – like the memorable occasion in the summer of 1978 when Stephen received an honorary doctorate from the University of Oxford – were enjoyable and gratifying, but that sort of limelight made not the slightest contribution to the help, both physical and emotional, which we needed more than ever because motor-neuron disease had not been conquered; it was still advancing at a slow but relentless pace. To the immediate family circle, the effects were devastating and the demands punishing. I could no longer keep up the pretence that it was just a background inconvenience, a fact of life. The disease dominated our lives and those of the children, in spite of all our efforts to uphold a precious veneer of normality.

Initially bright then reserved, Robert was now becoming so withdrawn that I feared that he was suffering from depression, a condition which, according to my doctor, was not unknown in children. For amusement he engrossed himself in computer manuals to the exclusion of other diversions. Stephen tried hard to fulfil his paternal role by buying elaborate electric train sets and complicated lengths of track, which Robert was not skilful enough to operate. Even when his old friend Inigo brought his more advanced electrical knowledge to bear, the trains never ran smoothly and Robert quickly lost interest. Apart from Inigo, who went to a different school, he had few friends and did not seem keen to cultivate new ones. It was obvious that Robert needed a male role model, someone who would romp and tussle with him, someone who would ease him out of a childhood already lost into adolescence, someone who would not expect anything of him in return, least of all help with their own physical requirements.

Lucy, effervescent and sociable, developed an early sense of independence, which enabled her to cultivate a wide circle of friends in which she found some compensations for the short-comings of her home life. From an early age she threw all her bubbling energies into a giddy social cycle of Brownies, swimming galas, Guide camps, sponsored runs, school plays and concerts and music and drama at the Saturday Music for Fun Club, as well as innumerable parties. Doubtless her huge collection of soft toys, and the fantasy world which she and Lucy Grace Cadbury invented for their Snoopy puppets, also played a part in helping her evolve subconscious methods for coping with her unusual background, though certainly she remained very sensitive to her circumstances. Both her age and her sex enabled her to avoid the some of the pressures that were falling upon Robert's shoulders.

My parents filled many of the gaps in the children's lives with trips to London, tea at the Ritz and visits to the theatre. However, there was a deep hole in my own life, which I could not even begin to broach to them. Thelma Thatcher was astute and forthright enough to identify it in one of her very last remarks to me before she died in the summer of 1976. "My dear," she said, leaning across her highly polished table and looking me straight in the eye, "I simply can't imagine how you survive without a proper sex life." I was so astounded by such candour from an octogenarian that I could reply only with a shrug of the shoulders. I myself did not know the answer to her question, but my sense of loyalty to Stephen forbade any open discussion of that topic, which for him was as taboo a subject as his illness. I did not allow myself to confide in Thelma Thatcher on that occasion and there was never another opportunity. Nevertheless I badly needed a confidante in whose age and wisdom I could trust. Quite apart from the physical aspects, the marital relationship was acquiring profoundly irreconcilable undertones. Intellectually Stephen was a towering giant who always insisted on his own infallibility and to whose genius I would always defer; bodily he was as helpless and as dependent as either of the children had been when new-born. The functions I fulfilled for him were all those of a mother looking after a small child, responsible for every aspect of his being, including his appearance – only just short of a nurse in that I refused to give injections or intervene in medical matters where I had no training. The problems were exacerbated by the sheer impossibility of talking about them. This was an intrinsic part of his battle against disease, which, with better communication, we could have fought together, side by side, supporting each other and developing strategies for coping with the difficulties. Instead it became an alienating force, bringing down a barrier of anguish between us.

Not for the first time, I sharpened my eyes and my ears, on the lookout for similar situations, words of advice or crumbs of comfort. My hopes were raised on a rare visit to Lucy Cavendish not long after kind Kate Bertram's retirement, when the new President was to introduce herself at a feast, a singular event for that College, and one which, despite my reservations about my own academic failings, I was reluctant to miss. After dinner, the new President rose to her feet and recounted the events of her life and of her academic career. Tears came to my eyes as she spoke of her marriage: her husband, too, had suffered from an incurable, disabling disease. Again it seemed for a brief moment that I had met someone with whom I might be able to talk freely, someone who would intuitively understand the tiredness and the despair behind the smiling but now hesitant façade. To my confusion, I heard her inviting the audience's sympathy for a choice that had faced her – between her academic career and her husband – when she was offered a prestigious American Fellowship. She had taken up the Fellowship.

Finally, in embarrassed desperation, I spoke to Dr Swan in the clinical atmosphere of his morning surgery. If his tone was one of concerned detachment, his words were as candid as Thelma Thatcher's. "The problems you are facing, Jane, are much like the problems associated with old age," he said candidly, "the irony is that you are a young woman with normal needs and expectations." He paused. "All I can suggest," he said, glancing up at me over his gold-rimmed spectacles, "is that you should make a life of your own."

In an unparalleled moment of chumminess that same autumn, Philippa coolly advised me that the time had come for me to leave Stephen. "Really, no one would blame you." she added condescendingly, as if in such facile advice lay the solution to all the problems. Whatever her motives – and certainly I had little enough cause to trust them – her advice struck me as being singularly ill judged. Certainly such a solution would have expelled me from the Hawking family circle with alacrity. She failed to understand that I could no more have left Stephen than I could have abandoned a child. I could not break up my family, the family that I myself in my optimism had created. This would effectively destroy the one achievement of my life and with it myself.

To pretend that I had never found other men attractive would be dishonest; however, I had never had an affair and my only relationship had been with Stephen. Those passing attractions had never been more than the briefest of encounters that consisted of no more than a fleeting eye contact. Indeed, I had long since lost my sense of individuality and any sense of myself as an attractive or desirable young woman. I saw myself as part of a marriage, and that marriage had grown from the original bond between two people into an extensive network, like a garden full of diverse plants and flowers, not only comprising parents and children but grandparents, loyal friends, students and colleagues. The central tree in that garden was the home, which I had created over the years, whether in Little St Mary's Lane, Pasadena or West Road. The relationship from which it had all sprung was now but one aspect of that complex diversity and, although that relationship had changed dramatically, the marriage itself was of much wider import and transcended the personal needs of the two people who had initiated it. A brittle, empty shell, alone and vulnerable, restrained only by the thought of my children from throwing myself into the river, I prayed for help with the desperate insistency of a potential suicide. The situation was such that I doubted that even God himself, whoever he was or wherever he was, could find a solution to it, if indeed he could hear my prayer – but some solution had to be found if our family were to survive, if Stephen were to be able to carry on with his work and live at home, and if I were to remain a sane and capable mother to the children.

It was an exceptional friend, Caroline Chamberlain – Stephen's former physiotherapist – at once sensitive and practical, who suggested that I might benefit from some diversion, such as singing in the local church choir. "Come and sing at St Mark's," she said, "we need extra sopranos for the carol service." Late one afternoon in mid-December we left the children with her husband Peter, while we went to the final rehearsals. This was the first time that I had sung in a real choir, as opposed to the choral class in Pasadena, and although my voice was developing nicely, sight-reading and counting were conspicuously absent from my skills, soberly reminding me of my teenage experiences as a hopelessly incompetent secretary. The other sopranos patiently measured the beat for me, a musical dyslexic, while the young conductor, pale and thin, politely internalized his dismay at the musical ugly duckling that Caroline had introduced into his organization. With practice my efforts improved, so that, come the carol service, my contribution was not as dire as he feared, and I was invited to join the choir for carol-singing round the parish later that week.

Lucy came carol-singing with me and trotted along from street to street, from house to house, calling at many homes, where the members of the choir and their choirmaster seemed to be not only well known but well received also. This was the area of Cambridge where Lucy went to school, yet apart from the school and the shops, I scarcely knew it at all. Here was a tightly knit community of friends and neighbours, elderly people and families, for whom the red-brick Edwardian church seemed to represent a nucleus, whether or not they attended it regularly.

In the dark winter night, as the choirmaster, Jonathan Hellyer Jones, walked beside Lucy and me, balancing on the edge of the pavement to protect us from the passing traffic, we struck up conversation. I talked as I had not in years and had the uncanny sensation that I had met a familiar friend of long acquaintance, a shadowy recollection brought sharply back into focus, given shape and form by this stranger. We talked about singing, music, mutual acquaintances – of whom there were several – and travels, particularly in Poland, where he had sung with the University Chamber Choir in the summer of 1976. He told me about St Mark's and its extraordinarily dedicated, warm-hearted vicar, Bill Loveless, who had given him great support and strengthened his faith through a very difficult period. He did not say what that period was, but I already knew from Caroline that eighteen months previously, Janet, Jonathan's wife of one year, had died of leukaemia.

We did not meet again for several weeks and our next encounter was quite by chance. In January 1978, while Stephen was away in America with his entourage for three weeks, I went with Nigel Wickens and a group from his singing class to an evening of Victorian entertainment given by the baritone soloist Benjamin Luxon at the Guildhall. In the crowded auditorium, I noticed Jonathan immediately, a strikingly distinctive figure, tall, bearded and curly-haired, on the other side of the hall. I was surprised when in the interval he recognized me and I introduced him to Nigel. "What a nice man!" Nigel remarked on the way back through King's College to West Road where he had parked his car. I agreed guardedly, preferring to concentrate on the other main topic of conversation, Nigel's forthcoming marriage to a talented American singer, Amy Klohr.

As a result of that chance meeting, Jonathan came to teach Lucy the piano on Saturday or Sunday afternoons, depending on his availability. She quickly warmed to him and his serious-minded hesitancy was soon dispelled by her liveliness. At first he came strictly for the length of the lesson, then he stayed a little longer to accompany me in the Schubert songs I was learning – while Stephen alternately directed the railway operations in Robert's bedroom and provided us with an audience of one for our own private *Schubertiades,* as we called them. After a few weeks of this routine, Jonathan began to stay for lunch before or supper afterwards, and to help with Stephen's needs, relieving Robert of all the chores which had oppressed him for so long. Then when we had got to know Jonathan a little better, Robert would lie in wait by the front door and pounce on him on his arrival, throwing him to the floor and wrestling with him. Jonathan took this unconventional form of greeting in good part and responded in kind to a growing boy's need for a good rough-and-tumble to release his excess energies.

Often during the course of each week we would come across each other quite by accident and wonder at the extraordinary coincidences which seemed to be bringing us together. We would stand by the roadside, talking, oblivious to what it was we were supposed to be doing or where we were going. We had so much to discuss, his bereavement, his loneliness, his musical ambitions on the one hand, and my fears for Stephen and the children and my despair at the difficulty of doing everything that was required of me with tolerance and patience on the other. Although younger than me, he had so much wisdom, so broad a perspective on life with which to enlarge my restricted view, so strong a faith and so luminous a spirituality with which to light my black horizon, that we truly trod the holy ground which, in Oscar Wilde's words, is present where there is sorrow. I had met someone who knew the tensions and the intensity of life in the face of death.

Other circumstances conspired to bring us together in the strangest of ways. I still attended dinners once a term or so in Lucy Cavendish – simply to maintain the contact rather than because I derived any pleasure from them. On one such occasion, having exhausted my own limited fund of conversation, I was listening to the talk across the table when I heard a distinguished elderly Fellow of the college, Alice Heim, singing the praises of a young man who visited her house regularly to play piano duets with her. The warmth with which she described him, his kindnesses to her and his musical talent startled me. He was unique, a veritable Apollo. Her ageing companions were more than a little perplexed by the effusions of their colleague. "What was his name?" they asked. When she replied, "Jonathan, Jonathan Hellyer Jones," my ears burned and I felt myself colouring with pleasure, as though I was the only person present who could share her appreciation of this champion who had entered our lives. Nor could anyone have been more surprised than I was, as much at my own blushing reactions as at Alice Heim's enthusiasm. I was uncomfortably aware that the warm glow resulted as much from embarrassment as from pleasure, as if I stood accused of a guilty secret. Yet there was no apparent reason for this friendship either to be a secret or to be tinged with guilt. It was based on our shared interests, on our concern for each other's situation, on the support we could bring to each other, and above all, on music. Nevertheless, though we had never touched and would not do so for a very long time, we were both aware that the guilty secret was an admission of the potentially physical nature of the relationship. The attraction between us was strong, but adultery is an ugly word, contrary to the ethical basis on which our lives were built. Was this the price I should have to pay to rekindle the flame of my passionate spirit? Was it a price that, in all honesty, I could allow Jonathan to pay? If I were to find myself in the company of the adulterous heroines of the nineteenth century, the price might be even higher. The end result might be only the jarring sound of Flaubert's cracked kettle rather than music to move the stars to pity.

8

A Helping Hand

During the following term Jonathan suggested that I might like to join the church choir, which was rehearsing excerpts from *Messiah* for an orchestral performance at Easter. As Robert and Lucy were old enough to be left for an hour in front of the television in the early evening, I joined the handful of choral parishioners for the Thursday rehearsals in the church. To me, a comparative beginner, the graphic complexity of Handel's choruses – in which sheep ran astray with alarming rapidity "turning everyone to his own way" – represented a challenge which I countered with an obsessive enthusiasm. In joining the choir, I also joined the church, where services fell loosely within the bounds of the Church of England formats that I had known since childhood. But this was Anglicanism devoid of sanctimonious dogma and stifling pedantry, thanks to the visionary dynamism of the vicar, Bill Loveless, whose surname could not have been more ill suited to his personality. Once a journalist on the *Picture Post*, actor, soldier and businessman, Bill had come to ordination in middle age. Happily still blessed with phenomenal vitality, he brought all his experience from other walks of life – and all his contacts too – to assist him in his pastoral work and in his unending search for relevant themes for his sermons, while for his monthly forum on topical matters he invited a succession of guest speakers – doctors, policemen, social workers, political activists and so on.

For Bill, true Christianity did not deal in absolutes, bargains with God or divine punishments. Its one guiding principle was a passionate love of humanity, affirming God's unequivocal love for all people, whoever they were, whatever their imperfections. The only command of this loving doctrine was to love one's neighbour. In this realm there was rest for all the weary and heavy-laden, and there I found solace. At last the crumpled rag of my spiritual being began to revive, but, although I derived comfort from my return to the Church, it also set me imponderable questions. What was being asked of me? How great a sacrifice was required of me? The circumstances in which I had met Jonathan, when I was at breaking point, were so extraordinary – and yet so ordinary – that I could not avoid the bizarre, perhaps naive impression that that meeting had been deliberately engineered by a benevolent power, acting through our good and caring mutual friends. We were both lonely, deeply unhappy people, in desperate need of help. Could that meeting really have been part of a highly unorthodox divine plan? Or was I just being absurd, even heretical and hypocritical? I knew my Moliere too well to want to find either myself or Jonathan being cast in the role of Tartuffe, the arch hypocrite.

Some people might regard the support that had appeared at my side, lifting the burden from my shoulders, as a happy chance, for others it might seem just a coincidence. For me, tense and overwrought to breaking point, it had the hallmark of divine intervention – although at that stage, in the spring of 1978, Jonathan and I had scarcely begun to confront our feelings, let alone give them any expression. The fundamental question was how to handle this heaven-sent gift. It could be used hurtfully, destructively, with the potential to break up the family in which I had invested so much of myself, if Jonathan and I even momentarily contemplated going off and setting up a home together. It would not be enough to claim that I had fulfilled my promise to Stephen in outrageously difficult circumstances over a very long period, because this was not a viable rationale in terms of the teachings of our church, which both I and Jonathan believed were the only true basis for human living. The alternative course was the only one we could follow. Then, that special gift could be used well, for the benefit of the family as a whole – for the children and for Stephen, if he were prepared to accept it as such. The latter course would not be easy since it would require a rigorous amount of self-discipline. In caring for Stephen we would have to try to maintain a distance from each other, living apart and not allowing ourselves to show any outward signs of affection for each other in public. In principle, our social lives would always focus on at least three, if not five people, never an exclusive twosome. The well-being of Stephen and the children would be the justification for our relationship with no thoughts for the future. In effect there was no obvious future for anyone who became involved with me. If it was selfish of me to monopolize the life of a young man who had already suffered so much tragedy, the answer was always the same: with his help we could survive as a family, without it we were doomed.

As, hesitantly, we began to admit to the attraction that was drawing us to each other, Jonathan would dispel these doubts by reassuring me that through us – all of us – he had found a purpose which was helping him to alleviate the hollow pain of his own loss. It was during the course of a rare visit to London, sitting in a quiet side chapel of Westminster Abbey, that he announced that he was prepared to commit himself to me and to my family, come what may. That most selfless and most moving of pledges lifted me out of the dark void that my life had become. The relationship was ennobling and liberating. It was still platonic and would long remain so. The mutual attraction, and the unruly emotions it threatened to provoke, were sublimated in the music we practised and performed together, usually in Stephen's presence at the weekends and sometimes on weekday evenings as well. It was enough that someone had come into my life on whom I could depend implicitly.

Stephen at first reacted to Jonathan with a certain male hostility, trying in true Hawking fashion to assert his intellectual superiority, just as he might when faced with a new research student. He was soon disarmed on discovering that this technique was unavailing, since Jonathan was not competitive by nature. Highly sensitive to the needs of others, he responded much more readily to Stephen's helplessness and to the charm of his smile than he did to the sonority of his reputation. Stephen became gentler, calmer, more appreciative, more relaxed. It even became possible, in the dead of night, for me to confide in him in an unprecedented manner. Generously and gently he acknowledged that we all needed help, no one more than himself, and if there was someone who was prepared to help me, he would not object as long as I continued to love him. I could not fail to love him when he willingly showed such understanding and, most importantly, communicated it to me. On the occasional days when Jonathan was attacked by the black dog of depression, it was Stephen who would reassure me that Jonathan would never let me down. Otherwise, once accepted, the situation was rarely mentioned. It was however greatly reassuring to me that I could trust Stephen with my confidence.

All pulling together, the three of us embarked upon an exceptionally creative period. There were still those times when the combination of my tiredness and Stephen's innate cussedness would bring me to the verge of collapse, but generally we operated on a much more even keel. For Stephen, it seemed as if the respectability conferred on him by his Fellowship of the Royal Society and by the Papal medal constituted an automatic passport to a cornucopia of other honours. While he continued to advance his understanding of the universe, all sorts of august bodies continued to trip over each other in their eagerness to cover him with medals, prizes and honorary degrees. These had already included the honorary doctorate from his Alma Mater, the University of Oxford, and to his special gratification, an honorary fellowship at University College. The atmosphere at the six-monthly feasts in the College was warm and friendly, and Stephen's undergraduate excesses were a recurring topic of jovial reminiscence. As if to lend substance to the recollections, we were regularly accommodated in undergraduate rooms at some distance from the nearest bathroom across cold, damp flagstones.

In March 1978, Caius College, not to be outdone, commissioned a line-drawing portrait of Stephen from David Hockney. While Hockney sketched and drew, Lucy sat curled up, reading and drawing, in an armchair in a corner of the living room. Doubtless to the surprise of the Fellows of Caius, Hockney included her in the final version, a gentle acknowledgement of Stephen's family background to offset the official formality of the portrait. On the second day of the sitting, Lucy paid her own tribute to Hockney. We were sitting on the lawn, drinking coffee and taking advantage of a brief spell of spring sunshine, when she burst out of the house, bouncing across the lawn on her hopper, a big balloon made of tough rubber. Her dungarees were pulled up to the knee, deliberately revealing that like Hockney she was wearing odd socks, one white and one brown.

One cold wintry evening that February, Stephen and I had joined the distinguished gathering of Fellows on the coach going down to the Royal Society for the admission of Prince Charles as an honorary Fellow. (Before coaches were fitted with wheelchair lifts, Stephen had to be hauled aboard bodily – by the coach driver and me. This however was easier than driving and parking in London.) The occasion gave Stephen cause for much mirth, a welcome reminder of the old irreverent student, scarcely discernible under the present, weighty trappings of

Establishment recognition. At the ceremony, the new President of the Royal Society complimented the Prince on the dedicated royal patronage of the Society, founded as he said by Prince Charles's namesake, Charles II, and "continued by his son James II". Stephen guffawed and, in the loudest stage whisper of which he was capable, gleefully announced, "He's got it wrong! James II was Charles II's brother!" At the reception after the ceremony, Stephen enjoyed himself even more by demonstrating the turning circle of the wheelchair to Prince Charles and in so doing, ran close to – or over – the highly polished royal footwear, an exercise which he was to inflict at a later date on the Archbishop of Canterbury at a dinner in St John's College, Cambridge.

Jonathan's career was much less meteoric than Stephen's; in fact it had scarcely begun. Quite apart from the devastating tragedy he had suffered, the frustrations of being a struggling musician contributed to the gloom of the bleak, black days he sometimes endured. A former chorister and prize-winning scholar of St John's College, he was sufficiently ambitious to find the prospect of a life spent teaching the piano disheartening, yet his natural reticence and modesty tended to conceal his very real talent as an organist and harpsichordist. His intense love and knowledge of baroque music, particularly Bach, especially when performed on authentic instruments, found scant outlet in the humdrum routine of piano teaching in schools. Convinced that he had a mission to wean the ears of the public away from resonant modern instruments and Romantic interpretations to the subtleties of baroque performance technique, he hardly knew where to begin. Authenticity in performance became one of the subjects under discussion at mealtimes, when the children's chatter allowed the adults to get a word in edgeways. Stephen would tease Jonathan about the difficulties of managing a harpsichord, insisting that a steel frame would solve all the delicate time-consuming problems of tuning and retuning. Jonathan would point out that the instrument would then not only be unsuitable for authentic baroque performance, it would no longer be portable either. In fact it might as well be a piano.

Good-humoured banter notwithstanding, Stephen and I inevitably became more and more involved in music and encouraged Jonathan to take the plunge, to move away from teaching into performing. This proposition presented him with a dilemma of which he was already only too well aware. To become a performer he would have to give up most of his teaching and devote the time to practising and rehearsing, yet he depended on teaching for his income. It would be a long time before he could make enough money from performing alone. He did have one great advantage however: he possessed his own instrument. Not only did he have a fine upright piano in his tiny house – so reminiscent of 6 Little St Mary's Lane – on the other side of Cambridge, but most of the rest of the living space was taken up with a harpsichord which he himself had built. He was therefore well equipped to begin performing; he simply lacked the right opportunity.

The more the three of us discussed the dilemma, the more we realized that the only way for Jonathan to build up a repertoire and to become recognized as a performer, in a highly competitive environment, while still earning an income from teaching, was for him to create his own opportunities. This he could do gradually by self-promotion and by offering his services to charities. A symbiotic relationship developed between him and the various charities to which he subscribed, particularly the societies concerned with leukaemia and other cancers. He gave recitals free of charge and in so doing trained himself in the techniques of performance, not simply in playing the notes but in overcoming nerves and in planning and presenting the programmes, while the charities benefited from one hundred per cent of the takings, minus the costs of publicity.

Meanwhile I was at last catching tantalizing glimpses on the horizon of the end of my own intellectual pilgrimage. I scarcely liked to confess how long it had taken me to reach that point, for it was all of twelve years and two children. Alan Deyermond, my supervisor, had been right to insist on registering me as a student at London University, as any other university would have thrown me out long ago. The way had been hard and tortuous and just when I was despondently thinking that there was no end to it, Jonathan had appeared to cheer me along the final stretch. He showed a sufficient interest in the subject to spur me on; he would ask me at the end of each day what I had achieved, listen to just a few lines of the poetry and lend a hand in sorting out the card index and the masses of notes, scribbled on odd bits of paper. That interest and a little practical help was all I needed to bolster my resolve for the final hurdle, the last chapter of the thesis which was to be an analysis of the language of the popular poetry of Castile in the later Middle Ages.

The Castilian lyrics were lively and colourful, full of the medieval iconography of gardens, plants, fruits, birds and animals, symbolizing the multiplicity of the aspects of love. Many of them were also of religious significance and were common to the rest of Europe. The garden epitomizes the attractions of the beloved as well as the virtues of the Virgin Mary. The fountain at the centre is both the spring of life and the symbol of fertility. The apple is the fruit of the Fall and the pear the fruit of divine redemption, but, in the secular context, both are potent metaphors for sexuality. The rose is the emblem of the martyrs and of the Virgin, yet it is also the most appealing image of the sensual beauty of the beloved. Spain introduces its own set of vivid images, drawn from its flamboyant landscape. The fruit which the unhappy nun tastes is the bitter lemon, while happy lovers walk in the shade of the sweet orange grove. The olive grove, similarly, becomes the scene of lovers' meetings. The fact that many of these images have reappeared in the poetry of the Sephardic Jews who were expelled from Spain in 1492, and in the poetry of the New World, is indicative of their early folkloric composition. Thematically these poems present an unbroken tradition with their Galician and Mozarabic forebears, the *cantigas* and the *kharjas*. The songs are usually sung by girls, the motif of the lover's absence recurs, the lovers meet at dawn and the mother is a constant figure.

During sparse weekday minutes and half hours, the writing began to flow with an unaccustomed ease. At weekends, on Saturday and Sunday afternoons, the songs began to flow as well. I voraciously attacked whatever Nigel, my personal Svengali, put before me, whether Schubert, Schumann, Brahms, Mozart, Britten, Bach or Purcell. Thanks to Stephen, I rapidly acquired my own library of music as he showered me with volume upon volume of music for birthday and Christmas presents. Sometimes I would be called upon to sing a solo verse in church. Initially the stage fright was terrifying, but eventually, with practice, it subsided and then the voice, which Nigel had painstakingly crafted into an instrument, surprised even me. I was producing the sound but it bore little relation to my light, unsure speaking voice. It was strong and confident, the voice of someone else, poised and assured and affirmed.

One weekend that spring my brother Chris and his wife Penelope brought their baby daughter to stay and I introduced

Jonathan to them as a new friend. They did not demand accounts of a situation which I myself could not fully explain. They were also a receptive and appreciative audience for a few songs. Afterwards, Penelope remarked on the atmosphere in the living room that Sunday afternoon. She said that it was magical, as if a great sense of peace and calm had descended on our house. That comforting remark increased my confidence in my new friendship. Chris was much taken with Jonathan, and before he left he deliberately drew me aside to tell me what a wonderful person he thought Jonathan was, especially remarking on his magnificent Byzantine eyes. Later he rang from Devon. We talked for a long time, discussing my situation and the way that it was changing. I took Chris's advice very seriously to heart. "You have been steering your little boat single-handedly across a very stormy, uncharted sea for many years," he said, and then continued, "If there is someone at hand, willing to come on board and guide that boat into a safe harbour, you should accept whatever help he can offer."

Later that summer we received a visit from my old head-mistress, Miss M. Hilary Gent, who regularly included us in her annual progress round the country, taking in former colleagues and pupils from her long career in teaching. Miss Gent's memory for names, faces and circumstances was formidable. She relayed her own news network, linking old girls with old teachers and vice versa, and establishing acquaintanceship between people from different periods of her life who had never even met. Keenly observant, she had shown herself sensitive to my tiredness and low morale over the past few years and had done her quiet best to help by writing formal but encouraging letters, and by putting me in touch with old girls from St Albans who had come to live in Cambridge. I rarely followed up her introductions as my life had become too complicated and I preferred the company of the elderly – especially since I myself, at the age of thirty-three, was acknowledged to be living the life of an old person and I needed the philosophical reassurance of someone who had come to terms with the dilemmas of old age and mortality which beset me.

Once a fortnight or so I would visit the oldest person I knew, a diminutive, white-haired former artist, Dorothy Woollard. As I sat with her in her sheltered accommodation, listening to her tales of the past and commiserating with her malaise at her present restricted circumstances, her room represented a quiet oasis of solitude and reflection in my otherwise frenzied routine. DW, as we called her, had trained in the Bristol School of Art, and as a girl she had seen Queen Victoria, a tiny old woman in a black bonnet, on a royal visit to Bristol. She had painted the pictures for Queen Mary's doll's house in Windsor Castle, and during the First World War she had worked in the Admiralty, drawing charts. She had never married but had devoted many years of her life to caring for her adored teacher who was wheelchair-bound in old age. His portrait, her greatest treasure, hung in her room among a vast collection of her own masterly etchings and watercolours. At an age when most people would have retired from all activity, she kept herself occupied by translating books into Braille. She was still quick and nimble, even in her nineties, so much so that once she left the dinner table to demonstrate her ability to touch her toes to my astounded parents. She attributed her longevity – she lived to the age of a hundred – and her sprightliness in part to her afternoon tea, *yerba mate*, a South American brew which she served to me when I visited her. Amongst my elderly acquaintance only Miss Gent, who was probably at least ten years younger, could compete with her in alertness, clarity of thought and quick-wittedness. Both were blessed with the perceptive wisdom of old age and a sensitivity to the problems of illness – attributes which, in my experience, younger people often lacked.

Jonathan was with us when Miss Gent arrived one Saturday afternoon for tea. Immediately she and he began to talk. They talked for the rest of the afternoon while Stephen – the famous old boy of the preparatory department of St Albans High School for Girls – and I sat listening. It transpired that Jonathan, in his late twenties, and Miss Gent, in her late seventies, had many acquaintances in common, since music and the musical arena were but one of the many topics in which she was intimately knowledgeable. She interrupted their conversation to follow me into the kitchen when I went to fetch the tea. Unhesitatingly, with an openness which I found extraordinary for a wizened, elderly spinster, let alone my former headmistress, she declared, "I am so very glad that you have Jonathan." She looked at me searchingly, as though wondering whether to be more explicit. "You have struggled on for so long alone," she went on, "I don't know how you have managed; you really need someone to help and support you. He is a splendid young man." It was as if Thelma Thatcher with all her years of experience was talking to me, telling me that my relationship with Jonathan bore the mark of destiny, that the gift was really to be accepted.

My parents met Jonathan that summer. As usual they were reticent about expressing their opinions, traditionally indicated by their reactions rather than words. In this instance they behaved exactly as if Jonathan had been a presence in our lives for as long as they could remember; they did not stand on ceremony, nor did they pass any comments on his regular appearances in our household. For his part he tactfully ceded his place at the piano to my father, whose passion for Beethoven had fired my own love of music. So while my father pounded out the *Appassionata* and my mother plied her needle, replacing the buttons and repairing the cuffs and seams which had fallen off or apart since her last visit, Jonathan would discuss the merits of early instruments with her and tell her about his crusade for authentic performance. It was after we had met Jonathan's parents that I remarked to my mother what wonderfully kind people they were. My mother looked at me in some surprise. "Well, you ninny, what would you expect?" she said. "People who have a son like Jonathan are bound to be wonderful. How could they be otherwise?"

At the end of the summer we parted company, already anticipating our reunion in the autumn. Jonathan left England to attend and teach at a baroque summer school in Austria, and we set out, with Don in attendance, for Corsica. Now that the children were growing up and my self-confidence was re-emerging, the fear of flying was beginning to dissipate a little. Air travel no longer held the dreaded threat of separation from tiny dependent beings; instead it held out the enticing promise of a holiday by the Mediterranean on a French-speaking island. The fact that the holiday was also a conference in physics was not a hindrance to enjoyment. In fact it was the perfect compromise because Stephen and his colleagues would be doing what they liked best – physics – while the families would be enjoying the best sort of beach holiday, within a stone's throw of the conference centre. I was particularly looking forward to seeing the Carters again. I intended to confide in Lucette. With her intuitive understanding of people and relationships, she would be bound to offer good, sound advice.

9

The Unexpected

Cargese, the conference venue on the west coast of Corsica, was certainly the happiest compromise ever devised for single-minded physicists and their young families. While Stephen revelled in the physics, the children and I enjoyed the bright sun, the sand and the sparkling sea. The occasional bomb outrage and high prices preserved the island from mass tourism, keeping its beaches and coves clean and uncrowded, as Majorca used to be. Cargese was established as the home of a colony of Greeks seeking refuge from Turkish persecution in the eighteenth century. Their presence was still very much in evidence in street names, family names and in the name of our hotel, the Thalassa – the Sea. On promontories overlooking the town, Cargese proudly sported two churches, one Latin and the other Greek. The same priest officiated at both, alternating between the two on consecutive Sundays. Lucette and I attended the Greek rite, fascinated by such an exemplary display of harmony in what might otherwise be a divided community. Both churches contained images of John the Baptist; the Greek icon was compelling for its sharp Byzantine clarity, especially for the haunting depiction of the saint's long, slanting eyes, so reminiscent of Jonathan's. Even that image was not able to inspire me with the courage to tell Lucette about my friendship with him. Whenever I tried to summon the words, whether in English or in French, they stuck in my throat, trapped by my sense of self-reproach at the merest hint of disloyalty to Stephen. The glorious new relationship, which promised so much, was awakening doubts. Was it going to force me to live a lie, to lead a double life? That could turn out to be as difficult as the strain and distress of the preceding months and years. I took heart when I recalled Chris's advice and Miss Gent's encouragement, but in the company of physicists and their families – among whom Stephen was an awe-inspiring hero – my courage failed me.

In a quiet bay, away from the children's shouts, I wedged myself into a corner in the rock and wrote a long letter to Jonathan, trying to organize my thoughts and sort out my troubled conscience. I told him how much I missed him and how eternally grateful I was for the light he had brought to my life, like the light of the Corsican sun searching out the green depths of the ocean. I said how appreciative I was of all the unstinting help he had given us, of the transformation he had brought about in our home, easing the tensions and assuming much of the strain – but I also said that I could not risk damaging my family, that my first duty was to Stephen and the children, that since Stephen and I had lived through so much hardship together, I could not renege on my marriage when he, more helpless than a small child, needed me more than ever. Resting against a warm rock with the waves splashing at my feet, I was preparing myself for the worst. I knew in my heart of hearts that it would not be at all surprising if, after a period of reflection during his stay in Austria, Jonathan were to decide that association with the Hawking household presented too many physical challenges and too many emotional difficulties. Such a decision would be understandable. Why should he want to burden himself with all our problems and willingly walk into an emotional trap when he was young and free, with the well-deserved prospect of a full, happy life before him?

Memories of Corsica faded fast on our return home, but those weeks had bequeathed us a long-lasting memento. As I took up the reins of the Cambridge routine that autumn, it began to seem even less likely that Jonathan would want to involve himself with us again, and the prospect of a happy reunion faded into the mists with the waning light of the September sun. As the days grew shorter and a chill crept into the air, I anxiously studied the dates on the calendar, starting to suspect in bewildered amazement that I might be pregnant. For some time I had ceased to bother about contraception as it hardly seemed relevant and simply added to the difficulties. In every waking hour and many a sleepless hour at night, the realization grew that, in the carefree abandon of the Mediterranean climate, I had been wrong. Passionately though I had adored my babies, the thought of caring for another little person, who would be totally dependent on me in an intolerably demanding situation, without the benefit of Jonathan's help, was terrifying. That Jonathan should have considered shoring up the existing family, as he had done for nearly a year, had been remarkable. To expect him to take on another small Hawking, especially when he had no children of his own and no prospect of ever having any as long as he associated with us, was inconceivable. I was resigned to losing him and, with his loss, to losing all hope for the future. I would be alone again.

The pregnancy had only just been confirmed when Stephen left for a conference in Moscow. Since I was already suffering badly from morning sickness, his mother agreed to go with him in my place. Don was also away with his father on a well-earned break from all those duties, which he fulfilled most conscientiously. As winter approached in Cambridge, the icy claws of the dark, inner winter from which I had so nearly escaped began to reassert their grip. I wrote Jonathan a note telling him about the baby, wretched in the certainty that this note would amount to a signing-off, an abrupt end to those few months of recovery and blissful platonic happiness. I did not know whether he was back from the summer school in Austria and did not expect a reply. For some time I heard nothing, but he replied eventually, apologizing for having taken time to digest the news and to adjust to it. He declared that his commitment to us was unchanged. Although he knew nothing at all about babies, he was sure that I would need his help more than ever and he was ready to offer it.

I was deeply grateful and felt myself blessed with the support of someone whose own early tragedy had awakened a sympathy and a consideration for the misfortunes of others which were exceptional almost to the point of eccentricity. His hand reached out and rescued me from death by drowning, not just in deep water, but in deep water under a sheet of ice. His encouragement transformed the long months of pregnancy from a time of desperate anxiety and foreboding to a period of hopeful anticipation and even enjoyment. He gave me the fundamental emotional reassurance that restored me to my old optimistic self and enabled me to prepare for yet another challenge, safe in the knowledge that for the first time in many years, this was a challenge I should not have to meet alone.

There was no escaping the fact that a very definite time limit had been sprung on the thesis. It had to be finished by the time the baby arrived, otherwise it might as well be thrown in the bin. I recovered my incentive, setting to work with renewed purpose even though it was fated always to be done in fits and starts. As usual, the writing had to be fitted in among the accustomed round of domestic chores, Stephen's care, children's parties, children's illnesses, speech days, dinners, lunches, visitors and travels. The latter included a physics conference in Dublin. It was our first visit to Ireland and Lucy came with us. Her picture, not unlike the Hockney drawing of her, appeared on the front page of the *Dublin Times* when a reporter found her hiding behind a door reading a book at a formal government reception.

Because Jonathan gave so much help with Stephen's needs, with the children and with the chores, even with the shopping, it was actually possible to make good, if fragmentary progress with the thesis, although my writing was also competing for time with music and hospital appointments. It was at the first hospital appointment in November that I suddenly became aware of the reality of the fourteen-week-old embryo, a mysterious, ethereal creature, whispering the message of its existence through the clinical medium of a new scientific invention, the ultrasound scan. After putting me through the barrage of usual tests, the doctors wired me up, and when they were satisfied with their findings, they asked if I would like to listen too. The rhythmic swish-swish of the tiny heart – beating rapidly against the background of my own, slower and louder – was poignantly moving, awakening in me a deep bond with the new life I had heard but not seen. It was as if the child was appealing to me through the music of its heartbeat, and so, long before the birth, I began to cherish that unseen presence, already loving the child as much as I loved Robert and Lucy.

Music accompanied the baby's gestation throughout the winter. Jonathan, our self-appointed entertainments officer, frequently brought home tickets for concerts, many of which were in the newly opened university concert hall only five minutes away. We sat on the stage alongside the performers in full view of the audience, since there was no other provision for wheelchairs. Often the performers, a host of celebrated musicians, from Menuhin to Schwarzkopf, would delay their exits after their curtain calls to come over and greet Stephen. At home I sang whenever I could, practising my repertoire for its first public performance. The baby responded with animated appreciation, kicking hard in time to the music. We were rehearsing with two musical goals in view. One was my entry in the Cambridge Competitive Festival in March, the other in February was a concert we and some musical friends of Jonathan's were giving at home for charity. We invited as many people as would fit into the living room and, in the tradition of the numerous parties in our establishment, laid on food and drinks in the interval. Afterwards, in an advanced state of pregnancy and an even more advanced state of nerves, I stood up to give my first public performance – other than the occasional solo in church. It consisted of two folksongs by Benjamin Britten and a couple of songs by Fauré; which were also to be my entries in the competition. The audience were kindly appreciative and on their departure made generous donations to our two charitable causes, leukaemia research and the Motor Neuron Disease Association, which had been recently founded and for which Stephen had become the Patients' Patron. When, long ago, his condition was diagnosed, we were told that it was very rare, that little was known about it, and that since so few people suffered from it there was no basis for a support group. None of this was true. Through the Association we discovered that the illness – also known in America as Lou Gehrig's disease, after a sportsman who suffered from it in the Thirties – was in fact quite widespread. At any one time there could be as many diagnoses of motor-neuron disease as there were sufferers from multiple sclerosis, which until then had received much more publicity because there were more survivors. Motor-neuron disease ran its course much more quickly – usually within two or three years – distorting the statistics and leaving patients and their families crisis-ridden, with neither the time nor the opportunity to set up support organizations or self-help groups. On the founding of the Association, some information at last became available. It emerged that motor-neuron disease could erupt in one of two forms. The acute form paralyses the victim's throat muscles, precipitating an early death. The rarer form, the one which had attacked Stephen, resulted in a creeping paralysis of the voluntary muscles of the whole body – including eventually the throat – over a longer period, perhaps five years or, at the outside, ten. Stephen's survival for sixteen years since the time of diagnosis in January 1963 made him a medical phenomenon, as unexplained as the illness itself.

Over the course of the next few years, Jonathan and I gave many joint recitals of baroque repertoire for the fledgling Motor Neuron Disease Association in churches throughout East Anglia, managing to raise quite respectable amounts of money, and since Stephen usually featured prominently in the audience, the illness and the Association came to the notice of the public. As a local volunteer, I visited some of the afflicted families in the area, whose lives were being shattered by a diagnosis that had left all of them shocked and bewildered, as it had left us years before. I felt that I had a duty to try and give these families the benefit of our experience, passing on to them the practical techniques we had devised for managing the condition, and pointing to the fact that Stephen, the survivor, was the living proof that the diagnosis was not necessarily a death sentence if one had the will to fight. Perhaps it was because the people I met were all much older than ourselves that they did not seem prepared to fight with the same vehemence. They were hurt and troubled, certainly, but they revealed a much greater calm and acceptance than I expected. The frenzied lifestyle, which had become the mark of our rejection of the disease, was not for them. Instead, they lived quietly, appreciating whatever was done for them, thankful for all the love and care they received from their families, often awaiting their fate with resignation. I trod warily, fearing to trespass on their privacy by introducing bright, well-meaning proposals for exercises, diets, injections or vitamins. There was, it seemed, an element in their lives which ours lacked and which I found myself envying. It was not defeatism but inner peace.

Stephen's position as Patron of the Association, and my attempts to help as a fundraiser and volunteer, brought me face to face yet again with one of those ironies of our situation. Once more we were elevated to a pedestal and there we found ourselves aloof. We needed advice as much as anybody, but we could not seek it because the admission of our needs would have been a denial of the confident façade on which other people depended for boosting their own morale. The number of people blessed with the perspicacity to see behind that mask were not many. They included my family, Jonathan and his parents and a few exceptional friends.

Just before the baby was due, we were fortunate to get to know some new friends of comparable sensitivity in Stephen's Australian colleague Bernard Whiting and his wife Mary, when they came to one of our musical gatherings. Relaxed and easygoing, Bernard was to give Stephen a hand, in much the same way that George Ellis had in the past. Mary, a classical archeologist, was writing a PhD thesis and working in the Fitzwilliam Museum on a catalogue of the museum's extensive gem collection. She was no fossilized museum piece. Her flowing, prematurely grey hair framing finely etched youthful features lent her a graceful distinction, like a Raphael madonna. Her appearance was well matched by her personality, for she was both learned and spirited, her interests extending far beyond archeology into art, literature and music, especially baroque music, so that when she and Jonathan met they immediately had plenty to discuss.

Towards the end of March 1979, Robert, who was in the first year of the Upper School at the Perse, went away to scout camp. I was not at all happy about this camp for eleven-year-olds since it was to be in the corner of a field in north Norfolk, exposed to the biting winds of a reluctant spring. The field, by all accounts, was sodden under a couple of inches of water. There was a fall of snow during the camp and Robert came back exhausted, soaked to the skin and coughing persistently. Stoical as ever, he declared that the camp had been "all right". After a couple of days in bed, he recovered sufficiently to be able to go away with Lucy to the cottage in Wales, where they were to spend Easter with Stephen's parents. Meanwhile I made my debut on the concert platform at the Cambridge Competitive Festival, singing the Fauré and Britten songs to Jonathan's expert piano accompaniment while Stephen smiled his cheerful encouragement from the audience. The adjudicator politely commended the timbre of the voice, otherwise only allowing himself to remark that he realized that my breath control was somewhat inhibited. With the competition over, back at St Mark's we were rehearsing for the devotional service on Good Friday and for the Easter Festival, at which I was to sing a solo, 'Now the Green Blade Riseth', accompanied on the flute by Jonathan's old school friend, Alan Hardy. After rehearsing in the church in the early part of Holy Week, we were all set for the performance on Easter Sunday.

The thesis was very nearly finished; all that remained was the mind-bogglingly boring task of ordering the bibliography alphabetically and attending to all the minutiae therein, upon the insistence of my supervisor. Every comma, full stop and bracket had to be in its correct place, otherwise he would not pass the thesis for submission. On Maundy Thursday, with an almighty flourish, I put the final full stop to the final entry in the bibliography, thus bringing to a conclusion thirteen arduous years of seminars, research, annotation, card-indexing, organizing, compiling, writing, editing, footnoting and referencing.

The next day, Good Friday, during the devotional service, I felt dejected to the point of tears. Perhaps this was a reaction to the emotive force of that particular religious commemoration and the music that went with it, perhaps it was the anticlimactic effect of finishing the thesis, or perhaps I was missing my children, who were to stay with their grandparents until after the baby was born in a week or two's time. The following day the melancholy lifted. Very strong physical symptoms took its place, leaving little doubt that the baby was going to be born quite soon. I spent most of the afternoon in the garden with Stephen beside me, relaxing in the sun and picking bunches of violets. Don drove us to the maternity hospital early in the evening, but a routine inspection revealed little movement of any significance, so we were sent away again. We called at Jonathan's house on the way home and stayed for a takeaway curry, inserting ourselves as best we could in among the musical instruments in the restricted space of the living room. As Jonathan and Stephen were partial to curries, he often arranged a takeaway, especially on Sunday evenings when the kitchen, after seven days of churning out three-course meals for all-comers, only ran to scrambled eggs. Exceptionally, this was a Saturday-evening curry and it was an exceptionally hot dupiaza.

Back at home I spent a most uncomfortable night and, at dawn, woke Don to ask him to drive us back to the hospital. Because Stephen wanted to be present at the birth of his third child, special provision had been made to accommodate him in the delivery room. Joy Cadbury, who presided over the Friends of the Maternity Hospital, had kindly conferred with the matron to make suitable arrangements for the wheelchair. The only space large enough for Stephen and Sue Smith, his physiotherapist, who came in to look after him – plus the medical team, not to mention me – was the delivery room, so I had to spend the rest of the day lying on the hard surface of the delivery table waiting for the birth to happen. Don sat out in the corridor, occasionally peering round the door, while Jonathan wisely took himself off to spend that hot, sunny Easter Sunday at his parents' parsonage in the country. In such inclement conditions, the birthing processes slowed down to a standstill. I sent messages to Don that he could safely abandon his post in the corridor to attend morning service in one or other of his ecclesiastical locations, and while I lay awkwardly trying to ease my bulk into a comfortable position, I rued the urgency with which we had come to the hospital, especially when I realized that I could have been singing in church. There, Bill Loveless had to announce the cancellation of the musical interlude on account of the absence of the singer who was otherwise engaged.

The various attempts made to accelerate the birth had the sole effect of turning me into a human pin cushion as the morning slid into afternoon and the afternoon into evening. Don returned and went out again – this time to evensong. While he was away, a crisis developed: the foetal heart, that infant heartbeat that had introduced itself to me many months ago, showed worrying signs of fatigue. While the medical team had their backs turned, preparing their instruments of torture to bring the baby into the world without delay, I hastily summoned all my remaining energies into an almighty push and my Easter child was born. When they gave him to me to hold, my heart went out to him. Wrapped in an old green blanket, his face was blue from the battering he had received. Although he was larger than either Robert or Lucy at birth, he did not display the energy with which they had greeted the world but lay limply, whimpering in my arms. For a moment I was oblivious of the commotion of the cleaning-up operations around us, absorbed by the little creature whom I already knew so well. Then Don burst triumphantly into the delivery room. He was pleased to make the acquaintance of his godson and was even more pleased with himself on account of a little ditty that he had thought up on returning from church. To my embarrassment he would repeat it to everyone he met for several weeks after the event. It went like this:

> On Easter Day,
> the disciples went to the garden
> and found the empty tomb;
> I went to the hospital
> and found the empty womb

10

Dissonance

During the week that Timothy Stephen (the baby's full name) and I stayed in hospital, Lucy was brought back to Cambridge to meet her younger brother – but Robert was stranded in St Albans for reasons which were not fully explained. Apparently the children had been playing barefoot in the stream in Wales and he had caught a cold. He was coughing again, so badly that when the children called on my parents for tea in St Albans, my mother put him to bed. There he stayed for the next week until Stephen's sister Mary, the doctor, decided that he was well enough to come back to Cambridge. His return coincided with our homecoming. He nursed his little brother on his knee, sitting in an armchair in the living room, but looked suspiciously flushed and unwell. The mother of one of Lucy's friends, Valerie Broadbent-Keeble, a respected pediatrician, came on a social call to visit Timothy and me. By coincidence, she arrived at the same time as Dr Wilson, my GP. The two doctors glanced only briefly at Timothy, who had adjusted to the business of living and was glowing with health; Robert, on the other hand, commanded their full attention. Both were visibly alarmed at his state of health and were fairly sure that he was suffering from viral pneumonia. Valerie went away to organize Robert's immediate admission to the children's ward at Addenbrooke's while Dr Wilson wrote out a prescription for penicillin.

It was a blessing that the new baby was still tired from the ordeal of his birth and consequently slept for long periods by day and, amazingly, by night as well, otherwise the weeks after his birth would have been an even worse nightmare than they actually were. I was needed by everyone all the time. Stephen's needs were obvious, the baby's needs were undeniable, Lucy needed reassurance now that there was a rival usurping her place as the youngest member of the family. Above all, Robert was seriously ill in hospital and needed me most. After one night on the children's ward, he awoke covered in weals from head to foot.

Either he had contracted an infectious disease or he was allergic to penicillin. As there was no way of telling which of the two was the cause, he was moved to an isolation ward at the top of the hospital for fear of infecting the other critically ill patients on the children's ward. In isolation, his meals were passed to him through a hatch, and the medical staff donned gowns, gloves and masks when they entered his room. He was allowed only restricted visiting and the visitors had to dress up in the same protective clothing as the nurses. Bored, lonely and ill, he lay in bed with the tears streaming down his hot cheeks.

My visits to the hospital had to be timed precisely in between the week-old baby's feeds. Once he was fed, changed and settled, I would dash off to spend the next few hours at Robert's bedside, reading books and playing games, before dashing home again for the next feed. This became my routine until Robert was discharged from hospital. Stephen's mother did her best to keep the home fires burning, shopping and cooking wholesome meals, but there was too much for her to do alone. Never was Jonathan's help more urgently required. He looked after Stephen, he did the heavy shopping, he took Lucy to school and he visited Robert, enabling me sometimes to take a break from a rigorously pressurized routine. It was unfortunate that he had only been introduced briefly to Stephen's mother before this crisis occurred. Since her visits to Cambridge had been much rarer than my parents', the opportunity had not arisen. I realized that I could not expect any of the Hawkings, unlike our close and tactful friends, to divine the significance of Jonathan's presence in our household. But I hoped however that I had earned their respect well enough over the many years in which I had cared for their son for them to trust me at least to try to do my best for him and for the children in the present demanding situation, and I trusted that they might muster some sympathy or discreet toleration. Above all I wanted to reassure them that I was not about to abandon Stephen or break up the home, nor was Jonathan encouraging me to do so.

There was no suitable opportunity to broach the matter to Isobel. When eventually she and I found ourselves alone in the house with the new baby one afternoon, she took the initiative, catching me unawares. She looked me straight in the eye. "Jane," she said, adopting a stentorian tone, "I have a right to know whose child Timothy is. Is he Stephen's or is he Jonathan's?" I met her steely gaze, dismayed that she had so readily jumped to conclusions – and the most uncharitable conclusions at that. All the discipline with which Jonathan and I had forced ourselves to try to sublimate our own desires and maintain a discreet relationship was being trampled underfoot. The simple truth was that there was no way that Timothy could have had any other father than Stephen. Isobel was not content with this statement of the truth; instead she carried on, as if riding the crest of a wave, "You see," she went on, "we have never really liked you, Jane, you do not fit into our family." Later she apologized for her outburst, but from my point of view it was too late.

The following day Frank Hawking responded to his wife's urgent summons and came over to Cambridge in the early morning. I watched from the house as, together, they went out onto the lawn and disappeared into the shrubbery, engaged in conspiratorial conversation. Soon afterwards they left, huffily defiant, scarcely bothering to acknowledge me at all. The combination of so many traumatic events in such a short space of time after the birth had the predictably disheartening effect of diminishing my ability to feed the two-week-old baby, who was emerging from his post-natal stupor, exercising his leonine lungs and his vocal chords with hearty enthusiasm. Stephen brooked no opposition in resolving the situation in his own fashion. He dragooned eight-year-old Lucy to accompany him into town and help him shop at Boots, where he bought an array of bottles, teats, sterilizing fluid and dried milk powder. Thus ended my pitiful attempts to nurse my third child and thus commenced a new chore for Jonathan. Every evening before leaving West Road for his own home, he would make up the next day's supply of baby milk and store it in the fridge, ready for use on demand.

Some weeks later, as I was making the preparations for Timothy's christening in early June, Stephen received a letter from his father. The letter announced that he had been in touch with an American team of doctors in Dallas, Texas, who were treating motor-neuron disease with a new drug. These doctors were issuing an invitation to Stephen to become one of the first patients to test the drug. It seemed that it was a fait accompli. We would all, Stephen, Robert, Lucy, Timothy and I, with the mere waving of a wand, move lock, stock and barrel to Texas, where Stephen would undergo an extended course of treatment lasting months if not years. The letter was passed to me without comment, without explanation, the tacit implication being that the decision rested on my shoulders.

My head swam and my heart sank at the complexity of the responsibility that I was being asked to assume. First and foremost, if there was a chance of a cure for Stephen, I could never deny him that chance. Yet I was only too aware that the demands on the family and on me would be monumental, far in excess of anything we had ever experienced before. The children would be summarily removed from the schools, the environment and the home where they were happy and secure, and would be dumped down in a huge, strange, American city. This would not be Pasadena. It was not clear where our income would come from, nor was it clear how our housing or transport would be organized. I, the mother of a six-week-old baby, was being asked to uproot the whole family, the three children and their paraplegic father, transport them a third of the way round the world and set up home for an indefinite time. There was no indication of how I was to achieve that objective, no promise nor any likelihood of help in this mammoth task other than young Robert's, nor any certainty that the treatment would be successful. Painful memories of Seattle in 1967 came crowding to the fore, multiplied a thousand times by the experiences of the past several years.

As the date of the baby's christening approached, I could not keep this most painful of dilemmas from my parents. The christening party divided squarely into two opposing camps. In a situation which required extreme tact on all sides, the Hawkings stood in one corner of the living-room, ostracizing the rest of the gathering – my parents, Tim's godparents and their families, and a few friends. The atmosphere was so unbearable that at one stage I left the room and took refuge in the bedroom. My father followed me, only too conscious of the intolerable pressure I was under. An intellectual match for the Hawkings but devoid of all affectation or snobbery, he pulled a piece of paper from his pocket. "Jane," he said, "just have a look at this, will you? If you approve, I am going to send it to Frank Hawking." As I read, gratitude for my father's intervention flooded through me: the letter was a masterly resolution of the dilemma, without in any way jeopardizing my loyalty to Stephen. Quite simply it stated that we all wanted Stephen's best interests, but that the Hawkings must be aware that the care of two young children and the new baby – their grandchildren – in addition to the burden of Stephen's care, made it impracticable for me to travel to Texas. He suggested that if they were convinced of the efficacy of the treatment, they should consider accompanying Stephen to Texas themselves. Yet again my father, sometimes exacting, always honourable, always unpretentious, had by quiet, intelligent application behind the scenes come to the rescue. The letter was sent. He did not receive a reply.

After so many years of thinly veiled tolerance, they had expressed their dislike of me with caustic bluntness when I was at my lowest ebb, soon after the birth of my third child, while my eldest child was critically ill. Their dislike had emerged and spread into unconcealed hostility. It was stupid of me not to have recognized their animosity and resigned myself to it sooner; it was stupid of me to have lived in innocent hope of better things. As they were Stephen's closest relatives, I had been bound to try to get on with them as best I could. In fact for this very reason, I was still obliged to maintain a veneer of civility. Whether I liked it or not, the close blood tie was the one invariable factor in this predicament.

The following winter news came that the Texan team were offering to send their treatment to Cambridge. However the consultant neurologist at Addenbrooke's stated quite firmly that the treatment was untested, unproven and inappropriate for motor-neuron disease. He suspected that Stephen would be used as a guinea pig, and that the researchers were looking for the scientific respectability and publicity associated with his name, possibly to attract funding. The treatment would have to be administered in hospital and the time involved would be considerable, with minimal chance of a positive outcome even in the short term. Motor-neuron disease had already done its worst to Stephen; there was little more that it could do and it was a well-known fact of medical science that the body was not able to repair damaged nerve tissue. The greatest risk to his survival these days came from pneumonia, not motor-neuron disease per se. The proposed treatment would be a waste of Stephen's precious time and scarcely more than one of those chimeras against which Frank Hawking had himself warned so decisively in the Sixties.

11

Turbulence

Perhaps I might have been less distressed at the behaviour of the Hawkings had I realized how implicitly I could rely on Jonathan's family. With unassuming goodness, they dedicated themselves tirelessly to other people, whoever they were, whatever their origins. They made no distinction between family, friends, parishioners or strangers. Anyone in trouble, rich or poor, could arrive on their doorstep by day or by night and be assured of help and a sympathetic ear, and probably a filling meal into the bargain. I could not believe that any parents, however well-intentioned, would welcome the sort of family that their eldest son had become involved in. I was wrong. On our first visit to their rectory, they treated us, Stephen, the children and me, as if we were the most welcome visitors, as if they were really pleased to see us. Never did they pass even the slightest hint of judgement on us or on our situation.

Like Bill Loveless, John Jones had been a late ordinand. He had come to Cambridge to train for the ministry, after his first career as a dentist in Warwickshire. In this mid-life change of direction, he was encouraged unequivocally by his wife Irene, so like my own mother in her quietly assured faith. From their hilltop vantage point, just outside Cambridge, they tended to their flock in the surrounding fenland and worshipped with a practical tenacity which would have been extraordinary in a young incumbent, let alone in one of advancing years. Not only did John, with Irene's assistance, look after the souls in his charge in Lolworth and its associated parishes, he also mended the fabric of the medieval building entrusted to him by an impecunious diocese. In the early Eighties the tower of Lolworth church was badly in need of repairs. As there were no funds available to repair it, John and Irene donned hard hats and overalls and set about removing several tons of bird droppings from the inside before relining and strengthening the structure themselves.

I found it unbelievable that these people, not related to us in any way, could find any good reason for wanting to welcome me and my family, nor could I understand why they should show such genuine interest in us and so much concern for us. They spread the light of kindness, sympathy and selflessness in darkness. It was not only Jonathan's parents who took us to their hearts but, inexplicably, his entire family as well, his aunts, uncles and cousins, his brother Tim and sister Sara. Formerly a physiotherapist, Sara was blessed with the same sort of intuitive good sense as Caroline Chamberlain in her approach to severe disability; she knew the toll that a paralysing disease could exact on the immediate family as well as on the patient. Sara and I quickly became the closest of friends. We were more or less the same age and we had our babies at more or less the same time. Sara's first baby, Miriam, was born in February 1979, two months before Timothy.

Thus I no longer had to look to the Hawkings for support. Instead, I began to foster the cool detachment that they had shown for years. Surprisingly, other more distant relatives of Stephen's stepped into the vacuum left by their absence. Michael Mair, a cousin of Stephen's who had been an undergraduate in Cambridge in the late Sixties when Robert was a new baby had returned to work in the eye department of Addenbrooke's Hospital. He and his South African fiancée, Solome, a radiographer, were enthusiastic cooks. Every so often they would bring a delicious, ready-prepared, calorie-rich meal for the whole family. In anticipation of their arrival, Robert and Lucy would stand in the porch, peering through the glass door and salivating long before they drew into the driveway. Never were those meals-on-wheels more welcome than in the months after Timothy's birth, as we struggled to get back onto an even keel, desperately weary from the gruelling effort of steering our little boat through turbulent seas.

The truth was that one adult minder was required to attend full-time to each one of the less able members of the family. Disabled to the point of not being able to do anything for himself – except handling the simple joystick controls of his wheelchair and of the computer which he had bought in celebration of Timothy's birth – Stephen had to have a well-known person, whether me, Don or Jonathan, in constant attendance. The baby, previously so docile, had begun to assert himself, responding to all the attention lavished on him with huge captivating smiles, so wide that they could have swallowed us up, but he protested loudly when our attention was deflected elsewhere. On these occasions my mother would laughingly point out his resemblance to his father. He had certainly inherited Stephen's cherubic dimples, but also like Stephen his mouth had the comical habit of drooping downwards at the corners to express affronted indignation, especially when he was hungry. In other respects, though a larger baby, he was the exact image of his older brother. I called them my twins – twins nearly twelve years apart. Indeed more than once, passing acquaintances would glance at Tim and cheerily call "Hello, Robert!" then in some bafflement would think they must have fallen into a time warp before they realized their mistake.

Luckily we were now able to afford the luxury of a nanny on a couple of mornings a week, so that I could see to all the administration involved in the production of the four bound copies of the thesis demanded by officialdom. My helper, Christine Ikin, later christened Kikki by infant Tim, was also the mother of three children. She came in from the country as regularly as the unpredictable bus service would allow, and cheerfully hoovered and cleaned and looked after the baby, while I contacted typists, proofread the results of their labours, collated hundreds of pages and sought out bookbinders. My association with medieval Spanish poetry had run its course and was coming to a grand finale. Since the thesis did not hold out the promise of any very obvious career, I had already reconciled myself to its being an end in itself rather than the means to greater advancement. In any case, a career was completely out of the question since ninety-nine per cent of my attention had to remain focused on the home and the family. Somehow I had to divide that attention fairly between the children and their father while still finding time to keep my brain alive.

Robert and Lucy were both finding it hard to adjust to new circumstances. Lucy now found herself in an uncertain situation in the middle of the family as neither the eldest nor the youngest child, and not until Robert went away to another scout camp later in the summer did she show any interest in the baby. Then she was suddenly called upon to fetch and carry bottles, nappies, pins and powder – chores that Robert had previously undertaken. At first she resisted defiantly, and then she burst into tears. At that moment I realized how badly she too had been affected by the trauma we had undergone since little Tim's arrival. Lucy had been left to fend for herself when in fact she needed as much reassurance as anyone else. I hugged her and told her that I had not stopped loving her just because there was another person in the family to care for. She warmed to her little brother straight away, as if in all those miserable weeks she had been longing to show her true feelings but had not known how. She fetched and carried just as willingly as Robert had done, and thereafter no one could have been more devoted to Tim or more susceptible to his winning ways.

Robert had been very ill, and although he had made a good recovery and was back at school, he often seemed subdued and forgetful. Dyslexia was still a severe handicap in his schooling. The school arranged a few sessions with an educational psychologist, who tried to instill into him techniques for coping with dyslexia, but she failed to identify the true extent of the problem. It was not until many years later that I discovered that at the root of it lay an overwhelming sense of inadequacy. From a very early age he had become aware that his father was a scientific genius and that people, in particular his teachers rather than his parents, had expectations of him that he knew he could not fulfil. His belief in himself swamped by self-doubt, his solution was not to bother with his studies at all since he felt himself doomed to failure in the eyes of the world, however hard he tried. The saddest part of it was that from as young as seven years old, when he first became aware that his father was a genius, he felt himself to be inferior. Robert had the doubtful advantage of a quick, scientific intelligence which destined him for a scientific career without achieving his father's fame. As for Lucy and Tim, they were later to suffer for not being scientific, and they were both acutely humiliated when told how disappointed their teachers were in them. Really all three children were in a no-win situation. But although their teachers' prejudices cast a passing shadow over their education, Lucy and Tim did not suffer as badly as Robert, for whom the expectations of society in general cast the long shadow of his father's reputation.

In the autumn of 1979 Stephen's reputation was enhanced very publicly in Cambridge by his appointment to the coveted Lucasian Chair in Mathematics. The chair, endowed in 1663 with one hundred pounds by Henry Lucas, was one of the most prestigious professorships in one of the most prestigious universities: it was Newton's chair. Stephen was now unequivocally ranked with Newton. He celebrated his elevation to the dizziest of academic heights by availing himself of the opportunity to give an inaugural lecture, a custom which had fallen into disuse, at least among scientists. A student stood beside him on the stage of the Babbage lecture theatre and interpreted his speech, which had become so faint and so indistinct that only a handful of students, colleagues and family could even begin to understand it. The rapt audience of scientists, many of them young hopefuls, strained to catch his utterances. The words were not designed to offer them the comfortable prospect of a secure future, for Stephen gleefully predicted that the end of physics was in sight. The advent of faster and more sophisticated computers meant that by the end of the century, in a mere twenty years' time, all the major problems in physics would have been wound up, including the unified field theory, and there would be nothing left for physicists to do. He, himself, would be all right, he declared jovially, as he would be retiring in the year 2009. The audience loved the joke, though I could not see that they really had much to laugh about...

Nor in fact did Stephen have much to laugh about. In summarily predicting the end of physics he had well and truly made himself a hostage to fortune, and his own Nemesis, the affronted goddess of Physics, caught up with him very quickly. Just a few weeks later, the new decade opened very inauspiciously for us all, especially for Stephen. After Christmas we all went down with bad colds, including the baby. By the New Year, the cold had settled on Stephen's chest, racking his body with harrowing choking fits at every sip of water or every spoonful of finely chopped food, even at every breath. These fits would come on at the end of the day and would last well into the night. Using the techniques I had learnt in yoga, I would try to encourage him to relax his throat muscles by quietly and monotonously repeating calming phrases. Sometimes I would succeed and would register the change from gasping panic to regular breathing, as sleep took over his sad, persecuted frame. Sometimes the sheer boredom of repetition would send me off into an interrupted doze while he continued to cough and wheeze beside me into the early hours. We would both be drained by the next morning, though he with true courage would never admit as much and would embark on his normal schedule undeterred by the events of the previous night.

While we all feared a repetition of the 1976 bout of pneumonia, Stephen himself predictably would not let me call the doctor, nor would he take any patent medicines, since he was still scared that the sweetener in cough linctus – even in sugar-free linctus – would irritate the lining of his throat and the cough-suppressant ingredients would either befuddle his brain or plummet him into a comatose state. So he coughed and choked, and choked and coughed, day and night, while the baby snuffled and wailed with a blocked nose and I panted for breath, since I was feeling none too well myself.

As ever my mother promptly came over from St Albans to run the household, while Jonathan, Don and I tried against the odds to care for its ailing occupants. Mum insisted on sending me to bed, at least in between the various tasks that I had to attend to. Bill Loveless paid me a visit on the following Saturday afternoon. I lay on the bed prostrate from tiredness and breathlessness while Stephen, the real patient, sat reading the newspaper in the kitchen, determined to sit out the crisis. I poured out my troubles to Bill. I still passionately wanted to care for Stephen, to give him a happy home life, to make all things possible for him within reason. Sometimes, as at present, his demands were totally in excess of all that was reasonable and the wall of his obduracy was making life unbearable. In consequence I was becoming more and more dependent on Jonathan to preserve my sanity, to share my burdens, and to make me feel loved. That dependency only increased my burden of guilt.

Bill took my hand in his. "Jane," he said, thoughtfully but firmly, "there is something I want you to know." If I was nervously expecting a stern rebuke, I was much mistaken. Gently he went on, "In the sight of God all souls are equal. You are just as important to God as Stephen is." So saying, he left me to ponder this surprising revelation, and went to talk to Stephen. Later that day Dr Swan called and recommended a short spell in the local nursing home for Stephen who, although ferociously indignant, reluctantly accepted his advice. I knew in a sense that Stephen was right because in the nursing home he was not known. The nurses there did not understand his speech nor were they versed in the very precise techniques required for looking after him. As soon as word spread that the Lucasian Professor had been removed to the nursing home, there was no shortage of offers of help. Once more the loyal students and colleagues, particularly

Gary Gibbons, Stephen's former research student, established an attendance rota so that Stephen should never find himself unable to communicate his needs to the nurses. Robert's headmaster, Antony Melville, remembering similarly tragic circumstances in his own family, spontaneously offered to take Robert into his own home, should the need arise. John Casey, a Fellow of Caius who concealed genuine sympathy behind a somewhat mannered façade, decided that the College should pay Stephen's nursing-home expenses and undertook to persuade the governing body and the Bursar. Perhaps that task was less insuperable than it sounds since, it should be noted, the Bursar, a retired Air Vice-Marshal, Reggie Bullen, was the most humane Bursar ever to hold that office in the College.

The following week, while Stephen was in the nursing home, I answered an invitation from Martin Rees, the Plumian Professor of Astronomy and Experimental Philosophy since 1973, to meet him out at the Institute of Astronomy. Endearingly unconvincing in his efforts to appear a hard-nosed scientist, Martin sat me down in his office and emphatically declared, "Whatever happens, Jane, you must not let the situation get you down." The unintentional irony of his words baffled me, but as I was too tired and distraught to comment on them to any effect, I said nothing, simply waiting for him to continue. He repeated what he had just said and went on to suggest that the time had come for Stephen to have nursing care at home. If I could find the nurses, he volunteered to find the funds – from various philanthropic sources – to pay for them. I was deeply grateful for his concern and his very practical offer, so carefully and considerately proposed. My gratitude was felt as much for the fact that he had noticed that we needed help as for the help itself.

There were three elements involved in bringing nurses into the home and certainly Martin's benevolent offer would take care of one of them, the financial side. I had no idea how to tackle the remaining two. Where was I to find suitable nurses and, more significantly, how was I to persuade Stephen to accept them? Whenever the baby and I went to visit him, he ground his teeth in anger at his temporary imprisonment, keeping his eyes firmly fixed on the television screen in front of him and refusing to look at us. There was little fundamental consolation that I could bring him, rather my presence seemed to madden him; yet if I did not visit him regularly I would quickly stand accused of neglect. Panting for breath under the weight of the hefty infant, I would struggle down the long corridor twice a day, rehearsing all the gobbits of information and titbits of gossip that I had been collecting for him. Our reception would always have a dampening effect, washing the colour and life out of those little yarns, diluting their impact until they were about as interesting as a firework display in a rainstorm. Stephen's parents paid him a visit one day without bothering to call on us at West Road.

We were expecting my father to arrive in Cambridge for lunch the next weekend when there was a ring at the doorbell. Mum and I were perplexed to find an unfamiliar car in the driveway and a middle-aged woman standing outside the door. Her husband was ushering my father towards the house. This couple had been travelling behind Dad six or seven miles outside Cambridge when they had seen his car slither across the road on a patch of black ice and crash into the opposite bank. They had come to his rescue. Although the car was a write-off, Dad, miraculously, seemed to be unhurt, though badly shaken. Nonetheless, we thought it best to call a doctor to check that all was indeed well. John Owens, the doctor who had delivered Robert twelve years before – and who, coincidentally had also attended Jonathan's wife Janet – came promptly and pronounced Dad to be in remarkably good shape considering the life-threatening ordeal he had undergone. Only a couple of days later we had reason to call the surgery again. Lucy, who had also had a bad cold, gave us and herself a fright when a capillary in her nose popped and started to bleed. No sooner had one copious nosebleed dried up than another began. This time the duty doctor was new to us. Rather surprisingly since he was middle-aged, he introduced himself as a trainee. Dr Chester White had taken up medicine as a second career in middle age, and he had only recently qualified. He gave Lucy a check-up, assuring us that there was no cause for alarm.

As he was about to leave, he turned his attention to me. "What about you? Are you feeling all right?" he asked to my surprise, "you look pretty exhausted." He sat down while I told him about Stephen and the crisis we were in. Little explanation was needed as he knew Stephen by repute and had seen him out and about in the street. He did not know, however, that we had battled on for years with minimal help from the National Health Service and was appalled to hear that we had the benefit of home nursing only on two mornings a week, when the district nurse came in to get Stephen out of bed and give him a bath and an injection of hydroxocobalamin. Stephen had been obliged to let the district nurses bath him when, in a cumbersome state of pregnancy, I found my room for manoeuvre in the bathroom severely restricted.

As I recounted the same old story of our wearisome struggle to keep going and to find a way through the obstacle course that our lives had become, I was under no illusions: Dr White would listen with the utmost sympathy but would be powerless to effect any improvement. Who could, even with the funds that Martin Rees had promised? I anticipated that he would say, as so many others had said before, "Well, I'm terribly sorry, but I don't know what to suggest." I was scarcely inclined to take him seriously, therefore, when with unusual perception he thoughtfully suggested two courses of action. First, he said, he would prescribe some medication for me and, secondly, he would get in touch with a male nurse on his list who did some private nursing and might be able to arrange a regular roster of care for Stephen.

The hope that these proposals held out was too beguiling not to be considered briefly, even if with a well-worn scepticism. There was just a chance that the hurdle of finding suitable nurses might be overcome as a result of this chance encounter, and the last hurdle – and undoubtedly the highest – Stephen's resistance, might also yield in the face of this initiative, since it was being imposed by an outside authority. The blame for this most detrimental of steps would not fall entirely on my shoulders. Within days Martin Rees had found a provisional source of funding to finance some nursing care for Stephen on his return home – but, as I feared, it took longer for Chester to get in touch with his nursing contact. That prospect, it seemed, was after all no more than another of those deceptive will-o'-the-wisps, a glimmer of hope extinguished before it had even been ignited. Perhaps it was just as well: in my heart, I disliked conspiring against what I knew to be Stephen's wishes, however intolerable the situation might be.

Then, one morning towards the end of January, Dr White's contact, Nikki Manatunga, the nurse, materialized out of the blue. A quietly spoken, hard-working Sri Lankan who had settled with his wife and two children in a village outside Cambridge, he showed no disquiet at my account of the difficulties and the requirements. On the contrary, he was confident of being able to put together a team of nurses from among his colleagues at Fulbourn Hospital, the local psychiatric hospital where he worked. A week later, when he came for his first shift, Stephen adamantly refused to look at him or to communicate with him in any way, except by running over his toes with the wheelchair. I apologized to Nikki who persevered with a smile, unperturbed. "It's all right," he said, "we're used to dealing with difficult patients." The next week he brought and introduced another nurse to the system and then another. An established nurse came with each new recruit and passed on the details of the routine so that there was always a smooth changeover with minimal intervention demanded of us, the resident carers. Slowly Stephen's irritation subsided as he grew to accept the presence of these dedicated, patient people, and eventually he realized that he could call upon them for help outside the strict hours of their terms of employment. He could take the nurses on trips abroad and be independent of his students and colleagues, even of his family. No longer would he have to rely on a small group of intimates for help with his personal needs. A new era was dawning for the master of the universe and, by extension, for the rest of us.

12

Ad Astra

In lifting the weight of Stephen's nursing care from our shoulders, Nikki's team allowed us as a family to start living life rather than just struggling through it. Caring for Stephen was relatively easy by comparison with the previous routine, especially since Jonathan was usually with us most evenings and all day at weekends, helping to feed Stephen, take him to the bathroom and lift him in and out of the car. He too was a helpless witness of the terrifying choking fits, which at every meal seemed to be squeezing the last lungfuls of breath out of their victim. We would wait hoping that the fit would pass, ready to call the emergency services, knowing that at these critical times the thread by which Stephen clung to life was at its most tenuous. The fit would pass eventually, and after a few sips of warm water he would resume his meal, discarding whatever item he suspected of irritating his throat. Then just as we were all beginning to relax, he would fall prey to another attack.

Jonathan was by nature susceptible to hardship and struggle, sensing where and how he was needed, helping with all those necessary domestic chores which formerly I had always done unaided: he brought in sacks of potatoes, emptied rubbish bins, changed light bulbs, checked air pressures in tyres and filled the cars with petrol. Now there was someone to help me drag home the mountains of weekly shopping from the market and from Sainsbury's. For years I had struggled across the Backs either pulling the heavy bags in a trolley behind me or carrying them on the pram, slung from the handle and squeezed into the tray underneath. Together we looked after the three children, but it was usually Jonathan who provided the taxi service to ferry Robert and Lucy to and from their various engagements, and it was Jonathan who indulged the baby's favourite activity: Timmie liked nothing so much as being thrown high in the air, up to the ceiling, abandoning himself, open-mouthed and wide-eyed, to that split second of suspense before coming back to earth and falling into the safety of Jonathan's arms.

Throughout the early Eighties, Stephen's ambitions and his successes continued to know no bounds. The catalogue of institutions, universities and scientific bodies vying with each other to shower sonorously named medals upon him – the Albert Einstein Award, the Einstein Medal, the Franklin Medal, the James Clerk Maxwell medal – and other honours, notably honorary degrees, read like Leporello's list of Don Giovanni's female conquests in Mozart's opera. Unlike Don Giovanni however, Stephen's conquests were not all restricted to Europe. There was no shortage of award-giving ceremonies in Britain, however, and when they were near to home, I took Stephen to them myself. On one memorable occasion we drove over to Leicester for a degree ceremony at the University, where the Chancellor was Sir Alan Hodgkin, the Master of Trinity College, Cambridge; he had formerly been the President of the Royal Society when Stephen was made a Fellow in 1974. Genial and unassuming, with a beaming smile, even when standing on the platform attired in full black and gold regalia, he welcomed Stephen into the ranks of the honorary doctors of the university by firmly pressing his hand – the hand which Stephen was using to control the wheelchair. That pressure sent Stephen, the wheelchair and Sir Alan Hodgkin – who was still, so to speak, attached to the apparatus – off into a whirling pas de deux, bringing the ensemble of ceremonial robes, mortar boards, bodies and wheelchair perilously close to the edge of the stage. I leapt to my feet and switched off the joystick control just in time to avert a horrible catastrophe.

Most of the ceremonies were in the United States, however, and it was fortunate that Nikki and his team were willing travelling companions. Thanks to them, Stephen was able to take advantage of every award-giving ceremony on the other side of the Atlantic – for which his fare and theirs would be paid. Then he would go on to the serious purpose of his trip – scientific discussions with his colleagues in other more interesting venues elsewhere. At this time he was particularly involved in the production – often as joint editor with Werner Israel – of several tomes of essays and conference proceedings concerning relativity and attempts to reconcile it with quantum physics. The conferences – or rather "workshops" – recorded in these tomes were Stephen's new passion, for he found that his international renown and his distinguished position as Lucasian Professor afforded him an advantage in attracting funding to the Department, though one of his pet complaints was *still* the lack of money for science. We had been used to receiving and entertaining regular seminar and conference delegates for years on a modest scale. These days Stephen could invite his colleagues – even his adversaries – to Cambridge on a grander scale and preside over all their deliberations as the ultimate authority. The workshops grew into much larger and much more prestigious affairs, with money not only to invite the most eminent speakers and delegates, but also to provide dinners and entertainments. Consequently my role as conference hostess was mercifully diminished. The days were over when I found myself putting on buffet dinners for forty or more people; under the new system, the workshop dinners were usually held in the college where the delegates were staying. My involvement was generally limited to hosting receptions, and the tea parties on the lawn, for which plates of cucumber sandwiches were, as usual, ordered from Caius kitchens. Otherwise, dinner parties at home were more intimate affairs for the band of our closest friends from abroad.

The lion's share of the complex administrative arrangements for these workshops – the delegates' travel, the accommodation, the venues, the methods of payment and all the printed material associated with the conference – as well as typing up the proceedings after the event, fell to Stephen's hard-working secretary, Judy Fella, although she was in theory only employed part-time. This was all in addition to her regular workload as the secretary to the Relativity Group. Her children were about the same age as Robert and Lucy, but she often worked long into the night, sometimes having to resort to the more advanced, experimental technology – installed by the fluid-dynamicists down in the basement of the Department – to produce camera-ready copy of the hieroglyphic signs and diagrams of the conference proceedings. Although Stephen appreciated her dedication, many of her secretarial colleagues failed to understand the unconventional pressures under which she laboured, and made life very uncomfortable for her.

It was in the Department rather than at home that a new wave of pressures, in the shape of the world's media, first made its appearance. For some time Stephen's discoveries had been well documented in the British and the American scientific press; the attitude was always one of deference in the strictly scientific context, with little or no reference to his physical condition. In the early Eighties the popular press began to take a more active interest in the phenomenon of the man himself. The contrast between the restrictions placed on him by his shrunken frame and his croaking speech on the one hand, and the power of his mind which allowed him to roam the outer reaches of the universe on the other, provided a fertile source for many imaginative flights of fanciful prose. Moreover the subject himself was far from averse to publicity; indeed was a willing interviewee, despite the incursions that interviews made into his already overloaded timetable. Judy took the extra demands posed on her schedule by the influx of journalists and television crews – not just from national networks but from all over the world – in her stride, though there were quite a few academics in the Department who understandably objected to finding that their tea room had been turned into a television studio yet again.

Stephen enjoyed bewildering the visiting journalists. He would apologize for not being able to bring a four-dimensional model of the universe into his office to demonstrate his theories, or, when asked about infinity, would reply that it was rather difficult to talk about it as it was such a long way off. Quite openly he would admit to disappointment that black holes had so far evaded detection, since proof of their existence would assure him of a Nobel Prize. The journalists made what they could of these witty, often cryptic responses to their questions and then went away to compile reverential articles from their baffling assortment of notes. Very few of them managed to achieve a balance in their reporting. Often their attempts to describe Stephen's physical presence lacked sensitivity, while their accounts of the science, perhaps understandably, relied on the interpretations of Stephen's students and colleagues.

The most insensitive journalist of all was a television producer from the BBC's *Horizon* team. The earlier snatch of film made some six years previously by my college friend, Vivienne King, had been a resounding success; she had shown Stephen in context and had avoided the pitfall – or the temptation – of depicting him as Dr Strangelove. It was still one of my worst fears that, in the hands of the wrong producer, Stephen might be portrayed as some sort of grotesque, wheelchair-bound boffin, twisted both in body and mind, destructively intent on the pursuit of science at all costs, and that is more or less what happened in the second *Horizon* film. When I asked if he would like briefly to include the family in the film, the producer disparagingly observed that the children and I were nothing more than wallpaper in Stephen's life, and when the film appeared six months later, the lunch scene in the University Centre at which little Tim and I were present was dubbed with a voice-over spoken by one of Stephen's students. He said, "Neither Mrs Hawking nor their son Timmie are particularly interested in mathematics, so when they come to lunch, we try not to talk about work." Afterwards, I learnt that, to his great embarrassment, the student in question had been commanded to read this by the producer. My former supervisor, Alan Deyermond, gallantly wrote to the BBC in protest at the injustice of such a deliberate insult. Irony of ironies, *Professor Hawking's Universe* opened with a shot of one of our wedding photos. The sole people to derive any tongue-in-cheek amusement from it were my parents, who featured in the wedding photo: overnight they became television celebrities in St Albans.

Even before the *Horizon* programme, Stephen had become a household name. In the summer of 1981, Prince Philip, the Chancellor of the University of Cambridge, expressed his wish to meet Stephen in the course of his rounds of the university departments. It seemed most appropriate to invite him to come for a private visit to the house, where he would be able to talk to Stephen without background disturbance. Robert, definitely a budding scientist at the age of fourteen, interpreted his father's replies to the Chancellor's questions about the age of the universe and the nature of black holes. As the visit on 10th June coincided with our guest's sixtieth birthday, I made and iced a fruit cake, decorating it with half a dozen candles which Timmie and Prince Philip blew out together before the royal visitor was precipitately whisked away to his next appointment.

When Stephen's name appeared as a Commander of the British Empire in the New Year's Honours List of 1982, we decided that, given the potential for calamity involved in controlling the wheelchair, Stephen should not go forwards to meet the Queen alone, but that Robert should accompany him. The investiture at Buckingham Palace was arranged for 23rd February. The occasion demanded new clothes for all of us, except for Timmie who was too young to qualify for an invitation and had to stay with my parents. Robert was kitted out with his first suit – which he never wore again since by the time another formal occasion arose he had outgrown it. Lucy, who was going through a tomboy phase, made it quite plain that she would only allow herself to be forced into a dress and a coat as a never-to-be repeated exception to her usual jeans and T-shirt.

As Robert and I were managing the exercise alone, we knew that we would be hard-pressed to arrive at the Palace from Cambridge at 10 a.m., so we drove down to London the evening before. There we stayed in the flat reserved for the use of Fellows on the top floor of the Royal Society, overlooking the tree tops of the Mall and the turrets and crenellations around Horseguards Parade. It was not until I was busily stowing all the new garments and their accessories away in the wardrobes late at night that I realized Lucy's new patent leather shoes were missing. She was innocently lounging in her scuffed, old-school clodhoppers and seemed quite content to go to the Palace looking as if she had just come in from climbing trees in the garden. The caretaker's wife thought there might be a shoe shop at the end of Regent Street, but doubted whether they sold children's shoes. We resigned ourselves to starting even earlier than planned the next morning. Leaving Robert to feed Stephen his breakfast, Lucy and I dashed up to Regent Street as the shops were opening – to buy the only pair of shoes available in Lucy's size. Sensible and unremarkable in brown leather, they were suitably smart but not as pretty as the shiny buckled pair that had been left at home. Ironically, they were to see plenty of wear, whereas the patent leather shoes lay untouched at the bottom of the wardrobe and were eventually given away.

Despite the last-minute crisis, we were still just on schedule when we set out for the Palace. We had not reckoned, though, on joining the mother of all traffic jams in the Mall: the whole population appeared to be converging on Buckingham Palace, giving the Mall the same air of frenzied urgency as the roads leading to Heathrow airport. Just as at the airport, most of the arrivals were being dropped at the gate, but it was our privilege to drive through those ornate, oft televised portals into a world apart. This was a world which seemed to operate on a different timescale from our own, a world where everything ran with a clockwork precision yet where no one showed the least signs of fluster or impatience, a bland courtesy and an easy charm being the hallmarks of all encounters.

Leaving the car, which suddenly looked embarrassingly old, battered and dirty, in the middle of the courtyard, we were shown to a different entrance from the other arrivals and were taken up several floors in an ancient lift. Lackeys ushered us with a genteel rapidity through a maze of corridors where we were able to pause only momentarily to glance at the furniture, the paintings, the Chinese vases and the exquisite, glass-cased ivories which lined the walls. When we came out into the main gallery, we were separated: Robert and Stephen were led away to join the waiting queues of national heroes and heroines, while Lucy and I were shown to our plush pink seats at the side of the magnificent ballroom.

There was plenty to absorb our attention while we waited for the proceedings to begin. Huge crystal chandeliers sparkled against the white and gold decorations. One end of the immense room consisted of a sort of red velvet temple, bathed in a soft gilded light, where elderly beefeaters from the Tower mounted guard over the dais where the Queen was to stand. On a balcony at the other end, a military band played a festive repertoire before launching into the National Anthem on the Queen's arrival. The morning's business was briskly introduced and the investiture assumed a remarkably familiar format, combining the time-honoured British traditions of school-prize-givings and degree ceremonies with the national penchant for pageantry on a grand scale, as each candidate stepped forwards from a seemingly endless line for his or her moment of glory face to face with Her Majesty the Queen. Lucy nudged me in alarm when she saw an elderly beefeater, who was standing behind the Queen, keel over – a victim of the heat, the weight of his costume and the hours spent on his feet. He was discreetly removed from the scene, feet first, without any disruption to the ceremony.

When Robert and Stephen appeared at the side entrance awaiting their turn, about halfway through the proceedings, my spine tingled with love and pride. As they crossed the floor to the centre and turned towards the Queen, they made a dramatically impressive pair – the indomitable but frail scientist slouched in his chair grinning broadly, accompanied by our tall, shy, fair-haired son. Stephen had every right to grin in pleasure at his own achievements. Perhaps he was also grinning at the irony. The formerly iconoclastic, angry young socialist had been nominated by a Tory government to receive one of the highest honours from the sovereign and was being taken into the bosom of the Establishment which he used to despise so vehemently.

Afterwards, over lunch in a posh hotel in central London, we inspected the insignia, a cross finely worked in red-and-blue enamel suspended from a red ribbon edged with a grey stripe. The inscription, "For God and Empire", like the Palace itself, belonged to the mysteries and the mythology of another age. When we studied the booklet of information that came with the "badge", as it was officially called, the only privilege we could discover that might be remotely relevant to us was that Lucy, as the daughter of a CBE, could be married in the Order's chapel in the crypt of St Paul's Cathedral. "Let's hope she remembers her shoes," Robert observed drily.

It was not only the British Establishment which was keen to number Stephen among its scions. He had already received the Papal medal in 1975, and in the autumn of 1981 he was invited to attend a conference organized by the Jesuits at the Pontifical Academy in the Vatican. The Pontifical Academy is the close-knit group of eminent scientists of unimpeachable character who advise the Pope on scientific matters. This conference was called by way of a papal updating on the state of the universe. At that early stage Stephen's nurses had not yet begun to accompany him on trips abroad, so Bernard Whiting, the Australian post-doctoral researcher who had been working with Stephen, agreed to accompany him to the conference, interpret his lecture to the audience and help me with his general care.

Since Timothy's birth, all my anxieties about leaving the children had returned and I could only reconcile myself to going to Rome by taking one or all of them with me – if not Robert, for whom school was now serious business, at least Lucy and Timmie. Happily, Mary Whiting, who knew Rome well, came too. Without the Whitings, the trip would have been an unmitigated disaster. The Hotel Michelangelo, supposedly the closest hotel to the Vatican though by our standards a good twenty minutes away from the conference venue, served no meals, not even breakfast. There was a lift but to get to it one had first to surmount a flight of steps. As if that were not enough, Rome was in the throes of cataclysmic rains. The mornings would dawn bright and sunny and we would cheerfully accompany Stephen into the Vatican, bowling along past the Swiss Guards at the gate, through the grounds to the Residence of Pius IV, a beautiful, rustic Renaissance building, constructed for the Pope in the sixteenth century. Later it accommodated female visitors to the Vatican and, since 1936, had housed the headquarters of the Pontifical Academy. There we would leave Stephen gleefully preparing to fight the Galilean corner and instruct the papal cosmologists in his revised view of the universe which had neither beginning nor end, nor any role for a Creator-God.

Until lunchtime at the Academy, the one reliably good meal of the day, I would stroll through the groves of bay trees and the children would play in the ornamental streams which trickled down the hillside. But the fine mornings would deteriorate into sultry, overcast afternoons when majestic clouds, worthy of Michelangelo, would billow over the dome of St Peter's. They would burst spectacularly amid dazzling lightning and crashing thunder, and would go on rending the heavens apart well into the night. Mary took us on guided tours to the places she loved and knew so well – to the Colosseum, the Forum, the Baths of Caracalla and out to the Catacombs of San Calixto – but our excursions were always tempered by the knowledge that we would be drenched to the skin if we were not back in the hotel by four o'clock in the afternoon. Thereafter we would have to hope for a break in the clouds around dinner time to allow us to dash out, wheelchair and pushchair in tow, for supper. Needless to say, the permanently gridlocked state of Roman traffic made it impossible to get anywhere near the hotel before the rains descended. Usually four o'clock and the first flash of lightning and roll of thunder found us in the vicinity of the railway station, searching for a bus to take us back across the Tiber.

Little Tim proved to be the unexpected hero of the hour: he loved the buses, grindingly slow, packed with bodies and suffocatingly steamed up though they were, and the Italian passengers adored him. "*Che bel bambino!*" they would exclaim, making space for me to sit down with him on my knee. "*Carissimo, carissimo!*" they would smile, stroking his blond hair and tickling his chin. He had just begun to discover the art of stringing sentences together in precise, grammatical English and was delighted to have a captive audience on whom to practise his new-found talent. "Do you have a house?" he would searchingly ask the adoring, though uncomprehending secretaries, students, businessmen and corpulent grandmothers. "Do you have a car?" He would continue with his own answers. "We have a house. We have a car. We have a garage. We have a garden." They would laugh, nodding sentimentally, while the rain streamed down the windows and the Roman traffic honked and hooted itself to a standstill in the darkening evening outside.

Mary took her role as guide so conscientiously that she would not rest until Lucy, Timmie and I had seen every church of note in Rome, including her favourite, the church of San Clemente. The medieval church, noted for its radiantly colourful eleventh-century mosaic of the Triumph of the Cross in the apse, is built above the ancient church, with its early frescoes dating from the sixth century, beside the remains of a Roman house. Having admired the brilliance of the mosaics, we followed Mary warily down into the dimly lit, red-brick lower church which, unaccountably, echoed with the sound of running water. "Oh," said Mary blithely, "that's the Cloaca Maxima, the main drain built by the Romans. It comes through here." The main drain sounded to me more like a rushing mighty river, but I supposed that Mary knew what she was talking about.

The bus ride back to the hotel in the pouring rain took even longer than usual that evening. The whole city had ground to a halt. From the conversation of the other passengers with the driver, Mary found out that the delay was caused by flooding – the Cloaca Maxima had burst the bounds of its Roman conduit and was pouring out into the streets of the city. In idle amusement to pass the time, we discussed whether this was a portent, a sign, an indication of divine wrath at Stephen's temerity in professing his heretical theories within the sanctified walls of the Vatican itself.

The Vatican – one of the most powerful, dogmatic and wealthy city states ever known – was presided over by a man whose personal attributes of holiness and courage were not in doubt, yet he sought to impose limitations on freedom of thought – just as rigidly as those atheistic scientists who would dispute our right to ask the question "why" the universe exists. The very man who should have been addressing the question "why" was busy telling the scientists that they had no right even to ask the question "how" about certain aspects of creation. At the end of the conference, the Pope told the assembly in his address that, although scientists could study the evolution of the universe, they should not ask what happened at the moment of creation at the Big Bang and certainly not before it, because that was God's preserve. Neither Stephen nor I was impressed by such injunctions; they were all too reminiscent of the attitudes behind

Galileo's arrest and confinement three hundred years earlier. Only now was the Church beginning to catch up with the history of Galileo's discoveries. There was detectable embarrassment that his theories had lain proscribed for so long. Though they were kept under lock and key, the papers relating to his fate were readily, almost apologetically, produced for Stephen's scrutiny – the implication being that it was simply an oversight that no one had thought of rehabilitating his reputation sooner. Nevertheless, the papal pronouncement indicated that the Church was still seeking to restrict thought, giving the undeniable impression that not much had been learnt from the lessons of those three hundred years.

13

Harmony Restored

Music, through which I had come back into the Church of England, had become the gateway to my spiritual rebirth and growth, and it was thanks to Mary Whiting that I was able to take up my singing lessons again soon after Timothy's birth. She positively begged to be allowed to take him out for a walk once a week in the hope that association with babies might help her have a baby of her own. On Wednesday afternoons therefore, though often tired, I resumed my lessons with Nigel Wickens, who was no stranger to the demands of parenthood after the birth of his daughter Laura. Under his guidance and to Jonathan's sensitive accompaniment – as and when his teaching commitments allowed – I returned to the joys of Schubert, Schumann, Brahms and Mozart. Variously they intensified then assuaged those emotions competing within my deepest self. Meanwhile Mary and Tim went to feed the ducks, walk in the park, sit on the swings and bury their faces in ice cream.

There were many opportunities to perform the solo repertoire in fundraising concerts for the causes which Stephen and I had espoused, and sometimes I was brought in to fill the gaps in other programmes, which was how my singing career reached its extraordinary apogee in the summer of 1982 with a short burst of song in King's College Chapel as an interlude in an organ recital that Jonathan was giving for a medical conference. My confidence both in my voice and in my ability to learn music quickly had grown sufficiently for me to feel that it was time to branch out by joining a choral society. It was just possible to contemplate such a step since I now enjoyed an unprecedented degree of freedom. While Stephen basked in the deserved glory of international acclaim, those early years of the Eighties witnessed my own transformation. On the one hand, the team of nurses brought desperately needed relief from the unrelenting physical demands that had previously consumed all my available energy. On the other, through Jonathan's unwavering support, and his devotion to the family as a whole, aspects of myself, which had long been suppressed, lying dormant in a dark corner in the daily struggle, emerged into the light. Partial living was no longer called for. I was beginning to experience the fullness of life myself, realizing that the sands which had run through my fingers on the beach in Santa Barbara years before had not, with the passing of time, spelt the end of my individual aspirations.

At a concert in the university church of Great St Mary, I encountered the sort of choir I was looking for – a mixed bunch of people of all ages and all walks of life – performing a wide repertoire and aspiring to a high standard. The dynamic young conductor, Stephen Armstrong, a recent graduate of the University, took me on and thereafter I found myself attending the once-weekly rehearsals, which demanded intense application for two solid hours at the end of a long day, and a great deal of learning in the intervening week. The day of the performance, usually a Saturday, was hectic. Concert or no, the family had to be fed and cared for, and the final rehearsal was always gruelling. Then the concert itself would be over in a flash and eight weeks' work would vanish in a single evening, sometimes creating a wild sense of euphoria at phrases that had gone exceptionally well, sometimes leaving tinges of frustration that others had not come up to expectation. Concert succeeded concert with quick changes of idiom and musical personality from baroque to modern via the classical and Romantic periods. From Bach to Benjamin Britten, the exhilaration from each performance well sung was heady. I did not mind what we sang; each successive work, each successive composer became my passionate favourite for the duration of the rehearsals and the concert, bringing about a timeless distillation of the fragile pathos of our lives, transforming painful intensity into consoling spirituality.

It was at this time, when my star was in the ascendant, that my mother fell seriously ill. Recently she and her only surviving cousin Jack had been overburdened with worry on account of Auntie Effie, who was now well into her nineties. Nor, I knew, did one need to look further than my own household to find one very obvious cause of chronic anxiety which could have exacerbated Mum's illness. At least the profound change in our own circumstances, occasioned by the advent of Nikki's nursing team, allowed me to give my parents some moral support at that most critical time and try to repay some of the care that they had shown us for so long. The revised regime also meant that, less harassed and less haggard, I could also give the children more attention. The baby had grown into the most irresistibly funny little child, observant, endlessly enquiring, dancing with an impish vitality. At about eighteen months, long before his encounter with doting Italian bus passengers, he had started to develop a precocious fascination for astronomy. In the early evening he would watch the moon from his high chair in the kitchen, following its course, distracted from the important business of his supper. As it moved across the sky – and across the window – he would grow impatient with his food, clamouring to be released from his harness. When it disappeared from view, he would dash excitedly into the living room to await the reappearance of its white shafts through the bay windows there. Each evening was for him a triumph of expectation – until the moon waned, abandoning him in the darkness of mystified disappointment. Then, at twenty-two months, he demonstrated a poetic though unscientific awareness of other natural phenomena. One cold afternoon in February 1980 as huge snowflakes came drifting down in a leisurely fashion, white and delicately geometrical against a leaden sky, he raced to the living-room window, shouting "I see tars! I see tars" – *tars* being his way of saying *stars*. He danced round the room, excitedly chanting his little refrain to the silent music of those softly falling starry constellations.

Tim's exuberance was enchanting but it could lead him to attempt potentially dangerous feats of independence in imitation of his brother and sister if left unguarded for the merest second. A couple of weeks before his second birthday, I was preparing the supper in the kitchen when suddenly the house seemed unnaturally quiet. There were no sounds of childish play – toy cars being pushed across the floor, the tin drum being thumped, chattering voices and laughter. The blood froze in my veins at the terrible silence. I rushed to the front door, only to find it wide open. Timmie had run away.

Robert, charging at full pelt ahead of Stephen and me, had frequently run away as a small boy but always to some purpose, and he had always put himself in the position of being easily found. Lucy had disappeared only once – on a fine day in the middle of summer when we were still living in Little St Mary's Lane. Thelma Thatcher and I had been anxiously searching the lane and the churchyard for her without success, when some passing Americans told us that there was a tiny girl standing with a doll's pram on the Mill Bridge. There she was – in her Bermuda shorts, one hand resting on the handle of the pram and the other holding up her transparent green umbrella. She was surrounded by an admiring band of undergraduates, who were clearly wondering what to do with this very self-possessed infant phenomenon.

Some ten years later in the isolation of 5 West Road, where there were no friendly adoptive grandparents to call upon for help and where the grounds ran for acres with neither a fence nor a gate, I stood at the open door in a frenzy of blank indecision, not knowing which way to turn. Had Timmie run out onto the road and down to the river, or round the house into the garden? The college staff, who were closing up their workshops for the day, heard me frantically calling his name, and came to help. Eventually Pat, one of the maintenance staff, soberly advised me to call the police. He stood by while, with my heartbeat resounding in my ears and my hands shaking, I dialled 999. I was upset that the officer who took the call did not react more dramatically. He did not seem to register the urgency of the situation. "Hold on a minute ma'am," he said jovially. He returned to the phone a moment later. "Can you describe your little boy and tell me what he is wearing?" he asked, still in the same irritatingly cheerful tone of voice. "Fair hair, blue eyes, blue top and green trousers," I replied distraught with worry. "That's all right then," the policeman said. "We've got a little boy in one of our police cars, but as he couldn't tell us where he lived, the officer is driving round in the hope of finding his mother." Timmie was brought home in a police car by a policewoman and the kind person who had picked him up just as he was about to set foot on the road – on his way, it seemed, to visit his godmother, Joy Cadbury. That same kind person had held him on her knee until the rather damp, blond, blue and green bundle was delivered back into my trembling arms.

Although they were less dependent on my physical presence, the two older children needed a great deal of understanding. Robert seemed destined to be a lonely child with few companions, while the transfer to secondary school parted Lucy from her band of cherished local friends whom she had known from birth. Because Robert had received a private education, thanks to his inheritance, we felt that we could do no less for Lucy, but she was the only one of her year to go from primary school to the girls' Perse. We gave her a kitten to comfort her and distract her, and in the hope that it might help pay her school fees, Stephen decided that the time had come to write a popular book, describing his science – the study of the origins of the universe – to the public in accessible language, avoiding the barriers of jargon and equations. I had often urged him to meet the challenge of explaining his research, reasoning that I, in particular, would benefit from reading it, and so would the taxpayers, in general, who were financing that research through government funding.

Both Robert and Lucy sometimes came with me to St Mark's where, ever inventive, Bill Loveless continued to cater for all ages and tastes. Not only did he keep the congregation of Newnham morally and intellectually awake with his monthly reviews of the state of the nation, he also put a prodigious effort into attracting families to the church by means of the family service. This service, always entertaining, sometimes unpredictable in the responses it could provoke, influenced a whole generation of children in an increasingly secular age. Lucy, who always had a part to play, whether lighting the altar candles or snuffing them out, reading the lesson, participating in the quizzes or performing in various dramatizations, loved it. One Sunday when I had left the children lazily dozing at home, Bill announced the inaugural session of a new youth club to be led by ordinands from the local theological college; it was to combine games, fun and serious discussion. Robert showed little interest when I told him about it, but reluctantly agreed to go that evening just to please me. At seven o'clock I drove him to the vicarage, promising to wait outside for ten minutes in case he did not like it. He liked it so well that I went home alone after the ten-minute wait, and thereafter he never missed a session. He met old acquaintances from primary school and made new friends, both girls and boys. They formed a cohesive and loyal group from that day onwards, encouraging Robert to develop the self-assurance and sociability which previously he had found so difficult. Only two weeks later, he met Bill Loveless as he was cycling home from school, and told him that he wanted to be confirmed. Bill became the trusted friend and mentor to both Robert and Lucy. He often reassured them and gently explained the complexities of adult life to them when the anomalies of their background – whether the scourge of Stephen's illness or the unconventional nature of Jonathan's presence in the family – disturbed their preconceived idealized notions of how family life and parents should be.

The atmosphere of those years was generally so much more relaxed that I was able to resume contact with my school friends again. They would come with their husbands and families for a Sunday visit once or twice a year. After a leisurely lunch during which many a topic – political, environmental, scientific, literary or musical – would be intensively discussed, the adults would amble round the garden and join the children for a game of hide-and-seek in among the glades and bushes of Harvey Court, the Caius property next door. This game became a tradition. With Stephen acting as lookout, the rest of us shed our adult reserve and recaptured for just an hour the intense excitement of childhood.

In the comparative harmony of that period, my relationship with Stephen entered a new phase where the tendency for us to slip into the roles of master and slave was arrested. We were companions and equals again – as we had been in our campaigning in the Sixties and early Seventies. The CND badge, which Stephen regularly wore on his lapel in television programmes, was but one indication of the several causes which we championed jointly. The inexorable increase in nuclear weapons, of which Rob Donovan had chillingly warned us in the early Seventies, had developed into a fully fledged arms race, a mad, uncontrolled competition between East and West to reach Armageddon as soon as possible and annihilate all living creatures on the planet. The Campaign for Nuclear Disarmament once again became a national force and local groups sprouted all over the country.

Our group, Newnham Against the Bomb, met once a month in the house of Alice Roughton, a retired doctor. A figure of immense and generous energies, trenchant convictions and fabled eccentricity, she was reputed to serve stewed squirrel and nettles at dinner parties. Her husband was known to prefer the garden shed to the house. We dozen or so members of Newnham Against the Bomb would sit round her smoking fire warming our hands on a glass of mulled wine, while we listened to presentations by knowledgeable but pessimistic speakers. Then we would plan strategies, discussing what we could do to stop the arms race. The prospects were not encouraging. We were after all pitting ourselves against the military industrial complexes of the two superpowers. There was some slight consolation to be derived from the fact that we were at least making an effort – and in any case, Stephen and I were used to playing David against many a monolithic Goliath.

Together he and I composed a letter and sent it off to all our friends around the world, particularly to those in the United States and in the Soviet Union. We urged them to protest at the escalation in nuclear weapons, which threatened to destroy the population of the northern hemisphere and produce so much radiation that the prospects for remaining life elsewhere would be negligible. We pointed out that there existed four tons of high explosive for every man, woman and child on the planet, and that the risk of a nuclear exchange being set off by miscalculation or computer failure was unacceptably high. Stephen used the same theme in his address to the Franklin Institute in Philadelphia when he was awarded the Franklin Medal in 1981. He remarked that it had taken about four billion years for mammals to evolve, about four million years for man to evolve and about four hundred years to develop our scientific and technological civilization. In the previous forty years, progress in understanding the four interactions of physics had advanced to the state where there was a very real chance of discovering a complete unified field theory, which would describe everything in the universe. Yet all that could be wiped out in less than forty minutes in the event of a nuclear catastrophe, and the probability of such a catastrophe occurring, either by accident or design, was frighteningly high. He concluded that this was the fundamental problem facing our society and was much more important than any ideological or territorial issues.

We made roughly the same points when we met General Bernard Rogers, a former Rhodes Scholar and Supreme Commander of Allied Forces in Europe, at a feast in University College, Oxford. After the meal, Stephen barred his way with the wheelchair as he was about to leave the dinner table. The General listened considerately while, in some embarrassment, I recited my speech on behalf of Newnham Against the Bomb. He then politely acknowledged that he himself was very concerned about the situation and had in fact been engaged in discussions with his Soviet opposite number. Within a few years, the rapidly changing economic and political situation behind the Iron Curtain overtook our local efforts. We shall never know whether our modest individual and group protests had even the slightest impact on the course of history, whether any of our letters ever reached their targets or whether our messages ever struck home to the heart of the political establishments of the East or the West.

Closer to home our campaigns concerned less apocalyptic matters, though they were equally impassioned, especially when they related to the rights of the disabled. The Cambridge colleges were so remarkably slow in implementing the Disabled Persons Act – which in its initial form had first reached the statute book in 1970 – that in the 1980s new buildings which made no provision for disabled access were still being commissioned. One of them, Clare College, not a hundred yards from our house, was sending out an appeal to attract funds for a building containing a library and recital room, which was advertised as a public place but had made no provision for disabled access. We campaigned vigorously in the media against this two-faced attitude and were met with comments such as: "If Stephen Hawking wants a disabled lift, he should pay for it himself." When finally Lord Snowdon – who had come to photograph Stephen for a glossy magazine – took up our cause on the radio, the College was forced to capitulate.

Stephen and I – and Jonathan – had supported the fundraising activities of the Motor Neuron Disease Association since its inception in 1979. For some time, Stephen as the Patients' Patron and I had attended meetings and conferences. In the early Eighties he was asked to become a Vice-President of the Leonard Cheshire Foundation as well and, in October 1982, I was invited to join the Appeal Committee to raise funds for converting a Victorian house at Brampton near Huntingdon into a Cheshire Home for the disabled. I attended monthly meetings in Huntingdon and soon discovered that my catchment area for fundraising was none other than the University of Cambridge – each college within the University and each individual Fellow within each college. Armed with a copy of the University register, my task was to sift through hundreds of likely donors and personally address pleading letters to each one, in preparation for the public launching of the appeal in the summer of 1984. The launch in Hinchingbrooke House augured well for the appeal, but unluckily for the charity it coincided with a six-week postal strike, while the national consciousness was distracted from giving to local charities by the horrendous pictures daily on television of starvation in Africa. Consequently it took many years of fundraising before the Home was opened. For Stephen and me, however, these campaigns were a wholly positive and unifying activity which gave us a joint role – outside physics.

14

Unfinished Business

In the early Eighties, there were two areas of unfinished business which I had to settle. First and foremost there was the thesis. I was summoned to Westfield for my oral examination in June 1980 in the presence of Stephen Harvey, the Professor of Spanish at King's College and of my supervisor, Alan Deyermond. The previous evening in Cambridge, Stephen and I had attended a performance of a Handel opera, *Rinaldo*, as part of the end-of-year celebrations in Caius. Much lauded though the performance was, it failed to make any impression on me because music, even the famous aria, '*Lascia ch'io pianga*', had temporarily lost its appeal. Like those occasions when Stephen had unwillingly found himself at the ballet, I squirmed in my seat in impatience, resenting the misuse of valuable time. I was fraught with worry that I would never be able to remember every point, every date, every reference in the 336 pages of the thesis the next day at 2 p.m.

The next day, tense and partially sighted, having lost a contact lens on the way to London, I groped my way through the exam until, with a mischievous smile, Stephen Harvey asked if I had read a book by the author David Lodge. Somewhat taken aback, I searched his face for clues to his meaning. Surely he wasn't referring to *Changing Places*, the hilariously authentic account of an academic exchange between Philip Swallow of Rummidge University (alias Birmingham) and Maurice Zapp of Euphoric State University (alias Berkeley)? I could not remotely discern any connection between *Changing Places* and medieval Spanish poetry; nonetheless I plucked up the courage to ask whether he was referring to any of David Lodge's novels. "No, no," he replied, "I mean *Modes of Modern Writing*" – which critical study, I had to admit, I had not read. After that, the exam proceeded in a more relaxed atmosphere. Later Alan Deyermond confessed that he had not read *Changing Places*.

The following spring Jonathan and Stephen – who bought me the flowing red robes of a Doctor of Philosophy – accompanied me to the Albert Hall and patiently sat through the mammoth degree ceremony. It was the end of a long and arduous journey. The fact that it ended in a blind alley was not significant. I had certainly not entertained any great hopes of a teaching post or even of hourly paid supervisions at the University of Cambridge, since my tentative enquiries as to whether there might be some teaching in the Spanish Department were politely ignored.

The chance to begin an occupation, if not a career, came unexpectedly and centred upon my other language, French, the language I had first encountered with some puzzlement on the side of HP Sauce bottles at the age of three or four. Fortunately the fascination for French engendered by the HP Sauce – together with sympathetic teaching in early childhood – had been strong enough to outweigh the powerful disincentive of Miss Leather, the gaunt, feline senior French mistress who regularly meted out "fifty French verbs" as her preferred form of punishment. It was said in her obituary that she could keep a classroom in absolute silence, even in her absence.

In the early Eighties, just as I had finished the thesis and Lucy and her contemporaries were looking forward to learning French in primary school, language teaching was summarily removed from the curriculum, a victim of the Tory government's economy measures. One of my much valued friends from the school gate, Christine Putnis, the Australian mother of a large family of clever children, prevailed upon me and Ros Mays, another of the mothers, to teach French to a group of children after school hours. With some trepidation, we began a project which was to last for ten years. Every Monday afternoon we would greet our pupils with drinks and biscuits, and then subject them to an hour's worth of intensive learning, artfully concealed in puzzles, games, songs, drawings and stories.

A year or two later I found myself obliged to revise French for GCE O level with Robert. It was his school report, just before the O-level term, which spurred me into action. "He is unlikely to pass the exam," it said of his French. The thought of a child of mine failing French was so terrible that drastic measures were called for. Robert's friend Thomas Cadbury was brought in to provide some competition and to ensure seriousness of purpose, and a minimum of fifty verbs were conjugated in all persons in all tenses. This linguistic onslaught struck its target so successfully that after the exam results it was actually suggested that the chip off the old scientific block might consider French for A level, a suggestion given only frivolous consideration as he had been earmarked from birth for physics, chemistry, maths, more maths and, of course, computing.

Just as I was beginning to feel confident enough to take on further teaching more formally, in either French or Spanish, another meeting at the school gate provided a golden opportunity. One of the mothers put me in touch with a recently established private sixth-form college where she worked, the Cambridge Centre for Sixth-Form Studies (otherwise known as CCSS). The startling conclusion of an informal interview with the Principal was that I found myself agreeing to teach candidates for Oxbridge entrance, a challenging proposition, and one which I suspected to be some sort of initiation test. If I could get students into Oxbridge, then I myself would probably be taken on. The advantages were that I could choose my hours and, as the organization had only limited premises, I could teach at home.

I spent hours looking up old entrance papers in the university library, devising teaching programmes and ruminating on the moral and philosophical questions set in the general paper, which revolved in some way or other around those philosophical and linguistic brain-teasers so beloved of Bertrand Russell such as: "There is a barber in Athens who shaves everyone who does not shave himself. Who shaves the barber?" or "Generalizations are false". Epigrammatic quotations were also a favourite of the examiners, who found an ample supply in the works of Oscar Wilde: "The truth is rarely pure and never simple", for example. Such formulations rubbed shoulders with essay titles inviting discussion about the ethics of nuclear deterrence or the positive and negative values of science, as for instance, "The genius of Einstein leads to Hiroshima". All these topics and many others like them were food to my starving brain.

My appetite whetted by university entrance papers, I next devoured the stuff of the A-level syllabus. Grammar, translations, comprehensions, literary texts – all required hours of thought, preparation and revision, but provided a sumptuous feast on which to feed my hungry intellect. What's more, I actually found that I enjoyed teaching and I liked the age group of sixteen- to eighteen-year-olds who were put into my charge. As my pupils were always about the same age as one or other of my own children at some stage of their education, I felt a natural affinity with that adolescent age group and quickly found that even the most difficult pupils would respond to a friendly approach. Many of them had been placed in boarding school at the age of six, and by the age of sixteen had demonstrated their frustration in some dramatic way or other and had accordingly been expelled. Now they had a second chance and had to be eased into taking it. There was also a clutch of overseas pupils, often multilingual, whose parents wanted their offspring to benefit from an English education within the security of supervised accommodation. These pupils were usually the most highly motivated and the most stimulating, though often, because of their multinational backgrounds, they were uncertain of their true national identity, and lacked written fluency in any of their languages. The strength of the A-level course was that it taught pupils to think analytically and critically for themselves and it introduced literature to people who might never have read a book in their lives. It was particular gratifying when, after two years of study, a pupil would come and thank me for opening his or her eyes to the delights of reading.

The pleasure was the more intense when one of those appreciative pupils was dyslexic. Through my own family I had such wide-ranging experience of the multitude of problems associated with the condition that I knew I could offer special encouragement. In an uncomprehending educational system, whether state or private, the dyslexics in a class, like my own sons, would typically be told that they were slow, stupid or lazy and would be sent to sit at the back of the class. Dyslexics are not stupid. Generally their intelligence quotient is higher than the rest of the population but their overdeveloped brain has squeezed out some other facility, usually associated with language or short-term memory. An intelligent child whose powers of communication are limited and who is sent to sit at the back of the class becomes a frustrated child who needs patient and considerate teaching to recover his self-esteem and express his latent intelligence.

Teaching at home for a few hours a day at my own convenience was the perfect arrangement. Kikki's successor, Lee Pearson, a gentle, reliable girl, took charge of Timmie in the mornings while I taught. My pupils would arrive as Stephen was leaving for work and when the bell rang, I had only to shed my apron before answering the door. I felt intensely happy: the skills that I had to offer were being mobilized. I won the respect of my pupils, and gradually discovered a professional identity for myself as I awoke from an intellectual coma.

15

Departures

Although through teaching, first at primary-school level and then later for A level, I was beginning to find some sense of my own worth, there remained the other area of unfinished business, the one major barrier to the recovery of my true self: the fear of flying. Flying phobia, the black consequence of that fateful trip to Seattle so soon after Robert's birth when I nursed my small bundle on aeroplanes the length and breadth of the United States, had deprived me of many an exciting opportunity to accompany Stephen – to California in midwinter, to Crete in spring or to New York on Concorde. It had forced me to invent patently feeble excuses, because every suggestion of travel by air sent cold shivers down my spine, putting me immediately on the defensive. It had caused tension in the home and it had made me very unhappy. The anxiety had started to produce physical symptoms so marked that, before the trip to Rome in the autumn of 1981, I was actually sick. I was desperate to find a cure.

It was with great excitement that, while idly thumbing through a magazine in the dentist's waiting room later that winter, I came across a reference to a clinic where flying phobia was accepted without embarrassment as a treatable condition. Enquiries and a letter from my GP eventually put me in touch with the York Clinic at Guy's Hospital where Mr Maurice Yaffe, a senior psychologist, treated sufferers, either privately or in groups on the National Health Service, with a variety of techniques. There was nothing clinical about Maurice Yaffe: his personality and manner were absent-mindedly donnish rather than medical; he never mentioned the word "phobia", only "difficulty". As he enthused over the delights of cheap air fares, we, his patients, became adjusted to a perspective which encouraged us to concentrate on the pleasures of Paris, Rome or New York instead of on the agonies of getting there. Then a very basic course in aerodynamics left no doubt in the minds of the sceptical that aeroplanes were meant to fly. Finally Maurice Yaffe unveiled his own brainchild, a simulated aircraft cabin, housed in a small room in the basement of Guy's Hospital. Within minutes of taking our seats in the simulator, we found ourselves soaring away to Manchester – Manchester because the video film which appeared in the cabin window was of a flight to Manchester with all the appropriate sounds and sensations of take-off and flight: the announcements, the revving engines, the crying babies, the floor tilting, the undercarriage jolting and slight turbulence as the plane supposedly passed through cloud. After an initial feeling of panic followed by twelve or so flights to Manchester, the whole business became so boring that I forgot to be frightened and began to relax. The culmination of the course was a weekend in Paris, arranged in fine detail by Maurice Yaffe, though not of course paid for by the National Health Service.

If Paris was the first step on my road to liberation, California was but another short step away in psychological terms. There in the summer of 1982, we renewed old friendships the length and breadth of the state and revisited old haunts. Jonathan had arranged to attend a conference on early music in Vancouver that August and combined the conference with a visit to us in Santa Barbara, where he was often taken for one of Stephen's students. Indeed, he lived with the students in their accommodation and to all intents and purposes shared their rota of duties, although, unlike them, he was paying his own way.

Little Tim was amazed at the size of the country. "They did build a big country!" he would mutter to himself as he gazed out of the car window over deserts and mountains. As we watched the sun setting over the Santa Inés range from our apartment every evening, he would declare solemnly, "It's the end of the world, it's the end of the world." Some time later, I asked him what he liked best about California – the J. Paul Getty Museum, the deserts, the mountains, the sea or the Huntingdon Museum and gardens. It was a stupid question to ask a three-year-old. He answered me in what he considered to be my own terms, for, as quick as a flash he replied, "The Mickey Mouse Museum..."

I was now ready to fly east again as well as west. With a cautious eye on employment possibilities, Lucy had begun to study Russian for O level. In retrospect, this was not a good choice since, despite changing times, it did not lead to a brilliant career and produced only much frustration. However, the rigours of studying seventeenth-century church Russian at Oxford and a winter spent in Moscow amid the privations of 1992 were still on the distant horizon when Lucy flew with her father, a bevy of nurses and me to a conference in that city in October of 1984. Lucy's attempts to speak Russian were met with ecstatic delight, especially when she stood up to propose a brief toast to *"mir i drujba"* – "peace and friendship" – at the closing banquet of the conference. It was one of those Russian banquets where the hors d'oeuvre are lavish – caviar, smoked fish and meats, nuts, pickles and, of course, the ubiquitous cucumber – and last for hours, interrupted by toasts, speeches and, in the case of one misguided Japanese delegate, an endless dirge delivered in a monotone which he himself had composed in unintelligible English. The main course, the usual lump of unidentifiable meat and mashed potato, arrived at the tables just as everyone was leaving.

Eleven years earlier, our acquaintances had demonstrated the utmost caution in their dealings with us. Now they seemed not to care a fig for officialdom. The young guide who was sent to "mind" Lucy and me was much more interested in accompanying us to buy clothes in the hard-currency shops to which we had access than in directing our movements. Two of Stephen's closest colleagues, Renata Galosh and her husband, Andrei Linde, openly invited us to dinner in their small flat on the outskirts of Moscow. They provided a delectable meal, in part down to an amicable relationship with the manager of some restaurant or other, and in part because of Renata's preserves from her dacha in the country, among them home-made strawberry juice strained from precious home-bottled fruit.

Although the flying phobia was more or less under control, it was simply not practicable for me to accompany Stephen on each one of his international expeditions: travel had become an obsession with him and he regularly seemed to spend more time in the air than he did on the ground. He found it hard to accept that, quite apart from Lucy and Tim, I was not prepared to abandon either Robert or my students as their A levels approached in the spring of 1985, a period which he had designated for an extensive tour of China. Bernard Carr and Iolanta, one of his nurses, manfully took charge, heaving Stephen on and off aeroplanes and trains, and valiantly manoeuvring the wheelchair up onto the Great Wall. They came back exhausted nor was Stephen in the best of health, though he was triumphant at his achievement. He coughed frequently and appeared to be even more sensitive to irritants in foodstuffs. Many a night would be spent nursing him in my arms, trying to calm the panic which itself precipitated even worse choking fits.

However, the summer holidays promised a respite. We were to spend the whole of August in Geneva, where Stephen was planning to have discussions with the particle physicists at Cern, while the rest of us could enjoy the environs of Lake Geneva. At Cern Stephen would be working on the implications for the direction of the arrow of time of quantum theory and of the observations from the particle accelerator. This was a topic upon which he had expatiated at some length, with Robert's help, to the Astronomical Society at the Perse School. It was at this lecture that I resigned myself to the realization that physics had become so abstract that, even when explained in pictorial form, it was beyond my comprehension. No amount of film played backwards of broken cups and saucers jumping back onto tables and reassembling themselves could persuade me that the direction of time could be reversed. Such a supposition could potentially alter the course of human history if visitors from the future could interfere with the past. It seemed however that it was essential to prove mathematically that this was not a possibility, since the proof would ensure that nothing could travel faster than light.

Stephen's travels in time and space notwithstanding, it had been a good summer: it had begun when the cat had a large litter of kittens on the kitchen floor. The prettier specimens were farmed out to various friends and acquaintances, until eventually all that remained was one undistinguished black-and-white tom, which one of my more susceptible students, Gonzalo Vargas Llosa, a young Peruvian, insisted on taking to join his uncaged rabbit in his room. Lucy completed her first French exchange with a Breton girl whose boatman father had won the lottery, and there were parties. Robert set the style by celebrating his eighteenth birthday, just before the onset of his exams, with a ceilidh on the lawn on a warm clear night under a full moon. There were also concerts of every description, choral and instrumental, recitals and even a pop concert at the Albert Hall to celebrate Tim's sixth birthday, as he had become a great fan of Sky, devoting himself single-mindedly in his every waking moment to emulating their tremendous, sustained drum rolls. An unscheduled concert of a different nature took place on our back lawn when, one Sunday at the beginning of July, just as Stephen and I were returning home from an expedition into medieval Suffolk with the delegates to that summer's physics conference, the lights failed in the University Concert Hall up the road. Jonathan was to play the harpsichord in the concert that evening and brought news of the disaster. The weather was fine and dry, so the obvious solution was for the players to set up their instruments on the lawn while the audience grouped round, sitting alfresco on whatever rugs, cushions and mats we could muster.

Although Jonathan was regularly asked to play with modern and amateur orchestras such as the one which performed on our lawn, he had long lamented the lack of authentic baroque performance in Cambridge, where many young hopeful keyboard players vied for the few opportunities available. On the other hand, he was too remote from the London scene for involvement there to be a feasible prospect. Had it not been for his commitment to us, particularly to me, clearly he might well have moved to London, where he could have advanced his career much more easily. The only course was for him to start his own orchestra, but that was a daunting prospect in terms of the time, the commitment and the money required. He was becoming so frustrated by the musical isolation in which he found himself, and he hankered so desperately to perform as part of an ensemble that when, in the spring of 1984, he went into hospital for an operation, I decided to take charge of the situation. First I picked up the telephone and booked the University Concert Hall, and then I rang round various contacts and booked a small but complete orchestra of baroque players. Jonathan came round from the anaesthetic to the news that, in his temporary absence from consciousness, he had been appointed the director of the newly formed Cambridge Baroque Camerata which was due to give its inaugural concert on 24th June. Frenzied planning, programming and publicity filled the intervening weeks, which were also the weeks of his convalescence.

On the night, Robert ran the box office, Lucy sold programmes and various friends acted as ushers while I ran to and fro, liaising between front of house and backstage and attending to Stephen who sat at the side of the platform. To our amazement, the queue for tickets stretched out into the forecourt. We counted each and every member of the audience as they filed into the concert hall that June evening, since a full house was crucial to the financial success of the enterprise. "Financial success" did not mean making a profit; it merely signified breaking even. All seats were taken and the performance, entitled *The Trumpet Shall Sound*, received rapturous applause. Emboldened by the success of the 1984 concert, the Cambridge Baroque Camerata ventured onto the concert platform again in 1985 with another own-promotion, a programme to mark the tercentenary of the births of Bach, Handel and Scarlatti. Fortunately the gamble paid off a second time – although on some later occasions, unexpected rival attractions such as televised football finals would decrease the size of the audience dispiritingly. The London debut of the ensemble, planned for October 1985 in the Queen Elizabeth Hall, had to be regarded as an investment for the future, as it certainly would not break even, but it would bring the Cambridge Baroque Camerata to the attention of a wider public.

Our household seemed to have recovered a considerable degree of equilibrium. For no one were the results more satisfactory than for Stephen himself, who had finished writing the first draft of a popular book about cosmology and the origins of the universe. The book ranged wide, from a discussion of early cosmologies to modern theories of particle physics and the arrow of time – with particular reference, of course, to the significance of black holes. In conclusion the author looked forward to the time when mankind would able to "know the mind of God" through the formulation, at some not-too-distant date in the future, of a complete unified theory of the universe, the theory of everything. Stephen had been given the name of an agent in New York where the book was being offered to publishers, and meanwhile in England we discussed tax-efficient methods of receiving royalties, which we expected to bring in a modest supplementary income regularly over the years, like textbooks which were said to be far more reliable in the long run than bestsellers. It was unlikely to fulfil the original aim of paying Lucy's school fees, as she was already well into her secondary education.

At the end of July, a few days in advance of the rest of us, Stephen, his new secretary Laura Ward, some students and nurses, flew out to Geneva. I was anxious to stay to see Robert off on a scout expedition to Iceland before leaving Cambridge myself. The plan was that within the week we would meet Stephen and his entourage in Germany at Bayreuth, the Wagnerian Mecca, for a performance of the *Ring Cycle*, and then all travel back to

Geneva to a house rented for the duration of the holidays. At last I had begun to achieve a happy balance in my life and felt that with the help of Purcell, Bach and Handel, I could cope with the effects of Wagner's sinister modulations in a spirit of good-humoured tolerance.

It was quite casually, without a second thought, that I waved goodbye to Stephen as he left home on 29th July. Geneva after all was no distance compared with China and it was renowned for its standards of hygiene. We were all concerned for Stephen's father, who was in the throes of a chronic illness, and feared that he might die during our absence. He bore his illness with the same gruff pragmatic stoicism that he had brought to all situations and which he used to conceal pain or embarrassment. Despite the vicissitudes of my relationship with the Hawking family, I had not ceased to respect him, the more so because of late he had begun to write me truly appreciative letters, praising my care of Stephen and the children and my management of the letting house. However, my greatest anxiety at this time was for Robert, my eldest son, whom I saw off in the company of the Venture Scouts three days after Stephen's departure. Their plans – to trek across a glacier and to canoe round the north coast of Iceland – filled me with silent foreboding.

Part Four

1

Darkest Night

It was seldom that Jonathan and I were alone together for any length of time. We tried to observe a code of conduct in front of Stephen and the children whereby we behaved simply as good friends, suppressing, sometimes with difficulty, any display of closer affection in our attempts to avoid hurting anyone. Each evening I would stand behind Stephen at the front door as he saw Jonathan off, dispatching him to his own house on the other side of Cambridge. In our efforts to keep the home going by this unconventional method we had the support of many people, among them my elderly home help, Eve Suckling. These were people who had witnessed the situation from the inside and who were wise enough not to draw hasty conclusions. Even Don, whose absolute values had been shaken one evening in the spring of 1978, just before Tim's birth, when he found Jonathan and me comfortably lolling against each other on the sofa, had conceded that the situation often demanded of him much more than he had expected, and sometimes more than he could give – certainly more than he could give indefinitely. He admitted that he had lived with us long enough to find that the ceaseless rigours of our way of life often brought him into uncomfortable conflict with his own conscience. Always we knew too that we could count on the guidance of Bill Loveless to strengthen our resolve and help keep our perspective within the disciplined framework that we had tried to establish for it while viewing our weaknesses with compassion. More than once he was heard to say that our situation was unique and that he could not say how we should deal with it.

Occasionally, when Stephen went abroad or when we were to take the car to join him somewhere on the Continent, we tentatively allowed our relationship to blossom. But so sensitive was I to its unorthodox nature that the experience was often watered with tears of guilt, since an unthinking word from one of the children or an unexpected encounter on a beach or campsite could quickly destroy the brief, heady illusion of freedom and send my conscience plummeting into despair. Discretion and deceit were divided by only the finest line, and it was never easy to judge on which side of the line we stood. There were a couple of other celebrities in the public eye who were seriously disabled, and it was public knowledge that their spouses had found solace with other partners while still caring responsibly and lovingly for them. Perhaps it was because those spouses were husbands rather than wives that it was easier for them to bring their new relationships into the open than it was for me.

Nevertheless, those short periods of respite, even if spent under canvas in a raging wind or sometimes sharing a small foreign hotel room with two or three children, allowed us a freedom from nagging anxiety and constant care – they restored our flagging morale and, paradoxically, reinforced our loyalty to Stephen. Our travels would often take us through France, giving me the opportunity to introduce Jonathan to Brandon and Lucette, who were now living outside Paris, and to Mary and Bernard Whiting, who with their two small children were living in the heart of that magical city. They all wholeheartedly welcomed Jonathan as an essential element in our family life. In 1985 however, our route took us through Belgium and Germany rather than France. It had become an accepted part of the family routine that Stephen would attend a summer school in some desirable part of Europe, flying out with his students and nurses, and that Jonathan and the children and I would arrive by car in a more leisurely manner, taking a few days' holiday on the way. So on Friday 1st August 1985, after Robert's departure to Iceland with the Venture Scouts, Jonathan, Lucy, Tim and I set out for Felixstowe to board the ferry for the overnight crossing to Zeebrugge.

We had planned to spend the weekend by the sea on the Belgian coast before driving through Belgium and Germany to Bayreuth, where on 8th August we were to meet Stephen for the performance of the *Ring* – but just one night on the coast, where stinging sandstorms were blowing along the beach under leaden skies, was enough to turn us inland to look for campsites in the Ardennes, the hilly, forested area of Belgium near the German border. Not only did torrential rain begin to lash our windscreen before we had even reached Brussels, but a strange itchy feeling also began to creep around the nape of our necks, like prickly burrs caught in our pullovers and anoraks: the truth was that we were giving a free ride to the head lice that had infested Tim's school just before the end of term. We had all carefully washed our hair with the prescribed shampoo, while Stephen, for good measure, had insisted on also having his locks doused with a foul-smelling lotion, which he wore throughout a whole day in the Department. He remarked that evening that, apart from his faithful attendant-student, no one had come near him all day.

On that summer holiday in Belgium we were little better than tramps, soaked to the skin, and lice-ridden until I could find the appropriate shampoo. We ambled on still in the pouring rain from Belgium into Luxembourg, where we paused for a picnic lunch in Echternach, a leafy town on the German border. After being cooped up in the car all morning, Tim raced gleefully up and down a long alleyway of trees in a park. Inevitably he slipped and fell flat on his face in a muddy puddle. The apparition rising from the dirt was of an unrecognizable small boy, previously blond, caked in mud from head to foot, from the very tips of his eyelashes to his shoelaces – every item of clothing, including his anorak, oozed brown mud. Jonathan steered me onto the front seat of the car and then hastily brought out the washing-up bowl and set up the camping stove on the pavement. He warmed some water and then washed the offending creature and his clothes as best he could in full view of all the passers-by – to Lucy's intense mortification. The final leg of that journey took us via some friends of Jonathan's in Mannheim to Rothenburg, a medieval showplace within easy reach of the Wagnerian holy of holies. We pitched our tents in the early evening and lingered drowsily over food and wine in a pleasantly atmospheric restaurant. On the way back to the campsite, I stopped at a phone box to ring through to Geneva to check the arrangements for meeting Stephen in Bayreuth the next day. The phone was answered by Laura Ward, who had replaced Judy Fella when the latter had left to go on an extended trip to South Africa with her husband. Laura's voice was tense with unexpected urgency. "Oh, Jane, thank goodness you've called!" she almost shouted down the phone. "You must come quickly, Stephen is in a coma in hospital in Geneva, and we don't know how long he'll live!"

The news was shattering. It plunged me into a black pit of misery. Quite irrationally forgetting all those travels to distant places that he had survived perfectly well without me, I asked myself how I could ever have let Stephen go off alone with his entourage, deprived of the protection of my intimate knowledge of his condition, of his needs, his medicines, his likes, his dislikes, his allergies, his fears? How could I have seen him off without a qualm of anxiety and then have set out on holiday myself – with Jonathan?

While we were still in Cambridge, Stephen had rung, as he usually did on arrival, to say that all was well. He was living in a nice house in Ferney-Voltaire, well situated, if a little distant from the laboratory. He had wished us well for our journey and looked forward to seeing us in a week's time at Bayreuth. After that, in the mishmash of all my other concerns, especially my anxiety for Robert on his canoeing trip round the north coast of Iceland, I had scarcely given him another moment's thought, knowing him to be safe and in good hands. Apart from the troublesome cough, which he had brought back from China, he had been fine when he left home. It was incredible that he could have fallen into a coma in Geneva. We sat in the car numbly discussing the news. We decided to strike camp and set off for Geneva immediately, but on our return to the campsite we found everything closed for the night: the main gate was shut and the only entry or exit was by means of a wicket gate for pedestrians. There was no way we could leave until the early morning. I lay awake in my sleeping bag, listening to wolves howling and farm animals cackling somewhere in the distant black night. "Please God, let Stephen be alive!" I whispered, impatient for dawn.

As soon as the campsite opened, we loaded the car and set out on a mad dash across Europe to Geneva. Hundreds of miles of German pasture land sped by without our noticing as we raced to the Swiss border. The one advantage of being in Germany was that there were no speed restrictions. We paused at the frontier for some refreshments for the children, though I had no stomach for food, and then resumed our frenzied progress along the heartlessly tranquil shores of the blue lakes, Lake Neuchâtel and then Lake Geneva. We spoke little, each absorbed in an unhappy turmoil of confusing reflections. Even the children were quiet in the back of the car. Geneva glistened in the late afternoon sun as we approached it, but we had only one goal: the Hôpital Cantonal, where the fearsome truth of life or death awaited us. A combination of Jonathan's map-reading expertise and my ability to ask for directions in French brought us to it – a clean, clinical complex of buildings, white and glowing on the outside, highly polished and shining with stainless steel all over the inside. We were taken straight up to the intensive-care unit, and there Stephen lay, quiet and still, his eyes closed in a comatose sleep. A mask covered his mouth and nose, and tubes and wires, attached to various parts of his body, trailed in all directions; across monitors an endless dance of luminous green and white wavy lines traced the rhythmic patterns of his life forces battling to maintain their superiority over the old enemy, death. He was alive.

The medical staff on the ward gave me a curt reception. "How many years is it since you last saw your husband?" they asked coolly. It was obvious they thought that Stephen and I lived separate lives and that his illness had developed since we last met. They were baffled when I replied that I had seen him only last week. "Well, then, why is he travelling in his state of health?" they asked with the shocked incomprehension of inbred medical caution. I could no more answer that question than they could themselves, though I tried to recount the usual story of Stephen's indomitable courage combined with his scientific genius, etc. etc. – an oft-repeated tale that was too long and too complicated in the telling for my drained emotional state, and nobody believed it anyhow. Instead they gave me a garbled version of what had happened.

Apparently, Stephen's cough had worsened after his arrival in Geneva. Perhaps, as they did not live with him every day and every night, his companions had not realized that this was fairly normal. Much to his annoyance, they had insisted on calling a doctor. After hours of argument, the doctor in turn had insisted on consigning him to hospital. There pneumonia was diagnosed and, after more argument, Stephen was put on a life-support machine. He was not in fact in a coma, as his secretary had said, but had been drugged to permit a potent mixture of antibiotics and nourishment to be fed into his system through various drips, while the ventilator did his breathing for him. He was not at present in danger, since all his functions were governed by machines. I could all too easily imagine that this had been the realization of his worst, most terrifying nightmare. His fate, which lay in his own control of his medical care, had been taken out of his hands by strangers who knew nothing about him, not even who he was.

At the rented house in Ferney-Voltaire, our arrival was greeted with relief by the students, nurses and the secretary – all at a loss since, with the removal of the key player, their presence was superfluous. They also were all in a muted state of shock, silently questioning what else they could have done. While Stephen lay drugged in hospital, there was nothing for them to do. However, in the succeeding days, as I found myself sucked into a vortex of administrative, emotional and ethical problems, they invented new roles for themselves, which they fulfilled with quiet efficiency. The students did the shopping and the cooking, the nurses looked after the children and took them on outings – this, after all, was supposed to be their summer holiday – and Laura, the secretary, was in perpetual contact with Cambridge and Cern, trying to sort out our financial and insurance problems. The news was a bitter blow for Stephen's family, especially for his mother. Her husband was an invalid, and now her son's life was critically threatened too. We were in touch by phone daily, and she was consistently supportive and philosophical. In her unemotional way, she already seemed to have resigned herself to Stephen's death. It was cruel that three generations of Hawking menfolk were at risk at the same time, yet so far apart: Frank was old and ill in the small, manageable house in Bedfordshire to which he and Isobel had recently moved; Stephen was critically ill in Geneva; and goodness knows what had become of Robert. It was just as well that I did not know that his canoe had overturned in the North Sea off the coast of Iceland.

There was no anxiety about the well-being of the fourth and youngest Hawking, Tim. His immediate future was a problem however, since he had to be returned to England and my parents by some means or other; I was far too preoccupied in Geneva to be able to look after him, and the nurses would shortly be leaving. Although Lucy had her own passport, Tim was registered on mine, so I approached the British Consulate for help in getting him home. One could have been forgiven for thinking that the consular officials were being deliberately obstructive. The hard-faced, dark-haired woman at the consular desk summarily waved me away after I had spent ages waiting for an interview, even though I explained the extraordinary circumstances fully. There was no chance of Tim's returning to England without a passport, she said: for that, I would need to produce his birth certificate. I sighed. Tim's birth certificate was in the living room at home, in the William and Mary desk which had belonged to Stephen's grandmother.

On an off-chance, I telephoned our home number, not expecting it to be answered. To my surprise Eve's voice came on the line at the other end: providentially, she was in the house doing a spot of spring-cleaning. She went to the desk, found the birth certificate and sent it out to Geneva by express delivery. Triumphantly I waved the document at the same consular official a couple of days later, but she was not impressed. "That will not do," she said, as acerbic as ever, "that's only a short birth certificate, and we need the full one – from Somerset House." I stared at her in disbelief. "And in any case," she went on, "there are papers to fill in that your husband will have to sign." "I have already told you," I replied through gritted teeth, "that my husband is unconscious and paralysed on a ventilator in intensive care in the Hôpital Cantonal. He cannot possibly sign anything." "Well," she continued obtusely, "if your husband does not know that you are taking the child out of the country, you certainly cannot have a passport for him."

In one final attempt, near to tears in exasperation, I pleaded with her. "I am only trying to send the child home." She paused for a second, during which her mood mollified slightly, as if only at that moment had my words registered on her brain. "If you can get someone else, a British person with some qualifications, a teacher perhaps, to sign the papers and bring a photo, then we might consider it," she replied. To our private amusement, Jonathan filled in and signed the forms, since he fulfilled all the official requirements. We took Tim to a photo booth and made him practise his signature. At last, on 13th August, a full British passport was issued in the name of Mr T.S. Hawking; it bore the appealingly innocent photograph and the untried spidery signature of a six-year-old. Thus equipped, Mr T.S. Hawking travelled home – business class for want of a seat in economy – to England with Lucy and the nurses, and went to stay with my parents.

In his absence, Robert was the source of the sole piece of good news that summer. Bernard Carr, always a loyal ally in extremis, flew out to Geneva to take over from the students as the situation began to change. He brought Robert's A-level results, which were excellent, the only glimmer of light through the blackest of clouds. Those results assured Robert a place at Cambridge, at Corpus Christi College, my father's college, to read Natural Sciences.

2

A Slender Thread

If the comparative triviality of Tim's passport took an inordinate amount of time to resolve, it was in the topsy-turvy nature of things during that period that a far more serious matter was resolved in seconds. Two days after our arrival in Geneva, the doctor in charge of Stephen's case asked to see me as a matter of some urgency. He took me into a bare, grey side room. At first I thought that he simply wanted to verify the facts of Stephen's exceptional existence. The nursing staff had begun to accept that Stephen was no ordinary patient, nor was he the victim of neglect by his family. Having ascertained various details about his phenomenal longevity and his self-management, the doctor came abruptly to the point. The question was whether his staff should disconnect the ventilator while Stephen was in a drugged state, or should try to bring him round from the anaesthetic. I was shocked. Switching off the life supply was unthinkable. What an ignominious end to such a heroic fight for life, what a denial of everything that I, too, had fought for! My reply was quick and ready. I did not need either to think about it or discuss it with other people, as there was only one possible answer. "Stephen must live. You must bring him round from the anaesthetic," I replied. The doctor went on to explain the complications of the procedures that would ensue. Stephen would not be able to breathe unaided, and when he was stronger he would have to undergo a tracheotomy operation. This would be the only way of weaning him off the ventilator, as it would bypass the hypersensitive area in his throat, which had been giving him so much trouble. The technicalities of the tracheotomy, a hole in the windpipe below the vocal chords, would require permanent professional care. I did not pay much attention to this gloomy, if realistic, prognosis. I had made the decision that was required. The important truth was that Stephen was alive and would remain alive as long as I had any power to influence events.

I emerged from the interview room to a remarkable sight. There, standing in the corridor, was a Fellow of Gonville and Caius College, though not someone whom either of us knew at all well. James Fitzsimons and his French wife, Aude, had been on holiday with Aude's family in Geneva when word had reached them from the College that Stephen was ill in hospital there, and they had come to offer help. They could not have arrived at a more propitious moment. I was profoundly shaken by the events of the past week and was disturbed, though defiant, at the interview. I realized that the crises were by no means over, and indeed a worse crisis could be looming, for it was not at all certain that Stephen would even survive resuscitation from his drug-induced sleep.

James and Aude brought fresh energy and buoyant, though sensitive, resolve to bolster our resources. As Stephen was slowly restored to us, James joined our long vigils, taking a share in the rota, which consisted of Bernard, Jonathan, the remaining students and myself. We were not there to act as nurses – there were plenty of those in the hospital – but to strengthen Stephen's fragile hold on life and reawaken his interest and his curiosity from their unprecedented state of inertia. James was a fluent French speaker and was able to relieve me of some of the pressures of communicating Stephen's every indistinct request to the nursing staff. His attempts to mouth those requests were impeded by the tubes and masks covering his face. Those of us close to him had to try to anticipate his needs and ask the right questions; he would respond in the negative or the affirmative by means of his painfully expressive eyes, now open again, and by raising his eyebrows or frowning.

To alleviate the tedium, we read aloud from whatever holiday material we happened to have with us. With my student, Gonzalo Vargas Llosa, I had begun to explore the works of the blind Argentinian multilingual polymath Jorge Luis Borges, whose ideas excited me: I was particularly fascinated by his preoccupation with paradox and ambiguity, time and timelessness and the cyclical nature of historical events. His writing appeared to mirror in literary, even poetic, form much of the substance of scientific discovery in the twentieth century, and might be conceived as literary versions of Escher's spatially irreconcilable drawings, themselves artistic representations of a mathematical concept, the Möbius strip. I had intended to read Borges's *El*

Libro de Arena (*The Book of Sand*) over the summer holidays, so, hoping that its conundrums and enigmas might appeal to Stephen, I commissioned Bernard to bring an English translation to Geneva with him. Whether Stephen appreciated the rather complex, cerebral games of Borges's writing, I did not discover. I relished the stories for the intellectual escape they offered from the nerve-racking tension and clinical monotony of the intensive-care unit. But my fascination was even stronger when I found that I was being absorbed into the puzzle of the literature myself, especially through the first story, 'The Other', an apparently autobiographical story set in Geneva. Borges is seated on a bench in Cambridge, Massachusetts in 1969, looking out over the Charles river. A young man comes to sit beside him and the two converse. The young man, however, asserts that they are sitting on a bench overlooking the Rhône in Geneva in 1914. He is, of course, Borges's youthful self, and he recounts details of his home life at number 17 Route de Malagnou in Geneva. The ideas in the story – of identity, time travel, dreams, prediction, of history repeating itself and of knowing the future, were stimulating in themselves. But the coincidence that I had, unknowingly, chosen to read this story to Stephen in Geneva gave me the startling impression that I had entered it myself and become a part of it, adding yet another dimension. Bernard, still engaged on parapsychological research as an antidote to physics, enjoyed the coincidence. One afternoon, as Jonathan and I were leaving the hospital, I suggested driving out of the city to catch a brief glimpse of the Alps. Our route took us along the Route de Malagnou. On the way out of the city and on the way back, we scoured the street for number 17, the house in Borges's story. We could see 15 and 19, 14 and 16, but of number 17 there was no trace.

Once Stephen had regained consciousness, the pace quickened. As soon as possible an air ambulance, paid for by Caius, was commissioned to bring us back to Cambridge. Carrying an enormous amount of luggage, Jonathan set out for home by car on the same day that Stephen and I – accompanied by a doctor, paramedics, portable ventilators and other equipment – were loaded carefully into an ambulance, whisked to the airport, decanted into a small, red jet and sent hurtling into the sky the moment the hatch was closed. Had it not been for the circumstances of our flight, I might rather have enjoyed it – even Stephen roused himself sufficiently to peer out of the window as we soared above the clouds. This was the way to fly: our private plane was given priority over all the other airliners queuing up for space on the runway; there was no time for anxiety, none of the usual hassle and no delays. At Cambridge airport, John Farman, the head of the intensive-care unit at Addenbrooke's, was waiting to meet us with an ambulance on the tarmac.

Although Stephen had undeniably received excellent treatment in Geneva, there was an irrepressible sense of relief at being back home, where we and our situation were well known. Many a familiar figure appeared in the intensive-care unit that day, including Judy Fella, Stephen's former secretary. She had already been active on his behalf and was ready to give whatever help was needed. There were no gasps of surprise at Stephen's ambitious travelling schedule or incredulity at his domination of motor-neuron disease from the staff at Addenbrooke's. The minimum of general explanation was needed. Nevertheless, detailed explanation was required of the management of his case, of the routines that he himself had developed, of the precise quantities and frequencies of the medications he took, of the positions he liked to adopt when lying in bed, of his insistence on a gluten-free diet, even when being fed by tube. Each and every one of these matters, and many more like them, became the subject of lengthy discussions and investigations.

Three days after the flight, by which time Stephen's condition had stabilized in intensive care, John Farman thought it might be possible to ease him off his dependence on the ventilator; he was keen to encourage him to breathe unaided in the hope of avoiding the threatened tracheotomy operation. By Tuesday 20th August, Stephen seemed to be making good enough progress for the experiment to be tried. He was comfortable and gaining strength, and we – that is, as many friends and relations as could be mustered – had devised a rota, mounting guard over him by day and by night. Usually the long-suffering students, or our team of nurses or physiotherapists, including Sue Smith and Caroline Chamberlain, would sit with Stephen by night, and the family and other friends took turns by day. The nurses promised to ring if Stephen needed me that night, as they embarked on the delicate process of detaching him from the ventilator.

The telephone rang in my bedroom in the early hours of the morning. The ward sister said little, except that she thought

I should go to the hospital straight away. She offered no explanation. As my parents were looking after Tim, I had only to dress and leave a note before slipping out at first light. Stephen was very ill: a blotchy grey pallor had taken the place of his whitish complexion, and his bulging eyes were drained of all colour. His limbs were rigidly frozen in spasm, while a brutal cough had returned to torment his throat, like a cat toying with a mouse, letting it go, then pouncing with sharpened claws. In between each attack, he desperately tried to draw breath. Fear was written large all over his face.

The expression on the nurses' faces gave me to understand that they thought that very little could be done for him, and that the end was near. I thought differently. That the old demon was back and currently had the upper hand was obvious, but I detected a familiar element in the choking. That element was Stephen's own understandable tendency to panic. But it had been controlled before, and there was just a chance that it could be brought to heel, using the simple relaxation techniques that I had learnt in yoga classes and which I had practised successfully on him at home in past crises. I sat at the head of the bed and put one arm round the back of his neck. While I stroked his face, his shoulder and his arm with the other hand, I slowly whispered soothing words into his ear, as one might when calming a fretful baby. I chose my words carefully, and tried to create a gentle, rocking rhythm to ease away the panic. I conjured up scenes of calm, blue lakes and balmy, clear skies, rolling green hills and warm, golden sands. Gradually, over the next few hours, as the tension subsided and as his body relaxed, the paroxysms yielded to a quieter, more regular breathing pattern. Finally he dozed off. I was exhausted but jubilant: my homespun attempt at hypnosis had worked! There was no escaping the fact, however, that Stephen was still critically ill.

I went away for a rest, leaving the telephone number of our good friends, John and Mary Taylor, who lived close to the hospital. As well as being regular visitors to Stephen's bedside, the Taylors had offered me the use of their house. That morning I took up their offer at 7 a.m. Mary offered me a bed, but I preferred to sit for a while in the garden to breathe in the fresh morning air, so welcome after the sterile, dry atmosphere of the hospital, and to let the early sun caress my weary frame. Mary brought me some breakfast and we sat talking. I was incoherent with tiredness but I had one overwhelming desire, and that was to speak to Robert. It was so long since I had last seen him and so much had happened in the interim. I had to assume that he was well and that no news was good news. According to the schedule he was due to be back at base camp before setting off on the final expedition, and was therefore no longer incommunicado. I felt that the time had come to warn him that his father was critically ill, though I did not intend to ask him to come home. "Phone him from here," Mary suggested with her customary generosity. I had not the will to protest: I did as she said, and dialled through to Iceland with trepidation. When I heard Robert's voice, my resolve crumbled and I broke down. Whatever my intentions, they were overridden by a cry from the heart which escaped before I could suppress it. "Please come home!" I heard myself pleading into the phone. "Right!" he said, without the slightest hesitation. He came home the next day and was met by the Taylors at Heathrow. I did not realize that, had he completed the expedition, he would have qualified for a Queen's Scout Award. When later I heard about the canoe-capsizing episode, he laughed it off as a triviality.

My return to the hospital revealed the sort of variations on the theme of illness that had become familiar over the past two interminable weeks. Stephen's life still hung by a thread, new strains of bacteria had been found in his lungs and the medication had been changed. He was breathing through the ventilator again, but cheered up considerably at the news of Robert's return. I discussed with John Farman the possibility of bringing in a professional hypnotist to encourage him to alleviate the panic attacks and relax those muscles which went into spasm when he tried to breathe. John readily agreed and brought in a GP of his acquaintance who was also a trained hypnotist. She had moderate success, using the same techniques that I had been using, but not enough to warrant parting Stephen from the ventilator for any extended period. There was, it appeared, no alternative to the tracheotomy, the operation which would allow him to breathe through a hole in the windpipe, bypassing the troublesome membranes and muscles in his throat.

As August slid into September and the doctors started to talk seriously about performing the operation, the lung infection was at last responding to treatment and Stephen was getting stronger. Whatever they may have felt about the risks of such a step, I was beginning to feel confident that Stephen would survive.

How could he not survive with so many people contributing in every imaginable way to his recovery? Some offered invaluable practical help, at his bedside, nursing and communicating; some helped with the day-to-day administrative problems or with running our home; others, more distant, offered moral support; others prayed. Many, like Jonathan, who had arrived back from Geneva, and his parents and mine, did all of these.

The operation was a success, and Stephen made such a rapid recovery that after four weeks in intensive care it became possible to lift him out of bed into his wheelchair, though he was still too weak to operate it himself. The prognosis improved daily until it was considered safe to move him out of intensive care onto one of the neurological wards. There was a price to be paid for recovery however: the operation had deprived him entirely of the power of speech.

3

The Burden of Responsibility

In Geneva we had been protected from the bustle of the wider world. There we had been able to focus on Stephen and his illness, our movements restricted to the route between the hospital and Ferney-Voltaire. Of that small border town, I saw only the statue of Voltaire, its most famous resident, who had settled there in 1759, putting a comfortable distance between himself and the French government, ready to flee into exile in Switzerland at a moment's notice. Apart from the several arrivals and departures, the outside world which existed at the end of the telephone line was unreal, remote from the intensity of the tragedy of which we were part. In Geneva, too, we took each day as our measure of time. We neither looked forward to, nor planned for, anything weeks or months ahead.

Back in Cambridge that protection fell away. On the one hand, there were all the usual matters associated with our way of life at home that had to be dealt with; children had to be fed and cared for, bills paid, Tim taken to school every morning and collected in the afternoon, school functions attended and my teaching commitments fulfilled. On the other, the preoccupation with the fluctuations in Stephen's condition continued to be just as harrowing as in Geneva and the hospital visiting consumed just as much time. My teaching hours had to be squeezed into the middle of the day – after leaving the hospital in the morning and before returning in the afternoon. It was only because my parents and Jonathan operated a comprehensive back-up system, and because many friends, particularly Tim's godmothers, Joy and Caroline, generously offered help in some productive or reinforcing way or other, that as a family we survived this most exacting and exhausting period.

Keeping the home going while ministering to Stephen in hospital was by no means the full extent of my responsibilities. There were many pieces of business to be sorted out, not least the future of Stephen's book. It existed in a first manuscript draft which had been accepted by a publisher. As soon as the contract was signed, in the summer of 1985, a New York editor started working on the manuscript, and his letter outlining preliminary criticisms was waiting for Stephen on our return to England, though Stephen was in no fit state to read it. It was no surprise that the manuscript was not publishable in its draft form, as many of the concepts it contained were far too abstruse for popular consumption. I myself had read it and marked in red the passages where the science was incomprehensible, and the publishers pointed out that every equation would halve the sales. In his present circumstances, it was unlikely that Stephen would be able to effect the fundamental changes required. Unless the manuscript could be amended by a ghost writer, we might have to return the advance, paid just before the beginning of the summer holiday. I approached one of Stephen's former students, Brian Whitt, to enlist his help with the rewriting, but all other considerations on that score I put temporarily to the back of my mind, since there were others, much more pressing, in the forefront.

As Stephen began to make progress and was transferred to the neurological ward, his eventual return home was mooted as a distinct possibility. It was not at all clear how this was to be achieved since, plainly, Stephen would need specialist nursing twenty-four hours a day. Our previous, relaxed system of support by psychiatric nurses at specific times and for limited periods would no longer suffice, nor was their psychiatric training adequate to deal with what was essentially a critical medical situation. The tracheotomy operation which had saved Stephen's life also brought its own concomitant risks, because the tracheotomy tube, inserted in his throat, had to be cleaned regularly by a sort of mini-vacuum cleaner to bring up the secretions which perpetually accumulated in his lungs, and the device itself was potentially a source of damage and dangerous infection. He was frighteningly frail and vulnerable. It was impossible to imagine a more extreme disability of the body.

Twenty-four-hour nursing for three hundred and sixty-five days a year would cost a phenomenal sum; predictably only a tiny fraction of this expense would be borne by the National Health Service. Funding would have to be found privately and nurses engaged privately too. The philanthropic foundations that had funded nursing for a couple of hours a day would be unlikely to pay for twenty-four-hour nursing at a minimum of between thirty and forty thousand pounds a year on an indefinite basis. Then, at that most critical time, a message arrived from Kip Thorne in California. The news of Stephen's illness had travelled far and fast, thanks to Judy Fella's concerned intervention and, in response, Kip advised me, as a matter of urgency, to make a representation to the John D. and Catherine T. MacArthur Foundation, an American philanthropic organization based in Chicago. In Kip's opinion, there was a chance that the MacArthur Foundation might be prevailed upon to make a large grant, on the scale needed for permanent nursing for Stephen, if the case were well represented. Murray Gell-Mann, the particle physicist from Caltech, was on the board of the Foundation, and Kip was sure that he would encourage the other directors to give our case a fair hearing, though there was some uncertainty as to whether the Foundation would sanction a grant outside the United States. Speed was of the essence, since their next meeting was but a few weeks away.

I had no practice in writing begging letters, but whatever reluctance I might have otherwise felt about such an exercise evaporated in the face of the overwhelming need. I put down all the appropriate information which might influence the committee, not omitting to mention that Stephen had been a frequent visitor to the United States and had received many honorary degrees there. I also included photographs, taken in happier times, of smiling family groups. It was essential to assure the Foundation that any grant would be handled by a team of professional accountants, so my next task was to negotiate with the University authorities to persuade them to administer the fund on our behalf. The negotiations were both complex and time-consuming, though the goodwill demonstrated was encouraging.

The need to set up a private nursing scheme was the more pressing since certain aspects of the treatment Stephen was receiving in hospital were less than satisfactory. On the intensive-care ward he had received the full attention of the specialist nurses. The situation changed when he went onto the neurological ward. If the ward sister was generally cheerful and competent, some members of her staff appeared to be much less so. There were far fewer of them in proportion to the number of patients than in intensive care, but the lack of dedication, understanding and continuity was often alarming, particularly since many of the patients were in a vegetative state, unable to protest, think or even speak for themselves. One nurse, in particular, appeared to take advantage of that state to mete out treatment that was less than human. She was on duty when I arrived for an afternoon visit. Stephen, now sitting up in his wheelchair, was grimacing and squirming in discomfort while the young nurse, totally impassive in expression, busied herself about the room, deliberately – or so it seemed – ignoring his urgent need to pee. I helped Stephen myself and sent the nurse out of the room. That was her usual attitude, Stephen explained quivering with anger. She always ignored his needs when she was on duty. He did not trust her and was afraid of what she might do or omit to do. I could see what he meant. In her impervious expression and blank, pale blue eyes there was a chill hint of sadism which I, too, found very alarming. There was no alternative, I should have to move heaven and earth to get Stephen home, and that meant sorting out all the problems associated with twenty-four-hour nursing as quickly as possible.

That Stephen was able to protest about the nurse's behaviour was thanks to a miraculous piece of equipment which had arrived out of the blue for his use. We, the family, students and friends, had done as much as we could to make him comfortable: we had tried to keep the rota of attendance constant with no more than a gap of a few minutes here and there, and I had bought a television for his room. Nothing could compensate for the terrible loss of the power of speech, however, and just when that loss appeared depressingly irremediable, the new means of communication arrived unforeseen and unannounced. In fact it was the result of Judy's tireless efforts behind the scenes. She recalled having seen a feature about communication for the severely disabled on the BBC science programme, *Tomorrow's World*, and after a global search for information had managed to locate the British inventor of the equipment. She brought him and his invention – a set of electrodes which when attached to the head could measure rapid eye movement – to the hospital, and persuaded a Cambridge-based computer firm to contribute the necessary computer free of charge. Stephen balked at the intrusive discomfort of the electrodes attached to his temples, but when one of his students adapted the mechanism to a hand-held control box, he was more willing to experiment with the device.

The computer was loaded with a programme which combined dictionary and phrasebook. Using the control, the operator could scan the screen for the words he wanted to use: as he clicked on each one, it would take its place in the sentence which was forming in the lower part of the screen where the observer could read what the operator was wanting to communicate. Frequently used phrases could be incorporated complete, and verbal endings could be added to infinitives as required. Initially it was a slow, laborious and silent way to communicate, requiring patience and concentration both of the operator and the observer. I found that, given one or two words to point me in the right direction, I could often interpret Stephen's thoughts telepathically and save him the bother of tapping them all out, though often he insisted on writing out the whole sentence to give himself practice. Once his hand and finger muscles had recovered some movement, the new device absorbed much of the tedium of that final period in hospital. Albeit painstakingly, he began to master the novel technique which allowed him once more to reach beyond the drab surroundings of his hospital room and make contact with the outside world. He could begin to talk to his students about physics again and he could begin to experiment with writing, as well as directing his own medical care.

Having set the wheels in motion for raising money, Laura Ward and I embarked on the search for nurses. Neither of us had any experience in interviewing or employing staff, least of all nurses, but I hoped that the various social-service departments in the hospital and in the community would give us support and advice in this process. Many social workers and nursing officers called, and sat chatting and drinking coffee while they talked about their pet animals and suchlike. The amount of useful information I gleaned from them could have been consigned to the back of a postage stamp. Laura and I were left to advertise and engage nurses, and then set up a working rota of three eight-hour shifts, as best we could.

Laura repeatedly placed advertisements in the local newspaper and dealt with the responses initially, asking for references which she then followed up. As time was short, we decided to interview all the candidates who showed any suitability before receiving references. They all seemed plausible, likeable even, and I was in a hurry to set up the nursing system with as many nurses as possible, so that Stephen could come home. I assumed that nurses were by nature dedicated and idealistic, and that I could trust them. I explained the situation as best I could and made it clear that, although we wanted Stephen to be able to live at home, it was important that the home, also the home of three children, should not be turned into a hospital. I expected to treat nurses as guests in my house, and in return I assumed that they would respect our right to privacy. What a vain hope that was!

Even among the people we had interviewed and liked, my preconceptions of idealism and service were not always well based. When the references started trickling in, we had to discard many of the candidates we had thought to employ. Some were said to be slovenly, others unreliable, a few even criminal. How was it, we wondered, that there was no central regulation of the movements of this last group, when the jobs in home nursing for which they would be applying would almost all, by definition, take place in vulnerable and delicate circumstances? We were still left with a handful of good candidates, even after eliminating the undesirables but, alas, when Laura wrote to the promising applicants offering them work, a depressing number either declined to reply at all, or replied saying that they had found other jobs or that they did not think the situation suitable. To our own deep dismay, there were some eminently suitable people whom we had to turn away, on the advice of Stephen's doctors, because of their lack of training in tracheotomy technique.

The alternative was to employ agency nurses. The severe disadvantage of agency nurses was that the essential element of continuity would be lost: a different nurse at every shift could only add to the considerable frustrations which Stephen, and the rest of us, were bound to experience. Equally prohibitive was the financial aspect: agency fees, over and above the nurses' pay, would fritter away the MacArthur grant in no time at all. The money had been approved, despite some understandable suspicion on the part of the Trustees about the role of Britain's much vaunted National Health Service. Why, they had wanted to know, was Stephen's care not covered by the NHS? I had to choose my words carefully in explaining how the American-inspired monetarist policies of the Thatcher government – which had been in power for the whole of Tim's lifetime – were destroying our already overloaded, free NHS. The truth was that in encouraging a new self-seeking materialism, those policies were destroying not just the health service and our educational system, but the very fabric of society. Indeed Mrs Thatcher had denied the existence of society: for her it consisted of nothing more than a set of individuals with no sense of common purpose. It was an unfortunate time to be ill, unemployed, very young, elderly or otherwise socially disadvantaged.

A couple of months later, Laura Ward fell ill and had to leave. By great good fortune, Judy Fella, who had already given so much unstinting help, was willing to resume her old post as Stephen's secretary until a full-time replacement could be found. Judy was more circumspect than I was in selecting nurses, urging caution in the face of my impatience to bring Stephen home. She was wary even of some of the nurses whose written credentials appeared to be impeccable. Indeed, independently, reports had reached my ears about a particular nurse who had been engaged for a trial period; I was warned that although she had been given good references, she had a reputation as a troublemaker, and that there were nurses who refused to work with her because of her apparently unhealthy obsessions with some patients. In the circumstances, I refused to listen to gossip which, in any case might be maliciously inspired. I knew the nurse in question by sight; she was a mother and I had seen her at the school gate. She struck me as reliable and efficient, and because she was a regular churchgoer, I felt that I could trust her.

During the month of October, I brought Stephen – with a hospital nurse in attendance – home from the hospital each Sunday afternoon. It was a delicate, worrying undertaking. Sometimes the change of atmosphere would frighten him and precipitate choking attacks. He was still very weak and coughed a great deal. The mini-vacuum cleaner was often in use, clearing the sputum from his chest. Sometimes we would have to return to the hospital before the afternoon was out, because the strain was too great for him; occasionally he would relax and enjoy being at home, though I sensed that he found the outside world intimidating after three months' incarceration. In those three months of crisis, his indomitable instinct for survival had stubbornly maintained its hold on life. Now everything looked strange and unfamiliar to him, as if he could not trust what he saw. Part of him wanted to re-enter the flurry of unpredictable normality, part of him wanted the predictable security of the hospital. Nevertheless a date, Monday 4th November, was set for his discharge.

In those three months since early August, I had escaped for just one evening's respite from the harrowing routine in order to attend the London debut of the Cambridge Baroque Camerata on 1st October. The evening was warm after a hot, sunny day, giving London a carnival atmosphere in the midst of which I felt alien and uncomfortable. The concert, played to an appreciable audience, went well, though the atmosphere lacked the buzz of excitement which attended the orchestra's full houses in Cambridge. It was a mystery how Jonathan had succeeded in putting it on at all, since his every spare moment had been spent either in the hospital looking after Stephen or at West Road looking after the family. Unruffled, he had calmly pursued his own activities – organization, administration, practice and rehearsals – late into the night, tucked away in his own house. As he performed and directed beneath the lights on the stage of the Queen Elizabeth Hall, always with an unassuming simplicity and understated elegance of style, no one could have guessed at the pressures of the preceding weeks. I was glad to be there to witness his success, yet I was smitten with guilt at having left Stephen forlornly behind in hospital, sitting out of doors in the autumn sun on a bare patch of ground which euphemistically called itself a garden.

By the end of October, the situation was different: Stephen was much stronger, but I was completely exhausted. I had developed chronic asthma and I slept badly, increasingly dependent on sleeping tablets and also subject to welts which came and went, producing sore tingling spots on the palms of my hands and in my mouth. All these were, of course, nothing more than the symptoms of severe stress. The doctors recommended a break, even if only a weekend, before Stephen's return home. In September, Robert had left Cambridge to spend his gap year in Scotland. He went to live temporarily with the Donovans outside Edinburgh and started working on the shop floor at Ferranti, where he learnt basic engineering techniques under the eye of an exacting foreman. Eventually he moved into digs in Edinburgh. It was not an easy life for an eighteen-year-old, and I feared that he was not looking after himself properly. The last weekend before Stephen's return home – which also happened to be the first weekend of half-term – was an opportune moment to get away. I could benefit from a change of air and routine, calm my stinging nerves and see Robert's circumstances for myself.

I was comforted to find him in good form – and Edinburgh was at its glorious, autumnal best. But three days, however sunny and bright, however clear and crisp, however stimulating with new sights and sounds, were scarcely enough to erase the incessant, intense, traumatic strain of the past three months.

Not three days nor three months nor even three years could have prepared me, or anyone else, for what was yet to come.

4

Mutiny

Stephen returned home in the early afternoon of 4th November. It was like bringing a new baby home from hospital. There reigned a sense of excitement tinged with nervousness, a protective fear lest the helpless, fragile being might suddenly cease to draw breath within moments of entering the house. Stephen, too, was tense and nervous, suspicious of the competence of the nurses engaged to care for him and anxious about every speck of dust in the atmosphere which might upset his breathing. He had little respect for the intelligence of other people at the best of times. Now, at the worst of times, he was inclined to regard them all as morons. His fears were warranted, but not altogether for the reasons one might have supposed.

The nurse who came that first afternoon was herself unwell; she was little more than an elderly waif and, although she fulfilled her duties admirably, she rang afterwards to say that she would not be able to come again as the strain was too great for her. This was a bitter blow, because that particular nurse had been booked for many of the twenty-one weekly shifts. There were others like her, pleasant, well-meaning people who could not cope with the stress. The agency was the only recourse, whatever the cost. For the next few weeks, as Judy and I tried to shore up the collapsing rota with a frenzied round of advertising, interviewing and instructing of prospective candidates, the agency provided nurses of varying degrees of competence. In fairness, these nurses probably had little advance notice of what would be expected of them. Never were Stephen's worst anxieties – and mine – more fully justified: the agency sent a different nurse on every occasion. Although generally they were well intentioned and well qualified, none of them easily understood what was required. Either Jonathan or I spent the whole shift repeating the same instructions over and over again.

Some nurses never mastered the angle of the cup to prevent tea from dribbling down Stephen's front into the tracheotomy tube or onto his clothes. Some did not chop his food into small enough morsels, others mashed it to an unacceptable purée. Some tried to give him his pills in the wrong order. Some jogged his hand on the joystick of the wheelchair, sending him off into a spin. Others made a complete shambles of the bathroom routine. Despite their medical experience, they were all terrified of the tracheotomy tube in his throat and were nervous of using the suction unit. Very rarely did the same nurse come back twice. When occasionally one of them was brave enough to cross the threshold for an encore, I greeted him or her as a long-lost friend in my relief at not having to repeat the whole procedure until I was sick of the sound of my own voice. I tried hard to be patient and reassuring, but my nerves were on edge, bristling with exhaustion, worry and dejection. Stephen's frustration was understandable, of course, and he made no attempt to conceal it.

If the daytime routine verged on the impossible, at night the problems were of a different order. Once in bed, Stephen no longer had the use of his computerized means of communication and was again deprived of speech. There were just two devices to help him. One, an alphabet frame, must have been the stock-in-trade of occupational therapists in the Dark Ages. The alphabet, in groups of large letters, was displayed around a transparent frame: Stephen was supposed to fix his eyes first on a group of letters, then on an individual letter within that group to spell out his needs letter by letter. The attendant was supposed to follow his eye movements and construct his meaning from them. The device demanded extraordinary patience and remarkable powers of deduction from all concerned. I tried to simplify the procedure by developing a shorthand code so that Stephen only had to focus on one letter for his meaning to become apparent. Either my code got lost in the muddle in his room, or the nurses thought they could do better; in any event, my invention did not last long.

The other device, which eventually superseded the alphabet frame and marked a considerable technological advance over it, was a buzzer. All night Stephen would hold the control in his hand, in much the same way as he held his computer control by day, and would exert pressure on it to illuminate a small box where any one of a limited number of commands would appear in sequence on a panel to indicate his needs. For a long time, even when he was in good health, it had been difficult to settle his rigid limbs comfortably in bed, and now that he was seriously ill the process took most of the night. In those early months I would stay with him until I was confident that he was well settled, since I knew that he was afraid of being left with an unfamiliar nurse. Then at two or three in the morning I myself would fall into bed, often to be woken soon after by the night nurse, who found that she could not cope alone.

Quite apart from the day-to-day and night-to-night problems, the months after Stephen's return were marked by many other life-threatening dramas. These usually occurred late at night, when the tracheotomy tube either blocked off or came unstuck. While the nurse tried to clear it or adjust it, I would dial through to the intensive care unit in search of the doctors who were versed in the technique of changing it. A dash to hospital and endless hours waiting in the casualty department would follow, until a new tube was inserted and Stephen could breathe again. Since our last student helper, Nick Warner, a cheerful Australian, had left in the summer and had not been replaced, Jonathan slept in the upstairs room so that he could look after Tim and take him to school first thing in the morning when I was still recovering from the disturbances of the night.

As Robert had left home, his room, large and airy at the front of the house, was quickly converted into a room for Stephen. It was particularly suitable, because it had a washbasin and adequate cupboards for nursing and medical equipment – of which we received regular, massive deliveries. There was also plenty of space for an orthopaedic bed, bins, computers, desks, armchairs, all sorts of other paraphernalia and, of course, the wheelchair. This last item was becoming ever bulkier and heavier. The computer equipment which Judy had acquired for Stephen when he was in hospital had been superseded by a more sophisticated version, sent from California. The new computer had the added advantage of a voice synthesizer so that Stephen could be heard to speak the sentences that he typed up on the screen. No matter that the synthesized voice sounded unnervingly like a dalek: Stephen was once again endowed with the power of speech. The husband of one of the nurses, David Mason, a skilled computer engineer, set to work to adapt the computer and add its several parts to the wheelchair, so that Stephen would no longer be desk-bound but could carry his voice with him wherever he went. The weighty computer and voice box were strapped onto the back of the chair, and the screen was attached to the frame where Stephen could see it. Once, some time later, when we happened to come across an industrial weighing machine, we levered Stephen and all his contraptions onto it. The weight of the chair, batteries, computer, screen, various cushions and occupant amounted to one hundred and thirty kilograms.

There were recurring crises when the newly invented mechanism developed teething troubles, just as there were recurring crises with Stephen's own state of health. If David Mason were not called round as a matter of urgency at all hours of the day, then it was our faithful friend, John Stark, the chest consultant, or long-suffering Dr Swan or another duty doctor from the surgery, who would be summoned at all hours of the night. Physiotherapists were called out at weekends and our local chemist was roused after closing hours. In short, we floundered in an endless state of crisis throughout November into December, with its usual round of school carol services and other preparations for Christmas. We were again piloting our boat across troubled waters. These uncharted waters were shrouded in darkness, and we had on board a potentially mutinous crew.

The major share of my energies and my time were devoted to Stephen. I drank every sip of water with him, ate every spoonful of food and breathed every gasp of air. When my strength failed, Jonathan shared the burden, quietly and always reliably available in the background. What little time and energy I had left, I gave to my children and to my pupils. Teaching was my one opportunity to concentrate for a few hours a day on other matters – the time when language and literature could fill and enliven the vacuum created by despondency and crushing weariness. The pupils of that year became very special to me. Generally they showed an exceptionally mature understanding for teenagers, and from them I received the fulsome appreciation which strengthened my resolve to continue teaching, come what may, so long as I was capable of doing the job properly. It was essential to my own ragged mental health.

Stephen did not view my modest attempts to keep up my intellectual interests in the same light. He had suffered, and was still suffering, a horrendous ordeal, and was still very frightened; like Lear, he was child-changed – into a child possessed of a massive and fractious ego. On the one hand, his pathetic physical state expressed all too clearly his need for constant loving reassurance; on the other, he made himself inaccessible, barricading himself behind defiance and resentment. From being authoritative in the past, he became authoritarian, even – or perhaps especially – with those of us who had been through so much with him. He was indignant at some of the decisions I had been forced to take in family matters during his period in hospital, and would insist on his rights as a matter of principle. It was natural that he would want to reassert himself, but no one was disputing his right to be king of the universe and master of the house. It was difficult therefore to understand why he seemed to want to make the daily routine even more fraught than usual by means of various disobliging ploys, which usually involved deliberately stationing his wheelchair in the most obstructive position imaginable, or by disputing other people's right to privacy, particularly Lucy's. She and I were very close companions. Her open character, brimming with enthusiasm, and her independent spirit were endless sources of strength and encouragement even in the depths of despair. She and I talked at length, discussing all manner of subjects without constraint. It was obvious that in our extraordinary situation she needed space to herself. Her room had to be respected as her sanctuary, away from the constant commotion caused by nurses and wheelchairs. She was as intensely loyal to her father as she was to me, but she longed for privacy, away from the prying eyes, listening ears and gossiping tongues of the nursing staff. That privacy was constantly denied her.

I recounted my dismay at Stephen's apparently unreasonable attitudes to a doctor friend, who replied, "Just think, Jane, what he has been through! He nearly died, he was kept alive by machines and drugs. Can you tell me that all that would have no effect on his brain? There must have been times when his brain was starved of oxygen and it's more than likely that that shortage caused minute, undetectable lesions which are now affecting his behaviour and his emotional reactions, although, thankfully for him, his intellect is intact." Another friend, a senior nurse in a hospice for the victims of incurable degenerative diseases, was convinced that the families of those motor-neuron-disease patients struck down in the prime of life rather than in old age were the ones who suffered most anguish. In one sense these opinions and advice were comforting. They implied that Stephen was not completely responsible for his actions and that it was not just his excess of innate egoistic energy that was determining his lack of consideration, but the combined effects of motor-neuron disease and the recent trauma. These opinions, however, bore little weight elsewhere, even among medical circles, since it was apparent to all that, intellectually, Stephen had come through hell unscathed.

That, nevertheless, was not the full story. Judy, Lucy and I were well aware that Stephen's egoism was being fed and urged on by his nurses. I might as well have voiced my concerns – about keeping the home a happy place for all the family and not allowing it to become a hospital – to a concrete wall, for all the impact these concerns had on the nursing staff. They were indifferent to the fact that the house was also home to a shy, sensitive six-year-old and a spirited, intelligent teenager immersed in O-level studies. One of the very first nurses turned the whole house inside out as soon as she stepped through the front door. Fretting at the lack of sterility, she scrubbed everything in sight, trying to bring our home up to intensive-care standards, while Eve, who continued to give valiant service washing, cleaning and hoovering daily, watched incredulously. "She's daft!" was Eve's comment. Finally the new broom decided that it was too stressful to work in such an unhygienic atmosphere and left.

There were, it has to be said, nurses who were dedicated and perceptive, the most exemplary being Mr Jo, as we called him, who not only fulfilled all his nursing duties but occasionally brought us the most fragrant curries on Sunday evenings. Generally the dedicated people were older women – or men – trained in a more disciplined age, or people who had achieved a higher level of education than the norm, or people who were not strangers to problems themselves. There were others of similar ilk who promised to be as dependable but who, in the event, found the physical strain too much for them. For most, the words "professional discipline" and "understanding" were meaningless, and self-interest was paramount. Our tales of the harrowing months before their arrival meant nothing to them, nor did they give a moment's thought to the stress that we lived under all the time. A seven- or eight-hour shift might be stressful, but the nurse who performed that shift could go away to recover in his or her own home. That was not an option open to members of the family.

One common problem was that nurses, like social workers before them, were easily deceived by our surroundings. Because we lived in a large house, they supposed we must be super-rich. Discreet attempts to explain that we rented our flat from the College fell on deaf ears. None were deafer than those of the nurse who misread our outward circumstances and Stephen's professorship as evidence of wealth and power. Late one evening she came to me in the kitchen as I was putting out the breakfast things and brazenly demanded that I obtain a mortgage for her from the University. Not sure that I had heard correctly, I asked her to repeat her request in front of Stephen, who was already in bed. We went into Stephen's room where, standing beside the bed, she repeated what she had said. I explained that there must have been some misunderstanding as I had no influence with the University and was not in any position to obtain a mortgage on her behalf. Whereupon, at midnight, she started screaming and writhing, stamping and beating her chest, before whirling into a frenzied war dance round Stephen's bed. I ran to the phone and rang Judy, who came straight away. She smartly but tactfully removed the wailing banshee, who stood screeching her protests and threats of litigation out in the drive, while I rang the agency for a replacement.

Another nurse, a sad, lonely woman whom I befriended, soon turned out to be an alcoholic. She not only helped herself to judiciously measured thimblefuls of liqueur from our modest assortment of spirits stored at the bottom of the kitchen cupboard, she also picked up any loose change lying around. When she suddenly left, the taxi driver who drove her to Heathrow happened by chance to be an acquaintance of Judy's. He reported back that the nurse had not only paid his fee – some £45 – in two- and five-pence pieces, but had spent the whole journey regaling him with the intimate details of life in our household. That nurse might well have been party to everything that went on under our roof, because privacy was non-existent. It was virtually impossible to have a private, let alone intimate, conversation with Stephen – or anyone else for that matter – without first making an appointment and asking the nurse on duty to be so good as to leave the room for five minutes.

Because of the scarcity of time and the slowness of communication, I got into the habit of preparing what I wanted to say to Stephen in advance. I hoped that by presenting him with a succinct and logical argument, I could simplify the matter, be it financial or family, under discussion. Stephen objected to this, implying that yet again I was denying him his rights. He would insist on returning to first principles and would dispute my reasoning at every stage, sure of the superiority of his own arguments. Thus, minor matters became major issues, and the cheerfully optimistic frame of mind in which I had entered his room would quickly disintegrate into defeat and disillusionment. As Stephen recovered his power of speech, I became nervously withdrawn again, unsure of myself and so uncertain of my opinions that I ceased to voice them, as much the victim of psychological pressure as Stephen was the victim of illness. I observed this process as it happened, yet there was nothing I could do to stop it, because it was part and parcel of the situation. I was caught in a trap and began to have nightmares two or three times a week. The nightmare was always the same: I was buried alive, trapped underground with no means of escape.

In a last-ditch attempt to stem the tide of nursing insurrection, Judy and I decided to provide the nurses with uniforms in response to a request from some of them who complained that their clothes were getting spoilt by splashes and spills of fluid. One of the more senior of them had access to a supply of second-hand white overalls and brought us a dozen or so. A white overall worn with a belt and buckle would look smart and official; the agency nurses always wore uniform, so it seemed appropriate for ours to do so too. A uniform would also clearly draw a line between the nurses and the family and, we hoped, instill some sense of professional discipline. Stephen however refused to let his nurses wear uniform: he wanted to maintain the illusion that his attendants were just friends. Thereafter nurses had free rein to wear whatever they liked. Sometimes their dress and make-up would have been more appropriate to a street corner in Soho than to the home of a severely handicapped Cambridge professor and his family.

Lucy soon became used to having the newspaper whisked from under her nose by the duty nurse, as she sat eating her breakfast before school in her O-level year. It would then be ceremoniously set up in Stephen's place to await his arrival some ten minutes later. Quickly, the rest of the family became second-class citizens, as if we were the lowest of the low, crouching on the bottom rung of a ladder, at the top of which the Florence Nightingales administered to the master of the universe. In between there were the several echelons of students, scientists and computer engineers, all of whom were obviously more important than we were. When one of the nurses, Elaine Mason, asked why I did not give up teaching and take up nursing, learning to use the suction machine so that I could look after Stephen myself, it was the clearest indication yet that the rest of us, who had no medical qualifications, were being consigned to a despised obscurity. The facility with which Elaine Mason used her evangelical certainty to gloss over profound issues as being the will of God was disconcerting. When she airily announced in Stephen's hearing that looking after him was so much easier than bringing up her own two sons, I hardly liked to point out that she was nursing Stephen for only just a couple of sessions a week. Such remarks were all too reminiscent of the facile Hawking attitude that I had encountered in the past. As she was an efficient nurse, I tried to regard her insensitive pronouncements with the detachment they deserved.

In the face of such sanctimonious pseudo-philosophy, I found even greater solace in my attachment to St Mark's. I listened to Bill Loveless's sermons intently and also to those of his fellow preacher, a scientist and former missionary, Cecil Gibbons, who at an advanced age made it his duty to keep abreast of scientific developments and interpret them in a religious context. They both always had something pertinent and measured to say to me personally, whether about suffering, about man's place in creation or about good and evil, and under their guidance I began to formulate my own simple philosophy about some of the stumbling blocks to faith, principally by understanding that free will is a prerequisite of the human condition. If belief in God were automatically decreed by the creator, the human race would simply be a breed of automatons with neither evolution of thought nor motivation for discovery. Evil, I reasoned, was often reducible, even if distantly and hazily, to human greed and selfishness – predatory animal instincts, dictated by nature for survival in a distant evolutionary past, long before the development of finer intelligence and the dawn of conscience. Selfish, instinctive reaction, the root of evil, is outside the reach of God precisely because free will prevents His intervention. God could not prevent suffering, but He could alleviate its effects by restoring hope, peace and harmony. There was still the stumbling block of illness, degenerative, incurable, paralysing and devastating, which did not fit into this system – unless, that is, illness also sometimes happened to be the result, however remotely, of human fallibility, an error in research or treatment, in a chosen way of life or in the environment. If the cause of Stephen's illness was really a non-sterile smallpox vaccination given in the early Sixties, it might be accounted for thus. As for the present chaos, one could only hope that, by keeping faith, by still trying to give of one's best, a brighter, calmer day might one day dawn.

On the administrative front, Judy was beleaguered. She would prepare an agreed rota of nursing shifts a month in advance, only to find, in the event, that her careful organization had been mysteriously overturned and that the working rota bore little resemblance to the one she had prepared and distributed. Neither she nor I would have any idea whom to expect at any given time; the system would inexplicably break down, and agency nurses had to be called in. Shattered and demoralized by all the unforeseen – and often unnecessary – complications which had accompanied our best efforts to enable Stephen to return to the family and the community, Judy and I called a series of meetings to try and settle various differences once and for all. Word had reached her indirectly that, quite apart from the interference in the organization of the rota, trouble was being whipped up among the staff on issues which had no relevance to our private nursing scheme.

The grants from the MacArthur Foundation came in six month-ly instalments. Every sixth months the University accountants would prepare a balance sheet to show the Trustees of the Foundation how their money had been spent, and I would submit a report on Stephen's health and care, together with another begging request for a further grant for the next half-year. In my second letter to the Foundation in March 1986, I explained how we had tried to engage our own team of nurses by placing regular advertisements in the local paper. I referred to the "indescribable problems" that this method had occasioned, with the result that we had often had to resort to the agency – hence the considerable bills for agency nursing. The grants, though generous, were only just enough to cover the bills. They certainly were not adequate to meet the demands which some mischief-maker among the nurses was now devising and which Judy thought to answer by calling the first meeting. Having thanked those present for all their help, I explained how the finances were obtained and organized in the hope that they might have a better idea of the difficulties we had experienced. I pointed out that the nursing bill came to at least £36,000 a year and was financed from the United States. I also emphasized that there was never any certainty that it would be renewed. It was therefore impossible to provide the nurses with anything more than casual employment on a part-time basis, which was strictly how the work was advertised. Consequently there was no scope for sickness pay, holiday pay, pensions or any of the other perks for which they had begun to agitate.

Thereafter a more subdued audience concentrated their attention on practical requests for laundry baskets, towel rails, adequate lighting, shelving and suchlike, and repairs to the potholes in the driveway. Judy and I took the opportunity to distribute the UK Council of Nursing's code of conduct, and asked the assembly to give its fourteen clauses their attention. Those recommendations had as much impact as the concerns I had already voiced about keeping the home, our home, a happy and well-balanced environment for Stephen and the children alike.

5

Out of the Ashes

Despite the mayhem wrought in the home by outside intervention, Stephen rose like a phoenix, and by early December 1985 he was well enough to attempt short sorties to the Department. At first I drove him there by car but, unless the weather was bad, he was soon wheeling himself in his chair over his usual route across the Backs, the only difference being that he was accompanied by a nurse instead of a faithful student. All expeditions took longer than before, involving much careful preparation of the patient before setting out. Many essential accoutrements had to be strung onto the back of the wheelchair, giving the whole contrivance an extraordinarily cumbersome appearance. Lumbering and festooned with eccentric appliances, rather like a tinker's cart, the chair dwarfed its occupant who, small and wasted, drove it fearlessly into battle to reassert his sovereignty over his intellectual domain.

It was unwise to dwell for too long on the Stephen's vulnerability, though it was difficult not to fall into the snare of sentimental overprotection: many had fallen into that trap. Some of us had striven to achieve a balance between a deep concern for the minimal, evanescent, physical presence and a somewhat mischievous irreverence for the immense psychological and intellectual power. This delicate balance, so essential to a healthy family life where no one person should claim to be more important than anyone else, had become impossible to maintain. At best, it entailed nerve-racking attention to every detail of Stephen's care, yet a healthy scepticism at some of his more outlandish and outrageous pronouncements. On a Sunday evening, for instance, Jonathan would bring in the usual takeaway curry. Though neurotic and mistrustful of the ingredients of my carefully prepared, guaranteed gluten-free home cooking, Stephen would on Sundays consume a huge plateful of curry with gusto, with never a thought as to the ingredients. The children and I considered this glaring inconsistency fair game for a little gentle teasing.

These were also occasions for wide-ranging discussions. Private conversation had become impossible, but in the relaxed atmosphere of those Sunday evenings – sometimes too at Sunday lunch when Robert, who came back to study in Cambridge in 1987, would bring his undergraduate friends home for a square meal – questions of science and faith would form the basis of sustained, good-natured argument. Cecil Gibbons had pointed out in one of his sermons that scientific research required just as broad a leap of faith in choosing a working hypothesis as did religious belief. Stephen usually grinned at the mention of religious faith and belief, though on one historic occasion he actually made the startling concession that, like religion, his own science of the universe required such a leap. In his branch of science the leap of faith – or inspired guesswork – centred on which model of the universe, which theory, which equation one chose as the most appropriate object of research. Then this, at the experimental stage, had to be tested against observation. With luck, the guess – or leap of faith – might, in Richard Feyman's words, prove "to be temporarily not wrong". The scientist had to rely on an intuitive sense that his choice was right, or he might be wasting years in pointless research with an end result that was definitively wrong. Any further attempts to discuss the profound matters of science and religion with Stephen were met with an enigmatic smile.

Insensitive to the subtleties of our relationship and unable to distinguish the mind from the body, the nurses, on the other hand, tended to smother Stephen in a blanket of sentimentality. This belied his strength of mind and undermined my attempts to keep the correct balance. For them he had become an idol, immune from criticism or even from the healthy scepticism which the psychiatric nurses had generated. They concentrated on the calamity of the illness rather than the victory over it, kowtowed to the patient's every whim and interpreted any innocent bantering as an insult to their idol.

The same sentimental mistake had been made earlier in 1985 by an artist commissioned jointly by the College and the National Portrait Gallery to paint Stephen's portrait. The paintings, unveiled that summer, showed the pathos of the body, slumped disjointedly in the chair all too clearly, but failed to show the willpower and the genius, conveyed with such persuasion in the set of the face and the light of the eyes. I regarded the portraits as a travesty and said so – to the exasperation of the bodies who had commissioned them. However, in the early months of 1986, the light of determination returned to those eyes as Stephen recovered his mobility and with it his unassailable position in the Department. The effect of his period of illness was not unlike the effect that exile from Cambridge had on Newton when the University was closed because of the plague in 1665. In the isolation of the manor house at Woolsthorpe near Grantham, Newton had found time for the contemplation and calculation needed to develop his theory of gravity. In those months when he was too weak to leave home, Stephen had learnt to use the new computer with the same single-minded motivation which he had shown in memorizing lengthy equations when, in the late Sixties, he lost the ability to write.

Through the loss of his voice, he discovered that he had gained a much improved method of communication. He could converse with anyone, not just the small band of family and students as in the past, and he was no longer dependent on having a student at hand to interpret his lectures for him. By turning up the volume on the speaker, he could address an audience as effectively, if not more so, as anyone else. His synthesized speech was slow, since it took time to select the vocabulary, but there was nothing unusual in that since his speech had always been measured. Stephen had always taken time to think before speaking to avoid cliché or inanity, and to ensure that the last word on any subject was his and his alone.

Not only was he empowered to express his own thoughts direct ly, deliver his own lectures and write his own letters, he was also able to work again on his book. His former student, Brian Whitt, had over the past months begun to help him with the methodical organization of the material and continued to help, particularly with diagrams and seeking out research material; but the project was now firmly back in Stephen's grasp. The book gave him the motivation to exploit the full potential of the computer, and the computer gave him the means of writing a revised version of the manuscript, incorporating the suggestions of the American editor. It began to look as if the book might become a reality: not only should we not have to repay the advance, we had, at long last, the prospect of financial security. The book might not make a fortune, but it might bring in a regular supplementary income, heralding the end of nearly a quarter of a century of economizing.

At home I endeavoured to juggle my own interests, teaching, music and the children, with the tiresome demands of wayward nurses. With Judy's stalwart help, I fended off impending chaos by conducting weekly interviews with new candidates and by attending to the requests for improvements from those already on the rota. We sensed that we had become the scapegoats for the frustrations which the nurses could not vent on Stephen himself. I discussed our predicament with an old school friend who lectured in nursing. She recognized the syndrome. "Nurses, like soldiers, are trained to act, not to think," she said. "If there is a patient needing treatment, their first duty is to that patient to the exclusion of all else. They act at an intensely physical level, which does not involve the intellect. Imagination is not a quality that is prized in nursing." This information certainly clarified the problem, but offered scant comfort, since it implied that nurses operated at the opposite end of the philosophical spectrum from the rest of us and, however much we might try to compromise, they, by definition, were unable to do so.

Meanwhile Stephen celebrated his return to normality. In the immediate short term, this took the form of a visit to the pantomime for his birthday and to the College Ladies' Night two days later. In the long term, he was already planning his travels for the forthcoming year, rashly undaunted by the Geneva experience. Paris and Rome were on his itinerary for the autumn, to be preceded by an experimental trip abroad in June – to an island off the Swedish coast for a conference in particle physics. How all this was to be achieved was another matter, especially since the dates for the Swedish conference coincided with Lucy's first O-level papers and I was reluctant to leave her at such a critical time.

In fact attention shifted dramatically from Stephen to Lucy in the spring of 1986. In March, she set off with a school party to Moscow, but not, as we had all expected, under the exuberant auspices of her Russian teacher. Each year it was Vera Petrovna's custom to dress up her charges like Michelin men, in layer upon layer of clothing acquired from second hand shops and jumble sales. In Moscow the girls would tour the city, visiting all her friends and relations, peeling off a layer of charitable clothing at each stop. However in 1986 she was refused a visa for the first time, so other non-Russian-speaking teachers had to accompany the party to Moscow and Leningrad. It was therefore a potential catastrophe when Lucy fell ill in Moscow with only her own knowledge of Russian to help her. Terrified of being abandoned in a Russian hospital, she told no one how ill she was feeling; she ate nothing and clutched her stomach for ten days. When she arrived home, she was too ill with a high fever and excruciating abdominal pain to go anywhere except straight to bed. The doctor came and diagnosed acute appendicitis. So there we were again – walking the all-too-familiar corridors of Addenbrooke's Hospital, sitting on the same plastic chairs, though for a dangerously inflamed appendix rather than a dangerously obstructed respiratory tract. We were told the next day, when Lucy was already recovering, that she was very lucky not to have had a burst appendix in Moscow.

Nevertheless, the arrival of warmer weather alleviated some of the tensions associated with winter susceptibilities, and life began to assume at least a thin veneer of its former hard-won normality. Defiantly determined that the home should still be worthy of that name, I tried to consign the complexities of full-time nursing attendance to the background, pretending, as we had so often in the past, that it was just another minor inconvenience. Once more we gave dinners and drinks parties for scientific visitors and participated in local activities at the schools and the church. Tim invited seventeen of his classmates to his birthday party, where a good, old-fashioned Punch and Judy show kept the guests enthralled for part of the time while, for the rest of the afternoon, my father, in time-honoured tradition at the piano, kept them amused with musical games.

As Stephen's health gradually improved, I ventured to take up some of my old activities, notably singing in the church choir and with the choral society which I had joined in the early Eighties. Since the latter's weekly rehearsals took place in Caius College Chapel by kind permission of the Dean, John Sturdy, this activity was quite compatible with Stephen's movements. He, accompanied by a nurse, would dine in the College while I sang – or tried to sing my way through an endless succession of colds – in the Chapel. Often he would call in at the Chapel after dinner to listen to the final stages of the rehearsal and we would then go home together. Lucy was adopting an increasingly independent lifestyle, which revolved more and more around the theatre and kept her out of the house.

Three nurses and a doctor were engaged for Stephen's trip to Sweden, stretching the MacArthur budget to its limit. It was however a profitable investment, since Murray Gell-Mann, one of the trustees of the MacArthur Foundation, was also a participant at the conference. He could see at first hand just how dire Stephen's circumstances were and just how much costly professional care was needed to sustain his life and his contribution to physics. In my next application to the Foundation in September of 1986, I was able to refer to our meeting with Murray Gell-Mann and to report that Stephen's health, though much more stable, continued to require the same degree of professional nursing: I predicted that it would be required indefinitely. Thereafter, the MacArthur Foundation agreed to support Stephen's nursing expenses on an indefinite basis and accepted my explanation that the National Health Service provided only a fleeting morning visit from the District Nurse to check the supplies, a weekly visit from the GP, one eight-hour shift out of the twenty-one, and additional help with bathing on a couple of mornings a week.

The small, traffic-free island of Marstrand off the west coast of Sweden proved to be the most delightful and suitable place for a convalescent physicist to flex his intellectual muscles. While Stephen and his comrades explored the universe by means of the trajectories of elementary particles, I relaxed, cherishing peace and solitude in the rocky coves and walking along the woodland tracks where daffodils still bloomed in June and the sun shone late into the night. The freedom of those few days in Sweden was a rare luxury, but one which just occasionally came my way thanks to the unexpectedly helpful intervention of Stephen's mother after the death of his father in March 1986. Stephen's father was not an easy patient in his final illness; the frustration of immobility was too burdensome for one who in earlier years had thought little of driving single-handed across Africa to enlist for service at the beginning of the Second World War, and who habitually in his late seventies would spend whole weeks camping and walking in the Welsh mountains. His funeral marked a sad end to a distinguished but inadequately recognized career in tropical medicine. I suspected that I was not the only person whose feelings towards him were decidedly ambivalent. I admired him and respected him, for he could be sensitive and considerate, even appreciative, but he could also be cold, harsh and distant.

After his death, Isobel's formerly stringent inflexibility appeared to mellow as she showed signs of greater compassion.

She seemed anxious to share the stresses of our family life in a new way and became popular with the children for her coolly sardonic sense of humour and for her apparently easygoing nature, which made few demands of them. She also showed a surprising and benevolent tolerance of my relationship with Jonathan, as if she had finally come to realize that he was not intent on destroying the family but was genuinely supportive of us all, including Stephen. I was grateful for her help and grateful for her understanding, especially when she offered to keep house so that we could resume our camping holidays on the Continent. If I could reliably look forward to a couple of weeks' summer holiday away from the strains of a half-life in a house where I was on duty in every capacity for seven days a week for a minimum of forty-nine weeks a year, juggling all my roles, trying to be all things to all the inhabitants, I felt that I could summon the strength to continue, however onerous those duties might be. At the end of the allotted time, I returned without question to Stephen.

Having spread his phoenix wings in Sweden without mishap, Stephen was eager to use them again and again. In September, the travelling circus – which now included a young physics graduate as Stephen's personal assistant – set off for Paris for a conference at the Observatoire de Paris at Meudon, where Brandon Carter worked. I was delighted to be able to spend time with Lucette, bringing her up-to-date on the events of the past year, and there I also discovered a new role for myself – as chauffeur and interpreter for the party. At least the nurses could hear, if not see, that I was good for something.

Only a month later we found ourselves again in Rome, where Stephen was to be admitted by the Pope to the Pontifical Academy of Sciences, despite the heresies he was still preaching about the universe having neither a beginning nor an end. Tim came too, as did the retinue of nurses and the young personal assistant whose responsibility it was to attend to the workings of the computer and the mechanics of Stephen's lectures. We tried to choose nurses whom we knew to be Catholic and who would appreciate the significance of the occasion. We were lucky in that two of the most reliable and pleasant nurses on the rota, Pam and Theresa, were both Catholic and were overjoyed to be invited. We needed three nurses however, and not all were as keen as Pam and Theresa. It was only at the last minute that Elaine Mason agreed to come with us: she did so only on the understanding that she would not have to shake hands with the Pope, as such a gesture would be against her principles.

The second visit to Rome was more formal than the first in 1981. The weather was better, and so were the provisions made for us: we stayed in a much more comfortable hotel, closer to the Vatican, and special tours of the art treasures of the Vatican were put on for wives and children while the scientists conferred in the Renaissance headquarters of the Academy. The climax of the visit was an audience with Pope John Paul II, to which all members of Stephen's party were admitted. With his hand gently resting on Tim's head, the Pope talked quietly to Stephen and me, pressing our hands and giving us his blessing. He then shook hands with the others, none of whom resisted. I was moved by the genuine warmth of his personality, the softness of his big hands and the holiness of the light in his bright blue eyes. I had no religious prejudices, and had come to Rome with an open heart and mind. The Pope touched my heart and my mind, for – politics and dogma apart – I sensed that he sincerely cared about the people he met and kept them in his prayers.

Encouraged by the success of these tentative trips abroad within Europe, Stephen's aspirations knew no bounds. That December he soared away to the usual pre-Christmas scientific conference in Chicago to reclaim his place on the international circuit. These days he travelled with all the ceremonial due to an Arab sheikh, surrounded by hordes of minions, nurses, students, the personal assistant and the occasional colleague. He was attended by so much luggage that the chassis of the limousines that came to whisk him away to the airport often had difficulty in clearing the ground as they left the driveway. The airlines had learnt to treat Stephen with respect, as a valued customer rather than as an inconvenience, and accorded him the sort of deference and assistance which, had it come twenty years earlier when I was struggling to look after Stephen and a tiny baby, might have spared me much stress. Nowadays, ironically, my presence was almost superfluous on the international travels. Alone among so many people, I often took Tim along for companionship, just as Robert had been my small companion in days gone by. Tim fulfilled this role admirably. He loved air travel and, as the plane was gathering speed for take-off – my worst moment – he would gasp, "Faster! faster!" dispelling my lingering fears with his contagious excitement. There was much that I could teach him and interest him in on these travels, not least a grounding in the Romance languages. In Spain, with patience and a total lack of competitiveness, he taught me to play chess, something his father had never succeeded in doing.

6

Maths and Music

Although eighteen months previously Stephen's chances of survival had been dismissed as negligible, he had confounded the pessimists yet again: he had survived and was back in the forefront of scientific research, theorizing on abstruse suppositions about imaginary particles travelling in imaginary time in a looking-glass universe which did not exist except in the minds of the theorists. His phenomenal resurrection and the consequent transformation of his prospects had galvanized him into even more intense industry. He was travelling again, terrestrially and universally, whenever and wherever he chose. Above all, just over a year since his first painstaking attempts to come to grips with the workings of the computer and his cautious return to the Department, he had completed the second draft of his book and was searching for a title. His state of health continued to be extremely precarious, the subject of perpetual anxiety, but with all the aids of modern medicine and twenty-four hour nursing care at his disposal, he virtually carried his own mini-hospital with him wherever he went. The nurses had learnt emergency techniques for changing the tracheotomy tube, and Stephen himself had taken charge of his medication as he reckoned, rightly, that he knew more about his case than any doctor.

Another nurse – tall, aristocratic Amarjit Chohan from the Punjab – had joined the rota. By night she worked in the operating theatres at Addenbrooke's, and by day (and in her free time) she came to look after Stephen. In lonely exile from her own home, the victim of thinly veiled racism, she adopted us with a passionate intensity which soon began to upset the other nurses. Stephen was flattered to find himself the contested prize in the battles which the more volatile, less stable of his attendants fought for his favours, and regarded their squabbles with bemused complicity. In Spain, Tim and I were astounded to watch while one of the nurses flirted unashamedly with a student and then actually resorted to fisticuffs with another nurse over

403

some petty argument. Like distant thunder, rivalry between assertive personalities, each insisting on the superiority of her own method of care, rumbled menacingly. It was yet an additional wearisome problem at home and a source of embarrassment in public abroad.

The big event of 1987 which, among the imaginary trajectories and illusory universes, was exercising Stephen and all those caught up in his orbit was the celebration of the tercentenary of the publication of Newton's *Principia Mathematica* with an international conference to be held in Cambridge. Stephen was firmly established at the centre of this event, since the Newtonian tradition of leading cosmological research in Cambridge was consigned to his care as Lucasian Professor, and his work was the logical extension of Newtonian physics modified by the twentieth-century influence of Einstein's theory of relativity.

Isaac Newton was born in 1642, the year of Galileo's death and three hundred years before Stephen's birth. Although his education as a schoolboy in Grantham and as a "sizar" or servant-student in Trinity College was conservative, his major work *Principia Mathematica* was directly influenced by the mechanical and mathematical principles formulated by René Descartes, the great seventeenth-century French philosopher. In Cambridge in the 1660s Descartes' theories provoked "such a stir, some railing at him and forbidding the reading of him as if he had impugned the very Gospel. And yet there was a general inclination, especially of the brisk part of the University to use him". Newton took Descartes' principles home with him to Woolsthorpe Manor just after his graduation at the outbreak of the Plague. It was during that extraordinary period of creativity at Woolsthorpe Manor that Newton at the age of twenty-three developed his three major discoveries: the calculus, the universal theory of gravitation and the theory of the nature of light.

Newton may have been "brisk" in adopting Descartes' theories, but he was not at all brisk about publishing the results to which those theories had led him. *Principia Mathematica* was finally published in 1687 at the insistence of Samuel Pepys, the President of the Royal Society, and Edmond Halley, the young astronomer. In his *magnum opus,* Newton not only proposed the Law of Universal Gravitation, predicting the elliptical movement of the planets around the sun, but also developed the complicated mathematics of such motions. It is in *Principia Mathematica* that mathematics is harnessed to the service of physics and is rigorously applied to the visible universe. *Opticks*, Newton's other great work, also developed in the Plague years but not published until 1704, described light as a spectrum of colours which in combination formed white light, but which could be split into seven component bands. Newton set up a prism in the path of a sunbeam and watched as the white light entering the prism split into the colours of the rainbow, producing not the rounded image of the sun on the opposite wall, but an oblong image, where the seven colours from blue to red separated and fanned out "according to their degrees of refrangibility". If *Principia Mathematica* was inspired by the fall of an apple in the garden of Woolsthorpe Manor, the inspiration for *Opticks* was commercial – the improvement of the glass in the telescope, the instrument which Galileo had first turned on the heavens in the winter of 1609. Although Newton would have described himself as a natural philosopher, one might designate him the first great modern mathematician and physicist.

The product of an unhappy childhood, Newton could be dictatorial and not a little devious. He earned a reputation for vindictiveness in his treatment of the German philosopher Gottfried Leibniz, who claimed to have discovered the calculus first. Newton's discovery of the calculus, or fluxions as he called them, was prompted by his need in the mid-1660s for a general method of mathematical calculation, essential for dealing with the dynamics of planetary motion. It was put to immediate use in his theory of gravitation, but typically he failed to publish his results and was then incensed when Leibniz published his independent findings in 1676. There was nevertheless a humbler aspect of this embittered genius which appealed to me. When writing of his role in science, he speculated about his own importance, unsure of the significance of his discoveries: "I do not know what I may appear to the world; but to myself I seem to have been only like a boy playing on the seashore, and diverting myself in now and then finding a smoother pebble or a prettier shell than ordinary, while the great ocean of truth lay all undiscovered before me". "Collecting pebbles on the beach" was the very image Stephen had used in 1965 to pour scorn on medieval studies.

Newton left no stone unturned on his particular beach. Although in the opinion of contemporaries he was said to be tone-deaf, he had in 1667 produced a theory of music. *Of Musick* was a fairly unremarkable treatise containing nothing new; in it he considered questions of tuning the scale and compared in logarithmic terms the just and equal temperaments. He also used music to draw synaesthetic analogies between the seven notes of the diatonic scale and the seven bands of colour in the spectrum, basing those analogies on the breadth of the colour bands and the seven string lengths required to produce a scale.

The link between Newton's personal tastes and music was rather tenuous but, taken with all the other considerations, his theoretical interest was strong enough to justify putting on a concert of the music of his era to celebrate his tercentenary. Another of the considerations centred on the fact that Newton's genius was initially fired by the new approach to science coming from France, while with the Restoration of the monarchy in 1660 a wave of enthusiasm for the innovative French style in music came to England with Charles II – inspiring the other great English genius of the period, Henry Purcell. Since, together with the music of Bach and Handel, the music of Henry Purcell formed the basis of the Cambridge Baroque Camerata's repertoire, there could have been no more appropriate way of entertaining the delegates to the Newton tercentenary conference than with a concert of the music of that period. However much Stephen might have preferred it, a performance of the *Ring Cycle* was hardly feasible. The great advantage of such a prestigious occasion, to be held in Trinity College, was that it attracted commercial sponsorship for the orchestra at last, not only enabling Jonathan to put his musical enterprise on a secure footing, but also to make a recording of the programme, entitled *Principia Musica*.

Again, Stephen, Jonathan and I seemed to have struggled back to some sort of synthesis of our various talents and interests. Although the modern physics of quantum theory was completely beyond me, I could research Newtonian physics with some understanding of the concepts if not of the mathematics, and I could make myself useful liaising between the mathematical and the musical aspects of that summer's major endeavour. I enjoyed concert organization: it was hard work but, like teaching, it gave me a sense of self-worth. As well as the practical business of concert promotion, arranging the venue, the advertising, the ticketing and so on, there was the intellectual stimulus of researching the background to the music for the programme notes. In pursuit of information about the late seventeenth-century musical scene, I found myself drawn back into the precincts of the University Library, where the frenetic tempo of daily existence slowed to a reverent, unhurried pace. My researches yielded a welcome connection between Newton and Purcell in the writings of an eminent seventeenth-century musicologist and undergraduate contemporary of Newton's, Roger North, who concluded that the great "practical diversions" of his life had been "reducible to two heads: one, Mathematicks, and the other Musick". His delight in mathematics culminated in "Mr Newton's new and most exquisitely thought" hypothesis of light "as a blended mixture of all colours". As for music, there can be little doubt that "the devine Purcell" afforded him the greatest pleasure as he came "full saile into the superiority of the musicall faculty".

As in days past, the hours I could spend in the University Library were lamentably scarce. There was time only for dashing in to check a few references before rushing out with a pile of books under my arm. Before the Newton celebrations in July, there was a flurry of other activities to be fitted into the calendar. I was never at rest, propelled by an inner tension which pervaded every aspect of my being – physical, mental, intellectual, creative and spiritual. Yet again, I had to prove to myself that I was a worthy companion to Stephen's genius, and to the world at large I had to prove that we were still operating as a normal family. Apart from our academic activities, there were more parties and dinners, more work for charities, more concerts and conferences, more travel and more honorary degrees. Though other families led busy lives, by comparison with theirs ours was not normal: it was insane. I depended for my survival on all the support and reinforcement that my myriad activities and my family, friends and Jonathan could give me. Stephen's nursing companions, gifted in neither insight nor imagination, viewed these pit-props to be counter to Stephen's interests rather than supportive of them. Soon I, and the rest of the family, were made to feel that we should be apologizing for our presence, for our very existence, for breathing the same air as the man of genius. More often than not, it was Lucy who helped me keep a sense of perspective and Jonathan who encouraged me to retain some self-respect. Jonathan's frequent and comforting presence however had increasingly become the cause of much tight-lipped whispering and drawing-in of breath by those outsiders who, in their shallowness, sought to govern others by standards which, as events were to prove, they themselves were unable to sustain.

As Lucy was continuing with her Russian studies and was in her first year of A levels, she came to Moscow again in May 1987 with Stephen and me for yet another conference at the Academy of Sciences. The Academy, like so many other Russian institutions, was quietly dropping its former "Soviet" nomenclature in recognition of the dramatic change which was taking place in Russian society. "*Perestroika*" and "*glasnost*" were the words dancing on everybody's lips with an infectious excitement, bordering upon euphoria. "What do you think of the changing state of affairs in this country?" journalists asked Lucy and me after Stephen's public lecture. "The very fact that you can ask such a question is proof enough of the extraordinary change," we replied. Freedom of speech, freedom from oppression, freedom to travel – these were astoundingly precious liberties to people who had been restricted to the chilling, grey confines of a shadowy one-party state.

We too were much freer than on previous visits to Moscow. We could go where we liked without being accompanied or trailed, and the entertainment provided for us was not just the obligatory visit to the Bolshoi but a concert in a church outside Moscow as well. Religious fervour had gripped Moscow. In the church of the Novodevichy Monastery, for example, the air was thick with the smoke of hundreds of lit candles, around which the faithful were chanting and genuflecting as if to make up for lost time. By coincidence, I had spent the winter months rehearsing Rachmaninov's *Vespers* with the choir – in Russian – for performance in Jesus College Chapel in March. To my delighted surprise, the concert to which we were taken was performed by a similar group of amateur singers and consisted of unaccompanied Russian liturgical settings, sounding very much like the *Vespers* in an atmosphere that was tense with the novelty and promise of reawakening tradition. Against a richly gilded backdrop of icons, the majestic *basso profondo* voices summoned up dark Russian vowels, rolled them on the tongue and emitted them into the resonant spaces of the ancient church, where their deep-toned sonorities held the audience enraptured.

Through being in Moscow, I missed an occasion in Cambridge which was of profound significance not only to the children, Jonathan and me, but to the whole of the parish of St Mark's.

Our vicar, Bill Loveless, was retiring. So devastated was the congregation at losing its dearly loved incumbent that the parish went into a state resembling collective mourning for a long period after his departure. In the spring Lucy had taken the opportunity to attend Bill's final series of classes, leading to her confirmation. At about that time, in honour of his forthcoming retirement, the choir put on a concert at which I sang a couple of his favourite Schubert *lieder*, including *Die Forelle*, and afterwards we held a large farewell supper party at West Road. Even so, I was sad not to be present at his last Sunday service. He had a fund of wisdom of which I had only scratched the surface; indeed, one of his last sermons, on the theme of the search for a quiet mind, had impressed me deeply. In it he uncovered every aspect of my own lack of peace: my concerns, my fears – for Stephen, for my children and for myself – my inability to rest, the tensions and the cares, the frustrations and the uncertainties. He also broached that other group of emotional disturbances associated with an unquiet mind, those evoked by guilt, to which I was no stranger. Self-reproach trailed me like a menacing shadow. I listened for whatever scraps of comfort he could throw in my direction. Live in the present, he said, and trust in God through darkness, pain and fear. Then, as he quoted the biblical passage from Corinthians, "God will not suffer you to be tested more than you are able", I felt that his words were aimed at me alone. Guilt, he went on to say, is the risk that comes from striving always for the highest and the best; love is the only answer to guilt. Only in love can we sustain each other. His words offered a new resolution to the gnawing dilemma of guilt. Love was most certainly the force that sustained our household. According to that reckoning, I was being true to my promise: I had love for everyone, abundant maternal love for each of the children, love for Stephen as well as love for Jonathan. Love had many facets, Agape as well as Eros, and I wanted to continue to prove my love for Stephen by doing my best for him, but sometimes that love became so entangled with the legion of worries generated by the responsibility for his care that it was hard to know where anxiety ended and love began. Stephen himself was insulted by any mention of compassion: he equated it with pity and religious sentimentality. He refused to understand it and rejected it outright.

7

Extremes

With a little help from Shakespeare, Stephen had devised a title
for his book; the manuscript had been moulded into a form
acceptable to the publisher and a date in June 1988 was set for
publication. The American edition was to be published in the
spring, before the British edition. That first American edition
had to be pulped at the last minute because of the fear of legal
action on account of certain aspersions cast in the text on the
integrity of a couple of American scientists. This misfortune
allowed a minor omission to be rectified: Stephen had dedicated
A Brief History of Time to me, a gesture which came as a much
appreciated public acknowledgement, but the dedication had
been left out of the American edition. The presses were put into
overdrive to produce ten thousand copies of the amended edition
within days, the potential libel was erased, my name featured in
the dedication and the book was launched in the United States.

While Stephen was in America for the launch, Tim and I went
to stay with his best friend Arthur and his parents, who were now
living in Germany. The two little boys saw each other rarely these
days, yet neither of them had made other close friends; when they
met, they happily settled into their familiar routine, like long-lost
brothers. As there had been a late fall of snow in the Black Forest,
Arthur's father, Kevin, surprised us by asking if we would like to
go skiing. I had never skied in my life and never expected to do
so, although rumour had it that Stephen used to be a competent
skier and Lucy regularly went skiing with her friends. Indeed, at
that very moment she was in the Alps recovering from an arduous
run of rehearsals for a play which she and her companions in
the Cambridge Youth Theatre were to perform in Cambridge in
April before appearing at the Edinburgh Festival in the summer.
Tim and I jumped at the chance to learn to ski. He learnt quickly,
hurling himself down the slopes at breakneck speed, threatening
to overshoot the car park at the bottom. I watched helplessly
while Arthur's mother, Belinda, desperately shouted instructions

at him to snowplough – that is, to slow down by turning the skis inwards. The memory of broken arms when learning to ice-skate made me much more wary and nervous – until I realized that snow was a soft bed, if cold and wet, to fall into or onto. During that weekend in the Black Forest, I recovered some of my lost bravado. High up on the hillside, with the wind in my face and the sun shining on the glistening white snow, I rejoiced at the release from the treadmill of care and responsibility, and from the divisive, tedious squabbles of petulant nurses which had made our home life such an unendingly depressing struggle. Skiing demanded one-hundred per cent concentration, both physical and mental: the immediate objective was the bottom of the slope, and the only question the brain could accommodate was how to get there in one piece.

Stephen was in America for over three weeks. Soon after his return, we were to set off together to Jerusalem, where he was to collect the prestigious Wolf Prize, awarded jointly to him and Roger Penrose for distinction in physics.

My misgivings about the Israel trip were not solely caused by my reluctance to leave the family or to take time from teaching. Although I was looking forward to meeting Hanna Scolnicov, my friend from Lucy Cavendish days, I was not much looking forward to visiting the holiest, most ancient city in the world in the company of a party of physicists: I would have preferred a pilgrimage with more like-minded people, but I had no choice. There was a discernible tension in the air when Stephen said that, if I did not want to go, he was sure that Elaine Mason, the nurse who had accompanied him to America, would be happy to go in my place.

He had resented my refusal to go to America with him in March when Tim and I had gone skiing and, since his return, the communication lines between us had become brittle and taut. My suggestion that he should sack some of the troublemakers among the nurses met with the blank, incontestable reply, "I need good nurses". When I offered to collaborate with him on a proposed autobiography, a project which I hoped would bring us closer together, his reaction was dismissive: "I should be glad of your opinion." Only then did I start to perceive the truth of what other nurses had been trying to tell me for some time, namely that one of their number was exerting undue influence over Stephen, deliberately provoking and exploiting every disagreement be-tween us. Naturally my relationship with Jonathan featured large in the increasingly extravagant web of wile and deceit that was being woven and, as far as that was concerned, there was little I could say in my own defence, since clearly in the eyes of the world our relationship was a guilty one.

Before our departure for the Middle East, there was just time to see Lucy performing in the lively spectacle of *The Heart of a Dog*, a staged adaptation of the political satire written in the 1920s by the Russian writer Mikhail Bulgakov. The novella, in which Bulgakov voiced his concerns at the take-over of Russian society by the proletariat, was considered too abrasive for publication at the time and was not published in the Soviet Union until 1987, the year of our most recent visit. On the following Sunday, leaving my parents in charge of the home, we left for Israel.

Although there were delays at Heathrow, the main stretch of the flight passed without incident. Jonathan, who was away on tour with the Cam-bridge Baroque Camerata, had given me a Walkman and tapes of Bach's *Mass in B Minor* for my birthday, and with that I whiled away the time, occasionally peering out of the window down to the distant blue depths of the Mediterranean. As night fell and the sky and the sea darkened, a strip of neon lights appeared far below clearly marking the coastline, and we were told to fasten our seat belts for landing in Tel Aviv. The plane began its descent, and I watched as we skimmed lit buildings and roadways. I heard the rumble of the undercarriage being lowered and waited for the jolt of the landing on the runway. The bump never came. Instead the plane lumbered its way back up into the night sky. To my own surprise, I was fascinated, not frightened. There were no announcements. A hush descended on the cabin, and I sensed that the same questions were passing through the minds of all the passengers: had we been highjacked and were we heading for Lebanon?

Ten minutes later the captain's voice came over the address system. We had not been able to land in Tel Aviv because of sudden fog, he explained, and had been diverted to the only other available runway, a landing strip at a military airbase in the Negev desert, the neck of Israeli territory narrowing down to the Red Sea between Egypt and Jordan. The plane droned through the night to the desert, where it made an abrupt and bumpy landing on a short runway, not built to accommodate 747s – and there we stayed. By the time the fog had cleared in Tel Aviv, the period of duty for our crew had expired, so we – and they – had to wait for another crew to come out from Tel Aviv to collect us. I pulled down the blind, curled up and went to sleep. Stephen's assistant, Nick Phillips, nudged me the next morning just as the engines were beginning to turn. I drew up the blind and looked out on a perfect introduction to the Holy Land. Outside was a scene of timeless peace and beauty: golden sands, silken dunes and barren, purple hills, all tinged with the soft pinkish hue of dawn.

The focal point of the official visit was the presentation of the Wolf Prize in the Knesset against the backdrop of Chagall's immense tapestry of the history of the Israeli people. The ceremony took place in the presence both of the highly respected, liberal-minded President of Israel, Chaim Herzog, and the notoriously hard-line, right-wing Prime Minister, Yitzhak Shamir. They epitomized the two ends of the political spectrum in a country where good sense and fanaticism coexisted in equal measures. After the completion of the ceremonials, Stephen and Roger Penrose were so much occupied in scientific meetings, lectures and seminars with their Israeli colleagues that I was often left to wander and explore at will through Jerusalem. "Go into the Jewish quarter of the Old City, by all means," I was advised, "but don't go into the Arab quarter: it's too dangerous because of the *Intifada*." In my impatience to be independent of the official party, I shrugged off such caution with indifference, happy to find that the hotel, a modern block, was within easy walking distance of the Jaffa Gate of the Old City. Like a magnet, the grey walls on the opposite hill, as austere and forbidding as the walls of the Alhambra in Granada, drew me to them. Unprepared for the bustling, noisy mass of colourful humanity which ebbed and flowed in and out of the gate beneath David's Tower, I paused, looking about me and wondering which way to go, to the right or to the left. I was tempted to let myself be pulled along with the crowds and be sucked down the narrow street on my left, but mindful of the advice to keep out of the Arab quarter I set off to my right, past the grey-stone Anglican cathedral into a street which ran along the inside of the city walls. It was disappointingly dull and quiet. Hammering came from the occasional workshop, a few people going about their daily business hurried down the street, the sounds of a piano wafted from an upper window, otherwise there was little to claim my interest. It was pleasant but unremarkable. I carried on walking and came to a new housing development which was even more disappointing. However, an alleyway between the new houses on the left gave onto a steep flight of steps which descended to a leafy little square where I stopped for a drink, before carrying on down the next long flight. At the bottom was a broad open expanse, enclosed on the far side by a high wall of mellow, sunburnt stone. Black-coated men were praying and kissing the wall and bridal parties were being photographed against it. I had reached the Wailing Wall. I ambled across the open space, watching the crowds, some earnest and devout, others laughing and talking.

On one side of the space was a short tunnel, guarded by soldiers, under a mass of buildings. People were coming and going through it quite freely, so I joined them. In passing through that tunnel, I discovered – without the aid of complex mathematical equations – that time travel is a real possibility. In practical and political terms, that tunnel divided the Jewish and the Arab quarters of the Old City. In historical terms it divided secular modernity from an ancient past which vibrated with the sounds, the colours and the traditions of biblical times. Pilgrims and tourists mingled like visitors from another planet with the local inhabitants who, with their children and donkeys, got on with their daily lives as if the twentieth century had not happened. I walked on alone, pausing now and then on the edge of a group of pilgrims. I listened to the guide's explanation of each site and I joined in their prayers and hymns at a couple of the Stations of the Cross on the Via Dolorosa.

It was a strange experience suddenly to be alone, free to make my own discoveries and form my own judgements. I shuddered at the gloomy, repellent sense of intrigue which pervaded the Church of the Holy Sepulchre with its squabbling, rival sects and its queues of tourists waiting to pass through the inner sanctum. I could not wait to get out of its morbid atmosphere into the bright daylight. The view from the tower was its one redeeming feature. The panorama of flat, white rooftops was as striking as the view of the red roofs of Venice from the top of the Campanile. Far below, chickens cackled, cocks crowed and a donkey brayed.

It was with reluctance that I dragged myself away from the Church of St Anne, close by the excavations of the Pool of Bethesda, only a hundred yards from the Lion Gate with its views across to the Mount of Olives. The Church of St Anne, immense and domed, light and airy, was deserted when I went in. I clicked my fingers – a trick Jonathan had taught me to test the acoustics of a building – and was surprised to find that the church was even more resonant than King's Chapel. Emboldened by the silence of the empty church, I hummed a few bars of Purcell's *Evening Hymn* – "Now, now that the sun has veiled his light and bid the world goodnight…" – I listened in astonishment as the sound of my voice was caught by the pillars and flung up into the dome. There the song took on a life of its own and whirled in ecstasy before sliding back to earth in a whisper. The friendly Arab guardian of the Church appeared from a side door. He said that he liked to listen to the pilgrims who came to sing in his Church. Apparently I was lucky to have had it to myself, as usually choirs queued up for their turns. He invited me to return whenever I liked.

The Arab quarter of the city held no terrors for me; so, another day, I made for the Dome of the Rock, the spectacular holy place of Islam and the site of the stone where Abraham prepared to sacrifice Isaac. The entrance was closed and guarded by Israeli soldiers. It would be closed, except to worshippers, for the foreseeable future. In disappointment I made my way back up the street through the Arab bazaar with its motley assortment of tourist goods – Bethlehem blue glass, pottery and leather. I browsed among its antique stalls, which displayed bits of Roman glass, copper and coins, and its food stalls spilling over with all the delicacies of the eastern Mediterranean, nuts and olives, Turkish delight and halva as well as a cornucopia of fruits and vegetables. Like the stallholders I had met in Tangiers twenty-five years earlier, the Arabs here were polite and friendly. Having haggled over a pretty Roman glass bead at one of the antique stalls, a malachite and silver necklace at a ridiculously low price on another then caught my eye. The proprietor came out to talk to me without attempting to pressurize me into a purchase. He spoke good English and was just telling me about his cousin in Middlesex when he glanced down the street and hastily pushed me into his shop. He then took up a position, arms akimbo, in the doorway. His alarm was understandable. A troop of armed Israeli soldiers was forcing its way noisily up the alley. They did not seem concerned about respecting any property, barrows or stalls in their path and, from the stance adopted by my shopkeeper and others nearby, it appeared that they had a reputation for being light-fingered. When the noise of their passage, their boots on the cobbles and their shouts had died away, the shopkeeper came back inside sighing. He apologized for pushing me through the door and simply said, "You see, we have to be very careful." I bought the necklace and a richly decorated, hand-painted plate and said goodbye, promising to return. I did return on the last day only to find everywhere closed: the shops were boarded up and, apart from stray cats, the streets were deserted. The ancient pageant of light, life, noise and colour had vanished. Everywhere, every street, every corner, every square, was dark, eerie and intimidating – a ghost city which had closed its doors to time travellers.

As well as my sympathy for the Arabs, I felt a natural affinity with the Jewish people: many of our friends were Jews, highly intelligent, articulate and sensitive, whose families had been ravaged by the Holocaust. I could not, however, sympathize with the inhuman tactics of the Israeli army that I had witnessed in the Arab quarter of Jerusalem, even less could I sympathize with the loathsome driver who had been allotted to us. An American Jew of central-European origins, he voiced his opinions loudly and coarsely wherever we went. As he drove down the winding road to the Dead Sea, he gestured to a row of white houses up on the hills. "See there," he said proudly, "that's one of our settlements, we're building all those homes. The Arabs had this land for two thousand years and didn't do anything with it. They've had their chance, but now it's our turn and they want to push us into the sea." I had heard these wearying arguments before, delivered in the same Americanized monotone by other immigrant speakers. Further down the road, we came across a simple Bedouin encampment. "What can you do with people like that? Just look at them!" the driver expostulated, "they haven't advanced in two thousand years!" I could hardly contain my indignation. "Perhaps they like their traditional lifestyle," I retorted. I was saddened that peace was so elusive between two peoples of the same racial stock who had so much to offer each other. The best Jews and the best Arabs had a lot in common. They could both be intelligent, generous, friendly and amusing. Perhaps the Jews had the edge over the Arabs in rational argument, in science, technology and mathematics, but the Arabs had superior intuitive poetic and artistic skills. Between them, they held the key to the most successful and gifted culture the world has ever seen.

There were, inevitably, many official expeditions. Television cameras and reporters followed Stephen to all his meetings, eager for his reactions to a wide range of questions. Unfailingly one question recurred at every interview. I watched and listened from the sidelines and my heart sank as I heard it repeated again and again in some form or other. "Professor Hawking, what does your research tell you about the existence of God?" or "Is there room for God in the universe you describe?" or, more directly, "Do you believe in God?" Always the answer was the same. No, Stephen did not believe in God and there was no room for God in his universe. Roger Penrose was more tactful. When asked the same questions, he conceded that there were different ways to approach God: some people might find God in religious belief, others in music, others conceivably in the beauty of a mathematical equation. Roger's answers could not, however, dispel my sadness. My life with Stephen had been built on faith – faith in his courage and genius, faith in our joint efforts and ultimately religious faith – and yet here we were in the very cradle of the world's three great religions, preaching some sort of ill-defined atheism, founded on impersonal scientific values with little reference to human experience. The blank denial of all that I believed in was bitter indeed.

I sat in miserable silence in the back of the van as the driver conducted us round all the holy places of the Old and New Testaments – the dark little cave in Bethlehem, the bleached stones of Jericho, the parched mountains of the Wilderness, the rippling green flow of the River Jordan and the Sea of Galilee. Dumbly, in my corner of the careering van, I mused that this tragic land seemed to breed conflict. Against the impenetrable landscape, the sense of conflict was all pervasive and insidious. Even Stephen and I were in danger of succumbing to it, since we rarely seemed to be of one mind.

However, while Stephen finished his lunch in a lakeside restaurant at Tiberias, I swam alone in the turquoise waters of the sea of Galilee, and for a few precious minutes I felt myself to be at peace and in harmony with the landscape and its history. The threat of war over the Golan Heights had preserved Galilee from the ravages of the tourist industry, with the result that little could have changed in two thousand years. Tiberias was possibly even less of a resort in 1988 than it had been in Roman times, and the Lake was as calm and as unspoilt as a Scottish loch.

Had it not been for the heat, Galilee seen from the chapel of the Sermon on the Mount could well have been Loch Lomond. On the final day, we all bathed in the Dead Sea. Encouraged by me and supported by his entourage and the natural buoyancy of the salt, Stephen lay back, floating in the warm water, briefly re-establishing contact with the reality of nature, long denied him, rather than its theory with which he was in ceaseless communion. There was silence all around us. The only witnesses of Stephen's peaceful bathing were the hazy purple mountains of Jordan in the distance, the blue sky and a solitary bird of prey. It was impossible to drown or even to swim. My attempt to strike out in a breaststroke collapsed in splashing and floundering, and filled my nose with stinging salt. My swimming sessions would have to be reserved for the hotel pool, up on the roof where I swam a few lengths every evening after each day's hot, dusty excursion. The novelty of swimming with the whole of Jerusalem spread out below would have been entirely agreeable, had it not been for the presence of a suspiciously spotty child in the water. I recognized chickenpox, but trusted that I was well enough protected with antibodies against that virus as a result of my experience in Spain as a student.

8

The Red Queen

The trip to the Middle East was a prelude to the demands of that summer, which proved to be even more intense than usual. Although there was no escape anywhere from the endless bickerings of the nurses, the epicentre of the rumbling discontent had moved to the Department, as that was where Stephen spent most of his day. The young assistant, Nick Phillips, wrote to me to apologize for handing in his resignation, a move forced on him because he was so often the target of the ill-humour and criticism of one of the nurses. "Bad-mouthing" was the term he used in his note. I sympathized with him, but there was little that I could do to help. The nurses were a law unto themselves, and neither Judy Fella nor I had any influence. Whatever went on in the Department was completely beyond my reach: my concern had to be focused on maintaining a civilized atmosphere in the home.

With the start of the A-level exams and the end of those particular teaching commitments for the year, I turned my attention to the plans for Robert's twenty-first birthday party. We celebrated the actual day with a large family dinner at home, and planned another evening party a week later, on the lawn with a band, a repeat of his eighteenth birthday party – though this time it was to be a jazz band, and Robert sent out invitations to a "Mad Hatter's Fancy Dress Party". Just as preparations for the party were in full swing, three weeks after returning from Jerusalem, I awoke one morning with a splitting headache and itchy spots around my waist. The only comparable headache that I could remember was the one that had preceded the chickenpox in Spain when I was a student. Lucy took her younger brother to school and I fell back into bed. I saw no one until Eve came in, as usual, at ten o'clock. Her comforting Brummie accents were clearly audible outside my bedroom door. "Where's Jane?" she asked. Elaine Mason's languid tones rang out in prompt reply, "Oh, she's lying in bed... shamming." Eve took no notice, but came directly into my room. One look at me sufficed: "You need a doctor!" she pronounced firmly and loudly enough for all to hear.

The doctor diagnosed shingles, the reactivation of the chicken-pox virus, exacerbated by stress. He prescribed bed rest and a new drug to relieve the itching. Ruefully I remembered the spotty child in the rooftop swimming pool in Jerusalem and wondered how I was to fit bed rest into the long list of all those things to be done.

Thanks to Eve – who herself was suffering having broken her arm – and Lucy and Jonathan, I managed to rest a little. Jonathan shopped and ferried Tim to and from school and cub camp, in between organizing and rehearsing his next run of concerts, while Lucy interrupted her usual whirl of social activity to bring me cups of tea, cook and ward off unwelcome intrusions. Luckily Jonathan was no longer dependent on my administrative skills in the running of his baroque orchestra, since that enterprise was now established on a firm enough financial basis for him to be able to employ an administrator who attended to every minute detail of every concert. Since the Camerata was now a going concern and was giving concerts regularly, even in the remotest parts of the land, Jonathan was frequently away from Cambridge. He worked hard, rehearsing and performing, and often drove back from distant concerts in the small hours of the morning. His irregular schedule, typical of the life of an itinerant musician, was incomprehensible to the nurses. Not having witnessed or appreciated his talent in practice, the less imaginative of them supposed that his presence in the house during the day suggested that he was a ne'er-do-well, a lounger, sponging off Stephen's munificence. His presence gave rise to much whispering.

Lucy, meanwhile, was juggling her social life and rehearsals for the Edinburgh Festival with her summer exams. As my shingles improved only slowly, she found herself obliged to squeeze yet another unforeseen commitment into her already hectic routine. I had been intending to accompany Stephen to Leningrad for a conference in the third week in June, but it was obvious to everyone, except to Stephen and his subversive minions, that I would not be well enough to travel. As he made such a superhuman effort to overcome all obstacles, it was difficult for him to see why others, above all his wife, should not be capable of similar exertion and will power, especially since all other illnesses were insignificant by comparison with motor-neuron disease. It was clear that I could no longer live up to his expectations. I found myself having to open every sentence with awkward apologies, and each attempt to apologize for being me made me even more aware of my inadequacy. The more my sense of deficiency grew, the more intense the shingles became. The neuralgia and dizziness intensified to blinding proportions, while my nerves tingled like a thousand bee stings to the very tips of my fingers whenever I tried to communicate my feelings or my ideas over any family matter, however trivial.

There was one function which I could not miss, however ill I felt: that was the launch of *A Brief History of Time*, scheduled to take place at a lunch party for family and friends at the Royal Society on 16th June, a week after the shingles struck. *A Brief History of Time* was the tangible expression of Stephen's triumph over the forces of nature, the forces of illness, paralysis and death itself. It was a triumph and an achievement which involved us both in a way that was reminiscent of those passionate struggles and heady victories in the early years of our marriage. This triumph however was not a private affair but a very public event, attended by intense publicity. The figure I cut at that feast was little more than spectral: I lacked the stamina even to maintain a coherent conversation, let alone confront the onslaught of ensuing media interest with any display of confidence.

The day after the launch I rose from my sickbed again, donned my red dressing gown and a red paper crown, applied patches of violent rouge to my cheeks and appeared at Robert's party as the Red Queen: I made a rueful joke of the fact that, like the Red Queen, I was always running to stay in the same place. Perpetually tired and listless, I battled on to the end of term through a long string of engagements and the last classes of the academic year. I had neither the energy nor the inclination to intervene again in the feverishly explosive rivalries among the nurses, which grew ever more venomous with the meteoric rise of *A Brief History of Time* to the top of the bestseller list. So long as the nurses' squabbles did not further threaten the balance of life in the home, I tried to treat them with the contempt they deserved. The minimum amount of time I was – in theory – prepared to grant them, stretched to eternity as they aired their mounting grievances at length over the telephone, oblivious to the fact that I might have better things to do, but all too ready to be mortally offended if I replaced the receiver without hearing them out. Finally I found myself obliged to ask one of the nurses, Elaine Mason, whose behaviour seemed to be at the root of the troubles, to come for a discussion, in which I intended to tell her that I could not stand aside and see the nursing rota, my home and my family torn apart. I might as well have saved my breath. With a smug complacency, she condescendingly denied all such malicious intent, calling upon her husband to vouch for her immaculate character before sailing out of the house, head held high, while I sank into a hollow of all-enveloping despair.

By comparison the crank intruders who would ring – usually from America – in the middle of the night with no consideration for the time difference, seemed like light relief. At all hours, they would demand to speak instantly to "The Professor". Like a certain Mr Justin Case, they had all, to a man, solved the riddle of the universe, and were impatient to tell the Professor where his calculations had gone wrong. Mr Justin Case had to vie for the phone line at 3 a.m. with a Mr Isaac Newton, who was a regular caller from Japan. Lucy answered one call from a man who asked her to marry him. "Fair Lucy," he pleaded, "will you marry me? But read my thesis to your father first!" Another desperate caller from Florida insisted on speaking to Stephen because he was sure that the world was going to blow up in half an hour. "Sorry," we said, "he's away." "Well, then," came the forlorn reply, "It's the end of the world, and there's nothing I can do to save it!" Some actually turned up at the front door and lay in wait for Stephen there, not always to their own best advantage however. One, his upper half clad only in a string vest, was unprepared for the front door opening outwards. As the door was flung wide for Stephen to emerge at full pelt in his chariot, the poor man was thrown into a rose bush. His string vest caught on the thorns, and Stephen was well away by the time he extricated himself. There was also the Hollywood film star, who wanted to test out her own half-baked mystic theory of the universe; the fraudulent journalists, who promised to make donations to charity in payment for the interviews we granted them but never paid up; and the would-be unauthorized biographers, who were obviously out to make a quick buck at our expense. It was with impatience that I looked forward to the summer holiday, when we were to lay the ghost of the Geneva episode with a return to that city. Anywhere had to be better than Cambridge.

Hollywood stars and domestic difficulties notwithstanding, when we managed to communicate, Stephen and I gave some thought to the mundane matter of how to spend the Wolf Prize money. That and the anticipated proceeds from *A Brief History*, together with the modest savings that I had made over the years, amounted to enough to allow us to think of buying a second home. Stephen was interested in buying a flat in Cambridge as an investment, but I cherished the dream of a country cottage, somewhere away from all the razzmatazz, tensions and persistent invasions of our privacy. A cottage on the north Norfolk coast would have been my ideal, but that was beyond our means. A place in the country could give us longed-for peace and anonymity, the time and the quietude for Stephen to think and for the children to revise for exams, while I would be mistress of my own establishment, both house and garden.

It was not until we came across an eccentric Englishman – as Jonathan, Tim and I ambled through northern France on the way south to meet Stephen in Geneva that August – that the thought of buying a property in France began to cross my mind as a viable proposition. This gentleman, who had a minimal command of Franglais, was cheerfully setting himself up in business, buying and renovating French country properties and selling them to the British at prices which were extraordinarily cheap by comparison with those at home. As he unfolded his plans to a rapt audience of mystified French and fascinated English bystanders in a wayside restaurant, the exciting truth began to dawn that this was a possible outlet for our resources. We would enjoy all the advantages of a country cottage, abroad but less distant than Wales, and we and our children would be true Europeans, with a foothold in Europe, and hopefully bilingual into the bargain.

With all the hurly-burly of the start of the new academic year just after returning to England, I let the idea drop, and it passed into the category of a pipe dream. Our holiday with Stephen in Geneva had been a heartening success from the moment we met him at the airport, and after that harmoniously restorative spell, Jonathan, Tim and I had spent ten days camping in the south of France. We came back to Cambridge, refreshed and ready to take up the reins, altogether unaware of the new chaos that awaited us. First of all, Lucy's application to the University of Oxford – to her father's and paternal grandfather's old college, University College – had to be withdrawn and hastily resubmitted. The unexpected success of the Cambridge Youth Theatre's visit to the Edinburgh Festival had made it impossible for her to sit the entrance exams, so she would have to rely on an interview and her A-level results instead. Secondly, the tenant in the letting house belonging to Robert and his grandmother was threatening legal action, because in my absence in France Stephen had thought to resolve a problem that had arisen by ordering her to leave. Thirdly, the administrator of the Cambridge Baroque Camerata was finding the workload too great and wanted to resign. Fourthly, and most untypically for the discreetly private world of a scientific institution, the Department had turned into such a cauldron of intrigue that Judy, incapable of doing her job properly because of the indiscipline among the nurses, was brought to the point of tendering her resignation. This was a sad turn of events for those of us who had witnessed and appreciated her devotion to Stephen over a span of almost fifteen years.

I was afraid that the volcanic eruptions in the Department might overflow and engulf the house at the worst possible time – when Lucy was under greatest pressure. She was now studying for her A-levels and for Oxford entrance at the same time as rehearsing for yet another run of *The Heart of a Dog*, because the Youth Theatre's performance at the Edinburgh Fringe had been awarded one of the top prizes in the Festival, the Independent award for the best Fringe performance, which entitled them to a two-week run on a London stage. Unfortunately the London performances were scheduled to take place just before the crucial Oxford entrance interviews, so Lucy would have to go down to London to perform every day after school and then return to school as usual the next morning. As her resilience would be tested to the limits, it was essential for her to be able to count on a quiet, stable background at home. This simple piece of common sense did not impinge at all on the majority of the people who regularly came in and out of the house.

A rearguard action to keep the nurses' battles at bay was simply not enough to maintain calm at home. From being a well-known scientific figure in Britain and America, Stephen had suddenly achieved worldwide fame: he had become a cult figure with the success of the book. We had the first taste of this in October 1988, when Tim and I accompanied him to Barcelona for the publication of the Spanish edition of *A Brief History of Time*. He was recognized everywhere, attracting crowds who stopped to applaud him in the street. I was called upon to translate for journalists in press conferences and television interviews and, in my own right, was asked to give interviews for women's magazines. There was a satisfaction in working in tandem with Stephen again as his intellectual partner. However, the demand for interviews was reaching fever pitch, not only in Spain but everywhere, at home and abroad. It was easier to cope with the publicity abroad, because we were there expressly to sell the book, and that Mephistophelean pact required us to make ourselves available to the media. At home, where we had our daily routine to accomplish in quiet anonymity, the intrusions of the press became an irksome dislocation of family life. That television equipment had become a regular feature of Stephen's office, where nurses vied with each other to pose for the cameras, was not a problem. The problem arose when the journalists asked for an interview or pictures at home as well. This I was extremely loath to grant, and the children objected vociferously. It was bad enough having nurses in the house all the time. with television cameras and reporters as well there would be no privacy for anyone anywhere. My arguments cut no ice. They were represented as yet further evidence of my disloyalty to the man of genius. It was obvious that with my dependence on Jonathan and my refusal to train to be a nurse, I was already condemned. My reluctance to regale the press with stories of life with that genius within the walls of my home was just one more admission of my perfidy.

On 7th November, Lucy's two-week run in London began at the Half Moon Theatre on the Mile End road. She came out of school at 4 p.m., with just half an hour to spare before catching the coach. The play demanded huge reserves of energy and concentration of its young cast, who changed roles with every scene, sometimes appearing in individual parts, sometimes in the chorus. She would arrive home after midnight, and the next morning, by nine o'clock, would have to be back in school for a full day's work. Her schedule was punishing, but the general stress was eased somewhat by Stephen's decision to go off to California with his retinue for a whole month the day after the first night. Thereafter the quality of life improved dramatically at home, and we all heaved a long sigh of relief as we withdrew into comparative peace and seclusion.

With unaccustomed self-indulgence, I was sitting idly thumbing through the Sunday paper the next weekend when an article on the availability of property in France caught my eye. Beneath it there was a modest advertisement for an English agency, offering to search for suitable houses in the French countryside for its customers. I followed the telephone number up, and within a few days photocopies started arriving in the post from northern France. The photographs looked as if they had been taken in thick fog or a snowstorm, and the terminology used often sent me searching for the dictionary, but the prices were remarkably low. None of them were more than about half the price of a two-bedroom Victorian terraced house in southern England, and, although it was impossible to tell what state the properties were in, they were patently much more substantial in terms of ground area. Clearly further investigation was called for, which was how Tim, Jonathan and I came to be sailing to France one Saturday in mid-November.

9

Prospecting for Paradise

France in November was bleak and dreary indeed, and bitingly cold and dark. But at seven o'clock in the evening, Arras, our destination, was still brimming with life and activity as the shops disgorged their last customers out into the brightly lit streets. They were full of enticing displays of Christmas delicacies and toys, which promptly made a hole in our pockets. Moreover, much to our surprise, signs everywhere announced that *Beaujolais Nouveau* had arrived! The weekend began to assume a different perspective, especially after an excellent meal in the bar of our pension, where the ruby-red new arrival met with general critical acclaim. If all else failed, the weekend held the promise of dealing with most of the Christmas shopping and a certain amount of pleasure in liquid form as well.

The next day, the heavy sleet was hard and unrelenting, and although I could summon no interest whatsoever in quaint little houses dotted about the landscape, a pleasant, helpful agent and his assistant were waiting, prepared to give up the best part of their Sunday to escorting us round what they considered to be the most suitable properties on their books. What a Sunday that was, and what sights we saw as we huddled in the back of the agent's car! The rain beat down, now and then giving way to driving snow. When finally the sleet and snow had exhausted themselves, a dark, penetrating mist set in while we looked at tumbledown houses with leaking roofs, cardboard bungalows, and a house where the passage between the kitchen and the dining room was in fact the bathroom. We were looking for an old house with character, but basically in good condition, possibly with some opportunities for renovation, and with plenty of ground floor accommodation for the elderly and infirm members of the family, especially for Stephen. Nice views were desirable, and the distance from the main road was a prime consideration. Nothing we had seen that first day even approached our requirements.

As it happened, the next day dawned bright and clear and the countryside sparkled under a fine layer of crisp, fresh snow. On our way back to Boulogne we stopped at a small market town to call on just one more agent, Mme Maillet. She led the way out of town in the direction of the coast. The road climbed out of the hollow in which the town nestled, up onto the windswept reaches of an extensive plateau – in fact, a broad ridge between two river valleys. We passed a small race track on the right and sped through a tiny village. There was little sign of habitation, only the occasional church spire, water tower or ruined windmill. Then, suddenly, Mme Maillet turned right – we followed, and there it was, a kilometre or so away from the main road, long and low, whitewashed and red-tiled. "That's our house, Mum," said Tim, then aged nine. And so it was, unmistakably beckoning us across the fields, an old friend from a past existence, instantly recognizable, immediately appealing. "*Un vrai coup de foudre*", the French would say – love at first sight. Nor were we disappointed when we turned into the driveway of the Moulin – for that was what it was, an old mill house, its windmill long since destroyed. The low, smiling façade we had seen from the road proved to be but one of the three sides of the house, which embraced a courtyard, rather in the style of a Roman villa, the sort of house that Stephen and I had dreamt of in the golden days of our engagement. The aspect inside the courtyard was as delightful and welcoming as the exterior had been from the road. The living rooms, including the kitchen, all looked onto the yard or out to the garden and pasture at the back; they were wild and unkempt, at the mercy of a flock of hostile geese, except for a corner of traditional vegetable garden.

The sleeping quarters in the long side of the building which had first caught our eye and our imagination from the road were ideally suited to Stephen's needs, being on the ground floor, and the accommodation could be considerably expanded by completing the conversion of the vast, light, airy attic, which ran the whole length of that wing of the house. It was almost too good to be true. As far as we could tell, the house fulfilled every requirement; it was within an hour's drive of the coast, no further away from Cambridge than parts of the West country, and certainly closer than Wales. It enjoyed lovely views sweeping across fields to woods and it was well away from the main road although the access was easy. It was old and bursting with character but, apparently, in reasonably good condition. There was obvious potential for further improvements and, most significantly, the price left a sufficient margin for any renovations.

All the way home my mind was fixed on the Moulin, programming in the impressions, the excitement, the ideas. Once back in England, I hastened to write it all down and, with pen, paper and ruler, to make rough sketches of the property and plans for its adaptation to our needs, and fax them all to Stephen in southern California. Stephen replied positively. It was much less complicated to communicate with him by fax across the Atlantic than face to face, and I interpreted his terse comment "sounds good" as approval. Then the wheels for the purchase of the Moulin were set in motion at remarkable speed. Equally quickly I had to learn the language and the procedures for house purchase in France which, from the outset, proved to be very different at every stage from the English equivalents. I had to get to grips with French law and legal terminology, the French banking system, French building terms, insurance French-style, local taxation and the eccentricities of the public utilities. Sterling was buoyant against the franc at the time, so I had the consolation of benefiting from a favourable exchange rate. The comforting thought was that the same amount of money could not have bought us anything worth having in England. Deep down inside me I felt an assurance and a certainty that I had not known in years. This project, based on my input, my knowledge of French, would be my contribution to family life – although, of course, it would be jointly financed. So many of our excursions in the past had had a single objective, the pursuit of science. This project would combine all our interests and talents – languages, love of France and the French way of life, relaxation, gardening and music as well – with that scientific pursuit. The more I looked at my plans and drawings, the more I realized that the Moulin had an even greater potential than I had at first deemed possible. There was an old barn attached to the house which was ripe for conversion into accommodation upstairs, with potential for a conference room downstairs, permitting Stephen to have his own summer school, to which he could invite his scientific colleagues and their families. I had visions of establishing our own version of the Les Houches summer school in the undulating countryside of northern France, and it was my hope that there we would once again find the unity and the harmony which we had achieved before the events of 1985, and which since then had eluded us in England.

10

A Homecoming

My plans for the Moulin were put on hold at the beginning of 1989 because I was busy proofreading the French edition of *A Brief History of Time*. It proved not simply to be a question of checking the language, but of delving much deeper. The English edition opened with an introduction by the American scientist Carl Sagan; I was perplexed to find that this had not been translated into French and that, unknown to Stephen, Flammarion, the French publisher, had commissioned an introduction from a French physicist to replace it. I found the disparaging tone of certain remarks in the French introduction extraordinary, and I took it upon myself to delete them. The launch of *Une Brève Histoire du Temps* was scheduled for the beginning of March in Paris and would coincide neatly with the completion of the house purchase. The weeks before the launch brought a procession of French journalists and television cameras to Cambridge, while the completion of the conveyancing process focused my attention more and more on the other side of the Channel. My horizons were expanding, no longer constricted by the four walls of the home in England.

The intricacies of the French legal system, the mechanisms for setting up a bank account, the details of the insurance contract – all these I attacked with enthusiasm, helped by the delightfully idiosyncratic characters with whom I was coming into contact in the quietly rural Ternois region of northern France. The plans for renovation were already in the pipeline when, *en route* for Paris, I signed the house purchase agreement at a formal ceremony on 1st March, itself a considerable achievement, since all parties to the agreement had to be present and Stephen had decided that he could not spare the time to attend. He had after all only just returned from a trip to New York on Concorde. When news of the house in France began to percolate through to friends and relations in England, I was baffled by some of the reactions. "Stephen doesn't like the country," his mother announced adamantly in his hearing, as if intent on predisposing him against the Moulin. Had she forgotten Llandogo? Certainly Stephen's mistrust of the country might be justified after that experience. But to condemn the Moulin, which had been chosen so carefully and was being prepared so meticulously for his enjoyment, seemed very unfair. The image of Stephen that was being cultivated by his relations, and some of his nurses, was that of a playboy who lived for the bright lights of the city and who found the rural life boring. This image of him conflicted with my own perceptions of his character, and the aspersions cast on my venture were already undermining his interest in it.

The few days in Paris after the purchase of the house certainly intensified Stephen's love of the bright lights. He was fêted and pursued wherever he went, the darling of the media and the prized possession of the publisher. As I loved Paris too, it was no hardship for me to enjoy the bright lights as well. We dined at La Coupole; we ate in the restaurant on the Eiffel Tower, where Stephen was invited to add his name to the signatures of the rich and famous in the visitors' book; we visited the newly opened Musée d'Orsay and we entertained friends and Stephen's French relations, including his cousin Mimi, to a dinner in celebration of the launch. Photographers followed us everywhere, and journalists clamoured for interviews, for which either I or a French colleague of Stephen's did the interpreting. I was flattered to be asked for an interview by a leading radio journalist, Jean-Pierre Elkabbach, at the radio station Europe 1. When I arrived, my interviewer was involved in a long and heated discussion with Jean Le Pen, the nationalist leader. Jean-Pierre Elkabbach quickly recovered his composure and treated me with Gallic charm and deference. The interview was broadcast all over France, and as a result we and our circumstances were introduced to our new neighbours in our village in the north before we had taken up residence.

Within three weeks I was setting out for France again: this time with Tim and Lucy in a car laden to the roof with packaged cupboard and bookshelf kits, linen, crockery, cutlery, utensils and food. As if in our honour, we found that a new motorway had just been opened, cutting twenty minutes or so from the journey from Calais, so when we arrived, earlier than expected, at the Moulin, we found the house full of workmen, putting the finishing touches to the Herculean effort of making suitable arrangements for Stephen – and of converting the attic to bed-rooms, which they had completed in seventeen days. Their beaming pleasure in our delight was obvious as we toured the house that they had so swiftly transformed.

Stephen had recently bought a Volkswagen van which had been fitted with a ramp and fixtures to hold the wheelchair steadily in place. It also proved invaluable in transporting large items of furniture. Late that evening, Jonathan arrived at the wheel of the van, which was packed with yet more furniture and luggage. The next day he drove to the airport at Le Touquet – so fashionable with the British in its heyday – to meet Stephen, Robert and the entourage of two reliable and trusted nurses. The advances and royalties coming in from the several editions of *A Brief History of Time* permitted Stephen the rare luxury of chartering a small aeroplane from Cambridge airport to bring him to France by the simplest and most comfortable means possible. The genial Australian pilot had opened up spaces in the wing to store suitcases and bits of the wheelchair, and he invited one of the passengers, on this occasion Robert, to sit beside him in the cockpit of his tiny six-seater aircraft.

The weather was so kind during the Easter holiday that northern France acquired a deceptively Mediterranean aspect. The long white walls and low red roofs of the house and out-buildings glowed in the bright sun against an azure sky, while clouds of white blossom fluttered to earth like silken snowflakes in the meadow and the shrubbery. Even Stephen was impressed, though he complained that the countryside was as flat as Cambridgeshire. This was not actually true, as Robert was to discover when he set off on a bicycle ride. The house stood on top of a plateau, which was divided by many a meandering river valley with villages, water mills, ruined châteaux, abbayes, poplar trees and trout streams. Stephen appeared to like it – though, of course, he would never allow himself to admit it. Whatever his opinions about country life and quaint old houses, he certainly enjoyed the social scene. He and the children went out to buy pink champagne for the house-warming party, which we gave for all our neighbours and for all the people who had helped me with the purchase or worked on the house. Stephen was the willing centre of attraction: he demonstrated his computer and its ability to speak a garbled, Americanized version of the French language to everyone's amusement, and graciously acknowledged the abundant congratulations showered on him on the success of his book. The children had quickly made new friends, and even Tim was communicating effectively in French with a few well-chosen words and gestures, like *"football?"* or *"jouer?"*. He did however object to being kissed on both cheeks at every encounter, until Robert remarked to his mystification that in a few years' time he would be only too pleased to be kissed on both cheeks by the girls. As for me, in France I could be French, spontaneous and natural and true to myself, neither having to justify my actions nor apologize for my existence.

11

The Price of Fame

The shoots of my budding self-esteem, cultivated in the soil of French society, were to be quickly crushed back in England. Optimistic as ever, I did not anticipate that the arrival in late April of a Hollywood film producer would signal the opening shots in the next onslaught on our home life. He seemed friendly enough, inspiring my confidence with stories of his young family, and conveying a genuine sense of purpose in his plan to make a film of *A Brief History of Time*. His would be a serious, informative film of the book, and he liked my idea that it should take the form of a journey in time and the universe through the eyes of a child. The idea was appealing. So long as the film remained strictly scientific and could be imaginatively done, using the innovative technology of graphics, his plans augured well.

Hot on his heels came an American film crew, directed by a lively woman who also won my confidence with her sympathetic approach. It had become the accepted routine that film crews would first wreak havoc in the Department before turning their attention to our home for a reassuring touch of cosiness in the otherwise enigmatic portrait of the disabled genius. On initial acquaintance the directors would all appear to be pleasant, considerate, ordinary people, effusively promising that any disturbance would be kept to an absolute minimum. Their fly-on-the-wall approach would take no time at all and would require only a few shots, causing no disruption to our normal activities. Cameras, cables, arc lights and microphones would all remain at a discreet distance; the furniture would not be moved; we could dress informally and go about our daily business as usual.

The reality bore no relation to these promises. Without exception, in the short interim between pleasantries and filming, the procedures would – before our shocked eyes – become devastatingly intrusive. Disregarding the assurances they had given, all the producers and directors would plead shortage of time or scarcity of funds in mitigation of their sudden change of approach as soon as the cameras started rolling. Items of furniture would be shoved around, often damaged, never to be returned to their original positions; blinding arc lamps and glaring reflective screens on cold metal supports would supplant well-worn familiar clutter, obscuring the furniture and the books and newspapers; lengths of cable would snake hazardously across the floors in and out of every room; microphones would be hung from any available hook or shelf. We strangers in the harshly transformed landscape of our unrecognizable tubular steel home would be typecast in our parts: the principle (though untrained) actors in the drama, expected to react with natural grace and aplomb for the eye of the camera, that twentieth-century sacred object of worship. As I watched helplessly and participated reluctantly, a despairing voice inside me protested. Surely, it complained, there had to be a middle way between this insatiable nosiness and the starkly impersonal approach of the BBC Horizon film some years before. But an imaginative middle way would demand both more time and more money than any of the directors had at their disposal as they rushed frenziedly from one project to the next.

For want of any outlet, my silent rebellion at this extra burden rumbled beneath the surface. Despite the complaints of the children, especially of Lucy, for whom the glare of publicity and the intrusion of the cameras were most distracting as her exams approached, I was in no position to bar the cameras from the house for fear of further antagonizing Stephen, who positively relished the publicity. He had just returned from yet another trip to America, but the respite did not arm me with sufficient strength to combat the depredations of the film crew at what was always for me the worst season of the year, when tree pollens settled like pepper dust in my sinuses. The American director, who at first sight had appeared so friendly and likeable, rapidly became assertive, indeed embarrassingly so, when her cameras trailed us into town to film my usual routine of Saturday-morning shopping. It was unusual for me to be accompanied in this weekly chore by Stephen and his retinue, even more so that we should all have a fully fledged film crew trailing our steps. There was no possibility of taking evasive action. It might not have been so bad if they had actually lent a hand with the shopping instead of following us like shadows, poking their cameras and microphones into my face as I loaded the shopping trolley to the rim and dragged its heavy weight home behind me.

The primary function of this film was supposed to be a portrait of Stephen for an American television news channel; subsequently it was to serve the dual purpose of providing a snippet of biographical background for the other scientific documentary based on *A Brief History of Time*. Only the thought that this spate of filming would be serving both purposes made that horrible weekend bearable. By the time that an urbane interviewer-journalist and his wife arrived for drinks that Saturday evening, I was in no mood to welcome any more film or television personalities or technicians into the house. Scarcely had I introduced myself to them than the journalist's wife casually asked, just as I was handing her a drink, "Do you have a religion?" Her enquiry was delivered with an unabashed coolness which froze my frayed nerves. I turned on my vapid interrogator, more or less telling her to mind her own business, but then, instantly overcome with remorse, I heard myself foolishly inviting the entire team to dinner in compensation for my rudeness.

Alone, late at night, I lay in bed aware that a trap was closing over me. The stress of publicity was forcing me to behave in ways that were uncharacteristic and untrue to myself, yet there was no clear way out. It was obvious that, in the eyes of the media, I had become an appendage, a peep show – relevant to Stephen's survival and his success only because in the distant past I had married him, made a home for him and produced his three children. Nowadays I was there to appease the media's desire for comforting personal detail while inwardly my spirit rebelled both at the indignity and at my own helplessness.

Ten days after that bout of filming had come to an end, Stephen gave the Schrödinger lecture in a hot, stuffy lecture theatre, packed to capacity, at Imperial College, London. Schrödinger's equation, the fundamental equation for the science of quantum mechanics which he developed in 1926, bears the same relation to the mechanics of the atom as Newton's laws of motion bear to the movement of the planets. Stephen's lecture about imaginary time was as lucid as it could be, and afterwards he was fêted and pursued by representatives from IBM, the firm that had sponsored the lecture, who hankered for a photograph with him, presumably as one of the perks of their job. I stood diffidently to one side, thinking that I was the only non-scientist present, until I was introduced to Schrödinger's daughter, whom I had encountered once before at a similar occasion in Dublin in 1983.

She was quiet and unassuming, informing me for the second time that she was Schrödinger's daughter by someone other than his wife, but had later been adopted by Mrs Schrödinger. I was sorry for her; she was uncomfortably pursued by her father's legacy – as much embarrassed perhaps by his reputation as a womanizer as she was haunted by his scientific fame – and walked in his shadow. I feared for my children – hers was not a fate that I wanted for them.

The following Saturday, before setting off into town to sell flags for the National Schizophrenia Foundation, I opened Stephen's mail for him as usual. It contained a letter from the Prime Minister Mrs Thatcher in which she proposed recommending his name to the Queen as a Companion of Honour in the forthcoming Birthday Honours' List. The proposal sent us running for the encyclopedia. It revealed that this singular honour was one of the highest in the land, ranking above a knighthood and discreetly conveyed, without title, simply by the letters placed after the name. As Stephen was on the point of leaving for America, it fell to me to accept on his behalf.

Since Stephen had already been nominated for an Honorary Doctorate of Science at the University of Cambridge, the summer promised to mark the apogee of his career – though how that, with its inevitable flood of media interest, was to be reconciled with Lucy's A-levels and Robert's Finals, let alone stability and harmony, was not at all obvious. Our priorities were diverging drastically. Mine was the preservation of the sanctity of the home and the privacy of our family life – or such tatters of it as remained after the nurses had done their worst to tear it apart and after the media had plundered every corner of it. Stephen was, for all his fame, but one member of a family where no one person had the right to be more important than any other. Although his medical condition demanded more attention for him than for anyone else, the home had still to cater fairly for the needs of all its occupants, adults and children alike. The children must never have cause to resent the circumstances into which they had been born.

Stephen, for his part, delighted in the publicity. He revelled in his relationship with the media, who had made his name a household word all over the world. His fame, in the face of a sceptical and sometimes hostile society, represented the triumph not only of his mind over the secrets of the universe, but also of his body over death and disability. For him any publicity was good publicity and could always be justified by claiming that it would increase the sales of the book. A case of champagne arrived from Bantam Press later that summer in celebration of *A Brief History of Time*'s fifty-second week on the best-seller list. In the fifty-third week, it shot back to its commanding position at number one. It seemed that he had succeeded in reconciling two extremes in the task he had set himself: in his description of his branch of science, the most fundamental and the most elusive of all the sciences, he had managed to placate the scientific intelligentsia and attract the popular reader.

Although there was no denying that the book was a phenomenal success, I tried to keep the correspondence relating to the handsome royalties confidential. If our sudden flush of wealth were to become generally advertised, I knew that I risked losing many of my real friends with whom in the past I had scraped and saved to make ends meet, and I was also well aware that any publicity given to our enhanced financial status would attract exactly the sort of people with whom I did not want to associate. In the past, while Stephen's mind was focused on weightier matters, I had handled our financial affairs, always with an anxious eye on that uncertain future when Stephen might be too ill to work and the money might run out. I had run the family budget prudently and had accumulated sufficient savings to pay Lucy's school fees and to provide a buffer against the rainy day, which for us could run to months and years. Since the signing of the contract for *A Brief History* in 1985, I had also dealt with the correspondence on that subject with the agent in New York. Unaccountably, the arrangement whereby I handled the royalties was suddenly overturned behind my back. It was from the agent in New York that I learnt of this change: he told me that he had been instructed to send all correspondence relating to the book to Stephen in the Department and no longer to me at home. I had no idea what had provoked this change, and Stephen gave no explanation. It was as if, after many years of mutual trust, my ability to handle financial affairs efficiently and with discretion was being called into question. In the resulting confusion, even the most casual helpers were allowed to open and read private correspondence; it was spread out on desks and tables, left strewn around for all to see, as if in black-and-white confirmation of the undisputed supremacy of genius.

Stephen's second trip to America that spring allowed us all a breathing space from impossible tensions in which to return to those other elements of a more regular lifestyle, the teaching, the studying, the literature and the music, and to settle into simpler, more relaxed habits without the vain and wearisome distractions of fame, publicity and contentious nurses. Tim fulfilled one of his passions when we took off for a promised weekend to Legoland in Denmark, and later in May we returned to France for half-term.

The Moulin, welcoming us in its summer garb for the first time, opened its box of delights in a new guise. Further renovations had been completed, a bathroom had been added for Stephen's sole use, work on the barn had been started, and the garden was beginning to take shape. My dream of an English country garden was being realized in France so satisfactorily that even Claude, my valiant workman, confessed that he had begun to plant flowers in his own garden where previously he had grown only vegetables. Even more significantly, the Moulin opened the door to another world, the world of a past era, where the impossible whirlwind of our Cambridge lives slowed to a leisurely pace under the influence of the land and the sky, and where the only sound was the song of the lark, soaring high into the blue above the green cornfield in the morning sun. The place had already engraved itself on my heart. Its clean air and broad patchwork of fields fading to a distant grey horizon, its sleepy shutters and its aroma of newly chopped logs and old wood, its backdrop of tall conifers and shrubs shimmering in the sun, all sang of unaccustomed peace, solitude and salvation. There I could be alone, undisturbed by nurses, by the press, by cameras, by the clamour of incessant demands. I could dig my garden. I could immerse myself in books without fear of interruption and I could learn and listen to music without fear of criticism at such wasteful self-indulgence. There I could find my true centre, in close touch with nature, old-fashioned, perhaps, contemplative certainly, a daydreamer whose favourite occupation was gazing out at the wide expanse of the western sky each evening, standing spellbound at the everchanging magnificence of the setting sun as it dropped behind the silhouetted line of trees across the fields.

In those periods of reflection while I dug the garden, sowed seeds and planted rose bushes, I identified with the hero of one of the set texts that I had been teaching for the French syllabus in the past year. Candide, Voltaire's young hero, whose optimism in the "best of all worlds" – as taught by the philosopher Dr Pangloss – is sadly betrayed by experience, finally turns his back on the world and takes refuge in his garden. "*Il faut cultiver notre jardin...*" is his ultimate, pessimistic, personal solution to the malfunction of society. The clash of inexorable but often zany logic with searing, unresolved emotional problems lay like a corrosive material at the root of our existence in Cambridge, and that root was succumbing to the insidious effect of the invasive poison of fame and fortune. In France the soil was fresh and fertile, and there the garden was full of the promise of a future, a cyclical foreseeable future, decreed by the immutable laws of nature.

12

In the summer of 1989 all attention was concentrated on Stephen's multiple triumphs and the avalanche of media interest in them. The date for the conferral of the Honorary Doctorate by the Chancellor, the Duke of Edinburgh, was set for Thursday 15th June while, known only to ourselves, the royal honour from Buckingham Palace was to be confirmed the next day and published in the media on Saturday 17th. By a fortunate coincidence, this was also the date of a concert to be performed in Stephen's honour by Jonathan and the Camerata, two days after the honorary degree ceremony, also in the Senate House. Although in 1987 the Newton celebrations and concert had provided an attractive lure for commercial sponsors to support the Camerata, the sponsors themselves had become extremely vulnerable to the harsh vicissitudes of life in Thatcherite Britain. The ink was barely dry on the signatures to a generous sponsorship deal when the sponsoring business, a very gentlemanly British firm, was gobbled up by an American computer corporation that had no compunction in declaring that they were in business to make money, not to support the arts, music or any other charitable organization. They promptly pulled out of the sponsorship deal. This left Jonathan, whose schedule of contracted concerts for two years hence was based on the calculations of the sponsorship deal, potentially with a huge debt when he himself at the best of times earned little more than a subsistence income from music. At that most inauspicious moment for Jonathan and the Camerata, Stephen's fame and success offered the hope of salvation. A concert in Stephen's honour could be counted on to attract a large audience of people who would come to applaud Stephen as well as to listen to the music. It might also attract new sponsors for whom the high scientific profile would be attractive. Stephen would be fêted with his favourite pieces of baroque music and a retiring collection could be divided among the charities we all supported. This piece of planning augured well for everybody, and Stephen gave it his approval – along with his approval of the Prime Minister's letter, before he left for America in May.

The challenge of concert planning, forever flying in the face of sound economic sense, had previously added a certain spice and bravura to my other various dilettante occupations. That concert would have been no exception, had it not been for the perpetual incursions of the media. The journalists who came to interview me were a mixed bunch: some were reasonably pleasant, some were clinical, others were demanding. It was impossible to tell what sort of gloss they would put on an interview in advance. French journalists, Spanish journalists, representatives of all nations, came in an endless stream, all wanting a different slant on the science and on the background. They brought their superficial interviewing techniques to the situation; in turn, I developed my own techniques for dealing with them by deciding in advance how much information I was prepared to part with. I saw no reason why I should confide all the intimate complexities of my life to a journalist, a stranger whose interest in me was governed by the imperative to sell more newspapers. If I wanted to confess, I would turn to a priest, if I needed psychiatric treatment I would turn to a doctor, and if I had a story to tell I might one day write it myself, though regard for privacy – my own and other people's – might well outweigh the desire to tell that story. If, therefore, the questions posed by journalists overstepped my boundaries, I would turn the interview into a conversation, asking for their opinions and reactions rather than telling them my own. Inevitably I became the target of disparaging remarks. For example, one journalist reported that I had "cared for Stephen for just a couple of years after our marriage". My old Headmistress and stalwart supporter, Miss Gent, wrote to the editor of that newspaper, the *Times*, to rectify the mistake. She was shocked at his arrogant reply: far from offering any redress or apology, he asserted that he knew better than she did and he was confident that the facts in the article were correct. Our loyal friend George Hill, the husband of my school friend Caroline, ever anxious to protect us from the prying eyes of the gutter press, said that he knew about the misrepresentations in the *Times*, because he had peered over the journalist's shoulder when he was writing the piece. However, George had been so relieved to find no mention of Jonathan's part in our household that he had thought it better to let the article stand as it was rather than reveal Jonathan's close association with us.

If however, as once I did when being interviewed for the *Guardian*, I allowed myself to show any dissatisfaction with the trite old clichés about the rewards of living with a genius – those oft-repeated truisms which dwelt on fame and fortune as if illness and disability were not fundamental factors in our lives – I would be accused of disloyalty to Stephen. But as I saw it, if I continued to perpetuate the myth of cheerful self-sufficiency without even mentioning the hardships, I would be cheating the many disabled people and their families, who were probably suffering all the heartache, the anxieties, the privations, the stresses and strains that we ourselves had undergone in earlier years. It would be all too easy for an uncaring society to point accusingly at other disabled people and declare, "If Professor Hawking can do it, why can't you?" The hard-pressed carers might be pressurized into performing even more impossible tasks because of the unrealistic image of our way of life presented through the media. I could no longer truthfully offer the carefree, smiling façade, giving the erroneous impression that our lives were contented and easy, marred only by a little local inconvenience. For that *Guardian* interview my assessment was candid and truthful: I noted the triumphs but did not gloss over the difficulties. I voiced our criticisms of the National Health Service and emphasized the fact that Stephen's success, even in procuring funds to pay for his nursing, had been due entirely to our own efforts. I described how we fluctuated between the glittering peaks of brilliant success and the black sloughs of critical illness and despair, with very little level ground in between.

Such simple and fairly obvious truths proved most unpalatable to those people who had come to believe in Stephen's immortality and infallibility, and had conveniently detached themselves from the reality of his condition, namely his family and certain of his nurses. My comments were interpreted as treason where no hint of criticism could ever be countenanced. Such reactions only served to increase my sense of isolation. Were the people around me blind or mad, or was I losing my mind? Were those people living in a parallel universe where the roles were reversed and where, as they seemed to suggest, it was I who was infirm? Further accusations of disloyalty were flung thick and fast on the showing of a BBC film made that summer. In it I repeated the misgivings voiced in the two newspaper interviews, in a vain attempt to restore a sensible balance both to the depiction of our way of life and to the representation of Stephen's scientific theories as the basis for a new religion. My performance before the cameras, which rolled throughout the period of the honours and celebrations and afterwards, was not enhanced by a streaming cold and a raging sore throat – just a couple of the recurring infections and ailments which followed each other in quick succession from beginning to end of that decade. The heavy cold lent my interview and voice-overs a jaundiced tinge, deadening any humour and betraying an unintentional touch of bitterness.

Sadness there certainly was in my voice: it was the unfortunate outward manifestation of a profound inner sense of desolation and foreboding. Cassandra herself could not have forecast more accurately, or with greater dread, the catastrophe that I knew was looming over us all. Even Nikki Stockley, the young television producer, remarked how Elaine Mason had disrupted the filming process when she had tried to film in the Department. In public and at home, she was busily usurping my place at every opportunity, sometimes aping me, sometimes undermining me, always flaunting her influence over Stephen. She had engineered an unassailable stranglehold over the nursing rota, and had so successfully ingratiated herself that all remonstrance was useless: any comments would be reported back to Stephen, and I would be castigated for my interference. My appeals to the secretary of the Royal College of Nursing for help in enforcing the code of nursing conduct met with a flat refusal to become involved unless I could produce photographic evidence of malpractice. Such was the background of physical chaos and emotional torment against which the tapestry of the traditional honorary-degree ceremony unfolded, briefly transporting us into a fantasy realm of theatrical grandeur and champagne celebrations where all the froth of new clothes, archaic ritual, fixed smiles, polite chatter and endless handshakes spread like an insubstantial white layer over the smouldering reality beneath.

In a modest bid to ensure some privacy, Lucy had optimistically marked the calendar from 8th June as follows: *Lucy starts A levels and becomes a complete recluse(!).* The day of Stephen's Honorary Doctorate, 15th June, she noted as, *L does 2 A levels.* Although she missed the accompanying festivities on account of the exams, there was little hope of fulfilling her reclusive intentions, so it was hardly surprising that on 22nd June an impassioned appeal appeared in brackets: (*Give me the sympathy I deserve!*). In the circumstances, it was a credit to her that she managed to do her exams at all, let alone succeed in them.

15th June, the day of the two most intensive A-level papers was bright, hot and sunny – which was not of much help to Lucy. For Stephen's Honorary Degree ceremony, however, the weather was ideal. Never had the discrepancy between the best interests of different members of the family been more marked. Lucy left early for school in an advanced state of nerves, while the rest of us looked forward to a day of pomp and rejoicing, a true holiday from stress and dissenting voices. We left the house at 10 a.m. and strolled down the road to the Backs. The lawns and meadows by the river could not have looked more pastoral and peaceful: every blade of emerald grass and every leaf – green, gold or bronze – rippled in the bright morning sun, while the river gleamed like a silvery mirror, reflecting the infinite brilliance of the sky in mid-stream and the shady overhanging fronds of willow at the water's edge.

We arrived in Caius to find a buzz of unaccustomed excitement: the whole College had assembled to applaud Stephen in Caius Court, the Renaissance court near the Senate House. It took a few minutes to robe the honorary graduand in the ante-Chapel and a little while to get him comfortable in the chair in the heavy red gown, which would have been fine for midwinter, but was unbearably hot in midsummer. He refused to wear the gold-rimmed black-velvet bonnet, so Tim wore it instead. As we emerged from the Chapel, the Fellows, all begowned, preceded us taking up positions along the path to the Gate of Honour. From another gate, the Gate of Virtue, came a brass fanfare, and then the choir struck up the anthem 'Laudate Domino'. Another fanfare resounded round the court, chasing Stephen as he raced at full speed through the Gate of Honour, up Senate House Passage and into the Yard of the Senate House.

Robert had enlisted the help of muscular undergraduate friends to lift the wheelchair and its occupant up the long, winding staircase to the Combination Room in the Old Schools building, where the other honorary graduands, including Javier Pérez de Cuéllar, the Secretary-General of the United Nations, were assembling. Stephen just had time for a sip of apple juice before Prince Philip, the Chancellor, arrived. Good-humouredly he came over to talk to us and recalled coming to West Road in

1981. He teased Tim about his hat and stayed to watch Stephen's demonstration of the computer before being whisked away to meet the other dignitaries. We passed the royal personage as we made our way out to prepare ourselves for the procession in advance of the rest of the party. "Self-propelled, is it?" he asked. "Yes," I replied, "watch out for your toes!"

The procession, which had already formed by the time we joined it, began to move forthwith. The four of us – Stephen, Robert, Tim and I – walked slowly round the Senate House lawn at the tail end of the line-up, watched by the crowds outside the railings and the cameras within. The clouds of tension, friction and confusion evaporated in the fierce sunlight, and for a fleeting moment it was hard to believe that they had ever existed. In the Senate House all was cool, dark and solemn. The assembly of red-robed Masters of Colleges and Professors and the Chancellor in his gold-braided black robes took up their positions, and the audience of families and friends, dressed with the formality befitting an occasion of such pageantry, sat waiting in silent expectation. As the great oak doors closed on the midday brilliance and the thronging informal crowds of T-shirted tourists outside, the combined choirs of St John's and King's opened the proceedings with an anthem by Byrd, followed by a twentieth-century piece, and then the presentations began. A German theologian, the Lord Chancellor Lord Mackay, Pérez de Cuéllar and then Stephen, were all introduced by the Public Orator, and in a witty Latin delivered with such panache and such flourish that when he concluded his oration in honour of Stephen, Tim – not renowned for his Latin scholarship – burst into spontaneous applause. Pérez de Cuéllar was described as "having brought peace to the Persians and Mesopotamians" while the substance of Stephen's encomium was adapted from the first atomic theory as described by Lucretius in *De Rerum Natura*.

Amid much bowing, handshaking and doffing of hats, the Duke of Edinburgh conferred the degrees one by one, each presentation ending with a round of applause, which when Stephen's turn came attained rapturous proportions. Some of the graduands, such as the diminutive and frail figure of Sue Ryder, looked as nervous as young undergraduates; others, such as the opera singer Jessye Norman and Stephen himself, were old hands at the game and received their ovations with confidence and style.

The ceremony came to an end with more anthems and two verses of the National Anthem. Leaving Tim with his grandparents, Robert and I processed out with Stephen, sedately walking round the green again before heading down King's Parade in the blazing sun. Crowds cheered, smiling and waving, and cameras clicked.

When we reached Corpus Christi College – which by coincidence was Robert's college and the venue for the luncheon – we found ourselves surrounded by the nation's great and good, all wilting visibly in the heat inside the marquee, where champagne was being served, followed by lunch in another equally sweltering marquee. To add to Stephen's discomfort, the food was not suitable for him apart from the salmon. He was well entertained by his neighbour, but I had a fairly hard time with mine, a well-known authority on French history who seemed to have nothing to say for himself until I mentioned our house in France. Then he came to life. His wife had just bought a property in Normandy, he said, but he was a city man and did not much care for the country. Whereupon there was much mirth as he shared his views with Stephen and the latter grinned in agreement.

In the rising temperatures, the speeches were mercifully short. Starting with Stephen, "because everything begins with him", the Duke of Edinburgh expressed his admiration of the graduands, who "reflected the best of our civilization". Lord Mackay replied briefly, and then it was all over. The rest of the day was a disturbing mixture of frivolity and encroaching normality, as if the harsh reality of the gathering storm could not extend its reprieve for much longer.

At home a select group of relatives and friends had assembled, and the College had laid out a tea of smoked salmon sandwiches and strawberries and cream on the lawn, all to be consumed with champagne. Robert was not at that party, as he had another engagement: early that evening he was to row in the Corpus second boat, racing in the Bumps. I managed to dash away from the lingering guests just in time to see him row. The day, however long and eventful, was not yet over. Lucy came home in dire distress, as neither of her A-level papers had gone at all well, and then later in the evening, when all the guests had left and I was clearing up, the telephone rang. It was Robert. We chatted for a bit and then he blurted out that his Finals results were out and they were not as good as he had hoped. He was understandably very upset, and I too felt his humiliation and the irony of the situation keenly.

Robert, loyal and uncomplaining as ever, had dutifully assisted his father at the Senate House, had accompanied him in the formal procession, and had provided the team of helpers from among his friends to lift him up steps and over obstacles in Corpus Christi College. With thoughtful reticence, he had witnessed his father's good fortune without presuming on it, though always overshadowed by it. All through the ceremony in his father's honour, all through the excesses of media exposure, all through the compliments, the ovations and the accolades, Robert had kept to himself the galling news that his Finals results, published that very day, were disappointing. The underlying truth of the situation was that his profound sense of individuality had rebelled against the overpowering shadow of his father's genius by mutely refusing to compete with it. I could not help feeling a much deeper pain for my son in his dismay than joy for my husband in the full glory of his many-faceted success. I identified closely with Robert: I could only stand on the sidelines of Stephen's success.

If Robert had not achieved the academic success he had been hoping for, he made up for his disappointment on the river. Pursued by the BBC film crew, I took Stephen down to the races the next afternoon. Despite taking a wrong turning – the races take place on a stretch of the river at Fen Ditton five miles or so out of town – we arrived just in time to see the Corpus boat flailing past, hot on the stern of the Lady Margaret boat. News filtered back up the river in their wake that the Corpus boat had bumped its prey. My father, who in his day had also rowed for Corpus, was thrilled with Robert's prowess on the river. He always regretted that, under constant pressure to aim high, he had not been able to relax and enjoy his years at Cambridge in the 1930s – which is why, in his opinion, it was important that Robert had made the most of his time as an undergraduate.

13

Honourable Companionship

Late that evening of 16th June, we sat up to watch the announcement at midnight of the Birthday Honours. Inexplicably,
Elaine Mason, the nurse in attendance, was disparaging and
disapproving, but my father hopped up and down with excitement at his son-in-law's elevation to the higher echelons of the
Establishment as a Companion of Honour. Like Stephen's father
he derived a vicarious enjoyment from his proximity to the sort
of public success that circumstance had denied him. The next
morning I awoke to the more practical consideration of how to
open the day in a suitably festive manner. I had not given any
thought to the start of the day and Stephen's most important
meal, his breakfast. Then I remembered that there was probably
some caviar left over from a trip to Moscow and champagne
from Thursday's celebrations in the fridge. The consequence
of that extravagant breakfast was that none of us achieved very
much that morning, only managing to stumble across the fen
to the University Centre, where I had booked a table for lunch.
In the early afternoon, however, I cycled into town to check on
the organization of the evening's concert in the Senate House,
and found Jonathan's family busy arranging the seating and
the general layout while he rehearsed the orchestra. I left them
to it and raced back home to collect my father for a lightning
trip down to the river. We arrived just in time to see the Corpus
second boat rowing down bearing a willow branch, the sign that
it had made yet another triumphant bump.

That warm, cloudless June evening saw us back at the Senate
House, astonished at the sight of the long line of friends and
admirers who were patiently queuing to get in for the concert,
aptly entitled *Honoris Causa*. I steered Stephen away from
making a tactless beeline for the exam results, the Class lists,
which were posted up outside the Senate House, and left him
sitting on the same lawn around which we had processed only
two days before. There he had his photo taken in company with

various distinguished guests – from the firm sponsoring the concert, from his College and from the University – while I went to investigate why the queue was moving so slowly. Its length was partly explained by the fact that ten-year-old Tim was the only programme seller inside the building, though Lucy and my father were hard at work ushering the crowds to their seats. Having enlisted more help for Tim, I rejoined Stephen outside. The manager of the Senate House insisted to my embarrassment that Stephen and I should make a formal entry, and detained us outside until the rest of the audience was seated. We were greeted by a standing ovation. While Stephen beamed at the audience and pirouetted in his chair, I felt painfully shy and gauche and was glad to be able to sit down with my back to the audience.

A couple of minutes later, the sounds of the baroque trumpet in Purcell's sonata for that gloriously commanding instrument opened the concert, soaring above the heads of the audience to mingle with the ornate plasterwork of the eighteenth-century ceiling. Just as I hoped, the audience were so well satisfied at the end of their evening's entertainment that they contributed generously to the retiring collection, with the result that we were able to send handsome cheques to the three charities – the Motor Neuron Disease Association, Leukaemia Research and the Leonard Cheshire Foundation – as well as covering the costs of the concert from ticket sales. Ostensibly the evening had been a tremendous success: the charities had benefited; the Cambridge Baroque Camerata had secured a new sponsorship deal and had given a spectacular performance to a full Senate House; and, most importantly, Stephen had been lavishly fêted and applauded by hundreds of well-wishers. He, however, was edgy and disgruntled. His perceptions of the event were coloured by the grudging view that Jonathan and the orchestra had obscured his share of the limelight. This was as unjust as it was unlike Stephen's normal character. He had entered into the project with excitement and, when he had not been in America, had involved himself in its development with enthusiasm. Jonathan with his natural reserve had carefully stepped aside to allow Stephen to revel in the audience's adulation at the end of the performance, and indeed there could have been no doubt that it was Stephen's show. It was even less like Stephen that he should remind me that, since the honour bore no title, I had no part in it. The conclusion was as inescapable as it was unpalatable: he had fallen prey to flattery. The sycophantic sources of this flattery were not disinterested, and seemed to be feeding him ideas which were at odds with his formerly generous if stubborn nature.

The limelight was blindingly focused on Stephen for the rest of that summer, never more so than when we made our second visit to Buckingham Palace a few weeks later, though by comparison with the first visit, seven years earlier, this one was surprisingly intimate. We followed a similar routine – again staying at the Royal Society the night before – but with the difference that this time Tim and Amarjit Chohan, Stephen's Indian nurse, came with us, and Lucy had remembered to pack her smart shoes to go with the dark-brown dress which set off her blond hair beautifully. Again, just as before, the traffic in the Mall was at a standstill, though this time it was on account of the Changing of the Guard. To avoid the congestion around the main entrance, we were directed to the Queen's private entrance and were suddenly transported into a quiet, colourful country garden away from the hot stuffy turmoil of London and its traffic. An equerry, footmen and a lady-in-waiting greeted us with graciously imperturbable smiles and ushered us into the Palace, past the gleaming toy car that Prince Charles had had as a child and a couple of bikes, and up into the vast marble-pillared hall, which was lit along its entire length and furnished in red and pink damask. Huge displays of lilies stood like decorative sentinels, guarding the treasures.

We turned a corner and doubled back along the picture gallery, quickly retracing our steps over the marble hall, with scarcely a moment to glance at the portraits of Charles I and his family, gazing in mute detachment at each other across the floor. A couple of Canalettos, a Dutch genre painting and lots of portraits of Princess Augusta caught my eye. We turned into a passage so narrow that it might have led to servants' quarters, and were shown into a small side room full of paintings and furniture, the Empire Room. After a brisk briefing from the equerry, Stephen and I were hurried away from the family to meet the Queen, who was waiting in a room at the end of the passage. True to form, Stephen charged ahead towards the open door across the passage. There by the mantelpiece stood the Queen, wearing a royal blue dress streaked with white. She glanced in our direction with a friendly but apprehensive smile. This soon changed to a look of absolute horror when Stephen, bursting in haste into her reception room, rolled the carpet up in his wheels like a cowpusher on an American locomotive. The chair hoovered up the edge of the thick coffee-coloured carpet, tying it up in knots, bringing Stephen to an abrupt halt and blocking the way into the room. From behind the chair I could not easily see what was happening, and there was nothing I could do to release the royal pile. The Queen was the only person inside the room. She hesitated, and then for one moment made a gesture, as if she herself were about to step forwards and lift the heavy mechanism and its occupant out of the snare. Fortunately the equerry who had announced us squeezed past the chair, lifted the front wheels and sorted out the mess.

Naturally, Her Majesty was a little flustered – as was I – so we failed to shake hands and I forgot to curtsey as she uttered a short formal speech of welcome. After an awkward silence she must have decided that the best course of action was to go ahead with the presentation without delay, and so proceeded to announce that she was pleased to invest Stephen with the insignia of the Companion of Honour. I received the medal on Stephen's behalf and showed it to him, reading the inscription aloud as I held it out for him to see. "In Action Faithful, in Honour Clear" it read. The Queen remarked that she thought it was a particularly lovely wording, and Stephen typed up, "Thank you ma'am." We in turn presented her with a thumb-printed copy of *A Brief History of Time*, which rather nonplussed her – "Is it a popular account of his work such that a lawyer might give?" she enquired of me. It was my turn to be nonplussed, since I could not imagine anything remotely approaching a popular account of the law. I recovered my composure sufficiently to say that I thought *A Brief History* was more readable than that, especially the first chapters, which provided a fascinating account of the development of the study of the universe – before the physics became too complicated with elementary particles, string theory, imaginary time and that sort of thing. Thereafter the conversation continued haltingly for another ten minutes or so, ranging from a basic explanation of Stephen's science and interests to a demonstration of the workings of the computer and its American voice. The Queen directed her questions to me with a piercing, blue gaze, as bright as the large sapphire and diamond brooch on her shoulder. Although there was warmth and consideration as well as keenness in that gaze, it transfixed me. I was too terrified even to move my eyes, much as I should have liked to glance round the pretty turquoise reception room with its paintings and mementoes, and I stood awkwardly rooted to the spot, hardly daring to turn my head to left or right.

Over lunch on the top floor of the Hilton we recounted the details of the audience to the family, whose movements had been restricted to the Empire Room, not omitting the carpet episode, which appealed to their irreverent sense of humour. We described the subsequent conversation as somewhere between an oral exam and an interview with an intense but well-meaning headmistress, both equally terrifying. I had little doubt that the Queen had found it pretty difficult as well. Did we give the right answers, we wondered, as we looked out over the London skyline? There, directly beneath us, was the Palace, surrounded by the Elysian Fields where, after the audience, we had just walked. Stephen complained that he had not been able to converse as much as he would have liked because of a problem with the setting of the hand control of the computer, disturbed by the contretemps with the carpet. Be that as it may, the overall impression was that the occasion had gone well, and Stephen had yet another impressive medallion to add to his already extensive collection.

Just as we were leaving the restaurant, I was surprised to be presented with an enormous bouquet of orange and yellow lilies by the management. Although it came from a commercial institution, one of the chain of Hilton Hotels, the gesture was quite affecting. It reminded me of the pearl that Ruth Hughes had given me in California when Stephen was awarded the Papal medal in 1975, and it told me that somebody had noticed me.

14

Dies Irae

A week later Tim and I were in France again. The Moulin blinked sleepily in the evening sun as we drove towards it up the track and as I opened the gates. The crisp, fresh air penetrated deep into my asthmatic lungs, reviving my spirits, for I was physically tired after the long journey and emotionally taut after the recent peaks and troughs. The inner courtyard was quiet and still, enveloping us like a soft blanket and protecting us from the tyranny of the outside world. The silence was broken only by the chirruping of sparrows, echoing off the white walls. Then Tim added his piping voice to theirs, impatiently urging me to open the door so that he could get in and clamber up to his attic to check the state of his model aeroplanes, which swooped vertiginously over the stairwell, suspended from the banisters by an intricate web of thread and Sellotape. Inside we ran from room to room, inspecting every nook and cranny and renewing our acquaintance with every old beam. To our astonishment, the dusty black barn had undergone a Cinderella-like transformation and was ready to accommodate Stephen's entourage of nurses. The rubble, cobwebs and rotting rafters had disappeared, and in their place downstairs there was a large room with a tiled floor and a kitchenette, and upstairs two large bedrooms and a bathroom. A blend of solid new beams and usable old ones held up the structure, so confident in their age-old tradition that were it not for the sheen of newness on all the fittings, they could have been there from time immemorial. Then we ran out into the garden, anticipating more discoveries. Some strange enchantment had been exercised in our absence. Tim gasped, "It's just like Buckingham Palace!" – and indeed he was right. The plants and seeds in the herbaceous border had leapt to maturity, and where in May there had been small isolated clumps and diminutive seedlings, now a riot of densely nodding flower heads and dancing colour shouted ecstatic greetings. There were still things to be done, walls to be painted and floors to be covered, but the essential work was completed. The Moulin was ready to receive not only us, but the whole crowd of our summer visitors as well. My brother was to bring his family of four children at about the same time as Tim's friend Arthur, and his parents would be arriving for a weekend visit. Jonathan would be bringing my parents and Stephen would be coming out by air to Le Touquet, attended by Pam Benson, a most trusted nurse, and by Elaine and David Mason and their family.

Despite my mother's misgivings, I had in my optimism invited the Mason family, hoping that the experience of living with us in the same house but in more relaxed circumstances than in Cambridge would encourage a greater respect for the self-discipline which was basic to our routine. While I had no intention of interfering in any fond attachment that might have developed between Elaine and Stephen, I thought that, as a professional nurse, she might be persuaded to see that the success of our task depended on finely balanced teamwork. There was no room for troublemakers in this situation. Naively I trusted too that if she realized that Jonathan and I did not, as a matter of course, sleep together in the same room, she would learn to respect the modus vivendi which enabled us to go on caring for Stephen and the children indefinitely, come what may. Surely only the most bigoted fundamentalist could be blind to what we were trying to achieve and the effort and restraint that we put into that endeavour? It was ironic that in days gone by Stephen would have been scathing in his intolerance of fundamentalism and would have laughed to scorn anyone who tried to preach it.

We – that is me, Tim, my handyman Claude and a very helpful girl from the village – were still energetically applying white emulsion to the walls of the new part of the house downstairs when my absent-minded brother and his family of four children arrived a week early. Chris more than compensated for their unexpected arrival, however, by taking over the cooking. In his opinion, the best tourist attractions of France were the supermarkets, where he would happily spend his days browsing along the shelves in search of ever more extravagant ingredients to add to his cooking pot, the aroma of which, wafting from the new kitchen, made our mouths water every evening with the promise of gastronomic delights.

By the time Stephen and his motley crew flew in to Le Touquet in the middle of August, the new wing of the house had been well and truly tested by successive waves of visitors, including my parents, who had pronounced it entirely satisfactory both for its charm and its convenience. But a perceptible tension reigned among the new arrivals. My delight at seeing Stephen met with a cool response, arousing my suspicions that the underhand mutterings about his dislike of the French countryside had struck home, persuading him that he really did not want to spend any time on holiday in France, let alone in the country. All efforts to interest him in the glorious views from the house across sun-drenched fields to the distant blue line of hills and forests encountered the same bored, disdainful expression. Day after day, the truth forced itself remorselessly on me that his smiles and his interest were reserved for Elaine, and I had no doubt that he was being encouraged to despise me because I was flawed and did not conform to the image of perfection with which he was constantly being tantalized. He was being persuaded that I was no longer of any use to him, that I was good for nothing. Elaine was in a position of strength: her responsibilities were minimal and she could indulge Stephen by doing anything he asked; she could wheedle and coax, and her specialized training enabled her to attend to his every whim. Since his work and his physical condition were his two principal preoccupations, my role was logically much diminished, and hers was ostensibly greatly enhanced. The familial and intellectual bonds which I had valued and through which we maintained a semblance of normality had apparently become insignificant. Probably with her he had found someone tougher than me with whom he could again somehow have a physical relationship, whatever the other dimensions of their affair. I could not deny him this, and was prepared to accept it in our scheme of things – in the same way that he had generously accepted my relationship with Jonathan – provided that it was discreet and posed no threat to our family, to our children, to our home or to the running of the nursing rota achieved at such wearisome cost. It was also essential that it must not negate my relationship with Stephen, because I was convinced that without me he would be like a lost child, an unruly, assertive child but a helpless and naive one as well. My fate had been bound up with his so closely and for so long that I could never be indifferent to him, however difficult his peculiar set of circumstances – those of a disabled genius – had made him. Care for his well-being had become second nature to me. Whether it was the slightest sign of distress, discomfort or disapproval that his mobile features betrayed, I could not ignore him. The truth was that I still loved him with a deeply caring compassion. In that emaciated body, despite the power of the mind, his suffering was all too painfully apparent, and it was through that suffering that my feelings for him were constantly being aroused. These feelings were never intended to be patronizing; indeed often they could lead me onto an emotional tightrope, where despair and frustration at his stubbornness and unreasonable demands had always to be reconciled with deference for his dignity and respect for his rights as an extremely incapacitated person.

Our marriage, and the large and complex structure that it had become, was the definition of my adult life, summing up my most important achievements: Stephen's continued survival, the children, the family and the home. It was the long history of our joint battles against his illness and the story of his success against all the odds. I had dedicated most of myself to it – even if I had accepted help to allow me to persevere without becoming suicidal. True, I sometimes longed for more freedom of movement and resented the strict limitations it imposed, but I had never thought of running away from it except – when driven to utter despair – by drowning myself. The structure may have become dangerously top-heavy and unstable, but it was unbelievable that all that the marriage represented might now be swept away in a flush of passion. The fact that Elaine had an able-bodied husband and a family of her own was beyond the scope of my comprehension: that was a matter for her conscience in which I could not become involved.

The situation might have resolved itself peaceably had the personalities involved been different, had they been more considerate, less determined, less self-centred, less bent on the fulfilment of their own desires to the exclusion of all else. Perhaps, if I had been stronger and less confused, I could have handled the situation differently and with more assurance. As it was, the holiday was a disaster. Various mishaps combined to intensify Stephen's distaste for the country, even for the Moulin, which was so unlike his enthusiasm in the spring, and he became increasingly hostile to both the family and to Pam, the other nurse. When eventually I took it upon myself to point out to Stephen that his and Elaine's behaviour risked losing Pam from the rota, I inadvertently set fire to the conflagration which would consume us all. It engulfed the old house that day and the following night, shattering the cherished silence and shaking the aged beams, as it raged up around me. Flames of vituperation, hatred, desire for revenge leapt at me from all sides, scorching me to the quick with accusations – the unfaithful wife, the uncaring partner, the selfish career woman, work-shy and frivolous, more intent on singing than on looking after her frail, defenceless husband. I had had things my own way for too long, they said. I should "put Stephen first".

I faced the attacks alone. I would not demean Jonathan by bringing him into this uncivilized fray, but nor could I douse the flames. It was hopeless to try and point out that, throughout all the alienating distractions of physics and the grinding, ceaseless demands of illness, I had honestly tried to be a good wife to Stephen; that through the paraphernalia of medicines, medical equipment and nursing rotas, through the plethora of scientific papers, equations and meetings, I had honestly tried to do my best, however distorted my own life had become. That Jonathan's love and help had preserved us and saved me from ultimate despair would never be countenanced as a valid defence. My best was not good enough, and now I was being cast aside in favour of someone who beguiled the sick man with the flimsy straws of extravagant promises and unrealistic expectations. It was the beginning of the death of our marriage.

Alone in my room after the first wave of attack had finally subsided, helplessness reduced me to hot, angry tears. My spirit rebelled at the shallowness of so many of the people who had recently come into our lives. They had never come face to face with successions of multiple crises. They had never had to confront the overwhelming trauma of living in the face of death, day in day out for more than a quarter of a century. They had never plumbed the depths of emotion or been torn apart by moral dilemma. They had never been stretched to and beyond the utter limits of their physical and mental capacities. Their experience of these issues had been facile, skimming the surface of reality, motivated by self-gratification, dictating absolute values to others that they themselves could not observe. Indeed in their eyes I was a mere automaton with no justifiable claim to any human reactions at all. My need to be loved for myself alone was dismissed as preposterous.

After this fiasco Stephen and the Masons returned to England, and Tim and I stayed on at the Moulin. The lovely old house and garden gathered up my spent body and charred mind into the comfort of their embrace as the calm of rural France descended once more. If Stephen really did not want me, I reasoned, I could make a good life for myself in France. I could support myself by teaching English and Spanish, and Tim could become completely bilingual. At the beginning of September he started going to the village school, where he quickly made friends, unperturbed by the demands of the language. He would cycle off down the road to the village every morning while I stood waving and watching as he climbed the hill opposite and disappeared under the trees. At home we often spoke French. English and England had become alien to me, a country and a language which harboured and expressed extreme personal torment – not to mention the widespread political injustices of the Margaret Thatcher years – while France offered a new lifestyle, new friends and a sense of equality. Moreover France, a predominantly Catholic country, worshipped and prayed to the Mother of Jesus, the feminine intermediary to the masculine figures of the Trinity. There a woman had a recognized place in the divine order of things. Mary had a human presence which was tragic, loving and comforting. Often, in French country churches and cathedrals, I would be drawn to the figure of the Virgin Mary – a crudely painted plaster saint perhaps – who offered the solace of shared suffering.

Tim and I quickly settled into a routine which I was confident of being able to sustain. We could live in France permanently if need be, or eventually we could return to England when Stephen had resolved his problems. Jonathan, who had gone back to Cambridge to play a series of organ recitals, kept in touch regularly, urging us to stay in France if that was where we felt at ease.

Stephen also telephoned almost daily, but he urged us to return to England. He missed us, he said, and he needed us. He was so persuasive that I trusted that he really intended to restore some harmony to our lives and keep his nurses under control. Later that September, believing that my lost child really needed me, we set out for England across stormy seas, determined to avoid confrontation. The family, that is my parents and Robert, were delighted to see us when we arrived home late at night after long delays on the motorways. The reception I, but not Tim, received from Stephen was distinctly frosty. It was not the lost child who came to greet us, but the despot. At once I knew that I had made a grave mistake in coming back to England.

15

Too Much Reality

The following Monday, Tim returned to his primary school and I took up my teaching again, committing myself at least for the term if not for the whole academic year. Then, exactly a week after our return, Stephen gave me a letter announcing his intention of going to live with Elaine Mason. That evening, by a sorry coincidence, Robert was dealt a broken jaw by muggers who attacked him on his way home.

The execution of Stephen's decision was considerably delayed for the extraordinary and eminently practical reason that he and Elaine Mason had nowhere to go. In the meantime we lived in a maelstrom of chaos and confusion, while I clung like a limpet to the belief that the storm would eventually wear itself out and that, despite his present sad emotional disarray, Stephen would choose to stay with his family. As if blown along like a dry leaf in a gale, he came and went, often without any notice. Extreme pressure from outside was exerted on him, and each explosive episode would be succeeded by a period of calm as if nothing had happened. Those periods, though, were just the eye of the storm, only presaging further unforeseen elements which blew in at hurricane force. Reports reached me that the nurse was already announcing her forthcoming marriage to Stephen. I lived with the constant fear that there might well be a battle to gain custody of Tim, and Jonathan was banned from West Road under threat of a court injunction, so he had no choice but to keep to his own home. Open discussion was impossible, because an insurmountable barrier had arisen between Stephen and me and, the more he appeared to lose control of his own situation, the more I felt he sought to control me, as if I was simply a piece of property. The duty nurses posted unpleasant letters through my car window just as I left for work each day, and impossible demands were made of me each evening. Unpleasant remarks and false motives were attributed to me. I was told to give Jonathan up and "put Stephen first in everything". I even found myself reluctantly drawn into clashes about money, not just with Stephen but with Elaine Mason as well. Through the concentration required by teaching – especially by teaching the absorbing, intellectually teasing novels and short stories of Gabriel García Márquez – I managed to preserve some sanity, while among my colleagues in the staffroom I found a quiet sympathy and supportiveness which brought a sense of stability to the few hours each day that I spent away from home. At other times music soothed and solaced my battered emotions, though often its intensity caused my voice to falter and fade. Otherwise bedlam reigned and our home became the scene of unprecedented violence as other people's madness forced its way into our household and left Tim and me terrified, with not the least gesture of support from the two professional nursing bodies, the Royal College of Nursing and the UK Nursing Council, who refused to become involved.

Later that month, as I waved the two eldest children goodbye on consecutive days – Robert to Glasgow for a postgraduate-degree course in Information Technology and Lucy to Oxford – it seemed that my entire existence and the structure on which it rested were crumbling away. My personal identity, which I had desperately tried to construct over the years from all the disparate fragments – the jigsaw pieces of everyday life – had been shattered. I was alone and without shelter in the midst of a private war. Wherever I looked, I saw the rubble and ruins of the brave, bold but fragile edifice that Stephen and I had built. A dark chasm had opened up in the ground, swallowing up that edifice and with it more than twenty-five years of my life – all the years of my youth and young adulthood, all the hopes and all the optimism. In their place there was left little more than an insubstantial, vacant shroud, ghostly and withdrawn, the object of daily mental torture. The only certainty for the future was that my youngest and most vulnerable child, Tim, had to be protected and, however crushed and broken I might be, I had to muster the strength and the courage to fight for him.

Jonathan and I had never contemplated the possibility of a future together without Stephen. We had no fantasies, no dreams. The thought of change was alien to our thinking: I had closed my mind to it and did not seek it. In the past I thought that we had achieved a balance whereby everyone could flourish, even if that demanded considerable contortion, restraint and self-discipline at a personal level. This had evidently proved to be nothing more than complacent wishful thinking, for I was now forcibly given to understand that Stephen had been dissatisfied with our way of life for some time. I found this revelation quite surprising. If Stephen had been seething with resentment for so long, why had he not told me about it? How had he managed to be so successful, creative and dynamic if he was really unhappy? Apparently he had not liked being treated as but one member of the family when he considered his rightful place to be on a pedestal at the centre. Someone had come along who was prepared to worship at his feet and make him the focal point of her life. That someone was promising him that he would never have to employ nurses again, since she alone would care for him twenty-four hours a day, seven days a week and would travel everywhere that he wanted to go. Patently I could not match such single-minded devotion and, as a result, change of the cruellest kind was being forced upon me. I was threatened with being thrown out of the family home, and my role in Stephen's life was being systematically denied, as if all reference to me, all memory of me, had to be erased from all the records.

Once the term had started and Tim and I were entrenched in the Cambridge routine, there was no going back to France, yet I badly needed a bolt hole. Jonathan's house was out of the question, since a move there would signify that I was ending the marriage, which was not and never had been my intention. Any bolt hole had to be neutral territory, where Tim and I could escape the tensions, the battles, the venom and the recriminations which were creating bitter chaos at 5 West Road. There was just one option open. Although the College had been in possession of our house in Little St Mary's Lane for years – in part-exchange for the College flat – the property still technically belonged to us. As I knew that the house was unoccupied, I wrote to the Master pleading with him to allow Tim and me to use it temporarily until the battles had died away and the crisis had resolved itself for better or for worse. The Master was new to the College – I scarcely knew him nor he me. His reply was unequivocal: much as he regretted it, there existed a formal agreement between Stephen and the College for the exchange of the two properties, and until Stephen revoked that agreement, I could have no access to the house.

By day asthma stifled my breathing and befuddled my mind, while my hands tingled to the tips of my fingers with fright each time Stephen announced that he wanted to speak to me. Every night the terrible nightmares returned, waking me in a terrified panic: my heart pounded as buildings collapsed on top of me, burying me in a dark underground tomb. Tim too had nightmares in which he dreamt that he was being chased by baddies along corridors and down streets. By day he became excessively introverted and anxious. The doctor prescribed beta blockers for me and sent me to see a counsellor. The only remedy for Tim was to distance him from the troubles, but since Little St Mary's Lane was denied us, that was not easily done. I asked his headteacher to warn his staff of the intolerable strain that Tim was under at home. Too late I discovered that he had omitted to pass my anxieties on to his staff, and poor Tim often came home from his primary school in tears.

The battles continued to rage furiously for the rest of the term with only a short truce during the visit to Spain for the presentation of a prestigious award by the heir to the Spanish throne, the Prince of Asturias, in Oviedo. Being in Spain lifted my spirits and made that visit bearable. Although the truce brought its own minor superficial tensions in the form of repeated public appearances, press conferences and interviews, at least these gave me the opportunity to prove myself professionally again and reassert my own qualifications as a linguist and as Stephen's companion. The underlying tension which resulted from his lately announced resolve of buying a flat for his favourite nurse was much more severe. The mind which had mastered the mathematical secrets of the universe was no match for the emotional upheaval which now overwhelmed it. Like his Wagnerian hero, Siegfried, Stephen had wrapped himself in a protective cloak, the stiff cloak of determination – inspired by unrelenting reason, steeling him against sentimental frailty in the belief that he was invincible. But like Siegfried he was vulnerable, and helpless when his vulnerability was exposed to attack. Stephen's physical weak spot had been his throat, but he also had a second, psychological weak spot, which was an utter lack of resistance to manipulative, emotional pressure. He had never been subjected to it before and had no armour against it. This was the sort of pressure being exerted on Stephen: it built up a head of steam, hissing with relentless energy until it erupted in a series of emotional surges of volcanic force, which engulfed all obstacles with a red-hot flow of anger and passion. Then, quite miraculously, each new eruption would subside as quickly as it had exploded, and peace would descend once again on our home life. He would become gentler, more docile and regretful, genuinely concerned to put the turmoil behind him and resume the family life on which he had thrived in the past. Then he would admit that he was being tossed by conflicting emotions and needed support, understanding and the possibility of a reconciliation. This I was all too willing to give, for I shared the tragedy of his situation and wanted to help him get through it – but the lull would last only until the awful moment when another missive, another ultimatum, another summons, would seek out its target. I learnt to dread the outcome as Stephen dashed off, abandoning meals and social engagements to appease and become even further enthralled. And so it went on until Christmas. My parents' plans for celebrating their Golden Wedding were a catastrophe on the ebb and flow of that tidal force. With a randomness which had become perversely predictable, Stephen spent Christmas Day in the bosom of his family, but then late at night his van drew up outside and he vanished into the darkness, leaving home with Elaine to go and stay in a hotel before setting off for a conference in Israel the next day.

We did not see him or hear from him again until early January, when the children, Jonathan and I arrived home from a blissfully untroubled break in France to find him waiting for us as if he were expecting to resume business as usual. No explanations were proffered, and I knew better than to ask for any. That evening we gathered round the candlelit table, feasting on roast duck and orange sauce in celebration of Stephen's birthday. The cheerful letter I wrote to Stephen's mother the following morning, genuinely expressing my joy that the disruptions appeared to be over and that we could resume our attempts to lead a creative family life, received an entirely negative response. From that letter it became clear that Isobel discounted, even doubted, the effort that I had so long put into caring for Stephen and, on the contrary, saw me as the hedonistic beneficiary of his fame and success, intent now on denying him his chance of happiness with someone she really approved of and liked.

The stability was short-lived: all too soon the situation began to deteriorate again. After several more weeks in which the threats, the recriminations and the abuse once again gathered force, the children and I left to join Arthur and his parents for a few days' skiing in Austria at half-term. On our return to Cambridge, there was no sign of Stephen. He had gone. He had finally moved out, aided apparently by Elaine's husband, on the day we had left for Austria, 17th February 1990. The end had come. I felt neither sadness nor relief. I was numb.

It was not the end however. The very next day, Stephen telephoned from Elstree Studios, where the film version of *A Brief History of Time* was being shot, and asked me to join him there to participate in a family portrait, a biographical background for the film. It was an astonishing request. It was incredible that, having just left his family, he could expect us to go on performing like puppets for the cameras, still conveying the outdated happy and united façade. There was no longer any timid hesitancy in my voice. In taking his decision to leave us, Stephen had unwittingly relinquished his power over me, leaving me free to make up my own mind, no more in dread of his imperious reactions. I refused to go to Elstree. I had gained control of my life.

Thereafter, the high tragedy descended into farce. The phone rang incessantly as one after another the American producers and directors tried to cajole, flatter, persuade me to participate in their film. When they moved to Cambridge to set up an exact replica of Stephen's office in a disused church, they beat a path to the door, bringing with them their pathetic arguments. Millions of dollars were at stake, they lamented, wringing their hands; my absence would upset all their plans; without a substantial biographical element, the film would be unbalanced. I shrugged my shoulders and quoted back their original assurances, enshrined in the contract, about the nature of the film – a purely scientific documentary with only the briefest of biographical references. The more they revealed their lack of integrity by denying all such promises, the easier I found it to hold my ground – and the easier I found it to hold my ground, the stronger I became.

16

Null and Void

Whatever small comfort I may have derived from my new-found independence of spirit, the cataclysm had in truth left me a shattered wreck. In the darkness of defeat, I felt myself discredited and disowned, fumbling to find an identity, as if the preceding twenty-five years had been erased without trace. Indeed that impression was not simply subjective: it was given substance by the two charities for whom I had worked so hard. They could not risk their public credibility, they said, by continuing to have the two partners to a separation or divorce associated with their efforts, so they both dispensed with my services. Naturally Stephen's name was more useful than mine. This was a bitter blow. As I had suspected, outside the marriage and apart from Stephen, I was nothing.

It was nonetheless from this blind maze of disorientation that I began to sense the stirrings of an unprecedented, almost palpable strength in the air around me, a spiritual force, unrelated to my sapped physical state. It revealed itself in the spontaneous expressions of concern and love, reaching out telepathically to me from our many friends worldwide. These were the true friends, people who had known us for many years, friends who had witnessed the struggles and had often helped in times of crisis, friends who had generously delighted in the successes without being blinded to the harsh underlying reality. These were friends, too, from whom my attempts to come to terms with the situation had been no secret, friends who had known and admired Jonathan for his dedication to the family as much as for his musical talent. Many said that they wept when they heard the news. They brought me a sense of peace which enabled me to look to my own resources. Rather than wallow in resentment, I would put the energy which I had previously devoted to Stephen's well-being into a new project, a project of my own: it would be a book, but not the book of memoirs for which various publishers were already clamouring, since that was far too painful a subject and still lacked a clear perspective. My book would describe our experiences in setting up home in France, and would consist of amusing anecdotes and practical information, aimed at the considerable market of British buyers of homes in France. As not many of those Francophiles seemed to have any great command of the French language, I would compile a phonetic lexicon of useful terms relating to all areas of house purchase and residence in France: legalities, insurance, renovation, the utilities, the telephone system, local government and healthcare.

Most of the time which used to be spent running the home, attending to Stephen's needs, accommodating his nurses, organizing rotas, answering the phone to disaffected carers and putting on parties, I gave to that book. In writing it and compiling the lexicon, I learnt – like Stephen in the period after his critical illness – to use a computer. How I wished that one had been available in those years when I was working on my thesis! The computer and printer were a magnanimous parting gift from Stephen. Quite why he bought them I never discovered, but I suspected that the gesture was typical of the state of confusion in which he found himself, and which as ever he was too proud and self-contained to admit. I was, however, duly appreciative, since I could not have compiled the dictionary of useful terms without it. Although the French aspect of the project was endlessly entertaining and stimulating in the research and the writing, the publication was fraught with difficulty because, in my naivety, I fell into the wrong hands. A seemingly sympathetic literary agent took the book on board, but in fact, like so many others, he was interested only in the memoir.

Devious literary agents notwithstanding, the news of the separation fortunately remained concealed from the press for several months. Because it had not hit the tabloid headlines, we were allowed a beneficial period of respite. This limbo enabled Stephen and me to try to put our relationship on a new footing without the rub of media attention. We could meet as old friends without the stress of the day-to-day friction which had soured our relationship: he could come to West Road to see Tim at mealtimes, and we could discuss matters of family concern calmly and sensibly. The only difference was that he lived elsewhere with someone else.

The press finally learnt of our separation, literally as the result of an accident. One night, as Stephen was on his way back to his flat, he and the nurse in attendance (not Elaine) were knocked down by a speeding taxi. The wheelchair was overturned and he was left lying in the road in the dark. It was a miracle that he suffered nothing worse than a broken shoulder and spent only a couple of days in hospital. Inevitably the press got to hear of the accident, and naturally they wanted to know why his home was no longer at West Road. Reporters and cameramen, especially from the tabloids, came clustering round the gate like a pack of baying hounds, scenting scandal and terrifying Tim and me. We were being hunted. It was thanks to the good sense of the head porter at Harvey Court that they were put off the scent, and Jonathan, of whose existence they were unaware, managed to escape out of the back door.

Once the separation had entered the public domain, the College lost no time in sending the Bursar across to enquire when we were going to move. He was quite explicit: the College felt itself under no obligation to house the family if Stephen, with whom the College had signed the agreement, was no longer living there. He was in effect giving me notice to quit. I had neither the presence of mind to protest nor the will to fight. The previous day would have been – technically was – our twenty-fifth wedding anniversary. On that Monday morning in July it was made quite clear to me that everything that had occurred in those twenty-five years was of no importance to anyone else. The records had been wiped out. Those years might as well never have happened. Stephen was the only person who mattered. I was of no consequence, nor were the children. I had been given my marching orders and we were effectively being thrown out into the street. It was time to wake up to a new reality.

The only concession was that we were given one year's grace in which to readjust. This was particularly important, as Tim had been entered for King's College School, directly across the road, and it would have been the height of irony if we had been forced to move just as he was changing to a school less than five minutes from our front door. A further advantage of King's for Tim was that his friend Arthur was coming to school there as a boarder, so whatever the upheavals at home he could count on seeing his best friend every day in school. In fact Tim not only saw Arthur in school, but at home as well, because for the next two years Arthur came to live with us. It was a very happy arrangement for all concerned. Arthur became part of our family and gave Tim invaluable moral support in his changing circumstances.

It was my infinite good fortune that I was not alone. Jonathan had stood discreetly and steadfastly by my side despite being the target of considerable hostility. Equally discreetly and steadfastly, and with endless patience, he began to reassemble the broken shards of what used to be my personality, the while trying to come to terms himself with what had happened. From the outset he had been under no illusions: he knew that our relationship depended on a fine balance and on Stephen's acceptance that it was dedicated to the survival, not the destruction, of the family. Jonathan had feared the possibility of Freudian repercussions, but had underestimated the havoc that the intervention of an outside party could wreak by gossip and misrepresentation. There had not been any viable alternative, since he cared so deeply for me and for the family, including Stephen. For my part, not only could I not cope, I could not survive without him: he shouldered the physical burdens, and in his arms I found a longed-for emotional security. The new reality flung us together, though not with any joy or elation, only with sadness at the betrayal of our best intentions, coupled with muted relief that the long ordeal was over. Although Jonathan and I started to live together and began to look for a suitable house to buy, we were not intending to rush into marriage. We were committed to each other, but I was in no fit state, physically or emotionally, to marry anyone, let alone someone who deserved so much more than I could offer. In any case, since there had been no mention of divorce, I was technically still married to Stephen.

It was some consolation that, for all the chaos that *A Brief History of Time* had plunged us into, at least it had not left me destitute. We were able to buy and enlarge a detached house on a modern estate on the same side of Cambridge. At first sight I found the house and its garden dispiriting to the point of heartbreak. The house was cramped, featureless and uninspiring – a modern brick-and-concrete box, its inner walls covered in torn and faded hessian; the garden was pitifully bare and sombre, shaded from the neighbours by a row of overgrown leylandii. Yet again I would have to start from scratch and try to recreate a home in that characterless house and a flower garden from the unyielding grey clay which passed for soil. The attraction of the house was its position: it was still within cycling distance of the centre of town and of Tim's school. It also happened to be quite close to Stephen's luxury flat, which had to be regarded as an advantage, since Stephen insisted on seeing Tim twice a week. With uncomplaining loyalty, Arthur accompanied Tim on these regular visits, the outcome of which was never predictable and always disturbing. I was relieved that Stephen showed no urgency in pressing for divorce, because I dreaded that Tim might become a pawn in yet a further acrimonious battle. Occasionally a demanding letter would arrive, but as this clearly was Stephen's response to domestic pressure, these letters could be taken lightly, whatever their contents. Generally our discussions were civilized and even affectionate whenever we met.

As long as no divorce proceedings were filed, Tim was safe from legal wranglings over custody. Eventually that potential problem, because of his age, ceased to be an issue. For my part, I was leading a normal life, a tremendous luxury after more than twenty-five years of a life which had never really been normal. Jonathan and I cherished our normality and our privacy, though still living in fear of abuse by the gutter press which, we knew, would not hesitate to exploit our situation to please the salacious tastes of their readership. Occasionally those fears were justified, though never to lasting effect.

It was no secret that both the University and the College had designs on the land on which the house at 5 West Road stood. The two institutions were engaged in negotiations for the redevelopment of the end of the garden as a library for the Law Faculty, while for many years the College had been intending to build a hall of residence on the site of the house. In that last year of our occupation, we watched from the house in a silent state of siege as surveyors stalked the garden, armed with measuring rods, marking out distances with stakes and poles, while down by the holly hedge a pile driver forced its way deep into the light alluvial soil. With our removal the fate of the whole property – the old house, its lovely tranquil garden and its majestic backdrop of trees – would be sealed. In the name of progress, the University and the College were predictably intent on destroying yet another shady green space. In the mayhem of moving, there was little that I could do to save the house and garden except to ensure that the trees, especially the two magnificent sentinels, the wellingtonia by the house and the western red cedar, the *Thuja plicata* at the end of the lawn, were protected by tree-preservation orders. The self-styled arboreal officers conducted a survey and assured me that I had no need to worry: the trees were protected already because they were in a conservation area. I moved house satisfied that I had done my civic and environmental duty.

During the course of the next year, I visited the garden frequently on my way home from town to check that nothing untoward had happened. The threat appeared to have receded. All was quiet apart from the constant grinding action of the pile driver. The garden, the lawn, the trees were untouched, just as we had left them. I wandered in that sanctuary of nostalgia, sadly remembering the parties, the dancing, the games of croquet and cricket, and gazing at the blank, unseeing windows of the house, those windows that had contained so much joy and so much anguish. The house guarded its secrets closely, revealing its past in only a few scattered remnants, like the forgotten spoils of a battle – the rain-washed remains of Tim's sandpit, a battered toy bucket, a deflated football, a cracked flowerpot and the rusting rotary washing line which had given such good service. They told of lives and events of which the current student occupants of the house were scarcely aware.

Lulled by the unchanging tranquillity of the scene, my concerns for the garden were replaced by other more pressing matters. The literary agent was having scant success in finding a publisher for *At Home in France*, my handbook about buying French property. After various failures on his part, I thought I might try publishing the book myself, whereupon he sent me a copy of his contract pointing out that I was bound by its terms for four long years – unless, that is, I would sign a new contract giving him rights in perpetuity over any biography I might write about Stephen. I was angry, as much with myself for being so naive, as with this slippery customer of an agent who had taken such blatant advantage of my inexperience and my dejection. His deviousness fired my determination to publish my French book myself whatever the cost and to deprive him in perpetuity of any commission on any other book that I might write.

At about the same time the Inland Revenue turned their attention to the profits made from *A Brief History of Time*. As a result of the high rate of unemployment caused by the Tory government policies, the Treasury was short of funds and was instructing the Inland Revenue to increase its income from compliance investigations, particularly by looking into situations where a marriage break-up might have caused fiscal confusion. Although I was no longer involved in the handling of Stephen's book, the tax inspector brought the full force of his bullying professional belligerence down on my weary head. He harassed me with letters and phone calls, even ringing up at Christmas when my hands were deep in flour and my mind on carols, puddings and presents.

These and other preoccupations distracted me from the issue of the trees and the garden at 5 West Road. It was not until one Monday in July 1993 that I found myself thinking about them again; strangely these thoughts grew in strength until they became an irresistible urge to go to the garden. My rational self suppressed that puzzling feeling, since I was far too busy that Monday with preparations for the summer holidays as well as other activities. It was not until later in the week that I found the time to call in at West Road on my way home from a final pre-holiday shopping expedition. As I rounded the corner of the house, I encountered a horrific spectacle. Where I expected to find the well-known, much loved haven of flowers and greenery, all I saw was mass wanton destruction. The far end of the garden had been ransacked, obliterated. Where previously there had been trees and shrubs, roses and poppies, birds, hedgehogs and squirrels, now there was nothing more than a huge black hole in the ground, a muddy crater where Mother Earth was laid bare, ravaged and exposed. A quick mental count suggested that as many as forty trees had been felled, the most spectacular being the western red cedar, under whose shady branches Cottontail, Tim's little rabbit, had had her hutch. As I stood paralysed with shock and disbelief at the scale of the devastation, I remembered the strange call I had felt earlier in the week. Could those trees really have been calling me to their rescue? What had become of my attempts to protect them with preservation orders?

In response to my enquiries, the City Council could find no record of my earlier requests for preservation orders to be placed on the trees. The plans for the new building when presented to the planning committee had made only passing reference to a few insignificant shrubs and saplings, so the planning committee had given the go-ahead without further enquiry. The protection to the trees afforded by the conservation area was worthless. There was however a sense of poetic justice in the tragedy. The fate of the trees and the garden mirrored the fate that had befallen us. There could not have been a more potent or poignant metaphor for the end of our family life than that black hole in the ground.

Postlude

I am beginning to write this new postlude while taking off for Seattle with a nine-and-a-half-hour flight ahead of me. Heathrow soon disappears below, yielding to an English patchwork of green fields as we bounce off the clouds. This is a journey I have flown many times since that first trip in 1967, and having a new grandchild on the other side of the planet is now a compelling cure for flying phobia. As we fly over the snow-dusted Scottish mountains, heading north-west to Iceland and Greenland, I travel back in time recalling that flight when Robert was a tiny baby and Stephen, his father, was showing the initial disabling effects of motor-neuron disease, and I marvel yet again at the coincidence that Robert should have settled in Seattle with his wife Katrina, a talented sculptor, and their baby son. I also marvel at the fact that Stephen, who was given approximately two years to live in 1963, is not only still alive forty-four years later, but has recently received the most prestigious medal of the Royal Society, the Copley medal.

In 1995, while visiting Robert, who had taken up a job with Microsoft six months earlier, I felt that there was a certain sense of poetry in the way that Seattle had described a circle around almost all the years of our marriage. Now I feel that poetry of coincidence even more strongly as we prepare to celebrate in that city the first birthday of our little grandson, named George, after my father. On this flight I am not alone: Robert is with me, returning to Seattle after my mother's funeral yesterday. Only a week ago she died very peacefully and quietly in her sleep after a sudden illness. I was at a rehearsal at the time and felt her passing as a slight frisson, a brushing of angel's wings. I scarcely needed to be told on my return home that there was a message for me from her care home, because I already knew what had happened.

It was in Seattle back in 1995, soon after the divorce had been finalized and a year after the eventual publication of *At*

Home in France, that I began to contemplate writing the long memoir of my life with Stephen. I was surprised therefore to find an invitation from a publisher to do just that awaiting me back in Cambridge. That September the words flowed quickly and passionately, as if urging me to free myself of a past that had often scaled the giddy peaks of impossible achievement and yet had plumbed the depths of heartbreak and despair. I had to exorcise that past and clearly define the end of a long era before embarking on a new future, and it was to their credit that the publication team allowed me to tell my story spontaneously. That first edition represented a great and cathartic outpouring of optimism, euphoria, despondency and grief.

My initial reluctance to tackle a biography – arising from diffidence about the loss of privacy that the exercise might entail – gave way before the gradual awareness that I had no choice in the matter. My privacy was compromised anyhow, because my life was already public property as a result of Stephen's fame, and it would be only a matter of time before biographers started to investigate the personal story behind his genius and his survival: that would inevitably include me. I had no reason to suppose that they would treat me with any more consideration than the press had in the past. It would therefore be far better for me to tell my own story in my own way. I would be revealing truths which were so deeply and painfully personal that I could not bear to think that their music might resound only with the ring of the *chaudron fêlé*, Flaubert's cracked kettle. Although my role in Stephen's life was drastically diminished – Stephen's remarriage had effectively slammed the door on our lines of communication – I could not close my mind to a quarter of a century of living on the edge of a black hole, especially when the undeniable living proof of the extraordinary successes in those twenty-five years was to be seen in our three handsome, well-adjusted, very loving children, as well as in the acclaim that Stephen enjoyed. As the words flowed, I discovered that the voice and the register were there within me, ready and waiting to surface and express that mass of memories accumulated over the years. They were memories which might simply be seen to relate the saga of an English family in the latter part of the twentieth century. Much of it would be quite ordinary, quite common to most people's lives, were it not for two factors: motor-neuron disease and genius.

Indeed motor-neuron disease provided a further equally powerful motive for putting pen to paper, in the desire to awaken politicians and government officials to the heart-rending reality faced daily in an uncaring society by disabled people and their carers – the battles with officialdom, the lonely struggles to maintain a sense of dignity, the tiredness, the frustration and the anguished scream of despair. The memoir would, I hoped, also reach the medical profession with the aim of improving the otherwise sketchy awareness within the NHS of the ravages of motor-neuron disease and its effects on the personality, as well as on the physical bodies of its victims.

As a result of the hardback publication in August 1999 of *Music to Move the Stars*, the original title derived from the Flaubert quotation, I received a sackful of supportive letters, mostly from women who empathized keenly with my situation, commended my decision to write and recounted the story of their own often troubled lives. Some had been carers themselves or had struggled to bring up families in adverse circumstances; others simply found resonances with which they could identify. Many admitted that the book had made them weep. From within Cambridge the expressions of support were quite overwhelming. All said they were gripped by the story, including a ninety-four-year-old who refused to go to bed until she had finished reading it! Many people, deceived by Stephen's television appearances into thinking that we enjoyed all possible help, were appalled to discover how little assistance we actually received, thus confirming my long-held suspicion that the public face and the private reality were far removed, if not at odds with each other.

The past had largely been consigned to computer, if not fully exorcised, when Jonathan and I were married in July 1997. Our wedding day proved to be an island of respite against the tumultuous background of illnesses, accidents and disasters which were affecting our families and some of our closest friends. We ourselves were not in great shape either: Jonathan had been taken ill with kidney stones while performing on the concert platform in Liverpool, and I had been hobbling about on crutches for some time with torn ligaments in both knees after a skiing accident. The multitude of problems that had befallen us and our near and dear had left scant time for the practicalities of planning, let alone for any mental, emotional or spiritual preparation.

In truth, nothing could have prepared us for the emotional and spiritual power of that day. Just a minute or two before leaving home, I suddenly became aware to my embarrassed amazement that a mile down the road there was a church full of people awaiting me. Then, on arrival at St Mark's in the company of my three children, even our new Vicar's calm, friendly greeting could not allay that mounting sense of awe and wonder. Perhaps her resplendent white-and-gold ceremonial vestments only added to the potent, dream-like quality of the occasion – a quality which became overwhelming as Robert, Lucy, Tim and I took up our positions in the porch from where we glimpsed my future husband, rising to his feet at the chancel steps. A wave of emotion engulfed us as the organist launched into the majestic opening chords of *The Arrival of the Queen of Sheba* and my children bore me, trembling and incapable of looking to right or left, up the aisle, depositing me at Jonathan's side. In a space to my left, looking wan and frail, sat my mother, in the wheelchair to which she had recently become confined.

There followed the hymns, the prayers, the readings and the anthems, their words carefully chosen, pored over, analysed, translated into French and Spanish, typed into and extracted from the computer many a time. All those words came alive in speech and song, lent breadth and depth, truth, urgency and clarity by the voices of the clergy, the readers, the congregation and the choir. The latter was composed of old friends, many of them professional musicians who gave a poignant rendering of 'How lovely are thy dwellings fair' from Brahms's *German Requiem*. As for the preacher, there was only one possible choice. Only Bill Loveless, who had known us both for so long and had sustained us through such times of trial, could have given the address. Despite ill health and old age, he climbed into the pulpit and launched into a passionate speech which bore all the hallmarks of his customary vigour and commitment. He spoke with heartfelt candour and honesty of the dilemmas and anguish of the past without glossing over the reality of our relationship. As he recalled former times, it occurred to me that so many of the friends from all over the world who had given us so much valuable support in days gone by, and for whom I regularly said a silent prayer from my pew on a Sunday morning, were all in the church, with us and around us – all that is except Stephen, my companion over such a long period and the father of my children.

The image of darling Lucy standing at the lectern to recite Shakespeare's sonnet about the marriage of true minds was quite unforgettable. She stood, radiant in cream silk, with her hands clasped under her six-month bulge as if to gain confidence from her tiny, fetal son while Alex, her fiancé, beamed with pride from the congregation. There were the odd distracting moments – such as the horrible scratchy pen which turned my signature on the registers into an untidy scrawl, bringing back humiliating memories of a failed art exam in calligraphy at St Albans High School. Then all too soon the service was over, and Jonathan and I were gliding down the aisle, borne aloft by the strains of Bach's 'St Anne Prelude' and by the joy on the faces of the congregation. We stepped out into the sun – it was the first fine day in weeks – there to kiss and hug all our guests and other well-wishers before setting off at the head of the long, slow-moving motorcade led by our friends from France, to Wimpole Hall for photographs, the reception, dinner and festivities which lasted into the night.

Jonathan and I were optimistically looking forward to a comparatively normal life together after our marriage. Since then I have learnt that there is no such thing as a normal life. Certainly we lead busy lives in which music plays a major role: I still revel in the choral repertoire and I also continue to give occasional solo recitals to Jonathan's accompaniment. I no longer teach – there are too many other demands on my attention, but I do manage to make time for dancing, which for so long in the past was not a feasible activity for me either as a practitioner or a spectator. Jonathan and I travel widely: as often as possible we step into that other dimension of rural France, where I work in the meadow garden I created to mark the millennium, while Jonathan plans new musical enterprises – either for The Cambridge Baroque Camerata or for the Choir of Magdalene College, which he has conducted and run for the past five years in his capacity as College Praecentor and Director of College Music.

Rarely however is there a time when we are not beset by troubles and anxieties. By the summer of our wedding my mother had become very disabled with arthritis, and was able to carry on living at home in St Albans thanks only to Dad's devotion to her care. Although I visited them regularly, there inevitably came the day when Dad, who was very hard of hearing, could no longer cope alone. Again we had to engage carers privately from an agency, again as no help was forthcoming either from the NHS or from Social Services. Our expectations that paid carers would be professional people were sorely disappointed. With a handful of shining exceptions, many proved to be of dubious character, doubtful honesty, uncertain qualification and inadequate training, and frequently Dad would have to call me to help out on a Bank Holiday when the replacement carer had failed to turn up. Often perplexed by the carers' idiosyncrasies, as for example when one of them served salad cream on a fruit pie, he never lost his sense of humour – but finally he took the decision to move with Mum into a care home just outside Cambridge.

Relieved to have them settled nearby and in good hands, I then found myself responsible for clearing and selling their house, a mammoth and exhausting task, but one that I was glad to be able to carry out while they were still alive. Still in full possession of his remarkable intellect, but sorely distressed by the perplexing contrast between his youthful inner self and his disintegrating outer frame, Dad succumbed to pneumonia, exacerbated by Parkinson's disease, in June 2004. He had refused to go into Addenbrooke's Hospital because he was so deterred by the terrible treatment Mum had received there only a few weeks previously, when she had had a chest infection. Against all expectations Mum outlived him, and not only celebrated her 90th birthday in March 2006 but also met little George, her fourth great-grandson and our second grandson.

Like so many of life's major experiences, there is no preparation for the stage when our parents become our elderly children and we are caught as the filling in a generation sandwich. Nor is there any warning of the trauma one feels at the death of one's parents, whatever their age. The two people who were always there unconditionally for me, and whom I have been able to depend upon unfailingly all my life, are no longer with me. It is as if a part of me is missing and now, just one week after Mum's death, I find myself flying halfway across the world in a miserably numbed state of shock. At home there are many encouraging messages of sympathy containing tributes to her selfless character, her genuine concern for and interest in other people, her dedication to good causes, her devotion to her family and her inspiring, deep-seated faith, but the sadness of the past week is very present. It travels with me wherever I go. Previously I could imagine how dreadful it must be to lose a child or a spouse, but I had no notion of how fundamentally shocking it is to lose a parent.

In the past ten years challenges other than attending to my elderly parents have arisen in the family. These I will not dwell on, but they have demanded special resources which I have found in the rock of faith that has sustained me from the early days of my marriage to Stephen. These days that faith is broader, more critical and more sceptical, but is nonetheless rooted in Christian ethics and finds its spiritual expression in music. The old optimism is gone and a determination to overcome adversity, probably learnt from Stephen, prevails in its place.

As far as the family are concerned, although Robert seems to be permanently based in the United States, we are lucky to have two of our children still living in Britain, and we see them often. Lucy is a full-time author as well as a single parent to her gorgeous son, William. A beautiful but difficult baby, he was diagnosed with autism in 2001.

Tim has rid himself of the self-doubt that characterized his childhood and has become sharp-witted and perceptive. Though he is proud of his father, he is particularly sensitive to the problems of living in the shadow of fame and would prefer to be considered for his own talents and hard work rather than because of his background. A linguist, like me, he read Modern Languages and then decided to do an MSc in marketing.

And Stephen... Remarkably since his second divorce Stephen has reasserted his control over his life, and despite bouts of illness, he has maintained his position on the world stage. We are able to associate freely again and enjoy many a family occasion together. It has been quite like old times, with plenty of banter and wit circulating round the dinner table while we wait for Stephen to have the last word. I was delighted to be invited to the Royal Society to witness the presentation to him of the Copley medal, the oldest medal of the Society. As on so many previous occasions I was touched with pride at his achievement, though quite what his science consists of these days I cannot tell, apart from his much publicized recantation of some of his former theories. I must admit I was less happy with his expressed intention, announced on radio on the day of the presentation, of going into space. Less ambitiously but perhaps more productively, he went off to Israel a couple of weeks later, a trip he undertook only on condition that he should be allowed to visit Ramallah and talk to the Palestinians. We gazed in awe at the double-page centre spread in the *Guardian* which showed Stephen driving his wheelchair through massed hordes of Palestinian onlookers. Before going into space he intends to bring his very special form of ambassadorship to Iran, though whether political circumstances will allow that to happen remains to be seen. On his return from Israel, he spent Christmas with us and we celebrated the New Year with him. Often he joins us for Sunday lunch and frequently we go to the theatre together. He and his mother came to my mother's funeral, and I was very pleased to see them there. Isobel looks frail but very fit, and is quite irrepressible, even if her memory is somewhat unreliable. In her jovial good humour and ready wit, she reminds me of the positive role model I once considered her to be. A couple of years ago she sent me a letter thanking me for all that I had done for Stephen. It was a noble gesture which helped alleviate some of the more painful memories, restoring our relationship to a civilized footing.

An enormous new hall of residence stands on the site at 5 West Road, where once we lived in that splendid house and relaxed in its beautiful garden. A few of the most significant trees however are still standing, a result of the campaign which I undertook in the 1990s when I discovered the havoc that had been wreaked in the garden after our departure. I watch as the plane en route to Seattle casts its shadow over northern Canada and releases its fumes over the receding frozen wastes of the Arctic, and I ask myself whether the bulldozing of our garden in the name of progress was not just another small symptom of the mad rush to exploit every available resource that is leading inexorably to the decline of the planet. Like that house and garden our lives were bulldozed, but the essential spirit of the family – truly the affirmation of all my young years – still exists and reasserts itself on those occasions when we can all meet and enjoy each other's company. Whether the spirit of the earth can eventually recover and reassert itself is the greatest question facing mankind, not unlike that menacing question way back in the Sixties, when Stephen and I first met, of whether the earth and all forms of life therein were destined to be obliterated by nuclear warfare.

Post Script – May 2007
Since I finished writing the Postlude, Stephen has completed his zero-gravity flight and returned to earth intact, giving rise to triumphant pictures in the media. The smile on his face as he floated in weightless liberation would have moved the stars. It certainly moved me profoundly and made me reflect what a privilege it was to travel even a short distance with him on the way to infinity.

Last Word – August 2014
Lucy's series of imaginative scientific adventures for children, beginning with *George's 'Secret Key to the Universe'*, has met with worldwide acclaim. She has battled tirelessly to obtain the proper provision for William, who has grown into a delightful, caring and very helpful young man.

Tim is now a successful marketing manager and travels widely in the course of his work.

Robert, still in Seattle, works somewhere on the Microsoft Cloud. He has a wonderful, very lively family who keep us interested, entertained and amused on their visits to Cambridge.

Stephen, the world's most famous scientist, remains at the centre of the family as well as at the centre of physics. In fact we are all just about to go on holiday together!

Acknowledgements

In *Music to Move the Stars*, the first edition of my memoir, I expressed my profound gratitude to all those people pictured within, friends, members of the family, colleagues and students, whose help and encouragement over the years had brought a positive influence to our family life. I also thanked my scientific friends, Kip Thorne, Jim Hartle, Jim Bardeen, Brandon Carter and Bernard Carr for their help in clarifying some of the more abstruse and intractable scientific issues which I had to address in the course of the writing, as well as gratefully acknowledging the advice of Peter Dronke in elucidating some of the finer points of medieval scholarship.

For *Travelling to Infinity*, the abridged version of the original memoir, I once again wish to express my thanks to all of the above and add the names of those who have made the new edition possible. Anthony McCarten has been a constant source of encouragement, and in his enthusiasm for *Music to Move the Stars*, introduced me to Alessandro Gallenzi and Elisabetta Minervini of Alma Books, who took the new project on with eagerness, alacrity and efficiency. I am extremely grateful to them for enabling my memoir to see the light of day again. I am indebted to Mike Stocks who took time from his own highly successful career as a writer to help tidy up the excesses of my prose. His tactful and supportive criticism has been invaluable and much appreciated.

Finally thanks are due to my family for once again allowing me to delve into their life stories and for showing forbearance and humour during the process.